Weekend Mechanic's Handbook

D0701321

Weekend Mechanic's Handbook

THE COMPLETE GUIDE TO DO-IT-YOURSELF REPAIRS

SECOND EDITION

Paul Weissler

PRENTICE HALL PRESS

NEW YORK   LONDON   TORONTO   SYDNEY   TOKYO

Dedicated to Ruth Rodgers

 Prentice Hall Press
Gulf + Western Building
One Gulf + Western Plaza
New York, New York   10023

Copyright © 1980, 1982, 1988 by Simon & Schuster, Inc.

All rights reserved
including the right of reproduction
in whole or in part in any form.

PRENTICE HALL PRESS and colophon are registered
trademarks of Simon & Schuster, Inc.

Library of Congress Cataloging in Publication Data

Weissler, Paul.
  Weekend mechanic's handbook.

  Includes index.
  1. Automobiles—Maintenance and repair—Amateurs'
manuals.   I. Title.
TL152.W428   1988   629.28′722   86-43151
ISBN 0-13-948100-1

Designed by Irving Perkins Associates

Manufactured in the United States of America

10 9 8 7 6 5 4 3 2

Acknowledgments

The author wishes to thank the following companies for their contributions of illustrations for this book: American Motors; Champion Spark Plug Company; Chrysler Corporation; Ford Motor Company; General Motors, Prestolite Division; Eltra Corporation; and the 3M Company.

Contents

Introduction   ix

1   **A Guide to Basic Tuneups**   3
2   **The Ignition System**   21
3   **Fuel Systems from Carburetors to Turbochargers**   100
4   **Air Pollution Controls**   172
5   **Basic Gas Engine Service**   189
6   **The Diesel Engine**   224
7   **The Cooling System**   234
8   **Exhaust System Service**   264
9   **The Electrical System**   275
10   **Air Conditioning Service and Repair**   307
11   **The Brake System**   318
12   **Basic Suspension Maintenance**   368
13   **Drive Train Fundamentals**   410
14   **Body Repairs**   431
15   **Parts Buying Guide**   443

Index   447

Introduction

As the cost of professional auto repair service rises, more and more people are saving big money by doing most of the work themselves. Although some jobs require major investments in equipment, the overwhelming majority can be done with inexpensive tools. Further, although some jobs require considerable experience to diagnose, in most cases a simple test or two and visual inspection will isolate the problem.

The second edition of *Weekend Mechanic's Handbook* has been written to enable you to diagnose and do the jobs that are within your ability to handle. In each section you will be shown what you can do and how to do it, or when you would be better off leaving the work to a professional. You probably will find that you can take care of virtually all the work your car needs.

If you have done some work on your car before, you can proceed directly into engine tuneup, the subject of chapters 1 through 4. Engine tuneup is becoming so popular as a weekend mechanic's service that you can readily obtain the inexpensive, light-duty testers and tools you need for a tiny fraction of the cost of professional equipment. You'll recoup the investment with the very first tuneup you do.

If you are a rank beginner, start with the easiest jobs, such as oil and filter change (see chapter 5), air filter replacement (see chapter 3), and cooling system service (see chapter 7).

Most important, approach each job with self-confidence but not cockiness. Auto repair requires attention to detail, and if you have the desire and the willingness to work carefully you'll consistently get results of which you can be proud.

Many weekend mechanics look under the hood of a new car and become bewildered as they attempt to absorb everything they see. This is a mistake. If you simply look for the familiar parts you want to service, you will find them. All engines still have filters (oil, air, and fuel) and spark plugs. Although an increasing number are being built without ignition distributors (see chapter 2), that has not been a major source of required service since electronic ignition became standard equipment for U.S.-built cars in the 1973 to 1975 period. Except for a handful of cars, they still have spark plug wires, however. And of course hoses, drive belts, and similar items remain. Although carburetors are giving way to fuel injection, many weekend mechanics will find this system easier to service.

Further, there's more to car service than the engine, and you still can work on the exhaust system, brakes, suspension, electrical problems, and the car body.

As new-car warranties are extended, you may think that you have little to do on a new car for the first six or seven years. However, you will be surprised to find that just as dents are not covered by the body warranty, virtually all the mechanical and electrical services covered in this book are also your responsibility.

Although you will be able to do many jobs on your car with nothing more than the instructions in this book, for the more complex jobs this book is intended to be a companion to a factory service manual for your car. Factory manuals are written for professionals using special tools and test equipment and they contain specific data that no general book can offer. The owner's manual for your car should include the ordering information for factory service manuals; if it does not, then check with the car dealer.

Chapters 1 through 4 cover tuneup services. At the end of chapter 4 is a checklist to follow to insure a long-lasting tuneup.

Weekend
Mechanic's
Handbook

1 A Guide to Basic Tuneups

Virtually every motorist knows that an automobile needs a periodic engine *tuneup*. In general, a tuneup is a group of services—replacement of certain parts, some testing of the engine's general mechanical condition, and a few mechanical adjustments. There is no uniform list throughout the industry, however. Mechanics don't agree because they are at the pricing end, and what they put into a tuneup varies according to the package price they feel is most marketable. If the situation is competitive, they make the package (and the price) smaller; if there is a market that is not price-conscious, the package is bigger.

What this all comes down to is that some services yield more obvious and immediate results than others, and the typical tuneup package always includes the services that the customer is more likely to notice when he or she drives the car out of the shop.

If you do your own tuneup, however, you can make it as extensive as you wish. Although some services do not produce immediately noticeable results, they do provide long-term benefits or assurances of reliable performance. By doing these jobs at little or no cost, you get a tuneup that most professional shops could not sell except to those few customers to whom price is no object.

Doing your own tuneup work provides another important benefit: You don't have to replace parts that are still serviceable. If you bring your car into a garage and ask for a tuneup, whatever is on the list will usually be replaced, even if it has thousands of miles of potential service remaining.

Engine Systems

The tuneup of a gasoline engine customarily involves the following four areas:

The ignition system. It has the job of producing high-voltage electricity and delivering it to each cylinder of your engine. Threaded into each cylinder is a spark plug, a device that turns the electricity into a spark that ignites the fuel mixture. The electricity must be delivered to each cylinder in precisely timed fashion, coordinated with other actions taking place, so that the burning of the fuel mixture produces maximum power.

The fuel system. It must combine fuel and air in the right proportions to produce a mixture that will burn readily when ignited by a spark. It then must deliver the gasoline mixture to each cylinder of the engine at the proper time.

Pollution controls. So that the engine releases a minimum amount of gases and fumes that could pollute the air we breathe, every car is equipped with a variety of control devices. Most of these devices are designed to regulate the way the engine operates, so checking their operation and performing certain services has two results:

1. The engine produces lower levels of polluting emissions.
2. Engine performance is maintained according to car manufacturer's specifications.

The engine itself. Actually, very few engine tuneups involve the engine per se, but there are a few. In no case, however, is any real disassembly of the engine required. The parts you must reach all are external, or just under a sheet metal cover held by a few screws (see figs. 1-1, 1-2, 1-3, and 1-4).

Because the tuneup is one of the most popular weekend mechanic's areas of operation, this book begins with the chapters that cover service on the systems you must know to do the work. Chapter 2 covers the ignition system; chapter 3, the fuel system; chapter 4, pollution controls; and chapter 5, the engine itself.

Before you begin these chapters, you should know something about the tools you will need, and replacement parts.

AIR CLEANER
PCV VALVE
OIL FILLER CAP
ALTERNATOR
ENGINE TOP COVER
CYLINDER HEAD
SPARK PLUGS
ENGINE BLOCK
IGNITION COIL
FUEL PUMP
IGNITION VACUUM ADVANCE UNIT
OIL FILTER
OIL PAN
IGNITION DISTRIBUTOR

CARBURETOR
FAN
INTAKE MANIFOLD
STARTER
TRANSMISSION
PUMP OIL RESERVOIR
POWER STEERING PUMP
THERMOSTATIC AIR CLEANER DUCT
OIL PAN

Figure 1-1. Side views of an in-line six-cylinder engine. Although many of the parts are unfamiliar to you, you will understand their function as you perform the jobs covered in this book.

FAN

PCV VALVE

COMPUTER

SPARK PLUG WIRES

ENGINE TOP COVER

SPARK PLUGS

TRANSMISSION

POWER STEERING PUMP

THERMOSTATIC AIR CLEANER DUCT

STARTER

CHRYSLER
Plymouth

AIR CLEANER

ENGINE TOP COVER

OIL FILLER CAP

IGNITION DISTRIBUTOR

ALTERNATOR

SPARK PLUG WIRES

SPARK PLUGS

CYLINDER HEAD

FUEL FILTER

FUEL PUMP

EXHAUST MANIFOLD

OIL FILTER

OIL PAN

ENGINE BLOCK

CHRYSLER
Plymouth

Figure 1-2. Side views of a V-8 engine.

Figure 1-3. This is a transverse-engine, front-wheel-drive installation; that is, the engine is mounted sideways, along with a combination transmission and final drive axle (set of gears that transfer power to the front wheels). Three-cylinder, four-cylinder, V-6 and V-8 engines are among the transverse engine installations. The steering gear and suspension also are shown and the view is from the driver's seat.

Carburetor

Air Cleaner

Spark Plugs

Thermostat Housing

Distributor

Oil Filter

Fuel Pump

Water Pump

Timing Belt Cover

Figure 1-4. Side view of a four-cylinder engine.

BASIC HAND TOOLS

If you do any sort of work around the house, you may already have an assortment of screwdrivers, pliers, and wrenches. If you don't, you will need them to do a tuneup and other work on your car. There are some buying guidelines you should follow.

Wrenches. There are three basic types of wrenches—the open-end, box, and socket (see fig. 1-5). The open-end and box wrenches are available in combination sets; that is, an open-end design on one end of the shank, a box on the other. Although the box wrench provides a better grip on the nut or bolt, there are often problems of accessibility when only an open-end will fit in.

Socket wrenches cannot be used by themselves, but instead fit into a tool called a ratchet wrench, which can be set to lock in one direction and free-wheel in the other. Set the wrench one way and it is used to remove spark plugs, nuts, or bolts; set it the other way to tighten them down. Although the socket is small and fits into many tight places, the size of the ratchet means it often cannot fit. To permit using the socket under such conditions, you can attach extension rods and flexible universal joints between socket and ratchet (see fig. 1-6). The size of the male and female squares in the tools is called the drive, and socket sets for automotive use are commonly available in $1/2$- and $3/8$-inch drives. The $3/8$-inch drive type is the one most suitable for weekend mechanics.

If you have an older American car with American-size nuts and bolts, these are the size wrenches you will find most useful for automotive service: $5/16$, $3/8$, $7/16$, $1/2$, $9/16$, $5/8$, $11/16$, $3/4$, and $7/8$-inch; in box, open-end, and socket styles. In addition, you will need a $5/8$- or $13/16$-inch deep socket (depending on your car) to fit the spark plugs. A deep socket is one that is taller than a standard socket, and one made for spark plug use will usually have a sponge rubber insert to grasp the body of the plug (see fig. 1-7). In addition, you will find a few short extension rods (2 to 6 inches) useful, which if necessary can be locked together to form one long rod. A universal joint also is helpful.

If your car has metric-size nuts and bolts, the key sizes are: 6, 7, 8, 9, 10, 11, 12, 13, 14, 15, 16, 18, and 19 millimeter, plus a spark plug socket.

Figure 1-5. Shown are the basic types of wrenches. *From left to right*, they are: double open-end, double box, combination box–open-end, and sockets. *Note*: A wrench may be a box-type on one end and an open-end on the other. Also note that two sockets are shown. The square end fits into a ratchet wrench; the other end shown up fits into the nut or bolt.

Figure 1-6. Ratchet, extension rod, and socket wrenches. The square hole in the end of the socket or extension rod fits into the male square on the ratchet or on an extension rod. A universal joint with one male and one female end also may be used for work in tight quarters.

Figure 1-7. Spark plug socket has sponge rubber insert (pulled halfway out for illustration) to grip ceramic insulator of spark plug during removal or installation.

Screwdrivers. Most screwdriver slots are either the simple slot or one of two Phillips types, the straight Phillips cross or a variation called Posi-driv. You can tell Posi-driv by what appears to be hairline cracks at each right angle of the cross. Screwdrivers are not interchangeable between the two, and in fact, you must have an assortment of sizes to properly fit the cross of each. Use of the wrong size screwdriver may gouge the cross; use of the wrong type screwdriver (particularly a Phillips in a Posi-driv slot) will create removal problems and may result in damage to the cross. Look carefully at the assortments in the stores, and try to find a small, medium, and large in both slot and Phillips and Posi-driv types. Select a quality screwdriver made of chrome vanadium steel. This designation will be found on the screwdriver shank. On slot screwdrivers, look for fine vertical lines at the tip, an indication of good machining. Make sure the screwdriver has a comfortable handle, whether it's wood or plastic.

Note: Many late-model cars have screws with hex or six-pointed-star slots cut into the heads. The hex-type is called an Allen head, the star a Torx head. In addition, some Torx-head screws have a head with an external star shape. Special socket bits are available for these screws, although in an emergency you can use an Allen wrench in a female Torx screw. With the male Torx head, you must use the proper wrench.

Pliers. The vise-type locking pliers that most people have for work around the house are the most useful. A small and a large pair will cover your needs. In addition, you can consider: needle-nose pliers (for tight quarters), cutting pliers for cutting wires and other jobs, electrical wire-service pliers (which may combine an insulation stripper and jaws to secure terminals [see fig. 1-8]), and hose clamp pliers for easy release of the spring-type clamps used on most cooling system hoses (see fig. 1-9).

Figure 1-8. Pliers for electrical service. Different sections of the jaws cut the wire, strip away insulation, and crimp solderless terminals to the bare wire.

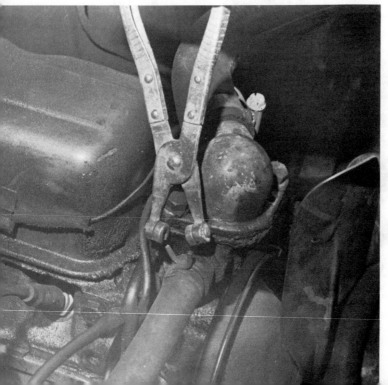

Figure 1-9. Special hose clamp pliers permit squeezing together the ears of a spring-type hose clamp.

SPECIFIC TUNEUP TOOLS

In addition to standard wrenches, pliers, and screwdrivers, you'll need the following tools specifically for tuneup work:

Tachometer. This is a meter that indicates the speed at which the engine is running. It's usually combined with a dwellmeter, which is necessary for ignition system work on cars without electronic ignition and to check electronically controlled carburetors. Although many inexpensive tachometers are made with analog (needle-and-dial) scales, your best choice is a digital meter, which is much easier to read. The reading you get is in crankshaft revolutions per minute (r.p.m.).

There are several types of tachometers:

Primary type. So called because it connects to the primary part of the ignition system (the low-voltage part), it can be used on all gasoline engines with distributors.

Caution: Some of these types may not indicate correctly on all electronic ignition systems. Be sure you can return what you buy if it does not work properly.

Secondary type. So called because it connects to the secondary part of the ignition system (the high-voltage part), this tachometer can be clipped onto a spark plug wire, making it much easier to use.

Electromagnetic type. It has an electromagnetic sensor that fits into a holder at the point where ignition timing is checked (see fig. 2-65), and therefore also is used to check ignition timing, as explained later in this chapter. The advantage of this design is that it permits reading ignition timing. However, it is useable only on U.S.-built Chrysler products and GM cars with distributors, plus (as explained later in this chapter) GM diesels.

Photocell type. It works in a manner similar to a flash-light. You make a mark on the exposed crankshaft pulley, then aim the light at the pulley and run the engine. The mark triggers the photocell to produce an engine speed reading.

Scan tester. This is a device that plugs into the computer on General Motors cars (and there are versions that also plug into Ford and Chrysler products), and on many models they not only produce engine test data but can display engine r.p.m. readings as well. If you have a GM car with distributorless ignition, this is your best choice.

Timing Light. This is a strobe-type light used to check ignition timing, which means the arrival of the high-voltage electricity at the spark plug. Timing is adjustable (on all but some Ford computer-equipped cars and engines with distributorless ignition) to match factory specifications, by loosening a lockbolt and turning the distributor body. First, however, it is checked, which is done by connecting the light and aiming it at a pair of reference marks on the engine (see chapter 2). There are many types of timing lights, including an inexpensive neon-tube design. However, the only type that will really provide a bright light to permit an accurate check is the "power timing light." For ease of use, buy a 12-volt power timing light, which connects directly to the car's battery.

Two additional buying factors you should consider are: the type of trigger wire connector on the timing light and where the timing marks are on your car.

The trigger wire is connected to a spark plug and/or plug wire so that the light is triggered when the spark plug is firing. There are many types of trigger mechanisms, but the only type that is suitable for all types of ignition systems is the "inductive pickup," which clamps onto the exterior of the spark plug wire (see fig. 1-10). Do not confuse it with the capacitive pickup, which physically resembles it. Ask before you buy.

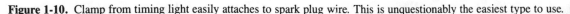

Figure 1-10. Clamp from timing light easily attaches to spark plug wire. This is unquestionably the easiest type to use.

If the timing marks on your car are really buried, as they are on some late-model cars, the brightest timing light won't help. To cover this situation, some late-model cars (primarily GM and Chrysler products) have special holders on the front of the engine for an electromagnetic probe, part of a timing indicator that reads at the meter (you don't have to look at marks). This type is often combined with a special universal tachometer suitable for General Motors diesel engines (see chapter 6). The price of this type of timing indicator is not low, but it can save you the inconvenience of making your own timing marks on the engine.

Or you may find the adjustable timing light shown in figure 1-11 suitable for this problem. Because it can delay the flashing of the light any number of degrees, it may permit you to set it to fire at a point you can see. Of course, the future is a car with nonadjustable timing and no timing marks for the timing light to illuminate. Some GM cars have this design already and others will follow. However,

if you have a car without this feature and plan to keep it for a while, you will need a timing light.

Feeler Gauge. The term is what the name implies. It's a set of strips of metal or pieces of wire of different thicknesses that permit you to measure gaps by feel. Why would you want to measure a gap? The answer is that in automotive work there are certain gaps—clearances—between parts that must be precisely correct (to within a thousandth of an inch in some cases) for the engine to perform correctly. If a gap is supposed to be .016 inch (sixteen thousandths of an inch), for example, you select the gauge marked .016 inch, hold it in your hand, and insert it in the gap between the parts. If the gauge can be inserted and withdrawn with just light-to-moderate drag, which you can easily distinguish, the gap is correct. If the gap is too large or too small, you make an adjustment on the parts to bring it to the specified number. A set of feeler gauges is very inexpensive, and you can buy either a combination set (of strip and wire types) or individual sets

Figure 1-11. This is a timing light that can be adjusted to delay flashing any specified number of degrees desired, so you can read timing even if it has advanced off the scale by turning the knob until timing is readable. This type of timing light also is useful if much of the indicator scale is not readily visible, also permitting you to retard the flashing of the light. Because you know how much you have delayed the flashing of the light, you know what the true timing is. There is also a timing indicator that fits into a GM or Chrysler probe holder and reads timing on a dial, so you don't have to read the timing marks on the engine.

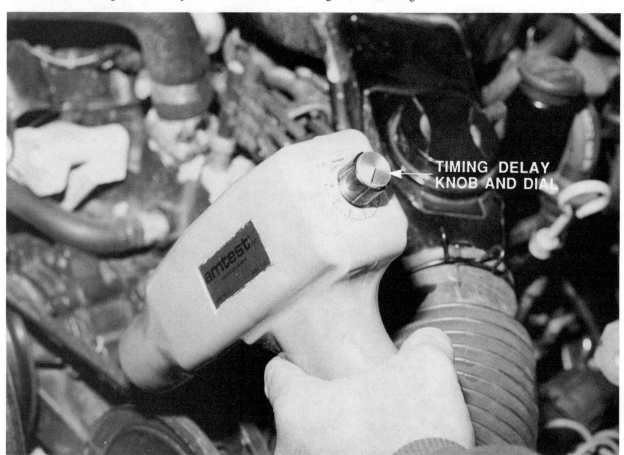

(just wire or just strips). If you have a car with electronic ignition, you need only a gauge for spark plugs, and that is commonly made with strips of wire (see figs. 1-12, 1-13).

If your car is an older model that does not have electronic ignition, you will also need the set with metal strips (see fig. 1-13).

Figure 1-12. These are three of the most common types of spark plug gauges. The rectangular one with U-shaped wires, the pocket-knife type with L-shaped wires, and the circular one with U-shaped bars are all readily available.

Figure 1-13. This feeler gauge with metal strips of varying thicknesses is used for adjusting ignition breaker points.

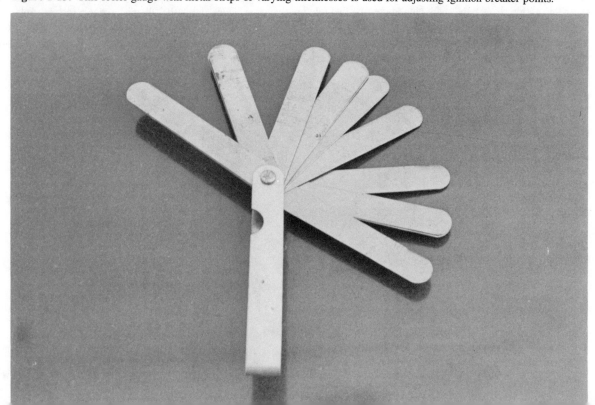

Compression Gauge. To understand the function of a compression gauge, you need a basic understanding of the piston engine and its four-stroke cycle (see fig. 1-14). When the piston rises on the compression stroke, it squeezes the air-fuel mixture. The more tightly the mixture is squeezed, the greater is the power developed when it is ignited. The compression pressure is determined by these factors:

1. The design of the engine, including the length of the cylinder, the shape of the top of the piston, and the size of the combustion chamber above the piston.
2. The condition of the seals—called the piston rings—that fit around each piston. If they do not seal tightly between piston and cylinder, some of the compressed fuel mixture can leak down from the cylinder into the bottom of the engine.
3. The condition of the intake and exhaust valves. If the valves do not seal tightly, some of the compressed fuel mixture can leak past them.
4. The condition of the gasket (called the head gasket) that seals the joint between the combustion chamber (in the cylinder head) and the cylinder itself (in the engine block).

By testing, the car manufacturer determines what pressure the engine should develop when it is in good condition, with only a minimum amount of leakage past the piston rings and valves, and provides this information for test purposes. The compression gauge is the tool used to make the test. With a spark plug removed, the gauge is inserted into the plug hole and the engine is cranked (see fig. 1-15). The compression pressure in the cylinder builds up a reading on the compression gauge, and this reading is compared with the manufacturer's specification. If the readings in all cylinders are acceptable, the engine can be given a tuneup. If the compression readings are too low, performance will be very poor and a tuneup will not correct the problem. The compression test is normally performed immediately before new spark plugs are installed; for further details, see chapter 2.

You can buy either of two basic types of compression gauges for gasoline engines: one that is hand-held in the spark plug hole, or one that is connected to a hose that can be threaded into the spark plug hole. The second type is the only choice if access to any of the spark plug holes is not good. Although it costs more and is not sold in most discount houses, it may be the only type you can use.

Ohmmeter. Resistance to the flow of electricity is an important factor in the operation of automobile ignition systems, particularly electronic ignition systems. An ohmmeter, which reads out in units called "ohms," is the instrument that measures resistance, and if you wish to be able to do detailed troubleshooting you may want to add this to your toolbox. The best ohmmeter is a digital type, and there are many moderately priced digital meters that include an ohms readout. Or you may get an analog (needle-and-dial) multifunction meter with a single ohms scale (typically up to 100,000 ohms). This scale is basically for checking spark plug wires. If you do not plan to do a wide range of work on your car, it may be enough. Although the digital ohmmeter would appear to be the "modern" choice, there are actually some tests of elec-

Figure 1-14. The four-stroke cycle of the gasoline engine. As the engine crankshift turns, a piston drops in the cylinder and the intake valve opens, allowing fuel mixture to flow into the cylinder (intake stroke); the piston rises and squeezes the mixture as the intake valve closes (compression stroke); the spark plug ignites the fuel mixture, which explodes and pushes the piston down (power stroke); the piston rises and the exhaust valve opens, permitting the burned gases to flow out of the cylinder into the exhaust system (exhaust stroke). The cycle repeats itself over and over. Each spark plug fires in a prescribed sequence, so there is always power from the burning gases pushing down on a piston somewhere in the engine.

INTAKE   COMPRESSION   POWER   EXHAUST

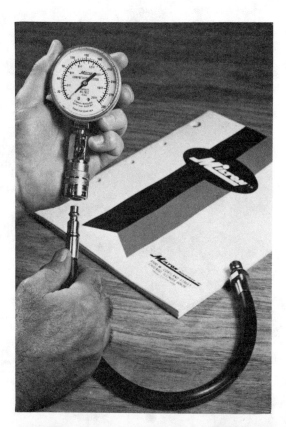

Figure 1-15. Spark plug is removed and compression gauge is held in spark plug hole as shown below. Engine is cranked and pressure builds up reading on gauge. As long as pressure readings in all cylinders are within specifications, the engine can be tuned. At left is a compression gauge that quick-connects to a long hose that threads into the spark plug hole. If spark plug holes are not easily accessible for the gauge shown below, this type is what you need.

Figure 1-16. Shown is a dial-type ohmmeter (digital types also are available). The knob at right permits you to multiply the dial reading as required for measuring high resistance. This meter reads from 0.1 (on the low scale) to 500,000 ohms on the high scale (times 1,000).

tronic components for which the analog ohmmeter is the only type of ohmmeter that works. However, the digital still is the best choice for readability. The ohmmeter is not a beginner's instrument, but as you advance to the more sophisticated work described in chapter 2, you may wish to acquire it (see fig. 1-16). A typical digital ohmmeter has a range of 0.1 ohms up to 100,000 and infinity.

Multi-meter. A multi-meter is a single instrument that combines the function of several. For example, it will often have scales that read engine speed (tachometer), dwell, resistance, volts, and amps. The price will be little more than that of a tach-dwellmeter; however, it is not always the bargain it seems. The multi-meter may not have all the useful scales, such as both low and high engine speed scales, all the resistance scales, and all the volt and amp scales you need for general electrical ser-

vice. Some multi-meters will meet many of your requirements, and if you see one with the right scales at the right price, it might not be a bad purchase.

Note: Electronic meters with digital displays are available that offer many meter functions and a wide range of scales. These are perhaps the best buy for a really enthusiastic weekend mechanic.

Additional Useful Tools.   You will find a 12-volt test light and a stethoscope useful; both are inexpensive items.

Test light. This tool looks like an awl with a clear handle and a wire with an alligator clip connected to it. Inside that clear handle is a bulb, and when you connect the clip to an electrical ground (metal part of the engine or car body) and touch the "awl" point to a source of current (such as the battery positive terminal), a circuit is completed and the bulb inside the clear handle should go on (see chapter 3 for illustrations). Thus, this tester is used to make sure a circuit is complete at various points and to test switches. If you plan to test computer systems, select one designed for them, often labeled "high-impedence."

Stethoscope. This tool is much like a doctor's, except that it has a long pointer you can use to touch various parts of a car. If an engine is performing poorly and you hear noise from the engine valves, you can find the ones that are making the most noise (and therefore are in need of service) by touching parts of the valve system with the stethoscope probe. The tool also is useful for locating other annoying underhood noises and defective fuel injectors.

SPECIAL WRENCHES

The general purpose wrenches described earlier in this chapter may be all you need for most jobs on most cars, but on some cars you may need the following:

C-shaped distributor wrench. The C-shaped distributor wrench permits easy access to the lockbolt that secures the distributor, the key component in the ignition system. The lockbolt must be loosened for a key adjustment—called ignition timing—so if you can't reach this bolt with a conventional wrench, the C-shape is required (see fig. 1-17).

Allen wrench. If you own a pre-1976 General Motors V-8 car (Chevrolet, Buick, Oldsmobile, Pontiac, or Cadillac) without electronic ignition, you need an $1/8$-inch Allen wrench (see fig. 1-18). The Allen wrench is a male hex that fits into a special screw with a female hex

Figure 1-18. If you have a General Motors car with a V-8 engine and breaker points, you need an Allen-type wrench, such as the one shown, to reach in through the access hole shown (metal window lifted up) to turn adjuster.

Figure 1-17. If the lockbolt that holds the distributor in the engine is not accessible with a conventional wrench, the C-shaped wrench is used. It is readily available in auto parts stores.

cut into its head, and is used for a key ignition adjustment. Although Allen wrenches are sold in sets, you can get a $1/8$-inch Allen type made just for General Motors V-8s.

Spark plug ratchet. If the spark plugs in your engine are not particularly easy to reach, a special ratchet is usually helpful. It's called a spark plug ratchet and it features a curved handle and a universal joint in its head. This permits it to work in very tight areas and around obstructions, as shown in chapter 2 (see fig. 1-19).

Figure 1-19. Ratchet with curved handle and universal joint in the head permits you to work around obstructions.

Figure 1-20. Two popular types of torque wrenches are shown. One has a dial gauge and a needle that deflects as a nut or bolt is tightened. The other has a torque-setting adjuster in the end of the handle. When you reach the preset torque, you hear a click.

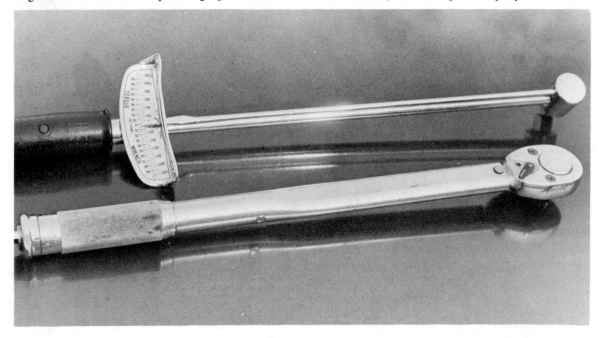

Torque wrench. Certain nuts and bolts must be tightened very precisely, and if a part is held by many of them, all must be tightened evenly. The torque wrench is the tool that is required. It's a wrench with a dial gauge (see fig. 1-20) that accepts a socket. As you torque (apply tightening force) the nut or bolt, the dial needle moves to indicate exactly how tight the nut or bolt is. Torque is measured in pounds-feet (abbreviated lbs.-ft.), or pounds-inch (lbs.-in.). On a metric scale, torque is measured in pascals or kilograms-meter (kg-m). The modern metric measurement is pascals, actually kilopascals, abbreviated kPa. However, on older imports the specifications in the shop manuals may be given in kg-m.

SPECIFICATIONS

The object of a tuneup is to install certain replacement parts, and in many cases to make adjustments to factory numerical specifications. The most common specifications are:

Gaps. Measured with feeler gauges in thousandths of an inch or (metric) tenths of a millimeter

Torque. In lbs.-ft., kPa, or kg-m, measured with a torque wrench as you tighten

Engine speed (r.p.m.). Measured with a tachometer

Dwell. On nonelectronic ignition systems, measured with a dwellmeter in degrees

Ignition timing. Read with a timing light on an indicator marked in degrees.

The specifications are supplied for each make and year car, engine size, and also according to some special characteristics of that engine, such as the type of carburetor and whether or not it has a manual or automatic transmission. Most public libraries have reference manuals that contain specifications sections, or the counter salesmen in many parts stores will provide a tuneup specifications chart you can consult.

Note: Some key tuneup specs are printed on an underhood decal (see fig. 1-21); if your repertoire is limited, they may be all you need.

Figure 1-21. Close-up look at the tuneup decal on all late-model cars. The decal, which lists important tuneup specifications, is located somewhere under the hood; in this case on the engine top cover.

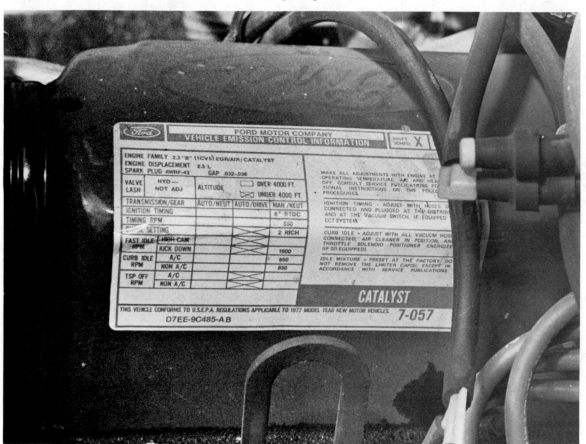

BUYING TUNEUP PARTS

When you buy the tuneup parts for your car, you must be sure to get exactly the ones specified for your car. Even if the wrong parts happen to fit, the performance of the engine will be adversely affected.

You can buy your parts from a wide variety of outlets, including discount houses, department stores, home-and-auto stores, car dealers, service stations, and the parts-only stores that serve primarily professional mechanics. This final choice, called a parts jobber, also is a good one for the beginning weekend mechanic, for these reasons:

1. The counter salesmen are more knowledgeable than at most other outlets, and they will look up the parts numbers for you and hand you the parts. Although they may make a mistake, this is less likely than at outlets where you have to read a catalog or where there are less knowledgeable personnel.
2. They are more likely to be able to supply advice on installation and look up service specifications.
3. They carry name brands, the top-quality lines used by service stations and garages.

Caution: Look closely at the package when buying a name brand. Some spurious brands are put in packages designed to closely resemble the name brand.

The only disadvantage of the parts jobber is that prices usually are higher than at discount houses and department stores such as Sears. Most parts jobbers will give you a discount from list automatically (and if they don't, ask for it), but it won't be as good as you'll get elsewhere. However, at least at the beginning, the extra service is worth the difference. The weekend mechanic's trade is of increasing importance to these stores, and they are becoming increasingly competitive on price, particularly for tuneup parts.

For details on general parts buying, see chapter 16.

THE WAY TO BEGIN

Before you buy anything, tools or parts, read chapters 2 through 5, with periodic references to your actual engine compartment, so you become basically familiar with what you will be doing. The general understanding will help you pick the most suitable tools and limit your parts purchases to what you will actually need.

2 THE IGNITION SYSTEM

Much of the tuneup is concentrated around the ignition system, and for good reason: Unless there is a consistent, healthy spark to the right cylinder at the right time, the engine will suffer. It may not start, and even if it starts, it will run poorly, suffer from stalling, and have many other problems.

With the exception of a few makes (primarily Chrysler, Plymouth, and Dodge since 1973), automobiles until 1975 were equipped with what is called a "breaker points ignition system." In 1975, the rest of the American car industry switched to electronic ignition; most imports did not begin to follow this lead until years later. If you have an older car that is equipped with the breaker points system, this opening section of chapter 2 is for you. If your car has electronic ignition, it does not have breaker points. Read the following descriptions of the basic electrical circuit and how breaker points ignition works, so you can also understand electronic ignition; then proceed to the next section of this chapter.

The function of the ignition system is to produce sparks at the ends of the plug wires, so if the system does this (and the spark plugs are good), it's doing its job and you can move on to other things if you are checking an engine for failure to start. See Page 43 for details of an Ignition System Quick-Check.

THE ELECTRICAL CIRCUIT—A SIMPLIFIED DESCRIPTION

The ignition system is a battery-powered electrical circuit and, as such, it bears certain resemblances to any battery-powered electrical circuit, including the lights on your car. The basic principles of the circuit are that it must have a current source (the battery) and that the circuit be completed back to the battery. Each battery has two posts, or terminals, one from which the current can flow and a

Figure 2-1. This simple battery circuit runs from positive terminal through wire to bulb terminal, through bulb filament to second terminal, through wire to battery negative terminal.

second to which it returns, depleted of its energy (see fig. 2-1).

It is impractical and expensive to have two wires for each electrical device in a car, so the electrical ground principle is employed (see fig. 2-2). The car body and the engine are metal, and therefore can conduct electricity. One post of the battery is connected by a wire, called a ground cable, to the car body and/or engine. The second post is connected by wiring to all the electrical accessories, and the circuits are completed by connecting all the accessories to the body or engine with metal mounting screws, or wires connected to the body by screws. The use of the engine or car body to complete a circuit is called *grounding*, and it is employed throughout the car, including the ignition system.

A final principle of general electrical circuits you must understand is the function of the switch (see fig. 2-3). You know that when you flip a light switch from off to on, a

Figure 2-2. This battery circuit uses a ground. The negative terminal of the battery is connected by wire to a metal part of the engine or body, such as a bolt. The positive terminal has a wire that runs to the bulb that fits into a socket. The other terminal of the bulb touches the metal socket that is attached to the car body, and so is in metal-to-metal contact with it, completing the circuit.

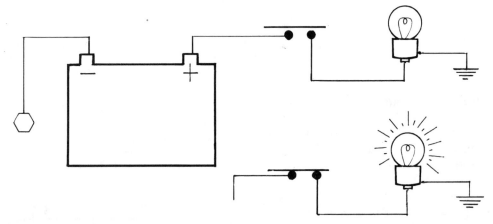

Figure 2-3. This battery circuit uses a ground and a switch. When the switch is open, the wiring from the battery positive terminal to the bulb is open, so the circuit is incomplete and the bulb does not light. When the switch is closed, the circuit is complete and the bulb lights.

bulb lights. The switch is actually a mechanical device that, when turned "off," breaks the completed electrical circuit by separating two contact discs (or something similar). When the switch is turned on, the discs touch, and current can flow through them. The switch, therefore, permits you to make or break the electrical circuit.

Now let's see how all this applies to the ignition system.

BREAKER POINTS BASICS

The source of current for the ignition system is the car's 12-volt battery. The following—like the description of the general electrical circuit—is a simplified explanation, but it will give you the basic understanding you need to service the system.

When you turn the ignition key on, current flows from the 12-volt battery into a device called a resistor (on most cars it is just a special piece of wire), which reduces the voltage to somewhere between 6 to 9 volts. The lower-voltage current then flows into the ignition coil, a high-voltage transformer that when triggered will build it up to as much as 35,000 volts or even more.

The current circuit is completed (see fig. 2-4) by a wire

from the coil to the breaker points (also called contact points or just "points"), which are located on a plate in the distributor, the heart of the ignition system. Opening the points triggers the coil, so let's look at them.

The points assembly consists of two parts, one a spring-loaded movable arm on a pivot, the second a stationary part held by a screw. When the contact discs of the points touch, the circuit from the battery through the coil is complete, just as if a switch were closed (see fig. 2-5).

The movable arm has a fiber block that bears against the distributor cam, which is the upper part of a two-section shaft that runs through the center of the distributor into the engine (which supplies power to spin it whenever the engine is running or being cranked).

The cam is a section with evenly spaced bumps (called lobes) around it, one lobe for each cylinder of the engine. As the cam spins, a lobe comes up against the fiber block and pushes on it, moving the arm away from the fixed point to trigger the coil. The opening of the points is the same as opening a switch, except it's done automatically.

The high-voltage electricity flows from the center of the coil into the center of a plastic cap on the distributor, and through that onto a part called the rotor. The rotor is attached to the top of the distributor cam, so it spins with

SPARK PLUGS

BALLAST RESISTOR

IGNITION SWITCH

IGNITION COIL

AMMETER

DISTRIBUTOR

BATTERY

Figure 2-4. This is the basic ignition system using breaker points. When you turn the ignition key, you close the ignition switch and complete a circuit from the 12-volt battery through a resistor to the ignition coil, in which a magnetic field builds up. When the ignition breaker points ("contact") in the distributor open, the coil builds up high-voltage electricity that exits through the center wire in the top of the coil, into the cap on the distributor, into a rotor in the distributor, then from the rotor out the distributor cap, through a spark plug wire to the plug, which fires the air-fuel mixture in the cylinder. On many cars a ballast resistor as shown is not used; instead there is a strand of resistance wire between the ignition switch and the coil.

Figure 2-5. This simplified illustration shows how the opening of the contact points creates a high-voltage spark. Notice that the coil has two windings, one in which the magnetic field builds up, a second (with much finer wire windings) onto which the electromagnetic field collapses when the points open. Because of the greater number of windings in the secondary windings, the voltage (electrical pressure) increases. In this illustration, the high-voltage electricity is shown going directly to the spark plug. Actually it goes to the distributor cap in the multi-cylinder engine.

12 VOLTS

WHEN THE DISTRIBUTOR CONTACTS ARE CLOSED, THE MAGNETIC
FIELD BUILDS UP IN THE IGNITION COILS.

25,000 VOLTS

Figure 2-6. This drawing shows the function of the rotor and distributor in the transmission of the high-voltage electricity to the correct spark plug (the one whose cylinder has the compressed air-fuel mixture ready for ignition). The cap and rotor are shown removed. The rotor is on the same shaft as the cam so both distributor cam and rotor are turned simultaneously by the engine. When the rotor aligns with a spark plug wire terminal, this coincides with the opening of contact points by the distributor cam, and therefore, with the discharge of high-voltage electricity from the coil, into the cap, to the rotor, and from the rotor to a spark plug wire and spark plug.

Figure 2-7. A look inside a distributor cap shows the button in the center and the buttons around the inside circumference. These buttons are electrical terminals that project through the cap to the spark plug wires and the center wire from the ignition coil. The center button inside the cap transfers the high-voltage electricity to the rotor, and the circumferential buttons take that electricity from the rotor to a spark plug wire.

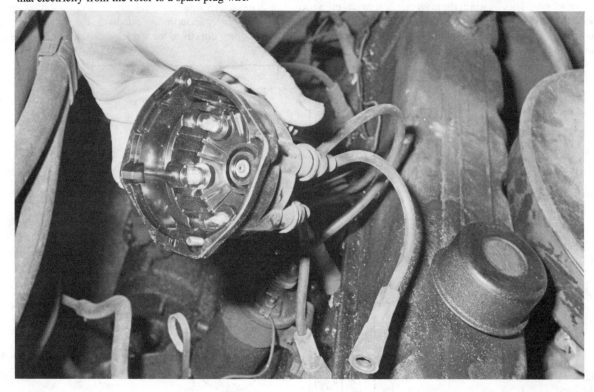

it, and as it does, its tip aligns with electrical contacts that pass through from the outer circumference of the cap. Each of these contacts contains a wire connected to the spark plug, the part threaded into the cylinder to ignite the fuel mixture (see figs. 2-6, 2-7).

The distributor is so designed that whenever the points are opened, triggering the coil, the rotor tip is aligned with the distributor cap terminal for the spark plug of the cylinder that contains a fuel mixture ready for ignition.

The spinning of the distributor cam carries the lobe past the fiber block of the movable point, and the spring on that movable point pushes it closed—into contact with the fixed point. The circuit is complete once more, the coil gets ready, and in another instant the next lobe will push open the movable point and trigger the coil. This action occurs thousands of times per minute.

Condenser

There's so much high-voltage electricity in the coil that some of it could flow through to the breaker points and arc across them while they are open. This would have two undesirable effects:

1. The contact discs would be burned very quickly, and soon fail to complete the circuit.
2. Since electricity takes the path of least resistance, most of the high voltage would leak across the points rather than go to the spark plugs. In either case, the engine might not start.

To prevent this, the condenser is used (see fig. 2-6). It's a small cylindrical can that is wired to the movable point, and it absorbs any stray high voltage before it can arc across the points. When the points close, it discharges the electricity safely.

Ignition Advance

It is desirable to slightly change the instant the spark fires the fuel mixture—called "ignition timing"—in accordance with changes in engine speed and engine load (how hard the engine is working).

The typical distributor has two automatic controls:

The mechanical advance. See Figure 2-8. The distributor cam is actually not a part of a solid shaft that goes into the engine, but really just fits over the shaft and is connected to it by a pair of weights and springs. As

Figure 2-8. Here's a cutaway view of a breaker points distributor. You can see the metal strip that transfers the high-voltage electricity from the coil wire to the appropriate spark plug wire on top of the rotor. You also can see the "automatic advance unit," a set of centrifugal weights that at high engine speed shift the position of the breaker points plate to change the time at which the points open and therefore the time the high-voltage electricity is transferred to the plug wires.

Figure 2-9. This is the vacuum advance mechanism. At low engine speed it changes the time the points open. The unit is a spring-loaded diaphragm, connected by a hose to a source of engine vacuum (usually at the base of the carburetor). Vacuum sucks on the diaphragm, which is connected to the breaker points' plate by a link. The diaphragm moves against spring pressure and turns the breaker plate so the distributor cam lobe opens the points earlier than otherwise. When vacuum drops as the throttle opens wide, the spring returns the diaphragm, link, and breaker plate. However, at this time a mechanical advance system sensitive to engine speed takes over.

DISTRIBUTOR

CARBURETOR AIR INTAKE

DISTRIBUTOR ADVANCE DIAPHRAGM

CARBURETOR

ENGINE INTAKE MANIFOLD

engine speed increases, centrifugal force moves these weights outward against the spring pressure and the position of the distributor cam is shifted slightly. Moving the cam (clockwise or counterclockwise, depending on car) changes the time the lobes come up against the movable point's fiber block, so that the ignition coil is triggered at a different time.

The vacuum advance. See Figures 2-9, 2-10. The engine develops a substantial amount of vacuum, the exact amount depending on the engine load. Therefore vacuum is used as the control for changing ignition timing as the load changes. The distributor has a diaphragm device with an arm connected to the breaker plate, the

part on which the points are mounted. The breaker plate looks as if it's just bolted down, but actually it (or a section of it) can be pivoted back and forth. When vacuum is applied to the diaphragm unit, it sucks on the diaphragm, moving the arm and the breaker plate. This shifts the position of the points relative to the distributor cam, which also changes the instant the coil is triggered. Vacuum usually is supplied to the diaphragm unit by a hose or piece of tubing from a part on the engine called the "intake manifold" (a set of chambers that carry air and fuel from the carburetor to the cylinders). Or the hose may be from the base of the carburetor, which is bolted to the intake manifold.

Figure 2-10. Here's an in-the-metal look at the distributor and the vacuum advance unit. Fingers are holding the vacuum hose connected to it.

SERVICING THE DISTRIBUTOR

Now that you have a basic understanding of the ignition system, you can service the breaker points and condenser in the distributor. This is a key job in any tuneup.

Begin by locating the distributor (see figs. 1-1, 1-2). This should be easy—it's the part with the cap into which all the thick spark plug wires are connected. The job should be done with the distributor in the car, so if your car's distributor is not conveniently located and you must drape your body across the engine, use a foam cushion for chest protection.

Remove the distributor cap. In most cases it isn't necessary to disconnect any wires from it, but if it is, label each wire and the terminal from which you remove it with pieces of masking tape (marked with letters or numbers for easy identification).

The cap is held in one of three ways:

C-shaped spring clips. Just pry them off the squared sections of the cap on which they grip, using a screwdriver or your fingers (see fig. 2-11).

Screws. Just undo the screws and lift up on the cap. The screws are installed so they won't come out of the cap (to prevent you from losing them).

Figure 2-11. Using a slot-screwdriver to pry the spring clips off the distributor cap.

L-shaped locking rods. If you look at the cap, these appear to be screws, but if you check further, you'll see that the rods are L-shaped and lock under the main section of the distributor body (see fig. 2-12). To release them, insert a screwdriver into the slot at the top, push down (against spring pressure), and turn counterclockwise.

Most distributors have just two clips, screws, or locking rods, but a few (primarily ones with electronic ignition systems) have four.

With the distributor cap up and out of the way, you can see the points and condenser. On General Motors V-8 distributors, you also can see the mechanical advance weights and springs, for they are just under the rotor. On other distributors, the mechanical advance is hidden under the breaker plate. See Figures 2-13, 2-14.

Inspect the points before you disconnect anything. Just push the movable arm away and look at the contact faces, using a magnifying glass if necessary. If the points are burned black, they must be replaced. If there is a metal transfer between the two resulting in a hill on one and a valley in the other or pockmarks in both, a replacement also is called for. If, however, the contact faces are clean, or have no more than an even gray coating, leave them in place. They may need an adjustment, but that's all.

Note: It is possible that the fiber block of the movable point has worn down so much that you will not be able to readjust the points satisfactorily. In this case, the points will have to be changed even if the contact faces look good.

If you see an oily film in the distributor, this can cause premature failure of the points or other ignition problems. It should be cleaned off all parts, particularly the points' contact faces. The problem usually is caused by a clogged Positive Crankcase Ventilation system, discussed in chapter 4.

Figure 2-12. This distributor cap has locking rods. Insert screwdriver as shown, push down against spring pressure, then turn, and L-shaped bottom of rod will turn out of the way, permitting you to lift the cap.

Figure 2-13. This is a General Motors V-8 distributor. Centrifugal advance weights are on top of the distributor, just under the rotor. The rod is held by a pair of easy-to-remove screws.

Figure 2-14. With the rotor off, you can clearly see the centrifugal weights held by little springs.

Adjusting the Points

If the points are in good condition, the points' adjustment should be checked and corrected if necessary. Adjustment refers to the gap between the two contact faces when the movable point is pushed away by a cam lobe. The check is made when the fiber block is against the very peak of the cam lobe, and is done with a feeler gauge. You merely insert a feeler gauge (or combinations of a few feeler gauge strips) until you find the size that can be inserted and withdrawn with light-to-moderate drag. If the gauge just slides in and out easily, try a thicker strip. If you have to push against the movable point to get it in at all, try a thinner strip. No set of feeler gauges will have all sizes, but to measure precisely, combine two thin strips to get a thicker size. Example: The set has a .016-inch strip and a .020-inch strip. If you need something in between, perhaps you can combine .008- and .010-inch strips for a total of .018 inch.

Note: See pages 32 and 33 for adjustments to General Motors V-8s.

The major problem is getting the fiber block against the

Figure 2-15. Shown is what the distributor lock looks like. It's just a clamp part held by a bolt. Once you slacken the bolt, you can turn the distributor body. When preparing for a points adjustment, remove the distributor cap so you can see the points, then turn the distributor body so the points' fiber block is up against the peak of a cam lobe. Always make alignment marks on the distributor body and the engine so you can return the distributor to the same position after the adjustment.

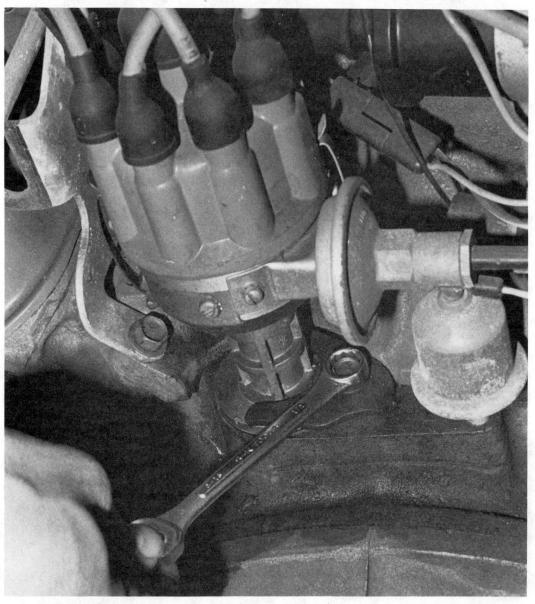

peak of the cam lobe. There are many methods, but the one that follows will give the beginner the least difficulty:

1. Locate the lockbolt at the end of the distributor body, where it mates with the engine (see fig. 2-15). If you need a C-shaped wrench to reach it, obtain one.
2. With chalk, tire marking crayon, nail polish, etc., make a thin mark on the distributor body and another just opposite on the engine. These are alignment marks.
3. Slacken the lockbolt with the wrench and turn the distributor body clockwise or counterclockwise until the fiber block is against the peak of the nearest cam lobe.

Now, you're ready for breaker points adjustment. The principle of the adjustment is this: The swing of the movable arm is determined by the distributor cam lobe; therefore, the gap is determined by the position of the fixed point. Although the fixed point is held to the breaker plate by a screw, it can be moved toward or away from the movable point when the screw is loosened.

Therefore, loosen the screw and move the fixed point toward or away from the movable point, to decrease or increase the gap. On most fixed points there is a little notch, plus another in the breaker plate, into which you can insert a thin screwdriver. Just turn the screwdriver one way or the other and the fixed point will move. Insert the feeler gauge and when you feel the correct gap (light-to-moderate drag as you insert and withdraw it) tighten the screw (see fig. 2-16). Recheck the gap after tightening the screw.

The maximum gap between the two points is extremely critical. The factory specification will give you a few thousandths of an inch of leeway (it might be .014 to .019 inch), but never exceed those limits. The reason is that the gap adjustment also determines how quickly the points will close when the lobe passes the fiber block, and how quickly they will open when the next lobe comes around. The closing of the points completes the circuit, so the charging up of the coil is affected. The opening of the points causes the coil to trigger, so the ignition timing is affected.

Next, turn the distributor body back until the alignment marks you made earlier are aligned once more. Tighten the lockbolt securely.

Figure 2-16. Checking gap between the breaker points with a feeler gauge of specified thickness. Once the gap is set so the feeler moves in and out with light-to-moderate drag, tighten the screw as shown.

Checking Points Dwell

The opposite of the points being open is when they are closed, which is called *dwell.* Whenever the lobes on the distributor cam do not hold the points open, they spring closed. The time they are closed (measured in degrees of rotation of the distributor cam) is important, for it is during that time that the ignition coil charges up. Just as the maximum gap between the points must be within specifications, so must the dwell.

Checking dwell is done with the engine running at idle, so begin by reinstalling the rotor (push it down firmly onto the top of the distributor cam, until it seats). Then refit the distributor cap and engage the clips, screws, or locking rods.

You're ready to use the dwellmeter. If it is a combination tach-dwellmeter, turn the knob to dwell, and the cylinders' knob to the correct number (4, 6, or 8).

Note: On some dwellmeters there is no 4-cylinder knob position; just set it for 8 and double the reading you get.

Before you make the connections, look at the top of the ignition coil. You'll see three wires, one wire with the thick jacket that goes to the top of the distributor cap, and one on each side of it. Of the two additional wires, one is to a terminal marked "SW" (for switch) or plus, the other "CB" (for contact breakers) or minus. Connect the test

Figure 2-17. How to connect a dwellmeter. The wire from the dwellmeter positive terminal is connected to the negative terminal of the ignition coil (also may be marked SW or CB). The wire from the dwellmeter negative terminal (usually black) is connected to an electrical ground, such as an engine or body bolt. Inasmuch as the dwellmeter also serves as a tachometer (engine speed indicator), this also is the way to connect a primary tachometer (see chapter 1).

meter wire with the red-covered clip (or from the plus terminal of the meter) to the ignition coil terminal marked "CB" or minus. Connect the other test meter wire (with a black clip or from the minus terminal of the meter) to an electrical ground, such as an engine bolt, or the metal body of the distributor (see fig. 2-17).

Start the engine and let it idle. Read the meter and compare the number of degrees shown with factory specifications. If you have set the breaker points accurately, the dwell reading should be within specifications. If the dwell reading is too high, increase the gap between the breaker points; if it's too low, reduce the gap. In either case, keep the gap within specifications; aim toward the high or low end of the car manufacturer's range.

Dual Points. Some older cars are equipped with two sets of points, which overlap each other and permit only one distributor cam lobe for each two cylinders. On this design, which improves spark at high engine speed, you must measure dwell both separately and with both points operating. To measure it separately, merely insert an insulator (such as a piece of cardboard) between the contacts of one set, and the dwell reading you get will be for the other set. Reverse the procedure for the second set.

Note: Although this book does not include Japanese cars, if you have a Japanese Datsun with two sets of breaker points, you should know that they are operated and adjusted differently from other types. Either obtain a Datsun service manual for specific instructions, or leave this job to a professional.

Next, perform a dwell-holding test. Switch the meter to "TACH" and have a helper step on the gas pedal—and hold it steady—so as to raise engine speed 1,000 r.p.m. over the idle speed reading. Switch the meter back to dwell, and at this higher speed the dwell reading should be within three degrees of the idle speed reading. If the difference is greater, it can be responsible for poor performance. The only cure, if you have a performance problem, is to replace the distributor, a job for a professional.

Notes: On some engines, the dwell variation may exceed three degrees without affecting performance noticeably. The criterion for replacement, therefore, is engine performance.

When you tighten down the fixed point screw(s), be sure to use the correct size screwdriver and tighten securely. If it is not tight, engine vibration allows it to loosen, and the point gap adjustment will be lost. In some cases, the initial movement may cause the engine to fail the dwell-holding test.

Adjusting Points—General Motors V-8s

On its V-8 engines, General Motors (producer of Pontiac, Chevrolet, Buick, Oldsmobile, and Cadillac) used what was called a Peek-A-Boo distributor with breaker points until 1975, when it switched to electronic ignition.

This distributor differs from others in several important ways. There is a metal window in the side of the distributor cap. Instead of removing the cap for points' adjustment, you just lift the window, insert a ⅛-inch Allen wrench into an adjuster, and turn it to change the point gap (see fig. 1-18). The point gap is adjusted with the engine running, using a dwellmeter.

Although you can, you need not remove the distributor cap and adjust the points with a feeler gauge. You should, however, take off the cap to inspect them (see fig. 2-18). On some distributors there is a two-piece metal shield (for radio interference suppression) on top of the breaker plate covering the points and condenser. Remove it and you can see the points. If they need only an adjustment, you can do either of the following:

Reinstall the metal shield (if used) and the distributor cap. Connect a dwellmeter, as with other types of distributors, and turn the adjuster whichever way is required to bring the dwell reading to within specfications.

As with other distributors, make alignment marks on the distributor body and engine, slacken the lockbolt at the base of the distributor, and turn the distributor body until the fiber block is against a peak of a cam lobe. Insert a ⅛-inch Allen wrench into the adjuster and turn to set the point gap to specifications (fig. 2-19).

Figure 2-18. To inspect points, remove the distributor cap (on GM V-8 distributors, also remove the rotor). Then push movable points away with a screwdriver so you can look closely at the contact faces.

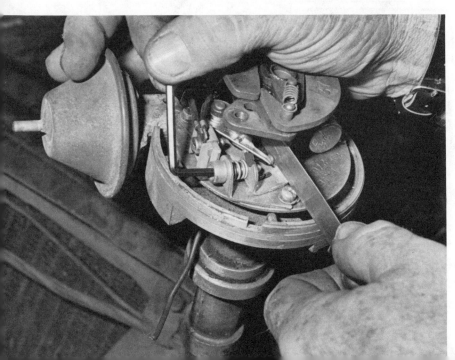

Figure 2-19. If you wish, you can adjust point gap on GM V-8 distributor with engine off and distributor cap removed. Just slacken the lockbolt and turn distributor body until fiber block is against peak of cam lobe. Insert specified feeler gauge between the points and turn the Allen head adjuster with an Allen wrench, as shown, until feeler moves in and out with light-to-moderate drag.

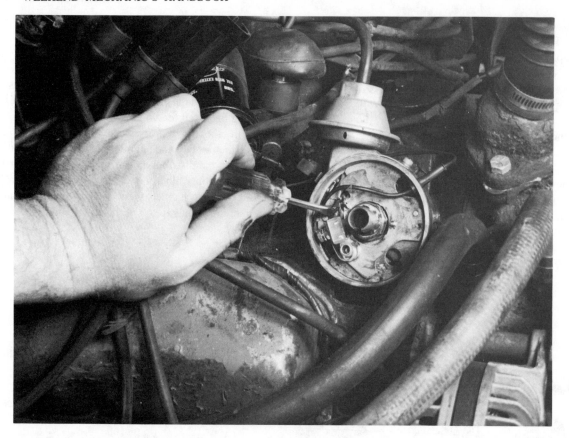

Figure 2-20. Installing a set of points with built-in condenser. The rectangular segment on top of the points holds the condenser, eliminating the need for an extra connection. Bottom illustration is a close-up drawing of the unified point set.

Replacing Breaker Points and Condenser

The condenser may last tens of thousands of miles. If you don't see metal transfers on the points (hill on one contact face, valley in the other), the condenser is apparently doing its job and need not be replaced. However, the easiest points and condenser to install is a combination assembly, in which the condenser is already a permanent part of the movable point rather than a separate item wired to it. With the combination assembly, you simply discard the old condenser and the job of installation is the same as if the condenser did not exist. The combination costs a little more than separate sets of points and condenser, and you may be replacing a condenser that's still serviceable. However, the assurance of a good condenser-to-points connection and the security of a brand-new condenser is well worth it (see fig. 2-20).

Begin the replacement job by removing the distributor cap and, on GM V-8 engines, the radio suppression shield if used. Observe how the wiring is connected to the terminal for the movable point, and check if there are any plastic or fiber sleeves or washers used (they are insulators) that must be reinstalled. Typically, the terminal will have a lockscrew to hold the wires from the condenser and the coil; there may be a nut threaded on a stud (see fig. 2-21); or finally, the wires could have push-in spades that are held by a spring lock in the terminal. With this design, you push on a tang on the terminal as you pull on the wire, and the wire will come out. Whatever arrangement is used (see also fig. 2-22), disconnect the two wires from the movable point terminal. If you have an access problem, perhaps you will find it easier if, as the next step, you unscrew the points and lift them up.

The points themselves are usually held in place by a single screw in the slot hole of the fixed point (see fig. 2-23). Or there are two screws, such as on some Ford and all GM V-8 distributors (see fig. 2-13).

Note: On the Ford distributors, the second screw will have a thin wire strap attached to it. This is a ground strap and must be reconnected.

If you have a magnetized screwdriver, remove the points' screws with it, so you don't drop the little screw and the washers.

To install the new set of points (see fig. 2-24), just put it in place (see fig. 2-25), install the retaining screw(s), and reconnect the wire from the ignition coil. If you are installing a separate set of points and condenser, make the second connection from the condenser and tighten the condenser mounting screw securely.

Figure 2-21. Nut threaded on stud is the terminal for wires from the coil and the condenser. Slacken nut and disconnect the wire as shown.

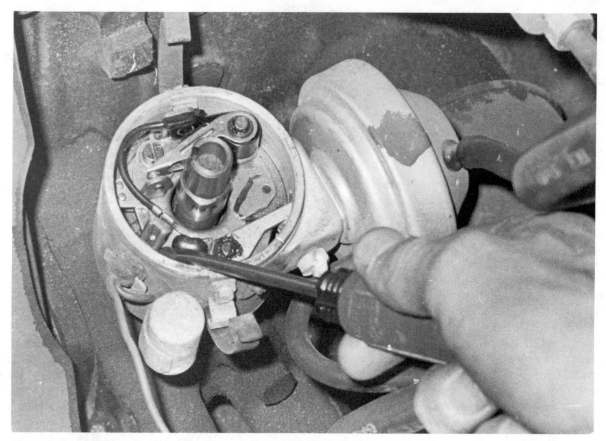

Figure 2-22. This distributor has a points' terminal with a male spade. Push up on the wire with the female spade, using a screwdriver as shown, to disconnect it.

Figure 2-23. A single screw in a slot hole holds this set of ignition points.

Figure 2-24. Here's another set of points with a lead wire that has a female spade terminal. You can see the slot hole and the notch for the screwdriver.

Figure 2-25. Putting the set of ignition points into place.

Figure 2-26. A dab of white grease, about the size of a match head, is all you need to lubricate the cam. Smear the grease evenly around the cam, using a fiber brush or your finger.

Apply a thin film of white grease using a soft fiber brush or your finger (see fig. 2-26) to the circumference of the distributor cam where it comes in contact with the fiber block. This grease is sold in tubes, or a small amount may be included with the set of points. If the point set comes with a lubricating wick built in, applying the grease is unnecessary.

Finally, adjust the points and check the dwell as explained earlier.

Other Distributor Checks

While you're replacing or adjusting the breaker points, there are several other checks you should make:

1. Look at the rotor. If the metal tip is burned, try to clean it with a wire brush or fine sandpaper. If the burn is severe, and a lot of sanding or brushing would be necessary, the metal removed from the tip might cause ignition problems. In this case, replace the rotor.

Figure 2-27. Notice that the rotor of the Ford distributor on an older computer system has two firing tips, one high and one low. The inserts in the distributor cap are also at two levels. This provides increased separation, so there is less danger of a high-voltage spark going astray. Only one rotor tip fires at a time.

Figure 2-28. Cleaning out distributor cap terminals with a wire brush. If cap has male terminals, wire brush their exterior. Also clean the spark plug wire terminals, male or female, with a brush, if required.

Figure 2-29. After cleaning, inspect the inside of the distributor cap, using a flashlight if necessary. If you see any cracks, including fine hairlines, replace the cap, as explained later in this chapter under the subject of spark plug wires.

Caution: Don't sand the rotor tip on a car with electronic ignition. What seems to be a brown mark on the rotor tip may actually be a special coating that should not be removed. However, if there's a clear-cut burn mark, replace the rotor. In fact, you should apply a fresh coat of that grease (called silicone dielectric grease and sold in tubes) to the rotor firing tip(s), and on Ford products with electronic engine control (fig. 2-27), to the rotor contact plate tips in the distributor cap too.

2. Disconnect one spark plug wire at a time from the cap and look at the terminal into which it fits. If you see whitish corrosion deposits, clean them out with a wire brush (see fig. 2-28). Also check the coil wire terminal in the cap.

3. Wipe the inside of the cap with a dry, clean rag and look for cracks (including fine hairlines). If you see any, replace the cap (see fig. 2-29).

4. On all but General Motors V-8 Peek-A-Boo distributors, which have it on top (and most computer-controlled electronic spark advance systems, which do not have it at all), the mechanical advance system is under the breaker plate, out of sight. You can quick-check it with the rotor in place. Just turn the rotor—it will go one way, about ¼ inch. Release it and it should spring back. If it doesn't, the mechanical advance is defective. Servicing it is a job for a professional.

5. On GM distributors with the centrifugal advance on top—that's the Peek-A-Boo—and on electronic igni-

tion systems (all without a computer), make a careful inspection of the centrifugal advance. Look for enlargement of the weights' holes and eating away of the posts on which the weights swing. If there is none, just spray on silicone lubricant. If there is erosion of either or both parts (fig. 2-30), you can obtain repair kits at auto parts stores to correct the problem. If the erosion is severe, a professional can repair the distributor by replacing the shaft-and-weights as an assembly. Detail parts are not available.

Erosion of weights and posts is rare on breaker points systems, but all too common on GM electronic ignition. The reason is the very high voltage the system develops. High voltage arcing in the distributor cap forms corrosive gases, which accelerate the erosion.

You also may see erosion of the distributor cap rotor button and the cap in the area around the button itself. In severe cases, high-voltage arcing from the coil to the rotor button can completely destroy the cap. Change spark plugs at reasonable intervals (maximum 24,000 miles) and apply silicone dielectric grease to the rotor tip if the car maker so recommends. Both these steps will reduce firing voltages and the corrosive gases that result. Also, spray silicone lubricant on the centrifugal advance mechanism at least once a year.

6. Check the vacuum spark advance, a feature on all engines except those with computer-controlled elec-

Figure 2-30. Centrifugal advance mechanism of GM electronic ignition (GM High Energy Ignition or HEI) distributors may wear away at the points shown at *top left*. *Top right* shows how holes in centrifugal weights wear into slots. Photo *at bottom* shows how posts wear away near base. Repair kits are available that permit installation of oversize plastic bushings to correct the problem if it is caught before excessive wear has occurred.

tronic spark advance mechanisms. With the engine running at 2,000 r.p.m. (fast idle), disconnect the vacuum hose from the advance unit (see fig. 2-9) and put your finger over the hose end. Let engine speed stabilize, then reconnect the hose. When you reconnect, the engine should speed up slightly if the vacuum advance is working. On all but General Motors V-8s, a defective vacuum advance can be replaced by removing a couple of retaining screws and unhooking the link from the vacuum advance at the breaker plate. An experienced weekend mechanic may attempt this. On the GM V-8 type, it may not be so easy on many models to unhook the link, so if you are not experienced, leave the job to a professional.

Note: If there are two vacuum hoses connected to the vacuum unit, it is a dual-action device that serves to both advance and retard the spark. With the engine warm and running at 2,000 r.p.m. (fast idle), disconnect both hoses and plug the hose ends. Reconnect the inner hose and the engine should respond by slowing down slightly. Have a helper hold down the gas pedal slightly, then reconnect the outer hose, and the engine should respond by speeding up. If there is no response, particularly from the outer hose reconnection, and you have an engine performance problem that other tuneup services do not correct, have the distributor checked by a professional.

ELECTRONIC IGNITION

Electronic ignition is standard equipment on all American cars today. If the thought of electronics frightens you, keep this in mind—the electronic circuitry does nothing more than replace the breaker points and condenser.

You need to know some basics about ignition.

Pickup Coil. Inside the distributor, where the points used to be, is an electronic device called a "pickup coil." It picks up a signal and transmits it to the car's electronic ignition unit. Most cars have electromagnets as their signaling device; others have a special type of solid-state device called a Hall Effect switch (see fig. 2-31), and still

PICKUP

ROTOR

ROTOR TIP

TRIGGER WHEEL

SHIELD

DISTRIBUTOR CAP

Figure 2-31. Here is one type of electronic ignition distributor (Hall Effect switch). As the teeth of the trigger wheel pass the electromagnetic pickup, they create a signal in the pickup that is transmitted to a transistorized control unit that triggers the ignition coil. Notice that the rotor is combined with the trigger wheel. If you have this design (Chrysler front-drive cars), you will notice a contact tab on the underside that grounds the trigger wheel. The tab must make good contact with the distributor shaft (or the car will not start).

others have a photoelectric type (a light aimed at an electronic device called a photocell, to provide a complete circuit). The pickup coil also is called a *sensor*, or as in the case of the Hall Effect type, a switch. It may also be called a *stator*. Do not confuse it with the ignition coil.

Reluctor, Trigger Wheel, Light-Chopper, or Armature. In the center of the distributor, replacing the cam and its lobes, is a wheel with teeth (one for each cylinder). The wheel may be called a reluctor, trigger wheel, light-chopper, or armature.

Figure 2-32. Schematic of an electronic ignition system showing the electronic control unit with its switching transistor, a part that opens the coil electromagnetic circuit just as if the breaker points were opening.

Figure 2-33. Here's a typical General Motors High Energy Ignition (HEI) distributor. Ignition coil is built into top of cap. Transistorized control unit is miniaturized and located next to pickup on what used to be called the "breaker plate." Notice that plug wires are held in place by the plastic cage on top and that the cap itself has male plug wire terminals.

As this device is spun by the distributor shaft, its teeth pass the sensor and trigger it. The sensor then signals the electronic ignition unit. On photoelectric systems, there is a disc with cutouts, so the light circuit from light to photocell is completed, then interrupted. When it gets this signal, the control unit electronically breaks the ignition coil circuit (just as the breaker points did it electromechanically). The coil discharges, and the high-voltage electricity goes to the rotor, the cap, and the appropriate spark plug wire.

In some cars the control unit is a sealed box bolted somewhere under the hood (see fig. 2-32). On others, primarily General Motors cars, it is miniaturized and placed inside the distributor, on the same plate as the pickup coil. On most 1982-on Ford products, there is a miniaturized unit bolted to the exterior of the distributor.

General Motors cars have another design wrinkle all their own. On many of their early electronic ignition systems, the ignition coil is built into the top of the distributor cap (see fig. 2-33).

IGNITION SYSTEM QUICK-CHECK

When a car won't start, but cranks normally, the ignition system is the first place to check, to determine if there is a spark to the plugs. This procedure can be used on all engines with spark plug wires.

All Systems

1. Disconnect the most accessible spark plug wire, insert a key or paper clip into the wire terminal, and hold the end of the key or clip within $\frac{1}{4}$ to $\frac{1}{8}$ inch of a metal part of the engine (see fig. 2-34).

Figure 2-34. Key is inserted into plug wire terminal to provide a projection from rubber nipple. If you hold edge of key to electrical ground while a helper cranks the engine, you can check for spark. *Note*: If the plug wire is even slightly deteriorated, do not hold it or you could get a shock. Use insulated hand pliers, electrical pliers, a couple of sticks, anything that will hold and insulate.

2. Have a helper crank the engine and you should see a steady spark from the key or clip to the engine. If you do, the ignition system is working, although worn spark plugs may be responsible for hard starting.

3. If there's no spark, disconnect the thick-jacketed wire from the center of the coil to the center of the distributor cap, at the cap. Hold the end of this wire within ¼ inch of a metal part of the engine (see fig. 2-35). Have a helper crank the engine and you should see a steady spark. If you now do, the problem is in the distributor cap, rotor, or spark plug wires.

   On General Motors High Energy electronic ignition, with the ignition coil built into the cap, the test in Step 3 is impractical. Instead, inspect the cap for cracks and make sure the pink wire in the cap flange is securely connected (see fig. 2-36). On distributorless ignition engines with spark plug wires, further evaluation should be left to a professional.

4. If you still have no spark on an electronic ignition car, remove the distributor cap and look for physical damage to the rotor, the pickup, or the reluctor (timing armature). If there is nothing obvious, proceed to a test instrument checkout as described elsewhere in this section. If you have a car with breaker points ignition, proceed to Step 5.

5. With the ignition turned on, flick the points open (see fig. 2-37) and allow them to close, using an insulated-handle screwdriver, with the tip wrapped with electrical tape. You should see a small electric arc. Or connect a test lamp to the movable point and electrical ground. Push open the points with a wooden stick, and the test lamp should light (see fig. 2-38). Let the points close, and the test lamp should go out. If the test lamp does not light in the first case, there is no current to the points (go to step 6). If it doesn't go out completely in the second case, the points are defective (go to step 7). If the test lamp results are normal, go to Step 8.

   Note: Points should be closed and touching for this test. Crank engine to allow this, if necessary.

6. Reconnect the test lamp to the negative terminal of the ignition coil (terminal generally marked with a minus sign or the letters "NEG") with the ignition on and the points pushed open. If the test lamp now lights, the wire from coil to points is defective. If the test lamp doesn't light, switch it to the positive terminal, and if it now lights, the ignition coil is defective. If it still

Figure 2-35. If there's no spark at the end of the plug wire, disconnect wire from center of distributor cap (not possible on most General Motors High Energy Ignition systems). Push back nipple and hold terminal close to electrical ground while helper cranks engine. As with plug wire, use special insulated pliers, sticks, etc., to hold wire if it's deteriorated.

Figure 2-36. Shown is pink "battery" wire in distributor cap flange of GM High Energy Ignition System. If necessary to disable this ignition system for any tests, unplug the pink wire.

Figure 2-37. You should see an arc across points when you flick them open with screwdriver with ignition on.

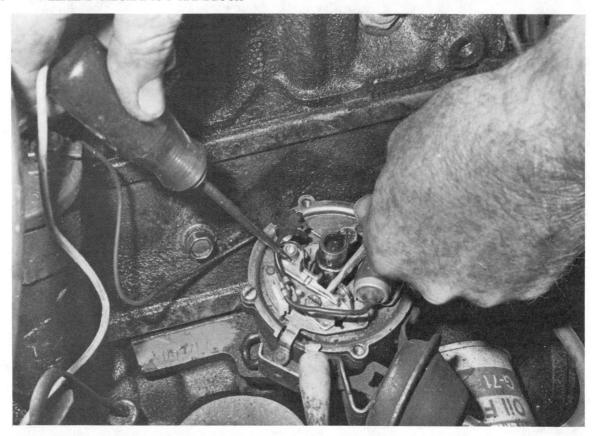

Figure 2-38. Connect test lamp to ground and hold its probe on movable point as shown. With ignition on, push away movable point with stick as shown, and test lamp should light. Let points close and test lamp should go out.

Figure 2-39. Testing condenser with test lamp. Wire from condenser is disconnected, and test lamp alligator clip is hooked to it as shown. Test lamp probe is touched to movable point, which is insulated from fixed point with piece of cardboard between the points. Turn on ignition, and if test lamp lights, it is because condenser is providing an electrical ground, which it *should not*. Replace condenser.

doesn't light, the resistor, ignition key switch, or wiring is defective—a repair job for a professional.

7. Replace the breaker points and adjust to specifications.
8. The condenser apparently is defective. If the problem is a grounded condenser, you can confirm this with the test lamp (see fig. 2-39). Disconnect the condenser wire, touch one lead of the test lamp to the battery starter terminal and the other to the end of the disconnected condenser wire. If the lamp lights, the condenser is grounded and must be replaced. Even if the condenser does not fail this test, test it by substitution with a new one. Test the ignition coil with the homemade tester as described in the electronic ignition service section earlier.

Servicing the Electronic Ignition

The electronic ignition components themselves require no periodic service, with the exception of some Chrysler designs, in rear-wheel-drive cars. The pickup coil position on those is adjustable (the part is held by a single screw, which passes through a slot hole in the pickup coil, as shown in fig. 2-40). The pickup coil must be a specified distance from the teeth of the reluctor, a gap which is measured with a feeler gauge. Because the pickup is magnetic, a nonmagnetic (brass) feeler must be used. A steel feeler (the conventional kind) would be drawn to the pickup, and a false feeling of drag would be provided, even if the gap were too great.

Dwell. Dwell is not measured on an electronic ignition system. It is a designed-in function of the electronic control unit, and unlike breaker points systems it normally will vary with engine speed.

Engine r.p.m. The "hot" tachometer connection (the one that isn't to the electrical ground) on some cars with electronic ignition is not quite the same as on breaker points ignition cars, particularly General Motors products with ignition coils built into the distributor cap. The hot connection must be made to a male spade terminal in the underside of a flange on the cap of GM cars (see fig. 2-41). It must be made to the "TACH" terminal of a plastic connector on the ignition coil of most older Ford cars (see fig. 2-42).

Note: On some tachometers made for electronic ignition systems, special connections are required. For example, you may have to connect to the positive battery

Figure 2-40. Some Chrysler distributors have adjustable pickup coil (screw goes through slotted hole). Line up reluctor tooth with pickup coil as shown, insert specified non-magnetic feeler gauge and, if necessary to change gap, slacken screw and move pickup as required.

Figure 2-41. Here's a look at the underside of a GM High Energy Ignition distributor cap. Wire connects to battery terminal from car's harness. The male spade *above* is for tachometer connection; however, you will probably need a special adapter, available in auto parts stores, since alligator clip on tachometer is too big to attach to spade. Adapter has female spade that plugs in, and adapter itself hangs down for easy tachometer connection. If you wish, you can make an adapter from a female spade terminal and a piece of wire. Then attach the alligator clip to a bared end of the piece of wire.

TACHOMETER TERMINAL

"BATTERY" TERMINAL

Figure 2-42. Here's an older Ford ignition coil with its special plastic connector. Insert male spade adapter or thin nail into location called "Tach Test" as indicated by arrowhead, then connect tachometer to adapter or thin nail. Also shown is a new coil design called an E-core. It is used on Ford and General Motors cars.

terminal, not to an electrical ground. Check the instructions furnished with your tachometer very carefully.

Electronic Testers. The best way to test an electronic ignition system is with an electronic tester made specifically for the purpose. Today there are many electronic testers that will check out virtually all cars, such as the inexpensive ones shown. The pocket-size tester (see figs. 2-43 and 2-44) has light-emitting diodes, little solid-state electronic "bulbs." When the tester is properly connected and some simple procedures are followed, certain light-emitting diodes will light up to tell you what is wrong. Then you replace the defective part.

Testing with Ohmmeter. If you have a multiscale ohmmeter, you can make some important electronic ignition tests, and they may be conclusive.

The basic test of an ignition system is to see if it produces a spark. If it produces sparks at the end of the spark plug wires and the spark plugs are good, it is doing its job.

Figure 2-43. This is one type of electronic ignition analyzer. It has light-emitting diodes (electronic bulbs) at left, and chart tells you what's wrong, according to which light-emitting diode(s) light up during test.

Figure 2-44. Tester also comes with spark-pluglike part that clips to an electrical ground as shown. A plug wire is disconnected, attached to this part, and the engine is cranked. If you see spark jumping inside the "spark plug," the ignition system is okay. This is ideal for electronic ignition systems, as it permits a spark check without the need to hold the plug wire, which could be dangerous on the ultra-high-voltage electronic ignition system.

Typical V-8

Typical 6 Cylinder

Figure 2-45. Illustrations show typical two-wire connectors from the pickup coil. Undo connector and check resistance across the dual-terminal arrangement of the wire section from the distributor.

Before you make any tests of the complex parts of the electronic ignition system when it does not produce a spark, look carefully for loose connections on the distributor and ignition coil, and if the system has a separate electronic module, at the module and from the pickup (see fig. 2-45).

Note: The connections inside a General Motors distributor are coated with a corrosion-resistant chemical that may look like corrosion, and this should not routinely be wire-brushed off, or the electrical terminals will quickly corrode and problems will occur.

To test each system if it does not produce a spark, in all cases, wiggle wires at connection points and recheck for spark. If spark appears, there is a wiring problem at the last point checked. Also check for current to the ignition coil with the ignition switch on. Do this by probing the coil's positive terminal (marked with a plus sign), using a 12-volt test lamp with the clip end grounded. The lamp should go on.

Note: On GM cars with the ignition coil mounted in the distributor cap, probe the pink wire terminal in the cap flange. On some computer-equipped cars, such as Chrysler front-drive products with electronic fuel injection, the computer does not provide current flow to the ignition coil until the engine is cranked.

General Motors. First, remove the distributor cap and unplug the two-wire connector from the ignition module in the distributor (see fig. 2-46). The two wires connect to an electromagnetic pickup, and testing it is important. Connect the two-wire leads from an ohmmeter to the pickup wires and take a reading, which should be within manufacturer's specifications (typically 500 to 1,500 ohms). If the car does not have an engine control computer

(most pre-1981 models don't), disconnect the vacuum hose from the distributor and connect an auxiliary hose. Apply vacuum with a manual vacuum pump (see fig. 2-47) or have a helper suck vigorously on the hose, and you'll see the distributor plate move. If the ohmmeter reading changes significantly, there is a problem, perhaps with the wiring at the pickup (where it's hard or impossible to see). The distributor must be disassembled for inspection and possible replacement of the pickup.

If the pickup passes the test, the ignition module or the ignition coil may be defective. First, if the system has a separate coil (rather than the one built into the top of the cap) check the ignition coil with the ohmmeter. Unplug the thin-wire terminals on each side and the thick-wire terminal in the center. Connect the ohmmeter to one thin wire terminal on each side and you should get a very low reading, typically 0.3 to under 3 ohms (see fig. 2-48). Next, (see fig. 2-49), move one ohmmeter lead to the thick-wire terminal (the one with the wire to the distributor cap) and again check resistance, which should be within specifications (typically 6,500 to 15,000 ohms). Replace the coil if it is outside specifications. On General Motors cars with the ignition coil mounted in the distributor cap, remove the cap and connect the ohmmeter to the terminals as shown in figure 2-50, and test as explained for that design.

An alternate way to check a separate ignition coil is with a homemade tester (see fig. 2-51). If the coil produces a healthy spark with the use of the tester, the coil is good. General Motors ignition modules are not very expensive, and substituting a new one in a no-spark situation should be less costly than obtaining a module tester. When installing a GM module, coat the underside with silicone dielectric grease, a special grease that transfers

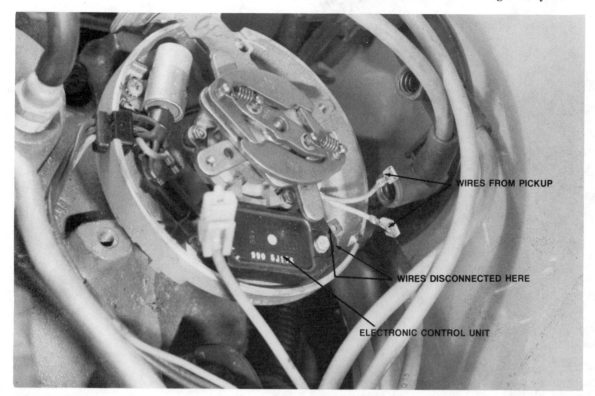

Figure 2-46. A look inside a GM High Energy Ignition system distributor. Wires from pickup coil, which is hidden underneath, have been disconnected from electronic control unit terminals. Connect ohmmeter across the two wires that are from the pickup.

Figure 2-47. Test GM module on cars with vacuum advance by activating vacuum advance with manual pump as shown or by sucking on vacuum neck, with ohmmeter connected. Ohmmeter reading should not change.

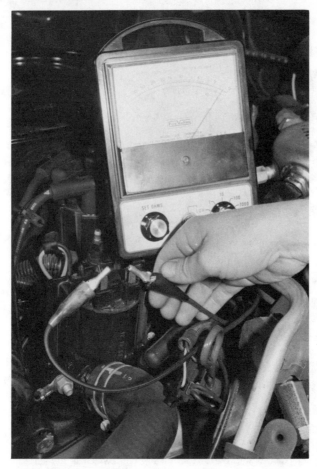

Figure 2-48. Test separate coil with ohmmeter across two thin-wire terminals (wires disconnected), and reading should be very low (0.3 to under 3 ohms).

Figure 2-49. Test separate coil with ohmmeter leads touching one thin-wire terminal and thick-wire terminal. Reading should be 6,500–15,000 ohms.

Figure 2-50. Testing GM ignition coil built into cap is different. Remove cap and turn over as shown. Connect ohmmeter leads to terminals numbered 1 and 2 and reading should be very low (under 3 ohms). Then connect between terminals numbered 1 and 3 and then 1 and 4. The coil is defective if it fails low reading test or is the ohmmeter reads infinity in both the second and third tests (not merely in one of them).

Figure 2-51. This is a homemade jumper wire arrangement you can use to test an ignition coil. Instead of the 0.33 microfarad capacitor, you can use a condenser from a breaker points system, if this is easier to obtain.

heat (see fig. 2-52). Failure to do so will cause early module failure. This also is true for Ford products with Thick Film Ignition (TFI) modules mounted to the distributors, covered later.

Caution: If you have to change an ignition module on a GM car, be sure the replacement is the correct part number. Even though another number may physically fit, it may not work properly under certain conditions. Also, there are two pickups and two ignition coils for coil-in-cap designs, and you must get the correct part. One pair has a yellow paint spot on the coil and a yellow wiring connector from the pickup; the other has a white or clear

connector on the pickup and a white or no-paint spot on the coil.

Chrysler Front-drive Cars. On carbureted models through 1986, turn on the ignition and use the special homemade jumper wire at the ignition coil. If there is no spark, unplug the 10-way connector from the underhood computer and recheck. Spark now? The computer may be defective (it is covered by a 5-year, 50,000-mile warranty). If there is a spark, unplug the three-wire connector from the distributor, and disconnect the center wire from the distributor cap, and hold it about 3/8 inch from a ground on the engine (taping the wire in place may be the practical approach if you don't have a helper). Turn on the ignition and connect a jumper wire to terminal No. 2 of the harness side of the distributor connector (the part that doesn't go to the distributor) and quickly touch and remove the other end of the jumper wire from terminal No. 3 of the wiring connector (see fig. 2-53). There should be a spark. If there is none, and if the coil tested good, the distributor pickup is defective. Unlike GM cars, it is not necessary to take apart the distributor; replacement is an obvious procedure.

On fuel-injected models, unplug wiring from the ignition coil and connect a jumper wire from the coil to the battery positive terminal, then use the special homemade jumper wire. If the coil passes this test, reconnect the

53

Figure 2-52. Apply silicone dielectric grease to entire base of electronic ignition module as shown, on GM and Ford TFI systems. The grease helps the module dissipate heat and if not applied, the module may fail quickly.

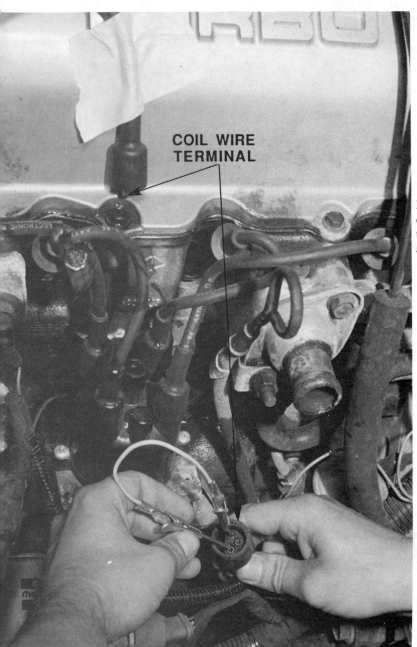

COIL WIRE
TERMINAL

Figure 2-53. To test for spark on Chrysler front-drive cars, separate connector from distributor, tape ignition coil wire so terminal is close to ground (metal part of engine) as shown, then connect jumper across terminals 2 and 3 as described in this chapter.

HALL EFFECT DISTRIBUTOR WIRING
HARNESS CONNECTOR

JUMPER WIRE

1

3   2

original wiring and probe the coil positive terminal with a grounded 12-volt test light while a helper cranks the engine. If the test light does not go on, there is an apparent problem with the computer system.

Ford Motor Company Cars. Ford has used three ignition systems—Duraspark, Thick Film Ignition (TFI) I, and TFI IV. On Duraspark, used exclusively through 1981, there is an electronic ignition unit mounted away from the distributor, typically near the starter relay. On TFI I, the pickup in the distributor is similar (an electromagnetic type), but the module is miniaturized (looks like the GM type) and is mounted on the side of (not inside) the distributor. TFI IV has a different pickup (a Hall Effect switch type) and it does not have a vacuum advance unit on the distributor. Instead, the timing is controlled completely by the Engine Control Computer (EEC), and because it is the fourth version of this computer, it is called EEC IV (hence the name TFI IV). On most 1988 Fords, the TFI-IV module was moved from the distributor body to a separate underhood location.

The ignition coil on all three systems can be tested as described for the GM types. To check the pickup on Duraspark, unplug the three-wire connector from the distributor, ignore the black wire, and check resistance across the terminals of the other two wires on the side of the wiring connector that goes to the distributor (see fig. 2-54). Resistance should be within specifications, typically 650 to 1,300 r.p.m. Recheck with vacuum applied as described for GM systems.

The best way to check the TFI I system is to first make a switching test, which tells you if pickup and ignition coil are basically operating. Pierce the green ignition coil wire close to the TFI I ignition module connector with a straight pin and connect a grounded test light to the pin (see fig. 2-55). Crank the engine and the lamp should flash reasonably brightly. If it doesn't, make tests of the ignition coil and pickup, and if they pass, the module apparently is defective (when removing a TFI module, remove the mounting screws and push down on it to disengage).

Because the pickup on TFI I is electromagnetic, it also can be checked with an ohmmeter (650 to 1,300 ohms), although the terminals are in the distributor and somewhat recessed. Refer to figure 2-56.

The Hall Effect switch means TFI IV requires a different checkout procedure. Make the switching test with the grounded test light at the coil negative terminal (may be marked "TACH" and/or with a minus sign). Also test the ignition coil.

Unfortunately, the switching test is not as positive as on

Figure 2-54. This is a Ford distributor on an older car with an electronic ignition system. Terminal from distributor has three wires. Disregard black wire and connect ohmmeter as shown, across the terminals for the two other wires.

Figure 2-55. To make switching test on Ford TFI I system, pierce green wire at connector and attach grounded test light, then crank engine and light should flicker. On TFI IV system, make test at ignition coil, as described in this chapter.

Figure 2-56. Test Ford TFI I pickup by connecting ohmmeter wire leads to pickup terminals indicated, and reading should be 650 to 1,300 ohms.

the TFI I system because you can't double-check with the ohmmeter test. Therefore, follow this procedure if the system passes the switching test but the car is suffering from cold rough idle and pinging noise:

Starting with an overnight-cold engine, unplug the "spout" connector (a black or white connector with two yellow wires that is in the harness close to the TFI IV ignition module on the distributor).

Ground the negative lead of a voltmeter to the distributor base, start the engine, and measure battery voltage at 1,200 to 1,500 r.p.m. (use tachometer). Then move the positive voltmeter lead from the battery to the TFI IV module side of the spout connector. If the voltage is not more than 40 percent of the battery reading, change the pickup.

Even if the voltage is higher, continue testing. Raise engine r.p.m. to 4,000 (keep hood down for safety), and take another voltage reading with the same electrical connections. It should be at least 90 percent of whatever you got at 1,200 to 1,500 r.p.m. If it's lower, change the pickup.

Here again, even if the voltage reading is at least 90 percent, continue testing. Warm up the engine and take another reading with the voltmeter connected to the mod-

ule side of the spout connector. This reading should be no more than 10 percent above the cold-engine 1,200 to 1,500 r.p.m. reading. If there's a greater difference, replace the pickup. If there is not, the pickup apparently is good.

Caution: When handling distributor rotors with the TFI system, don't bend the "cat's whisker" type rotor tips or engine roughness may occur (see fig. 2-57). Also, don't coat these tips with silicone dielectric grease.

On Chrysler rear-drive products, most of the electronic ignition systems have a dual resistor (see fig. 2-58). One section of this resistor is to reduce voltage to the ignition coil, as in a conventional ignition system; the other is wired to the electronic control unit. The resistance of each must be within specifications, as measured with a multi-scale ohmmeter. If either resistance section is outside specifications, the complete resistor must be replaced.

Other Checks. As with a breaker points ignition system, you must check the distributor cap for cracks, the rotor for burns, and on non-computer systems, the advance mechanisms. Details on these checks are at the conclusion of the previous section.

You should realize, however, that many rotor tips are

Figure 2-57. This is a cat's whisker type rotor used on Ford products. It should not be greased and it must be handled carefully to avoid damage to the whiskers.

Figure 2-58. Checking the resistance across one of the two resistance sections of a Chrysler resistor. The resistance being checked is for the wiring to the electronic control unit (upper section is for ignition system resistance to the ignition coil). Use the notch in the end of the resistor as a locator, as the resistor may be mounted upside down or vertically. The dual resistor was changed to a single resistor (with only a section to the ignition coil) in 1980 and was discontinued in 1981.

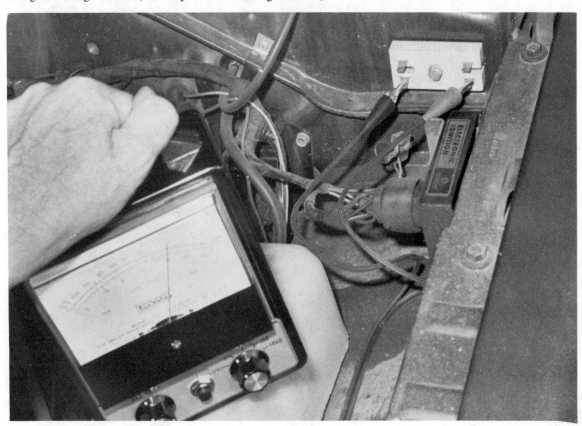

coated with silicone dielectric grease, and this may produce a brown coating on the tips that resembles burning. Do not sand off this brown coating, or you may increase the air gap between the rotor and distributor cap to the point where engine misfire will occur. If a rotor tip appears burned, replace the rotor.

Replacing Components

The control unit on virtually all systems is a simple unbolt-and-disconnect proposition. The only special procedure is on the modules in the General Motors distributors. A small capsule of special heat-sink grease should come with a replacement module, and you should smear this grease on the metal base of the module before installation. If you don't, the module will overheat and fail prematurely. The pickup coil on all but General Motors cars (and American Motors cars with GM electronic ignition) is easy to remove from the distributor. On General Motors systems, the distributor must be removed and partly disassembled, a job for a professional. On pre-1978 American Motors cars (Prestolite system), pickup coil service also should be left to a professional. AM cars made since 1982 have the Ford system. However, many AM cars have GM engines and use GM ignition systems. AM-built Renaults have a French ignition system.

Note: It is good practice to apply heat-sink grease to Ford TFI modules mounted on the distributor.

IGNITION TIMING

Ignition timing—the arrival of the high-voltage electricity at the plugs—is one of the most important tuneup adjustments you make. On cars with breaker points, it follows the points adjustment, for points gap changes can affect it.

All ignition systems have provided for automatically changing the timing according to engine operating conditions—speed and load, for example—but it is important that the engine begin with a basic setting that is correct.

Note: If your car has a computer that regulates spark timing, special procedures in addition to (or replacing) those given in this section are required. Computer-controlled spark advance is covered in the next section of this chapter.

Some engines (often those with turbochargers) have a provision for automatically setting back (called "retarding") ignition timing to prevent engine spark knock (ping). This is done by an electronic control unit or the engine computer, signaled by a knock sensor. See chapter 3 for testing information.

Here's how to check the basic timing and make adjustments if necessary.

Timing Marks

Except for those cars with distributorless ignition, all engines have timing marks for reference. Ignition timing is checked by aiming the timing light (see fig. 2-59) at the timing marks. There are two marks, one of which is fixed to the engine, the other of which is on a rotating part—such as the belt pulley assembly of the crankshaft, at the front of the engine, or the flywheel at the rear, visible through a hole in the flywheel housing. On a few cars, the mark is on the flywheel but the "viewing window" is at the rear face of the engine, covered by a rubber plug. On transversely mounted engines, the marks are at one side (see figs. 2-60 to 2-63).

Figure 2-59. Here is a typical timing light. Two alligator clips at bottom are connected to car battery, and clamp above them is clipped onto No. 1 spark plug wire.

Figure 2-60. This is a typical timing mark arrangement at front of engine. Degree indicator is fixed to front of engine and there is a notch on the crankshaft pulley that rotates adjacent to it. Although this degree indicator has many marks and numbers, plus the words "before" and "after," the typical indicator may have no more than a few lines and perhaps just a couple of numbers. The words before and after refer to "Top Dead Center," which is when the piston is at the top of its stroke (during compression of the air-fuel mixture). Some engines use a zero for this position. TDC is a common abbreviation for Top Dead Center, and many ignition timing specifications are BTDC (for Before Top Dead Center) and occasionally ATDC (for After Top Dead Center). If BTDC or ATDC is not specified with the number of degrees, the specification is for BTDC.

Figure 2-61. This is the VW BEETLE air-cooled engine. There is a notch on the pulley (if more than one notch, check specifications to see which one to use) and the fixed indicator is simply the joint between the two halves of the engine. *Note*: Water-cooled (front-wheel-drive) Volkswagens have a mark on the flywheel and a viewing "window" in the transaxle housing.

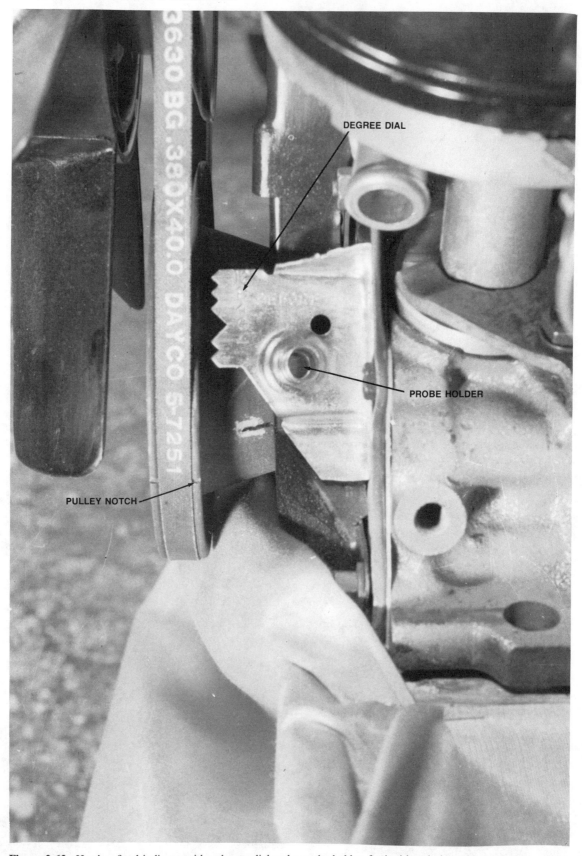

Figure 2-62. Here's a fixed indicator with a degree dial and a probe holder, for ignition timing with an electromagnetic probe instead of a timing light.

Figure 2-63. Many cars have timing marks at the flywheel. On this particular one, VW Rabbit, you remove the computer-timing sensor and either aim a timing light into the hole (the mark—a number—should show up in the middle of the hole when the light goes on) or use a probe timing indicator. On later VWs there is no sensor, but there may be a plastic plug in the hole. Remove it for a timing check.

These marks are so located that when they line up with each other, the spark plug on either one of two cylinders will be firing. All cylinders are numbered by the car manufacturer, but you won't find the numbers on the engine. Instead you must consult a reference chart (see fig. 2-64), which shows how the numbers are assigned.

It is customary for the car maker to position the timing marks so that they align when the No. 1 cylinder's plug is firing. If the timing is correct for the No. 1 cylinder, it will be correct for all.

With the timing light hooked up and the engine idling, the light will flash on when the spark plug to which it is connected is firing. If you aim the light at the marks, they should be aligned whenever the light goes on.

Finding the Marks. By reference to figs. 2-60 to 2-63, you should be able to find the fixed timing indicator. It may be just a pointer, or a dial with numbers. The rotating mark will usually be a notch, perhaps a dial, or occasionally a number. If you can't conveniently see it, crank the engine in very short bursts until it comes up into view.

Hard-to-see Marks. The fixed timing indicator may be badly obscured, such as by an alternator or air conditioning compressor. This is a common problem on cars with the marks at the front of the engine, the usual location on American cars.

If you can't see the marks, you can't aim the timing light at them. There are two practical answers to this problem:

Most rear-drive Chrysler products, and those GM cars with distributors, have a fixed indicator with a holder for a pencil-like probe (see fig. 2-65). You obtain a special timing indicator with the probe, push the probe into the holder, and read the timing on a meter (see fig. 2-66). This type of timing indicator is much more expensive than a conventional power timing light.

Note: If you can see part of the timing indicator, you can use a special timing light as shown in figure 1-10.

You can make a set of timing marks elsewhere, in a better viewing location. In some extreme cases, the only location may be from under the car, with the front jacked up (see chapter 5 for jacking instructions).

Making New Marks. To set up the engine for a set of new marks, you must properly align the existing marks once. This may pose some difficulties, but even if you have to use a flashlight and mirror to do it, just realize that after you make the new marks you won't have to struggle again.

FIRING ORDER AND CYLINDER NUMBERING OF POPULAR CAR ENGINES

Make of Car	Firing Order	Cylinder Numbering*	
AMERICAN MOTORS (except Renault models and GM engines)			
V-8	1-8-4-3-6-5-7-2	D: 1-3-5-7	P: 2-4-6-8
four	1-3-4-2	1-2-3-4	
six	1-5-3-6-4-2	1-2-3-4-5-6	
CHEVROLET, BUICK, OLDS, AND PONTIAC			
V-8	1-8-4-3-6-5-7-2	D: 1-3-5-7	P: 2-4-6-8
V-6†	1-6-5-4-3-2	D: 1-3-5	P: 2-4-6
four†	1-3-4-2	1-2-3-4	
six (in line)	1-5-3-6-2-4	1-2-3-4-5-6	
CADILLAC			
V-8 (except 350)	1-5-6-3-4-2-7-8	D: 2-4-6-8	P: 1-3-5-7
350 V-8	1-8-4-3-6-5-7-2	D: 1-3-5-7	P: 2-4-6-8
CHRYSLER			
V-8	1-8-4-3-6-5-7-2	D: 1-3-5-7	P: 2-4-6-8
in-line six	1-5-3-6-2-4	1-2-3-4-5-6	
four	1-3-4-2	1-2-3-4	
FORD			
V-8 (351, 400)	1-3-7-2-6-5-4-8	D: 5-6-7-8	P: 1-2-3-4
V-8 (other)	1-5-4-2-6-3-7-8	D: 5-6-7-8	P: 1-2-3-4
four (1600)	1-2-3-4	1-2-3-4	
four (2000)	1-3-4-2	1-2-3-4	
four (2300)	1-3-4-2	1-2-3-4	
V-6	1-4-2-5-3-6	D: 4-5-6	P: 1-2-3
six (in-line)	1-5-3-6-2-4	1-2-3-4-5-6	
VOLKSWAGEN			
Beetle	1-4-3-2	D: 3-4	P: 1-2‡
Rabbit, Dasher, or Scirocco†	1-3-4-2	1-2-3-4	
DATSUN			
four	1-3-4-2	1-2-3-4	
TOYOTA			
four	1-3-4-2	1-2-3-4	

*D indicates driver's side and P indicates passenger's side. On Chrysler Omni-Horizon models with Peugeot engines, the numbering begins at the transaxle end of the engine.

†On transversely mounted engines, numbers start at crankshaft pulley (drive belt end) of engine.

‡On rear engine, reverse the numbers if you are counting from the rear bumper: i.e., D: 4-3 becomes P: 2-1 counted from the rear bumper.

Figure 2-64. Chart gives the firing order and method of cylinder numbering of popular car engines.

SIX-CYLINDER ENGINES

MAGNETIC TIMING PROVISIONS

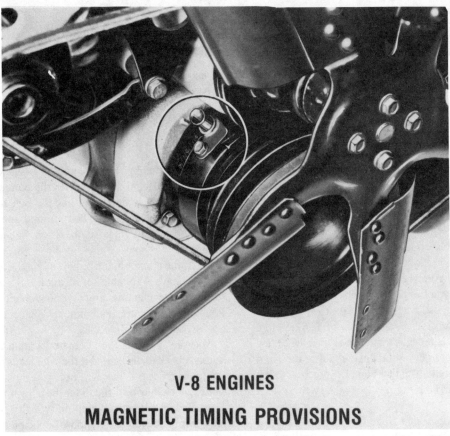

V-8 ENGINES

MAGNETIC TIMING PROVISIONS

Figure 2-65. This illustration shows the magnetic timing probe built into the fixed timing indicators on rear-wheel-drive Chrysler engines.

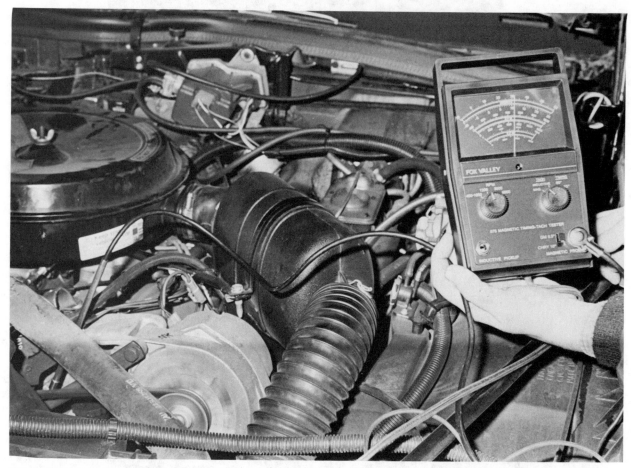

Figure 2-66. This is a magnetic timing indicator. Wire with probe goes into holder and other wires are connected to car battery and No. 1 spark plug wire. Ignition timing is indicated on meter, which also serves as a secondary tachometer.

Crank the engine in very short bursts until the rotating indicator (usually a notch on the crankshaft pulley) is as close as possible to the fixed indicator. Then grasp a drive belt that wraps around the crankshaft pulley at two locations midway between the crankshaft pulley and another pulley. Push the two sections together and simultaneously pull up on one section, down on the other. The crankshaft pulley will turn and you'll be able to get perfect alignment of the marks. Or if you can get a wrench on the crankshaft pulley bolt, you can use a wrench to turn it.

If the specification reads, for example, 8 BTDC (Before Top Dead Center), that means that the notch on the pulley must align with the eight on the degree dial of the fixed indicator. If there are two eights, align the notch with the first eight as you turn the engine clockwise (viewed from the front).

Now look for an open area around the circumference of the pulley, somewhere close to an engine bolt, to which you can attach a fixed pointer (see fig. 2-67). Make the pointer from a piece of metal, something substantial, at

least 1/8 inch thick. Make the pointer L-shaped (or as close as is practical) and drill a hole in the pointer for the bolt. The part of the pointer that has the bolt hole should be long enough so it can be bent around some part of the engine to hold it in position. Then tighten the bolt to secure it.

Next, file a mark in the pulley, aligned with the pointer, and you have a suitable set of marks. Because you have lined up the manufacturer's timing marks, these additional marks also are in alignment. You need never use the hard-to-see original marks.

Note: In selecting the alternate location for the timing marks, check to determine if the wire leads of your timing light will reach. If they will not, you must obtain extensions, which may be difficult for the trigger wire to the No. 1 spark plug if it is the clamp-on type that attaches to the plug wire. Or you may choose a location for the new marks that may not be quite as convenient, but which will not require modification to the wire leads of your timing light.

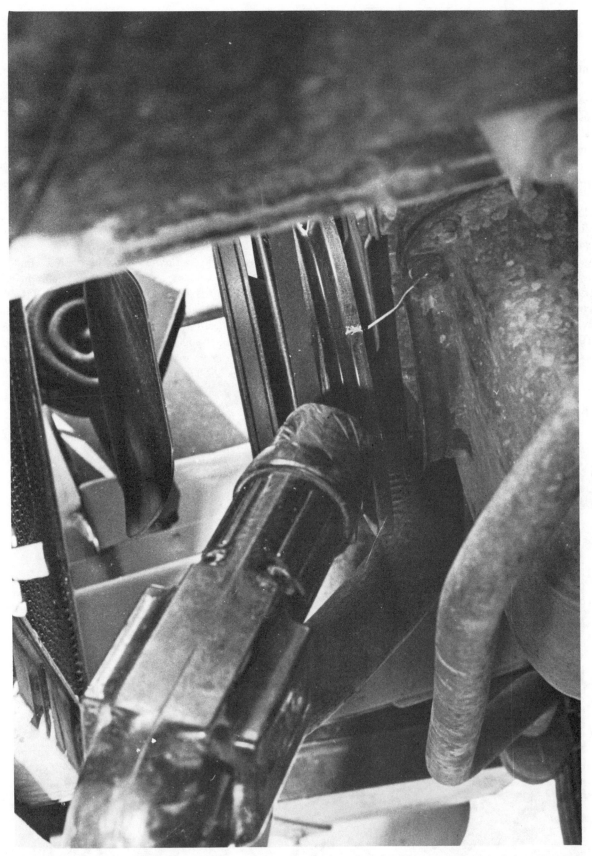

Figure 2-67. If timing marks are inaccessible, make your own elsewhere on engine. This pointer is attached to an oil pan bolt and the crankshaft pulley has had a notch filed into it, on the underside of engine.

Specifications

Timing is set to specifications provided by the car maker. In most cases the information is on an underhood decal (see fig. 1-21). On a car with breaker points ignition you must set the breaker points first (or be assured by a check that the gap is correct), for changes in point gap change ignition timing.

You must understand what the specifications mean and how to interpret them. If a specification reads 8 BTDC, that means eight degrees Before Top Dead Center, or before the piston reaches the top of its stroke in the cylinder. You can't look inside the engine, but there is a degree dial at the timing marks. As the engine rotates clockwise (as you look at it from the front), the first set of numbers before the zero or TDC (Top Dead Center) mark is *before*. Those that follow are ATDC (After Top Dead Center). On some cars, timing may be ATDC, but that is rare. In some cases the specifications may read BTC and ATC (Before Top Center and After Top Center). If neither appears, the timing should be set for Before Top Dead Center.

Checking Ignition Timing

To check ignition timing, follow these steps:

Warm up the engine.

Disconnect the vacuum hose. Or disconnect hoses at the ignition distributor's vacuum control unit (see fig. 2-68), and plug the hose(s) end(s) with a pencil(s). This may not apply to an imported car. Check the underhood decal on your car for precise details. Many cars with electronic ignition, even without computers, require special steps before ignition timing should be checked, and these steps are listed on the underhood decal. Failure to follow them often causes severe errors in setting timing and possible engine damage.

Connect the power timing light. Clip the red wire to the battery's positive terminal, the black wire to the negative terminal, and the remaining wire, called the trigger, to the No. 1 spark plug, or its wire. Exactly how you connect the trigger wire depends on the make of timing light you have purchased, so you must follow the instrument maker's instructions (see also chapter 1 and figs. 2-69 and 2-70).

Figure 2-68. Disconnect and plug the vacuum hose from distributor before checking ignition timing. If there are two hoses, disconnect and plug both.

Figure 2-69. Trigger wire on this timing light has alligator clip which attaches to spring. Disconnect No. 1 plug wire, push one end of spring onto end of spark plug, and reconnect plug wire to other end of spring.

Figure 2-70. This timing light has clamp-on pickup on the end of the trigger wire.

Figure 2-71. If timing is off, slacken lock-bolt or nut at base of distributor and turn distributor body as necessary to bring timing marks into alignment; then retighten bolt or nut to secure the timing adjustment.

As explained earlier, the timing marks line up when No. 1 cylinder spark plug is firing, so connect the trigger wire to No. 1 plug or its wire, in accordance with the instructions.

Start the engine and let it idle. On some cars timing is specified at a speed other than idle. Check the under-hood decal and if necessary operate the throttle to obtain the specified speed. You will have to connect a tachometer to be sure. If you find it difficult to hold the specified speed, you can have a helper at the gas pedal or obtain an inexpensive special tool that is installed to bear against the throttle linkage in any position and hold a desired engine speed.

Aim the timing light at the marks. If they are perfectly aligned, timing is correct. If they are not, loosen the lockbolt or nut at the base of the distributor (see fig. 2-71) and turn the distributor body in whichever direction is required to bring the marks into alignment. Tighten the lockbolt or nut and the adjustment is complete.

COMPUTER SPARK ADVANCE

Computer-controlled spark advance first appeared in 1976, when Chrysler introduced it on a small number of cars. Ford introduced its version, called Electronic Engine Control I, on some 1978 cars. General Motors had an early system in 1977 and 1978 (MISAR on Olds Toronado), then began heavier use in 1979, primarily on California cars. By 1981, all GM cars but the Chevette had a computer to control spark advance.

All these systems have certain things in common:

A miniature computer that signals the electronic ignition control unit, to tell it when to trigger the ignition coil.

A group of electronic and electromechanical devices called "sensors" wired to the computer and feeding it the information needed to make a decision as to the optimum ignition timing for each situation.

These computer systems were introduced because it was found that if the ignition timing could be changed radically according to a range of engine operating conditions, two things could be accomplished:

Exhaust emissions could be reduced.

Engine performance and gasoline mileage would be improved.

Prior to these computer systems, ignition timing was automatically controlled by a set of centrifugal weights on springs in the distributor (responding to engine speed) and a vacuum diaphragm unit bolted to the distributor (responding to changes in engine load). These mechanical devices are not nearly as precise as a computer, not nearly as fast, and they cannot make very radical changes in timing (see fig. 2-72).

Figure 2-72. This is the distributor of a Ford with a computer-controlled spark advance system. With the rotor removed and at left, you can see there's nothing inside except the distributor shaft.

Sensors

The sensors commonly used include the following:

Engine speed
Coolant temperature
Throttle position (see figs. 2-73, 2-74)
Engine vacuum (also measured as a form of pressure in General Motors and Ford systems, as in fig. 2-75)
Crankshaft position, so the computer knows which cylinder will be the next to require a spark, and when
Air temperature inside the engine compartment (see fig. 2-76)

The operation of a basic system to control ignition timing is shown in the early GM MISAR system (see figs. 2-77, 2-78, and 2-79).

Figure 2-73. Throttle position is an important consideration in ignition timing, and when a computer knows where the throttle is, it can make precise adjustments. This Chrysler device is a miniature electromagnet containing a movable iron core that is connected by wire to the throttle linkage. When the throttle is opened the wire is pulled, moving the iron core. This alters the magnetic field and sends a signal to the computer.

THROTTLE LINKAGE

THROTTLE POSITION SENSOR

Figure 2-74. This Ford throttle position sensor is a variable resistor. As the throttle linkage is operated, it also moves a contact inside the sensor, changing the resistance of a current flow transmitted by the computer. When the computer senses a change in this current flow, it translates this information into a throttle position indication.

Figure 2-75. This is an early Ford computer system that controls spark advance, fuel mixture by the carburetor, the exhaust gas recirculation valve, the air pump system, and the fuel vapor control cannister. The composite pressure sensor measures both atmospheric and intake manifold pressure (actually a vacuum in the manifold). The solenoids at the lower left are triggered by the computer as necessary to control the output of the air pump, a pollution control. The EGR solenoids regulate vacuum flow to the exhaust gas recirculation valve when they are triggered by the computer. The exhaust gas oxygen sensor tells the computer how rich the fuel mixture is, and if necessary the computer moves a device in the carburetor called a stepper motor to richen or lean out the mixture. The computer also uses information from the various sensors to control ignition timing and, if necessary, to operate a throttle kicker solenoid to increase the idle speed.

ELECTRONIC SPARK ADVANCE MODULE
- **Vacuum Transducer**
- **Ambient Temperature Sensor**

FRESH AIR INTAKE

WATER TEMPERATURE SENSOR

IDLE STOP SOLENOID WITH CARBURETOR SWITCH

THROTTLE POSITION TRANSDUCER

TO IGNITION

BALLAST RESISTOR

INLET AIR TEMPERATURE SENSOR

IGNITION COIL

MAGNETIC TIMING

DUAL PICK-UP DISTRIBUTOR

CHRYSLER Plymouth

Figure 2-76. This is a Chrysler electronic spark advance system. Vacuum transducer converts engine vacuum reading into an electronic engine load signal for computer; carburetor switch on idle stop solenoid tells computer if engine is idling or not; other sensors measure water temperature, ambient air temperature, throttle position, and inlet air temperature in air cleaner.

ATMOSPHERIC PRESSURE LINE   VACUUM PRESSURE LINE

IGNITION HARNESS

REFERENCE TIMING CONNECTOR

CONTROLLER ASSEMBLY

Figure 2-77. Here is the heart of the GM MISAR system, used on 1977–1978 Olds Toronados. Below is the crankshaft (position) sensor, aligned with a toothed pulse generator disc on the front of the engine. Each tooth triggers the crankshaft sensor that transmits a signal to an underdash computer, *above*. The computer then triggers the High Energy Ignition distributor. Note the timing adjuster bolt and the clamp bolts on the sensor. Also notice the reference timing connector wire, an unconnected wire hanging down from the computer. This connector must be grounded before a timing check can be made. If timing must be changed on this design, slacken clamping bolts and turn adjuster. In 1978, this system was changed so timing changes could be made in the conventional way, by turning the distributor body.

FRONT ENGINE MOUNT

TIMING ADJUSTOR BOLT

PULSE GENERATOR DISC

P/S PUMP BRACKET

CRANKSHAFT SENSOR

TIMING ADJUSTER CLAMP BOLTS

Figure 2-78. View of front of 1977 Olds Toronado engine shows how toothed pulse disc was mounted on crankshaft, just back of crankshaft pulley.

Figure 2-79. A look at the actual parts of the 1977 MISAR system.

Computer Failure

If the computer fails, the systems all have a "limp-in" feature that permits you to continue to start and operate the car, but with performance and gas mileage often so poor you'll bring the car in for service.

If you believe that a sudden substantial drop in performance may be caused by a computer failure, and there is no "Check Engine" light or similar dashboard warning to let you know, you can make this simple check: Connect your timing light, aim it at the marks, and start the engine. Have a helper operate the gas pedal, light on the gas, then heavy, then moderate. As the pedal position changes, you should see substantial changes in ignition timing, but if the computer has suffered a catastrophic failure, you'll see none—the timing will remain unchanged.

Note: Many cars have a warning lamp that will light in case of a computer failure, eliminating the need for this test. On General Motors cars, the "limp-home" feature includes provision for some changes in spark timing, built into the distributor electronic module. Therefore, you may see some changes (up to as much as nine degrees) on GM cars even after the computer has failed and the "Check Engine" light in the dashboard has gone on. The limp-home providing of a small amount of spark timing charge also may be encountered on other makes.

Checking Computer-controlled Timing

Except for engines with distributorless ignition, there must be a provision for checking ignition timing on computer-controlled engines. Just check the underhood decal for the details. Following are special guidelines for most U.S. cars that may be helpful.

Ford products from 1978 to early 1980 have Electronic Engine Control I and II systems. The basic timing should be 10 degrees Before Top Dead Center, and this is checked with the computer out of the picture. The way to do this is to locate the computer housing under the dashboard, remove the screws that hold the program module in it, then take out the program module. If timing is correct, refit the module. If it is off by several degrees, have a dealer check the system.

Ford products made from 1980 to 1983 have EEC III (you can tell the 1980 models by the gold underhood tuneup decal). You must put the computer into a self-diagnosis mode to check timing, and you need an adjustable timing light because the specification will be off the scale on the front of the engine unless you retard the flashing of the timing light. To activate the self-test you need a manual vacuum pump (sold in auto parts stores under Lisle and Mityvac brands) and a vacuum-fuel pressure gauge. Install the gauge with a plastic tee, an inexpensive part also sold in auto parts stores and shown in figure 2-80. The tee goes into the thin (vacuum) hose from the air pump bypass valve (see chapter 4). Then force the hose end of the manual vacuum pump into or onto the neck of the pressure sensor, marked "Vent." Both parts are on the passenger's side of the engine compartment, on the fender well sheet metal. Warm up the engine, run it at idle and operate the vacuum pump to draw over 20 inches of vacuum. Hold this reading for a minute, then release. The vacuum gauge needle should pulse two or four times (depending on the engine), which tells you that self-testing has begun. As you draw vacuum, the throttle kicker should go on automatically. This is a device on the throttle linkage at the carburetor that normally pushes on the linkage to maintain idle speed when energy-drawing accessories are turned on. When you release vacuum with the pump, the kicker should go off but come on again and stay on for the rest of the self-test, which takes about two minutes. You can tell when the kicker is on (engine speed rises) and when it goes off (engine speed drops). Only when it is on should you check ignition timing, which should be 27 to 33 degrees Before Top Dead Center. After about a minute, the vacuum gauge reading should go up and hold steady. Then the vacuum gauge needle should pulse two or three times (depending on model). Soon afterward, the kicker should go off (engine speed will drop slightly) and if you watch the vacuum gauge, you should see the needle pulse. The needle should pulse once, pause, then pulse once more, a "code 11," which means the computer system apparently is performing normally. If you get another set of pulses, such as one, pause, then four pulses, that is a "code 14" and means there is a problem. There is a chart of trouble codes and what they mean in the factory service manual. This system is covered by the 5-year, 50,000-mile emission control warranty on the car, so refer the problem to the dealer. Checkout procedures on other computers are covered later in this chapter.

On 1983-on cars with Electronic Engine Control IV and the TFI IV ignition system covered earlier, unplug the spout connector from the wiring to the electronic ignition module on the distributor, as shown in figure 2-81, and the ignition timing should match the "base timing" specification (computer deactivated). There also is a timing check you can make with the computer activated. Put the car into the self-test mode as explained under Computer Systems Self-Diagnosis later in this chapter. In this mode, timing should read 20 degrees greater than the number with the spout connector unplugged.

On General Motors cars with carburetors, there is a four-wire connector from the distributor. Unplug it to bypass the computer (see fig. 2-82). On GM cars with fuel injection the procedure is different. If you unplug the connector the engine will not run, so you may have to put the computer into test mode. This is done by jumping across two terminals (one with a black wire, the other

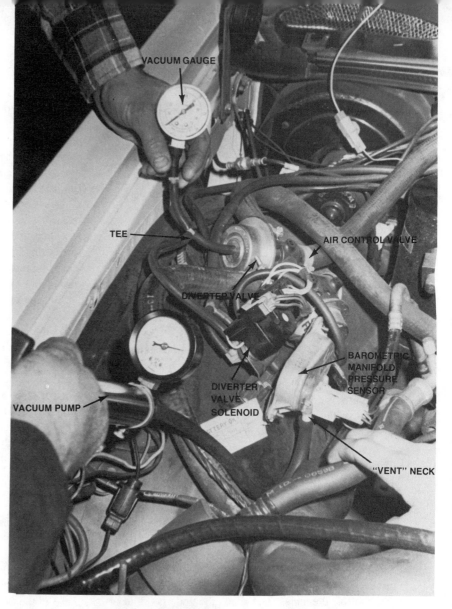

Figure 2-80. To trigger the EEC III self-test, connect a vacuum gauge with a tee and spare piece of hose into the vacuum hose from the solenoid to the diverter valve section of the air pump control valve, as shown. Then attach the hose from the manual vacuum pump securely into or onto the "Vent" neck of the barometric/manifold pressure sensor, also as shown.

Figure 2-81. Unplug spout connector from Ford TFI-IV distributor as shown. The entire connector has been unplugged from the ignition module on the distributor only for illustration.

Figure 2-82. Before checking basic timing on a General Motors computer-equipped car, unplug the four-wire connector from the electronic ignition distributor. Do not unplug any other connector. Unplugging this one will keep the computer from adding any advance to the ignition timing.

Figure 2-83. To probe the General Motors computer (all cars except Cadillac with throttle body fuel injection and all diesels), locate the special black/white wire hanging down under the dashboard. On pre-1981 models, it is a single wire hanging down on the passenger's side from the computer (*top photo*). On 1981 models, it is part of a five-wire connector just toward the driver's side of the dashboard (you may have to remove a trim panel underneath to find it). With the single wire, connect it with a jumper wire to an electric ground. With a five-wire connector, insert a paper clip as shown between the terminals for the black/white wire and the black wire next to it at one end.

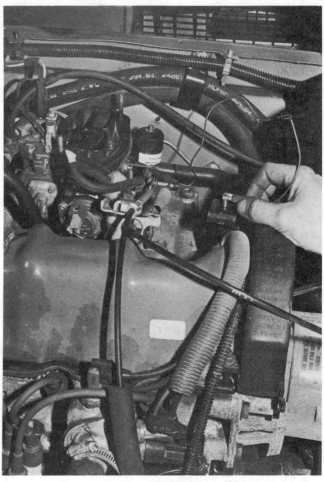

Figure 2-84. The Chrysler carburetor switch, which signals the computer when the throttle linkage is closed or open, should be grounded with a jumper wire as shown before attempting to check ignition timing. With the carburetor switch grounded, the computer will not change the basic ignition timing. The carburetor switch has a rod that bears against the throttle linkage and a wire from it to the computer. It is typically opposite the idle speed solenoid on front-drive Chrysler products.

Figure 2-85. Illustration shows vacuum transducer used on early-1980s Chrysler front-wheel-drive computers. If your car has one, disconnect hose and plug hose end for timing check explained in this chapter.

with a white one) side by side at one end of an underdash plug (plug is behind the cigarette lighter panel on Pontiac Fiero), as shown in figure 2-83. On others (except Cadillac), one of the four wires has a connector that must be taken apart for a timing check. Read the underhood decal to be sure. Refer to a service manual for the Cadillac procedure. Also, see figures 2-77, 2-78, and 2-79.

On Chrysler products with carburetors, connect a grounded jumper wire to the carburetor switch terminal (see fig. 2-84) and disconnect and plug the vacuum hose (if there is one) to the underhood computer (see fig. 2-85). On models with fuel injection, run the engine at idle, disconnect the wiring connector from the coolant temperature sensor (see fig. 2-86), then reconnect it, and the Power Loss lamp on the dashboard should come on (indicating the engine is in a mode with the computer control of spark advance bypassed).

On most 1980 and some subsequent models of Volkswagen with electronic ignition, a device called a digital idle stabilizer is used. This gadget (see fig. 2-87), mounted atop the electronic ignition unit, makes continuous small adjustments in ignition timing to maintain a consistent idle speed. To check timing, therefore, you must take this device out of the picture, which is done simply this way: Remove the two electrical connectors from the idle stabilizer and plug them into each other (they're made for this). If you have a starting problem on a VW with the idle stabilizer, the cause may be that the stabilizer is defective. You can isolate it from the circuit as explained, and if the car now starts, you know the stabilizer is defective and the cause of the starting failure.

Most 1988 VWs have Digifant II computers, with a totally different type of idle stabilizer. To check timing, warm up the engine, unplug the coolant temperature sensor (tower-shaped connector) from the engine upper radiator hose neck, raise engine r.p.m. to about 2300 (2000–2500), at which timing should read to specifications: 4 to 8 degrees Before Top Dead Center on 1988 cars, or the number on the underhood decal.

On 1982 AMC six-cylinders, unplug the black/yellow wire connector and hook up a jumper across the male terminals.

On Renault Alliance and Encore models, locate the electronic ignition computer under the hood on the firewall. Disconnect and plug the vacuum hose before checking ignition timing. See figure 2-88.

Figure 2-86. To put late Chrysler computers into Power Loss mode for timing check, unplug coolant sensor, then reconnect (engine idling).

Figure 2-87. If there is an idle stabilizer atop the electronic control unit on a VW Rabbit or other VW water-cooled model, remove both wiring connectors from it and plug them into each other before checking basic ignition timing on cars with electronic ignition. The electronic control unit is under a plastic shield on the driver's side, just back of the engine compartment in the air intake area. It is accessible with the hood up.

Figure 2-88. Disconnect and plug vacuum hose from ignition computer on U.S.-built Renault Alliance and Encore prior to timing check.

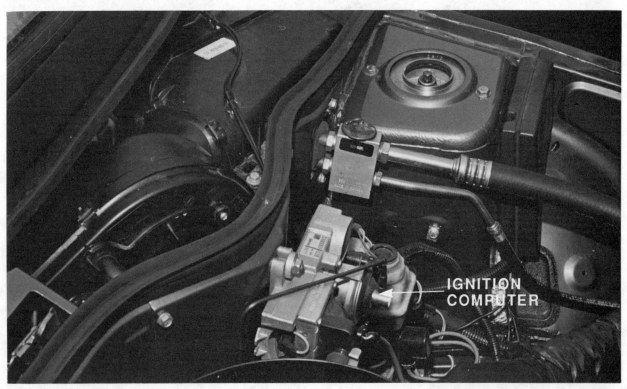

SPARK PLUGS

The spark plugs are the terminals of the ignition system (see fig. 2-89). When the rotor aligns with a terminal in the distributor cap, the high-voltage electricity goes into the terminal, along a heavily insulated wire, and into a metal rod (called the center electrode) embedded in the center of the plug. The electricity travels down that rod and when it comes to the end (inside the cylinder) it looks for a place to go. There is only one: an L-shaped metal prong that is anywhere from .025 to .080 inch away. That prong, called the side electrode, is part of the lower end of the plug that is threaded into the engine and is in metal-to-metal contact with it. The side electrode, therefore, is an electrical ground just like the engine itself. The electricity is sufficiently high-voltage to jump the air gap between center and side electrodes, and so it does, completing a circuit and forming an electric arc. That electric arc is what we call the spark.

Two things can happen to the plug to prevent that electric arc:

1. The inside of the plug can become fouled with deposits from gasoline or, if the engine is burning oil, from the oil. If the deposits coat the inside of the plug, they can provide an easier, alternate path for the electricity, so it doesn't jump the gap.

2. The constant electrical arcing across the electrodes causes them to erode, and the gap between them gets larger. If it gets too large, the high-voltage electricity may not be high enough in voltage to jump across.

Either of these conditions has the same effect: The mixture isn't ignited and we notice that the engine is misfiring.

Servicing the spark plugs is a multistep job:

1. Disconnect the spark plug wires.
2. Remove the old spark plugs.
3. Inspect the old spark plugs.
4. Perform a compression test (covered later in this chapter).
5. Adjust the new spark plugs.
6. Install the new spark plugs.
7. Inspect the spark plug wires and replace any that are defective.
8. Reconnect the spark plug wires.

Let's take a look at each step.

Note: Before you start, you should know that a compression test is best performed with the engine warm, so it's best to begin spark plug removal with a warmed-up engine. Wear work gloves to prevent burning your hands.

Servicing Spark Plugs

Disconnecting the Spark Plug Wires. The spark plug wires on all modern cars are the resistance type, for radio suppression. The conductor is not metal wire, but a fiber

Figure 2-89. This is a typical spark plug. When threaded into the engine its side electrode is an electrical ground. Spark enters electrode at top, travels down to electrode inside the cylinder, and jumps air gap to side electrode. As the electricity jumps the air gap, it creates what we call the spark. Circuit is complete when electricity reaches the electrical ground of the side electrode. The ceramic insulator prevents high-voltage electricity from leaking away to ground via another patch, which would eliminate the spark that fires the air-fuel mixture in the cylinder.

Figure 2-90. To remove a plug wire, twist the nipple to break heat seal, then pull off. Do not grasp wire itself or you could damage it internally.

Figure 2-91. If plug wire is in a tight area use a plug wire removal tool, such as these insulated pliers.

impregnated with carbon. Therefore, you must handle the wires with care to prevent them from breaking internally, which is damage you can't see, but which can cause the engine to miss.

Grasp the wire at the spark plug terminal's rubber nipple, twist back and forth to break the heat seal, then pull. Never pull on the wire itself (see fig. 2-90).

If the nipple is not easy to grasp, obtain a special tool (sold at auto parts stores) that is made to do the job. There are several types and all are inexpensive (see fig. 2-91).

To assure that you will reconnect each wire to the correct plug, label each wire. A simple way is to wrap a piece of masking tape around the wire and put a number on the tape, starting from the front of the engine. First plug is No. 1, second is No. 2, etc., except Peugeot engines (also used on some Chrysler Omni-Horizons) and Jaguar in-line six-cylinder engines.

Removing the Old Plugs. To remove the old plugs, you'll need a spark plug socket, which is a deep (tall) socket made to fit the hexagonal rim of the plug (see fig. 2-92). Most spark plug sockets are $^{13}/_{16}$ inch, although there are some that are $^{5}/_8$ inch.

Note: The engine should always be cool before you remove spark plugs. This is particularly important on engines with aluminum cylinder heads. If you are planning to make a compression test, for which the engine should ideally be warm, remove the plugs after allowing a couple of hours for the engine to cool.

If the spark plug is wide open, all you need to remove it is the socket and a ratchet wrench with the knob set to "loosen." This means it will lock when counterclockwise force is applied, and it will freewheel when the handle is turned clockwise. Just put the socket over the plug and move it down until it fits on the hex section securely. If you're not sure how this should feel, just take a new plug from the box and try the socket on it.

Move the ratchet handle into an open area, then apply steady counterclockwise pressure with one hand while you push down (to keep the socket in position) on the head of the ratchet. If the spark plug is very tight, whack the end of the ratchet handle with your palm to shock it loose.

Less-accessible Plugs. It is almost unheard of for all spark plugs to be so accessible that the ratchet and socket is all you need. At the very least, placing the ratchet on the socket will bring the ratchet so close to the engine that you won't be able to get a good grip on the handle. If this is the case, just place an extension rod between the ratchet and socket (see fig. 2-93).

If there is some underhood accessory in the way of a straight-on approach with the extension rod, there are other possible methods. Use a universal joint, inserted between socket and extension, or between extension and ratchet. That will permit you to work at an angle, around the obstruction.

Or purchase a spark plug ratchet, the type with a universal joint built into the head and a curved handle; it

Figure 2-92. With the plug wire off you can see the exposed hex in the middle of the plug, flush with the exterior surface of the engine's cylinder head.

Figure 2-93. If the plug is reasonably accessible, just the plug socket, an extension rod, and a ratchet will permit you to reach it.

Figure 2-94. If access is a bit difficult, perhaps this spark plug ratchet will help. It has a long curved handle and universal joint in the head, so it can work in tight places.

should be even better at clearing obstructions (see fig. 2-94). If the problem is lack of clearance between the spark plug and the side sheet metal of the engine compartment, perhaps you can use the socket without the ratchet. Just fit it onto the spark plug and put a box wrench over the hex end of the socket. Put a finger on the end of the socket to hold it in place and use the box wrench to turn the socket.

To some extent you have to look at the spark plug and see what tool arrangement is necessary. In some cases, a plug that looks buried may be reached with a combination of extension rods and a universal joint. Just remember, the spark plug must be removable, even if it isn't easy.

Don't fret if you crack or break the ceramic outer shell of the plug. Sometimes the wrench will slip and that's exactly what will happen during removal. Just reposition the socket on the hex section and get out the broken remainder. You're throwing it out and installing a replacement, so you don't need it for anything.

After loosening a spark plug, blow away any dirt before removal. If you don't have an air compressor or tank, you can use a can of compressed air available from a photo supply store.

Inspecting the Old Spark Plugs. As you remove spark plugs, keep them in order. Inspect them, looking for the conditions shown in figures 2-95 to 2-98. If a mechanical problem is indicated in only one cylinder, you'll know which cylinder it is. If only one spark plug is oil-fouled, for example, the problem might be a broken valve stem seal, something you can replace yourself, as explained in chapter 5.

Compression Test. Once the spark plugs are out, you can make a compression test, which will indicate if the engine can be tuned successfully. The gauge measures the pressure developed by the piston as it rises in the cylinder to compress the fuel mixture. If compression is good, it means that the sealing rings around the piston (the piston rings) and the valves that admit the fuel mixture to the cylinder and allow the burned exhaust gases to escape are not leaking, and that the cylinder head gasket (the seal between the engine block and the head) is holding. If they leak, the pressure is reduced, and so is the force of the burning fuel mixture. Less force means less power. A tuneup will not restore compression; that's a mechanical job for a professional shop.

Figure 2-95. This spark plug was damaged by preignition, which usually is indicated by a pinging sound from the engine. Some pinging is normal in a modern engine, but an excessive amount can damage the plug. Often this type of damage is caused by a plug with too high a heat range, so check the spark plug application chart carefully.

Figure 2-96. This spark plug has been fouled by sooty carbon deposits. Because the spark plug has too low a heat range for the engine or the fuel system is maladjusted or spark plug or plug wire is defective, the plug has been misfiring.

Figure 2-97. This spark plug is covered with oil deposits. Check for worn piston rings or defective valve stem seals or guides.

Figure 2-98. This plug is just worn out from excessively long use. Notice that center electrode is worn down from erosion.

The compression test requires a helper—someone to sit behind the wheel, hold the gas pedal to the floor, and crank the engine while you hold the gauge in place. You must make simple disconnections to prevent the system from building up high voltage while it is being cranked. If there is a separate ignition coil, remove the two thin wires attached to the top of the coil. On General Motors High Energy Ignition, disconnect the pink wire in the distributor cap flange (see fig. 2-36). If the pink wire is difficult to reach and there is a separate ignition coil (not built into the distributor cap as on most GM HEI systems), you may be able to reach and unplug all the wiring at the ignition coil. On distributorless ignition engines, unplug the thin wires' connector from the ignition modules.

As shown in figure 1-15, hold the gauge with the nipple in the spark plug hole. Push firmly, because the compression pressure will try to force the gauge nipple out. If you have a gauge with a long hose, just thread it into the spark plug hole and simply hold the gauge itself. This type is ideal for those spark plug holes in positions that make the other type impractical to hold.

Have your helper crank the engine for about three or four seconds, then remove the gauge and record the reading. Repeat this procedure for each cylinder. Reset the needle to zero after each reading.

Look at the readings. The lowest should be within 25 percent of the highest, and all readings should be at least 90 to 100 pounds per square inch (p.s.i.). If the highest is 160 p.s.i. for example, the lowest should be at least 120 p.s.i. If any one reading is unusually low, repeat the test on that cylinder. A low reading in adjacent cylinders only is normally caused by a defective cylinder head gasket. In any case of low compression, have the engine repaired before you tune it.

If the compression readings are within the acceptable range, proceed to adjust and install new spark plugs.

Adjusting Spark Plugs. The gap between the center and side electrode of a spark (see fig. 2-99) must be adjusted to factory specifications before installation, using a feeler gauge with a bending bracket.

First, pick the feeler gauge with the gap specified for your engine and insert it between the two electrodes. It should go between with light-to-moderate drag. If it does, the plug is ready for installation. If the gap is too large, tap down on the top of the side electrode with a wrench, light hammer, etc. If the gap is too small, position the bending bracket on the side electrode (see fig. 2-100) and gently apply bending force to increase it. You may have to bend and tap a few times to get the gap just right.

Figure 2-99. Checking gap between center and side electrode, using a wire-type feeler gauge. Gauge of specified thickness should move between electrodes with light-to-moderate drag.

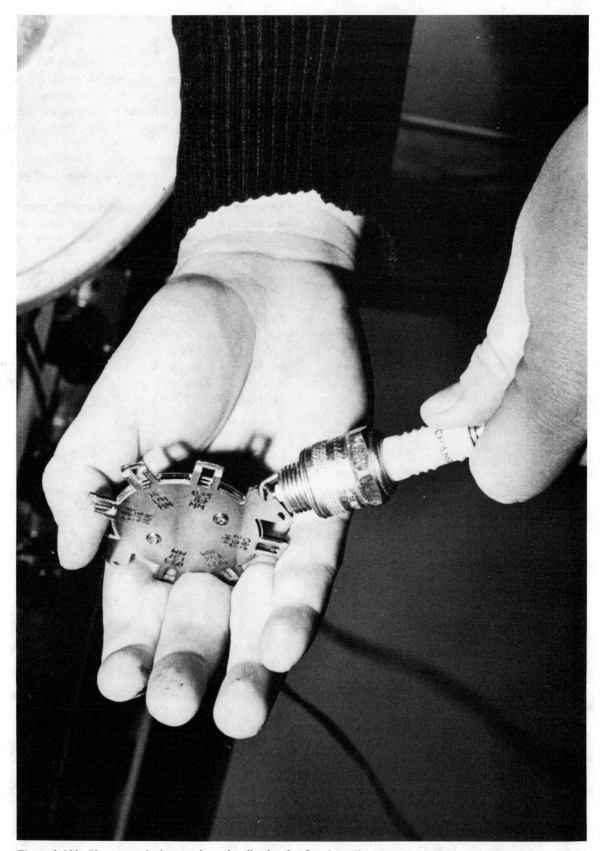

Figure 2-100. If gap must be increased, use bending bracket found on all gauges. Only bend on side electrode.

Note: If your spark plugs come with threaded caps for the outer ends, thread them on and tighten with pliers. The plugs now are ready for installation.

Installing Spark Plugs. If the cylinder head (the part of the engine with the spark plug holes) is aluminum, apply a thin film of "anti-seize compound" to the threads of the new plug. This compound, sold in squeeze tubes, is available in auto supply stores. If you aren't sure if the cylinder head is aluminum, put a magnet on it: The magnet should not adhere if it's aluminum.

Note: If the old spark plugs were very slow to unthread (constant wrench effort was necessary, as contrasted with a loose plug just spinning out), obtain and use a spark plug hole "thread chaser." This is an inexpensive tool that screws into the hole and cleans deposits from the threads. Before threading in the new plug, apply a film of anti-seize compound to the plug threads, particularly on engines with aluminum heads. This will make replacement simpler, avoiding the danger of damaged threads in the cylinder head, which could be a tedious repair even with one of the repair kits sold for this problem.

Start each spark plug in by hand, so you can feel if you have engaged the threads of the plug and the hole properly. If you feel resistance, remove the plug and try again.

On many engines, you will not be able to see the plug hole, and working purely by feel, you may have the plug at a slightly incorrect angle. Just keep experimenting and eventually the plug will thread in smoothly. Once you have it in as tight as you can with your fingers, you are ready for final tightening with a wrench.

If the plug hole is so inaccessible that you can't hold the plug with your fingers, make a plug-holding tool in either of two ways:

Obtain a short (about four inches long) piece of vacuum hose, a narrow-diameter hose used to connect the engine (the source of vacuum) to various accessories. Push one end of the hose onto the shank of a Phillips screwdriver, the other end onto the exterior of the center electrode of the plug (see fig. 2-101). The screwdriver serves as a handle and the hose as a flexible connector. Line up the plug with the hole and thread it in by turning the screwdriver.

If you have an old spark plug wire, push the terminal onto the plug and use the wire as a flexible tool, in basically the same manner as the screwdriver-and-vacuum-hose previously explained.

Tightening the Spark Plugs. Some spark plugs come with a metal gasket, others do not (see fig. 2-102). Those

Figure 2-101. If you have trouble starting a spark plug by hand because of limited clearance, a short piece of hose on a Phillips screwdriver can be used as a spark plug starter. Push open hose end onto spark plug as shown, then use screwdriver as a thread-in tool for the spark plug.

Figure 2-102. A look at two spark plugs. The *upper* plug has a metal gasket at the end of the threads, a thread-on cap for the outer end of the center electrode, and a 13/16-inch hex in the middle. The *lower* plug has a tapered surface at the end of the threads, so the plug wedges into place and seals without a gasket. The cap is a formed part of the center electrode, and the hex is 5/8-inch.

that don't have a tapered section above the top line of the threads that seats the plug in the hole when the plug is tightened. The tightening requirement for gasketed and tapered-seat plugs is different.

For a gasketed plug, tighten it with a wrench one-quarter to one-half turn past the finger-tight point. If a fractional turn is hard for you to visualize, just think of the wrench handle as the hand of a clock. A quarter turn is three hours on a clock face, a half turn six hours.

With the tapered seat plug, just a very slight tightening will secure it, normally no more than a couple of hours on the imaginary clock face.

Note: These references to tightening assume that the plug has been threaded all the way down by hand (or with one of the tools you have). It is not uncommon for a plug to bind on a slight burr on the threads of the plug hole, particularly if you didn't clean them with a thread chaser. Therefore, if you encounter slight binding and must put the wrench to the plug before it is threaded all the way, you must "feel" the finger-tight position through the wrench. It should be quite obvious.

Inspecting and Testing Spark Plug Wires. Before you reconnect the plug wires, you should inspect them carefully. If their exterior jackets are cut, oil-soaked, or heat-hardened and somewhat brittle, you should replace them.

You should also check the resistance of the plug wires to make sure it is within specification. If it is, the plug wires will make a valuable contribution to radio suppression without affecting engine performance. If the resistance is excessive, the plugs may not fire consistently.

The plug wires can be tested using one of the following methods:

Screwdriver and jumper wire. Connect one end of the jumper wire to an electrical ground, the other to the shank of a screwdriver with an insulated handle. With the engine running, move the screwdriver along the spark plug wire. If a spark jumps from the wire to the screwdriver tip, the plug wire insulation is leaking and the wire should be replaced. Watch particularly closely at each end of the plug wire. Also, spray water on the plug wires and watch them in the dark with the engine running. Leakage may show up under these conditions even without the screwdriver (see fig. 2-103.)

Ohmmeter. With an ohmmeter set on the high scale (or with a multipurpose meter that includes an ohms scale for plug wires), just disconnect a plug wire from the distributor cap and connect one ohmmeter lead wire to the metal terminal on each end of the plug wire (see fig. 2-104). The reading should not exceed 15,000 ohms per foot of length of the plug wire (for example, 22,500 ohms for a wire that is 1½ feet long). If it does, the wire must be replaced. If the reading is infinity, there is a break in the wire (if your engine is misfiring, this could be the cause).

Figure 2-103. Testing spark plug wires with a screwdriver grounded to the engine by a jumper wire.

Figure 2-104. Testing spark plug wire that leads from an ohmmeter. This spark plug wire has been removed completely from the engine. In most cases, however, you can simply disconnect at both ends and test by bringing the ohmmeter leads over.

Note: On some electronic ignition systems, the acceptable resistance can run as high as 60,000 ohms per foot. Check specifications if resistance is high.

Voltmeter. If you have, or can obtain, a voltmeter (a test instrument that measures voltage) you can check the wire this way: Connect the voltmeter's negative lead to the battery's negative post (the one to which the ground cable is attached) and the voltmeter's positive lead to one end of the plug wire. Touch the other end of the plug wire to the battery's positive post and you should get a reading of six volts or more. If the reading is less, the plug wire has excessive resistance. If you get a zero reading, there is a break in the plug wire.

Note: This test procedure may require disconnecting the plug wire from some of its retaining guides, so one end can reach the battery. In addition, this procedure should not be used on wires from electronic ignition systems.

Engines that require procedures different from the procedures described in this section are covered on page 95-97.

BUYING REPLACEMENT PLUG WIRES

Replacement spark plug wires are sold in various ways.

Rolls of wire. These you cut to size and attach the terminals and nipples. This is the cheapest way, but even a professional using special tools may have difficulty making good connections for the terminals on resistance wire.

Semicustom sets. The plug wires are precut and a terminal (and perhaps a nipple) is factory-installed at the spark plug end. You shorten the wire if necessary by cutting with pliers and attach a terminal to the distributor cap end. If you're going to attach a terminal, this is the less-critical end, for the connection will be disturbed less frequently, and it is a type that can be more easily inspected.

Custom sets. See figure 2-105. The plug wires are precut to length and the nipples and terminals are factory-installed. This is the most expensive type, but it's worth it. Shop around for the best price.

Types of Wires

The late-model cars all use resistance wire as original equipment, and so should you for replacement purposes. It's true you can buy metal core wire in rolls, plus the terminals and nipples you need, and suffer little risk in assembly because of the metal-to-metal connections. However, the entire ignition system is based on the use of resistance spark wires (and in many cases resistance spark plugs as well), so experimentation is not recommended.

If you'd like something less fragile than ordinary resistance wire, there are two choices:
1. Wire made with a core of aramid, a synthetic fiber also used in tires. In some respects it's stronger than steel.
2. An internally shielded wire with a metal core. This type does contain a resistor, but the reading you should get is only 400 to 700 ohms per foot. Keep that in mind when you test.

The type of insulation jacket is your other consideration, and there are three basic kinds:

Figure 2-105. If you need new plug wires, the completely custom set shown is the best choice. Nipples and terminals are already in place, and the length of the plug wires is very close to the originals.

Standard. This is an inexpensive synthetic rubber, such as neoprene. It will last only in a much older car. It may hold up on a later model you plan to dispose of within a year. Be sure it comes with silicone rubber nipples at the spark plug end for maximum heat resistance where it's hottest.

Premium. This is usually a material called EPDM or hypalon, which was used on original equipment through to about 1974 on most cars. It is really the minimum you should consider, particularly if the car has electronic ignition. If this is what you get, be sure it has silicone rubber nipples at the spark plug end.

Super-premium. This is silicone rubber, designed for today's combination of high engine compartment temperatures and the high voltages of most electronic ignition systems. Both the wire jacket and the nipples are made of this material.

Silicone rubber insulation wires are very expensive, but so long as they aren't cut they will really last, resisting not only high temperatures and voltages, but oil, grease, and road film deterioration. If you find just one bad wire, replace only that (see fig. 2-106). Unlike other, less-expensive types, silicone rubber wires can be purchased individually.

Note: On some cars the conditions are so severe that the manufacturer installs an extra-thick silicone rubber wire (8 mm instead of 7 mm), and if this is what the car maker uses, so should you.

Note also: Chrysler front-wheel-drive cars have a special spark plug wire with a spring clip that goes through a hole in the cap to also serve as the terminal to which the rotor transfers spark (see fig. 2-107).

Figure 2-106. The spark plug wires must be disconnected from both the cap and the plastic cage on General Motors High Energy Ignition distributors. This particular system does not have the coil built into the cap but mounted remotely, slightly to the *left* (it's the rectangularly shaped part that looks rather different from other ignition coils). *Caution:* If you also replace a distributor cap, be sure to align the new cap with the old (using locking rods or spring clip bosses for reference) before you begin to transfer wires. When transferring wires, move them one at a time into a cap terminal in exactly the same position as on the old cap.

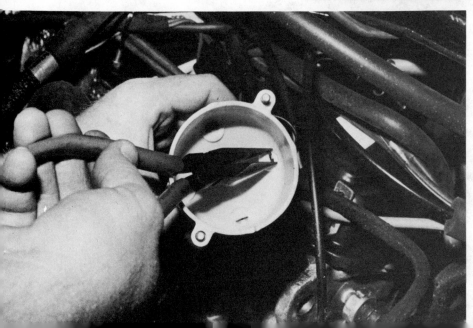

Figure 2-107. Distributor cap terminal of spark plug wire has spring clip. To remove plug wire, take off cap and squeeze together spring clip tangs as shown, using needlenose pliers. To install plug wire, just push its end into cap until you feel spring clip tangs seat.

Changing Spark Plug Wires

If you must replace spark plug wires, do the job one wire at a time, to prevent an incorrect connection. Always duplicate the routing of the original wire, even if it seems somewhat unusual (see fig. 2-108). The car makers attach the wires to little plastic holders and run the wiring so that the ignition system functions properly. Any deviation could cause the engine to miss.

Connecting the Wires. The spark plug wire must make a good connection at each end. If you have disconnected it from the distributor cap, push it into or onto the cap terminal until it seats, and then push down on the nipple.

At the spark plug end, first test the fit of the terminal by pushing it onto a used plug. If you feel any looseness, the terminal must be tightened. On a straight terminal, just push back the nipple carefully and squeeze the terminal together with pliers (see fig. 2-109). On a right-angle terminal, the nipple can't be pushed back, so wrap the pliers jaws with tape, then squeeze on the nipple (the tape will protect the nipple). Once you have the terminal tight enough, you can install it on the plug.

Note: It's a good idea to first spray the inside of the

Figure 2-108. Notice the unusual routing of these spark plug wires. It was done to prevent a phenomenon called "crossfire" that results in the engine missing.

Figure 2-109. If a plug wire terminal is loosely fit on the plug center electrode, push back nipple as shown and tighten terminal with pliers. If terminal is a right-angle type, cover pliers jaws with tape and squeeze carefully on the nipple, since you can't push it back.

Figure 2-110. Spray silicone lube (or dab silicone grease) on inside of nipple on spark plug end before installation.

nipple with silicone lubricant (see fig. 2-110) or coat it lightly with silicone dielectric grease (a special grease sold in tubes in auto parts stores). The lubrication will not only help installation, but will keep the nipple from heat-sealing to the spark plug.

NEW SPARK PLUG REMOVAL TECHNIQUES

New removal techniques are required for spark plug removal on some General Motors cars introduced in 1988.

If a GM car has the Quad-4 (a four-cylinder engine with two overhead camshaft chambers and four valves per cylinder), it does not have a conventional electronic ignition system or even a typical distributorless system. Rather, there is an electronic module assembly atop the engine between the camshaft chambers that connects directly to the spark plugs, so there are no plug wires. For access to the plugs, remove the bolts that hold the electronic modules and lift them up (fig. 2-111). Next, remove the boot over each plug for access with a spark plug socket wrench (fig. 2-112).

Figure 2.111. Remove the bolts that hold the electronic module assembly and lift it up as shown for access to the spark plugs on the GM Quad-4 engine.

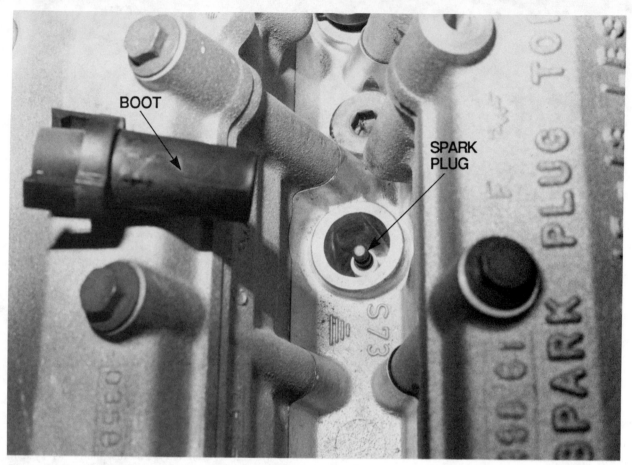

BOOT

SPARK PLUG

Figure 2-112. Lift off the boot, shown resting on the camshaft chamber, for access to a spark plug in the circular recess.

Figure 2-113. Disconnect both dogbone-shaped engine struts from the top front of the 2.8-liter V-6 in some new GM cars. Remove the bolt from one of the struts.

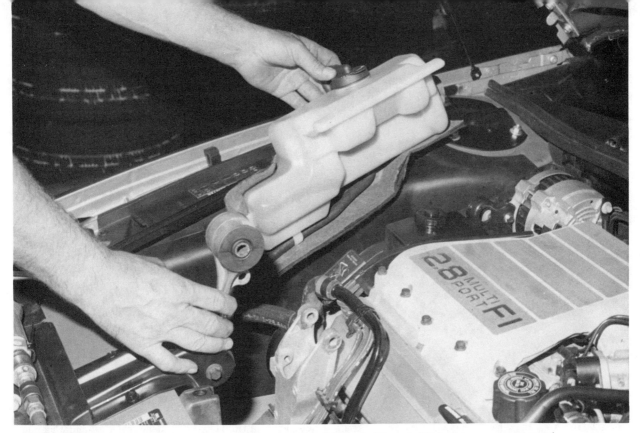

Figure 2-114. Next, disconnect the coolant overflow reservoir and lift out of the way. Tilt both torque struts upward.

The front-wheel-drive Olds Cutlass Supreme, Buick Regal, and Pontiac Grand Prix with the 2.8-liter V-6 have an arrangement that provides access to the rear bank of spark plugs, normally very difficult to reach on front-drive applications of this engine. For access, unbolt the two engine torque struts (dogbone-shaped parts as shown in figs. 2-113, and 2-114), disconnect and lift the coolant overflow reservoir out of the way and tilt the engine forward (fig. 2-115). The struts have a central bolt hole to hold the engine in the tilt-forward position while you reach the rear plugs (fig. 2-116).

Note: This procedure can be used only on those new applications of the 2.8-liter V-6 with the special dual-torque strut arrangement.

Figure 2-115. Tilt the engine forward. This can be done with a pry bar between the engine and a strut bracket or by two people. Once it is tilted, hold forward as shown.

Figure 2-116. Align the center hole of one strut with the engine bracket and reinstall the bolt to hold the engine forward while you service the rear bank of spark plugs.

COMPUTER SYSTEMS' SELF-DIAGNOSIS

All late-model engine control computers have a procedure for self-diagnosis of the entire control system, including the computer itself and sensors and devices the computer operates (motors, switches, solenoids, etc.). Before you go through extensive tuneup procedures, you may wish to assure yourself that any performance problem is not in the computer system, correcting which is a job for a professional and typically is covered by a 5-year, 50,000-mile warranty or more.

When GM computers detect a failure, a "Check Engine" light (or light with similar wording) is turned on to alert you to that fact. Chrysler products may turn on a "Power Loss" lamp. However, in some cases trouble codes may be stored without turning on a dashboard indicator, and if you encounter a performance problem you may wish to see if a trouble code has been found.

Note: Cadillac systems and 1986-on Olds Toronado and Buick Riviera systems are more sophisticated than those in other GM cars, and if you have one of these, you will need the factory service manual for self-test details.

When you activate self-testing, the computer gives you a trouble code if there is any it has detected. Many late-model computers have "memory," which means they are provided with a source of current even with the engine off (the current draw is small so the battery should not run down in normal situations). With this continuous current feed, the computer can "remember" any failures. If you are not sure your computer has memory, you should keep the engine running while you activate the self-test.

American cars typically provide a pulsing trouble code that works this way: an initial series of pulses, short pause, then a second series of pulses, longer pause, then initial series, short pause, and second series, etc. If the initial series is two pulses and the second series is four, that's a 2 and a 4, or number 24. Then you check a reference list in the factory service manual to find out what trouble No. 24 indicates. If there is more than one trouble code, the typical procedure is for the computer to go from one to the next, although it may start with a high-priority problem and not display another code until the problem represented by that one is corrected.

Many imported car systems have long and short pulses. For example, two long pulses, short pause, and four short pulses also equals a code No. 24.

Once a problem is corrected, the fuse for the computer must be removed from the fusebox to erase the memory; or you can disconnect the car battery cables and get the same result. However, any preset positions for an electronic radio or air conditioning (and the car's clock) would have to be reset. Further, on cars with fuel injection, a computer "learning curve" (minor adjustments for your style of driving) would be lost for a short period (no matter which erasure step you took), and you might notice poor driveability until the adjustments were "relearned."

Chrysler Front-Wheel-Drive Cars with Fuel Injection. Turn the ignition key on and off two times and then on again (within five seconds), and leave it on. The Power Loss lamp on the dashboard will pulse out any trouble codes. If it just goes from code 12 to code 55, all is okay if the engine starts. If the engine does not start, the code 12 may indicate a problem.

General Motors Cars. Locate the underdash (or behind the cigarette lighter on Pontiac Fiero) diagnostic plug (see fig. 2-83) and bridge the terminals of the black and white wires at one end with an opened paper clip or something similar. Turn on the ignition and the Check Engine light (which may say something similar, such as "Service Engine Now") should pulse out any trouble codes. As with Chrysler, a code 12 is meaningless if the engine starts.

Ford Motor Company Cars. The procedure for EEC III engines (1980 to 1983) is described earlier in this chapter. On later models with EEC IV, locate the underhood test connectors (see fig. 2-117). They are generally at the driver's side rear of the engine compartment, but if you don't find them there, look for the distinctive six-terminal pentagon-shaped main test connector and you'll find the other adjacent to it. Connect an analog voltmeter (one with needle and dial) as illustrated, put the transmission in Park, set the parking brake, turn the air conditioning or heater off, and turn the key to the run position. You should get a code No. 11 (one voltmeter needle pulsation, pause, then a second), which is a pass. Disconnect the jumper wire and voltmeter from the test connectors, start and run the engine for more than two minutes at 2,000 to 2,500 r.p.m. to warm up the oxygen sensor (see chapter 3). Activate the self-test once more with the jumper wire and voltmeter, and the voltmeter needle should pulse two to four times (frequency equal to half the number of engine cylinders). Hit the brake pedal only once and wait for a single pulse, then floor the gas pedal for an instant and then look for trouble codes or a code No. 11. After any trouble codes or a No. 11 occur, check ignition timing quickly (within two minutes) and the timing should be 20 degrees higher than the ignition timing recorded with the spout connector unplugged, as explained earlier in this chapter.

Figure 2-117. Illustration shows Ford Electronic Engine Control IV test connectors and how to hook up a voltmeter and jumper wire. The jumper wire goes from the single test connector to terminal 2 of the main test connector. The voltmeter positive wire lead goes to the battery positive terminal. The voltmeter negative wire lead goes to terminal 4 of the main test connector.

3 Fuel Systems from Carburetors to Turbochargers

How the Carburetor Works

The carburetor (see fig. 3-1) is the device that combines air and gasoline to produce a combustible mixture. The ideal air-fuel mixture depends on a number of factors, including engine temperature, so the carburetor must produce the correct mixture automatically. When the engine is cold, it requires what is called a "rich" mixture, one with more gasoline in it; as the engine warms up, a "leaner" mixture is desirable. Rich and lean are relative terms, for the mixture is always mostly air. Rich might be 10 parts of air to one of gasoline; lean would be 14 to 18 parts of air to one of gasoline.

The perfume atomizer, a gadget with which you may be familiar, illustrates one of the basics of carburetor operation. Squeeze the bulb and you push air quickly past the top of a tube that extends down into the bowl of perfume. The air rushing past the top of the tube creates a vacuum there that sucks up perfume droplets and expels them with the air as a spray.

In an engine, the movement of the pistons creates a vacuum in the engine. Nature abhors a vacuum, so air rushes in to fill it, through the only opening—a cylindrical barrel called the carburetor barrel (or air horn). As the air rushes in, it speeds past the top of a tube that extends from a bowl filled with gasoline. The vacuum created by the air rushing through draws out fuel droplets which mix with the air. The "spray" flows into a series of chambers—called the intake manifold—and through the manifold into the cylinders.

Now let's look at the controls the carburetor has which enable it to get the right amount of fuel, mix it correctly, and control the flow rate of the air-fuel mixture.

Venturi

If you look into a carburetor barrel you'll see it necks down at about the halfway mark. This restriction is called the venturi, and some carburetor barrels have multiple restrictions at the same point. The venturi restriction forces the air to speed up to get through to fill the vacuum in the cylinders. The higher speed creates a higher vacuum at the fuel bowl tube (called the main metering jet) so more fuel can flow. Don't confuse the vacuum in the cylinders and the little vacuum at the tip of the main metering jet. They're two different things. The air rushing in to fill the vacuum in the cylinders is being used to create a second, mini-vacuum at the tip of the main metering jet.

Throttle

There must be some way to regulate the flow of air-fuel mixture, or the engine would, once started, run at top speed. The throttle, a circular hinged plate that blocks off the bottom of the carburetor barrel, does that job. The throttle is connected by a linkage to the gas pedal, so when you step on the pedal you are pivoting the throttle. The more the throttle plate pivots, the more air-fuel mixture can rush through the barrel, speeding up the engine.

Idle Circuit

When the engine first starts, or if you take your foot off the gas pedal, there must be some way to keep it running. This is the job of the idle circuit, a passage with an opening above the throttle (a source of air) and an opening below the throttle (to permit it to bypass the throttle). The passage goes by the fuel bowl metering jet, and air flowing through picks up fuel droplets, with which it mixes. The fuel mixture is discharged below the throttle and flows to the cylinders to keep the engine "idling."

Figure 3-1. A drawing of a simple one-barrel carburetor. Although no modern automobile has such a carburetor, it shows the basic principles of carburetor operation. Fuel is pumped into the fuel bowl, and when the level is correct, the float rises and pushes a tapered needle into a seat, shutting off the flow. As fuel is consumed, the float drops and fuel under pressure pushes the needle off the seat, allowing additional fuel to flow in. The fuel bowl contains a metering jet, a nozzle that projects into a tapered section of the carburetor barrel. Stepping on the gas pedal pivots the throttle plate from horizontal toward a vertical position, allowing the engine to suck in air, which creates a mini-vacuum at the end of the jet, drawing out droplets of fuel that mix with the air to form a combustible mixture that flows into the cylinders. To provide some fuel mixture when the throttle plate is closed, the idle circuit, (a passage that runs from the top of the barrel to a point below the throttle) is used. Even when your foot is off the gas pedal, the throttle doesn't completely close; it is open just enough to allow some air to flow past it. This air combines with the air-fuel mix that comes through the idle circuit to form a mixture that is both combustible and sufficient to keep the engine idling. Notice the idle fuel mixture adjusting screw. Although preset and sealed on current models, on older cars the idle circuit permits adjustment of the idle fuel mixture for smooth idle. When you floor the gas pedal to accelerate, additional fuel is needed, beyond what the main metering jet will supply. At that time the accelerator pump is operated, permitting additional fuel flow.

Accelerator Pump

When you really floor the gas pedal, the fuel flow can't match the sudden need. To add extra fuel to the suddenly greater air flow, an accelerator pump is used. This is a mechanical device operated by the linkage from the gas pedal, and it squirts an extra bit of fuel into the barrel. The pump system will only work when the gas pedal is floored quickly, not when it is done gradually.

Choke

The choke is a hinged plate that resembles the throttle. However, it sits on the top of the carburetor barrel, well above the venturi, and can only regulate air volume into the barrel (see figs. 3-1 and 3-2). When it nearly covers the top of the barrel, there is little air flow, and the overall air-fuel mixture is richer with fuel (perhaps a 10:1 air-fuel ratio). When it pivots to the vertical position (open), maximum air flow is allowed.

The choke plate position is controlled by two things: engine vacuum and a temperature-sensitive coil spring (see fig. 3-3). Remember that the pistons are creating a vacuum and this vacuum exists in the intake manifold and up to the bottom of the throttle plate. Even when the throttle is opened, unless it's opened all the way there is some vacuum around.

A passage from the bottom of the carburetor goes up to either of two devices: a little piston in a little cylinder in the carburetor (see fig. 3-4), or an external diaphragm connected to the vacuum passage by a hose (see fig. 3-5). The piston or the diaphragm is connected by linkage to the choke plate, and because there's vacuum on the piston or diaphragm it's always trying to pull the choke plate open. The temperature-sensitive coil spring, however, keeps tightly wound up and holds the choke plate closed when the engine is cold. As the engine warms up, the coil unwinds and the vacuum piston or diaphragm pulls the choke plate open. Some carburetors have two choke diaphragms, designed to open the choke at different rates, for more precise operation.

Heat for the thermostatic coil typically comes from one of the following sources:

Exhaust manifold. A tube projects into the exhaust manifold, where the air inside is heated by exhaust gas.
Intake manifold. The coil itself sits in a well on the intake manifold (see fig. 3-6), which is warmed up by physically touching the exhaust manifold or by exhaust gas, which is run through a special passage in it.
An electric heater. In some cars, the heater is a ceramic device warmed up by current tapped off the ignition circuit. Or it can be wired through both the ignition circuit and the oil pressure warning light circuit so that current is supplied to the choke only when the engine is

Figure 3-2. Finger points to the choke plate on the top of the carburetor. When the engine is cold, this plate is closed as shown. When the engine starts, it cracks open a bit to allow some air flow; as the engine warms up, it pivots to the vertical position so air can flow through the barrel freely. The closed choke plate, by restricting air flow, richens the fuel mixture as necessary for cold starting and cold engine driveaway.

LINK TO CHOKE PLATE

THERMOSTATIC SPRING

CHOKE HOUSING COVER

Figure 3-3. The choke housing cover has been removed so you can see the thermostatic spring. When cold, the spring winds up tight and holds the choke plate closed by its link connection to the plate.

Figure 3-4. Finger points to little cylinder that contains a tiny piston connected by linkage to the choke plate. As the thermostatic coil heats and unwinds, the piston, which is open at the bottom to a source of engine vacuum, is sucked downward. The downward movement of the piston tends to tug the choke plate open.

Figure 3-5. Many chokes have an external vacuum diaphragm connected by links to the choke plate, instead of the little piston inside. An external vacuum diaphragm is shown. As soon as the engine starts, the diaphragm (connected by a hose to an engine vacuum source) tries to pull the choke open. As the thermostatic coil unwinds, it performs the same function as the little piston in Figure 3-4. The heat tube is run to a source of exhaust gas heat, such as the exhaust crossover passage in the intake manifold of a V-8, or to the exhaust manifold itself on an in-line-engine. As the exhaust gas heats the air inside the tube, the air transfers the heat to the thermostatic coil inside the choke housing.

Figure 3-6. This is a well-type choke. The thermostatic coil sits in a well in the exterior of the intake manifold, and is connected by a link to the choke plate. As the intake manifold warms up, it warms up the coil. *Note:* This choke system has a vacuum diaphragm.

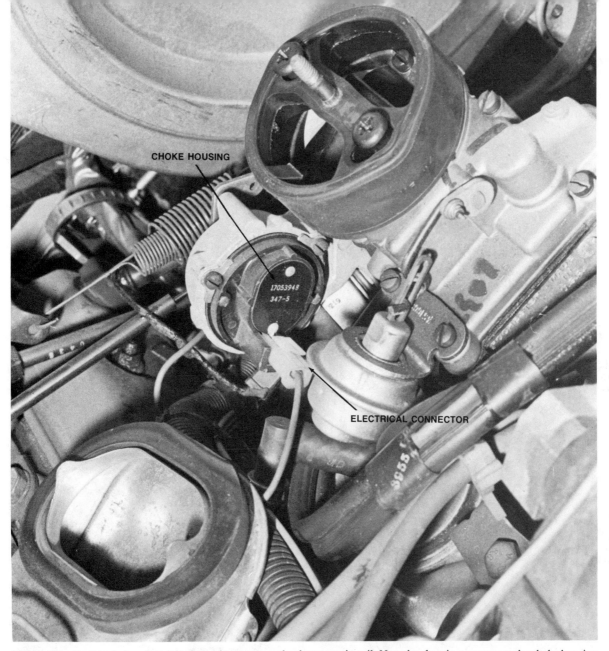

CHOKE HOUSING

ELECTRICAL CONNECTOR

Figure 3-7. On this choke, electricity is used to warm up the thermostatic coil. Note the electric connector to the choke housing cover. This choke cover is held by rivets, not screws, so if the thermostatic coil becomes weak, the rivet heads must be drilled out. This is done to meet exhaust emission regulations to prevent unneeded tampering with choke. A service kit available includes screws or studs and nuts to replace the rivets, which are threaded into the carburetor body.

running. This prevents premature choke opening if the motorist sits in the car with the ignition on for a few minutes before attempting to start the engine (see fig. 3-7).

The ceramic is so designed that when the weather is cold, only part of the heater warms up, so the choke opens very slowly. If the weather is warm, both parts of the ceramic heat up, and the choke opens more rapidly.

Fuel Bowl

The carburetor's fuel bowl is filled as necessary by the fuel pump, normally a mechanical device bolted to the engine and connected to both the gas tank (for supply) and to the bowl by steel and/or rubber lines. Some cars have an electric pump, operated by current tapped off the ignition circuit. This pump may be placed in the gas tank or mounted in the engine compartment. Most fuel pumps are sealed, nonserviceable units.

The pump (covered later in this chapter) forces the fuel into the carburetor bowl through a little valve called the needle-and-seat. A toilet-bowel-type float is mounted in the bowl, and when the fuel level is correct the float rises and pushes the needle into the seat, shutting off the fuel flow. As the engine uses fuel the float drops and more gasoline is admitted.

Figure 3-8. This is a two-barrel, variable-venturi carburetor. The venturi opening in each barrel is controlled by movable walls that are operated by a control vacuum diaphragm. As the venturi walls move to increase the venturi opening, they also pull tapered needles out of fuel jets, permitting increased fuel flow. This carburetor has proved to be extremely difficult even for professional mechanics to service, and for versions without the stepper-motor-controlled vacuum valve shown in figure 3-9, there are conventional Holley carburetors available as replacements.

VARIABLE VENTURI WALLS

JETS

TAPERED NEEDLES

CONTROL VACUUM DIAPHRAGM

JET

TAPERED NEEDLE

The level of the fuel is important, for if too low, the engine will starve for gasoline; if too high, it will pour out the main metering jet and flood into the engine. Either condition can cause the engine to stall.

Other Controls

The modern carburetor has other control devices for precise operation. It is unlikely that you would ever service them, because that's work for the carburetor rebuilder. If the carburetor does not respond to the service described later in this chapter, obtaining a rebuilt is the practical solution.

Variable-Venturi Carburetors

The venturi in the typical carburetor is a fixed restriction. If we could change the size of that restriction in accordance with throttle opening, the air-fuel mixture could be kept more uniform, and we wouldn't need such devices as the accelerator pump.

Some carburetors, called variable-venturi designs, do exactly that. One wall of the cylinder barrel is movable, and to that wall is attached a tapered needle that fits into the main metering jet. As the wall is moved to enlarge the venturi, it pulls the tapered needle out of the jet, allowing more fuel to be drawn out by the inrushing air. The shape of the needle is tailored to allow just the desirable amount of additional fuel flow (see figs. 3-8 and 3-9).

When you step on the gas pedal with this type of carburetor, you pivot the throttle plate as in a conventional carburetor, but this action also allows engine vacuum to pass into a chamber with a diaphragm. The diaphragm is linked to the movable barrel wall, and it draws it open, increasing the size of the venturi.

Gasoline Filters

All carburetor systems have filters to remove dirt particles from the gasoline. The main filter, which is replaceable, is located in any one of three places: at the carburetor fuel

Figure 3-9. Here you can see the tops of the movable venturi walls of a variable-venturi carburetor. This type of carburetor does not lend itself to the use of a choke, so instead there is a system that increases fuel flow when the engine is cold (this instead of restricting airflow as does the choke). This particular carburetor is used with a computer that regulates fuel mixture by operating the stepper motor and vacuum valve, shown removed *at left*. The position of the motor plunger (determined by computer) regulates the flow of engine vacuum to the top of the fuel bowl. As the vacuum is admitted, fuel flow is reduced; as the vacuum is reduced or cut off, the fuel flow is increased.

bowl inlet, where the line from the pump is attached; spliced into the line between pump and carburetor bowl; or mounted on the fuel pump.

Replacement of this filter is a standard part of a tuneup. Some filters, primarily those at the fuel bowl inlet, are designed so that if they clog, fuel can bypass them. Others are not so designed, and if they fill with dirt, gasoline cannot get through and the engine will starve and stall.

Electronically Controlled Carburetors

Electronically controlled carburetors are a product that results from strict emission regulations. To meet them, the car makers must use an additional catalytic converter, which functions properly only when the air-fuel mixture going into the engine is very close to 14.7:1. To maintain this mixture under all operating conditions, a computer or electronic control unit is used to richen or lean out the fuel mixture as required. The computer is often a multifunction control, the same one used to regulate spark advance on some cars. (See "Computer Spark Advance" chapter 2; see also Figure 3-10.)

Key to the system is an oxygen sensor (see fig. 3-11), an electronic device which checks for oxygen content in the exhaust, an accurate indicator of the air-fuel mixture that went into the cylinders. If the oxygen sensor indicates a rich mixture, it signals the computer to lean it out. If it indicates a lean mixture, it signals the computer to richen it. The electronically controlled carburetor may also be triggered according to information from sensors that measure coolant temperature, engine speed, and throttle position.

The computer gets the carburetor to respond in one of many ways. The three most common are as follows:

1. *Solenoid (electromagnetic switch) controls a metering rod.* This is the most frequently used arrangement. The metering rod normally pulses in a fuel passage, and by changing the pulsation, the computer can change the fuel mixture. If it keeps the rod more out of the passage than in, more fuel can flow and the mixture is richer with fuel. If it keeps the rod more in than out, less fuel can flow and the mixture is leaner. This is called mixture solenoid dwell, and it can be measured with an analog (needle-and-dial) tach-dwellmeter, an old test instrument you may have. Somewhere under the hood is an unconnected wiring connector. Often it is under the air cleaner projecting from the mixture solenoid on the carburetor, but it could be anywhere in the engine compartment. The factory service manual gives a test procedure and a specification for the number of degrees of dwell.

On some cars the metering rod is in an air passage, and the results are the opposite. If the metering rod is held more out than in, more air can flow with the

Figure 3-10. This is a schematic of a computer control for a carburetor. The computer housing contains circuit boards that control spark advance, the carburetor, and perhaps some other engine functions. An oxygen sensor in the exhaust manifold tells the computer whether the fuel mixture is too rich or too lean, and the computer makes an adjustment. In figure 3-9, the adjustment was to operate a stepper motor. In this case it controls a solenoid regulator, an electromagnetic switch that admits or denies engine vacuum to a diaphragm in the carburetor. When the diaphragm receives vacuum, it yanks on a tapered rod in a fuel passage to increase fuel flow. When vacuum is denied, a spring retracts the diaphragm, and the rod moves back into the fuel passage, reducing fuel flow.

ELECTRONIC SPARK CONTROL COMPUTER

HOUSING

FEEDBACK CARBURETOR CONTROLLER

COMBUSTION COMPUTER

COMBUSTION COMPUTER

AIR FILTER

COOLANT SENSOR

CARBURETOR

SOLENOID REGULATOR

MANIFOLD VACUUM

OXYGEN SENSOR

EXHAUST MANIFOLD

ELECTRONIC FEEDBACK CARBURETOR CONTROL SYSTEM

Figure 3-11. This is an oxygen sensor threaded into the exhaust system. If a trouble code indicates that it has failed, you may remove it. The physical positioning of some oxygen sensors requires a special wrench for removal. Always watch the routing of the sensor wiring, for if it touches the hot exhaust, it will be damaged and fail to operate.

gasoline and lean out the mixture; if it's more in than out, less air can flow, and the mixture is richer. One car at this time (the Subaru Justy) has a double-acting arrangement, where the solenoid controls rods in fuel and air passages.

2. *A solenoid (electromagnetic switch) operates a vacuum valve* (see fig. 3-10). The computer supplies or denies current to the solenoid so as to allow only the desired amount of engine vacuum to pass through this valve and through a hose to the carburetor. At the carburetor, the vacuum draws on a spring-loaded diaphragm connected to a fuel metering rod. If it pulls on the rod, it yanks it partly out of a fuel passage, and more fuel can flow through the passage to richen the mixture. When the computer wants to lean out the mixture, it denies current to the solenoid valve, no vacuum goes through to the diaphragm, and the spring pushes the metering rod back in, reducing the fuel flow through the passage.

3. *The computer supplies current to a stepper motor* (see fig. 3-9). The stepper motor is a little motor that can run forward or backward and stop in any position desired. The stepper motor operates a little rod in a carburetor vacuum passage up to the fuel bowl. When the computer wants to lean out the mixture, it winds out the motor so the rod allows full vacuum to go to the fuel bowl and suck out most of the air. This lowers the air pressure below atmospheric, and with less air pressure on top of the fuel in the bowl, less can flow out in response to the mini-vacuum in the carburetor venturi. To richen the mixture, the motor pushes the rod to close off the vacuum passage. Atmospheric pressure is instantly restored, and fuel flow increases.

CARBURETOR SERVICE

The carburetor normally requires little attention, and a basic rule is: With the exception of certain external maintenance and minor adjustment, leave it alone. The exceptions are: cleaning, replacement of fuel and air filters, minor adjustment, tightening, replacement of a leaking fuel inlet fitting, automatic choke service, and replacement of a defective mixture control solenoid. If the carburetor needs other service and you are not an experienced weekend mechanic with a factory service manual, you should limit yourself to installing a replacement rebuilt carburetor.

Cleaning

You can pour a can of gasoline additive into your tank periodically and hope that will keep the carburetor clean. However, it won't do the job that an at-the-carburetor cleaning will.

To a professional, at-the-carburetor cleaning means complete disassembly and a soaking in solvent. You can, however, get very close to the same results with this 2-prong approach, performed every 2 years or 30,000 miles:

1. Spray the carburetor barrel and the exterior of the carburetor, particularly the linkage, with an aerosol solvent (see fig. 3-12). When spraying the barrel,

block the choke plate open, perhaps with a rubber band on the linkage to hold it.

2. Run pure solvent through the internal passages of the carburetor with an on-the-car cleanout kit (see fig. 3-13). Disconnect the fuel line at the carburetor and plug it with a tapered stopper, then attach a suitable fitting and a hose from the kit. Attach the can of solvent to the other end of the hose, hold the can upright, and run the engine at idle until the contents of the can are exhausted. If the carburetor has not been cleaned in four years or more, use two pint cans of solvent. If the engine will not run (stalls out) on pure solvent, mix it 50:50 with gasoline.

Note: Either way this job will require removal of the air cleaner housing, which on the typical late-model car has several vacuum hoses connected to it. When you disconnect a hose, wrap a piece of masking tape on its end and another piece on the neck from which you disconnected it. Write an identification mark (such as the same letter) with a marking pen on each tape so you can reconnect accurately. Or you can obtain a set (six pair) of different-colored vacuum hose and neck plugs, sold in auto parts stores.

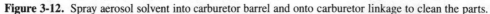

Figure 3-12. Spray aerosol solvent into carburetor barrel and onto carburetor linkage to clean the parts.

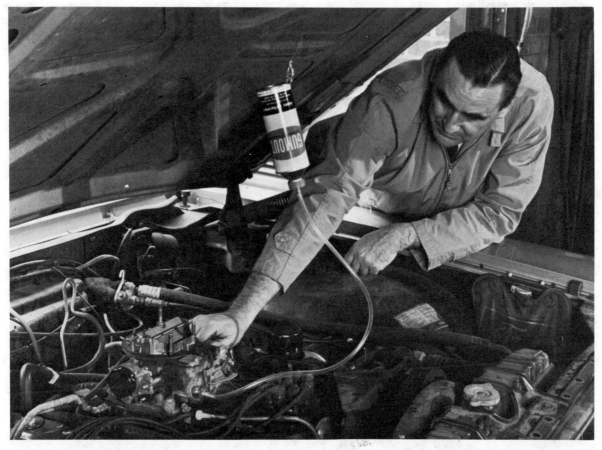

Figure 3-13. This is an on-car carburetor cleanout kit in use. Fuel line is disconnected from carburetor and plugged; kit is attached to carburetor inlet fitting as shown. Can of cleaning solvent is inverted as shown, and the engine is run at idle until the contents of the can are exhausted.

Fuel Filters

You will probably find one of the three types of replaceable fuel filters on your gasoline engine:

A *little filter in the fitting that holds the fuel line to the carburetor bowl.* This filter, made of pleated paper or powdered bronze, should be replaced annually, or every 12,000 miles, as follows:

1. Disconnect the fuel line (see fig. 3-14).
2. Loosen the fitting with a large wrench (an adjustable type normally will do).
3. Unthread the fitting by hand and carefully remove it. The filter element will pop out (see fig. 3-15). If a spring also pops out, note which way the spring faces. If the filter is powdered bronze, discard and obtain a pleated paper replacement for better filtration.
4. Install a new filter element and spring, and thread in the fitting finger tight. Give it a final tightening with the wrench.
5. Reinstall the fuel line and tighten.

An in-line filter, in the line between fuel pump and carbu-

retor bowl. See Figure 3-16. It is a pleated-paper or nylon filter that should be replaced every 2 years or 24,000 miles as follows:

1. Disengage the four hose clamps. If spring-type clamps are used, squeeze the tangs together with hose clamp pliers (see fig. 3-17) and move them off the overlap section of hose and fuel line or hose and filter neck. If they are the crimp-together type, pry them open and cut them apart with cutting pliers. If the filter is threaded into the carburetor fuel inlet (as on many Ford products), loosen the clamp and disconnect the fuel hose from the filter, then unthread the filter from the fuel inlet. Or the filter may be held by what are called "banjo" fittings (see fig. 3-18). When replacing a filter in this case, install new gaskets at the fitting joints and tighten securely to prevent fuel leaks.
2. Carefully work the short hoses off the filter necks or fuel line, whichever is easier. Be sure to hold the fuel line when you try to get a hose off so you don't damage the line's connection at the carburetor or fuel pump.

Note: Some replacement filters come with new

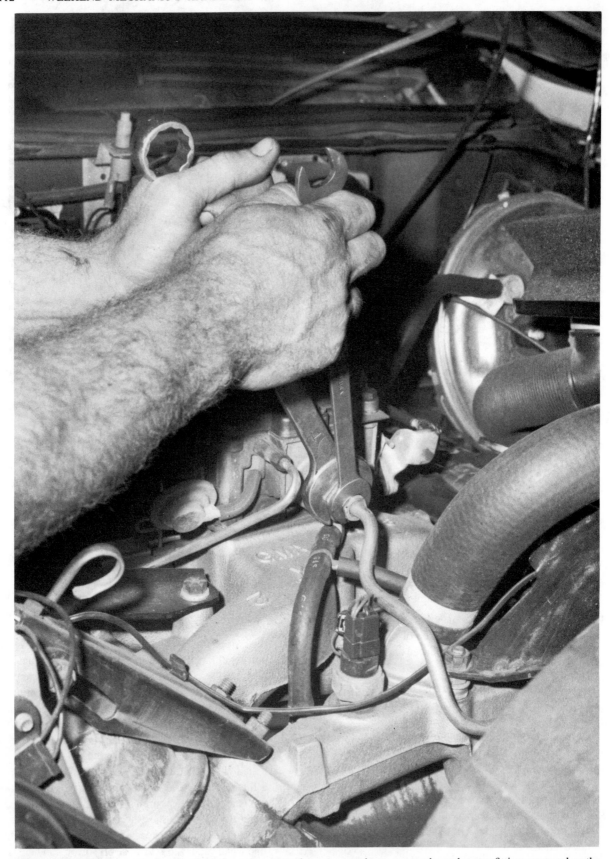

Figure 3-14. Disconnect the fuel line from the carburetor, using two wrenches—one on the carburetor fitting, a second on the fuel line nut. Apply tightening pressure on the fitting while you loosen the fuel line nut.

Figure 3-15. After disconnecting the fuel line, you can remove the carburetor fitting and take out the filter inside the fuel inlet. In this case it is a powdered bronze filter as shown.

Figure 3-16. This fuel filter is in the line between fuel pump and carburetor.

IN-LINE FUEL FILTER

Figure 3-17. If in-line fuel filter is held by spring clamps, move them off the overlap sections between flexible hose and steel line, or hose and filter neck, using hose clamp pliers as shown. Then remove filter and hoses from fuel lines. When installing a new filter on a car that has two nipples at one end, the two-nipple end should face the carburetor side of the fuel line. *Note:* On some cars, primarily Ford products, the filter threads into the carburetor at one end and attaches to the fuel line with a short hose and a clamp on the other.

Figure 3-18. To remove VW Rabbit fuel filter, use wrench on filter hex section to hold it while you loosen bolt that holds the fuel line to the filter. Place dry rag underneath to catch fuel dripping. Shown is a filter held by banjo fittings. Although this one is with a fuel injection system, the same arrangement may be used with carburetors. Install new gaskets when replacing.

Figure 3-19. Unscrewing fuel pump fuel filter cover.

pieces of hose. In this case, remove the hoses from the fuel line and discard.

3. Install the new spring clamps on the midpoint of each hose, then install the new filter so that the arrow on the filter points toward the carburetor. With the pliers, relocate each clamp so it secures the hose to the fuel line and filter necks. On Ford products with a hose neck that has two clamps, position each so it is not over the hose neck boss.

A filter element under a cover on the fuel pump. Like the in-line type, it is made of pleated paper and is of a size that should last 2 years or 24,000 miles.

To replace (see fig. 3-19) simply unscrew the cover (if it is tight, obtain a special band-type wrench, sold in auto supply stores). Remove the old filter element,

install the new one, refit the cover, and tighten with the wrench.

Automatic Choke Service

A choke that sticks closed will cause poor gas mileage and reduced high-speed performance. A choke that sticks open will make starting, particularly in cold weather, very difficult.

Checking the Choke. The engine must be cold, and ambient temperature must be 50°F or lower to check the operation of the automatic choke. Remove the air cleaner cover (see fig. 3-20) and look at the choke plate (see fig. 3-21). The plate should cover the top of the carburetor barrel. If it does not, floor the gas pedal, hold it there for an instant, then release. The choke should close.

Figure 3-20. Air cleaner cover is held by wingnut. Unscrew it and lift cover as shown. Air filter element can be lifted out for replacement if necessary at this time, but if it's clean just leave it in place.

115

Figure 3-21. With air cleaner cover off you can see if choke plate is closed, covering the top of the carburetor barrel, as shown.

If the choke plate does not close completely, move it back and forth by hand. If you feel stickiness, the choke should be cleaned, as will be explained.

If the choke plate closes, refit the air cleaner cover and drive the car for a couple of miles. Stop the engine, remove the air cleaner cover, and look at the choke again. The plate should be vertical. If it hasn't moved at all or has moved very little, try to operate it by hand. If you feel stickiness, cleaning is required. If the choke has an external vacuum diaphragm (see fig. 3-22), watch the link to that diaphragm as a helper starts the engine. If the diaphragm doesn't pull the link, check for a good hose connection, and if that's not the problem, unscrew and replace the diaphragm.

If the diaphragm moves the link, but not enough to crack open the choke about ⅛-inch, a choke vacuum break adjustment may do the job. The adjustment procedure is described later in this section.

Figure 3-22. This view of a carburetor clearly shows the vacuum diaphragm and the hose that connects from it to a source of engine vacuum (a neck that has a passage through the carburetor).

Note: Starting on 1981 models, the choke vacuum break adjustment may be sealed by a cover plate riveted in place. To make an adjustment, therefore, the rivets first must be drilled out to permit removal of the cover. When reinstalling the cover, use self-tapping screws.

Cleaning and Adjusting the Choke. Using aerosol spray solvent (see fig. 3-12), spray the choke plate, its shaft, and all the external linkage that moves when you operate the choke plate by hand.

If the choke is the type without an external diaphragm, the same job is done by a little piston inside a housing built into the carburetor under a plastic cover (see fig. 3-4). Take off the cover slowly so you can look inside and see how the tang on the thermostatic coil spring engages the choke linkage.

You'll see a little piston and linkage. Squirt them with solvent and work the choke plate back and forth until the solvent has done its job and the choke plate operates absolutely freely (see fig. 3-23).

Refit the cover disc, insert the screws (but do not tighten), then turn the disc until the mark on the disc aligns with the center mark on the carburetor (see figs. 3-24, 3-25). The choke plate should close, but if it doesn't, continue turning the disc until its mark is no more than two marks past center. If the choke plate still isn't closed, replace the thermostatic coil. If the plate is closed, tighten the cover disc retaining screws. Reattach the electric connector if used.

If a sealed choke won't close or open fully, and it is simply not sticking, it must be replaced. A typical procedure is shown in figures 3-26 to 3-33.

Well Chokes. The choke with a thermostatic coil in the well in the intake manifold (see fig. 3-6) may be adjust-

Figure 3-23. This view inside choke housing clearly shows linkage and piston. Spray with aerosol solvent until choke plate, linkage, and piston all move absolutely freely.

CHOKE PISTON
CYLINDER

CHOKE PISTON LEVER
AND LINK ASSEMBLY

CHOKE PISTON

Figure 3-24. With the cover screws loose, you can turn the choke housing cover clockwise until the choke plate closes and the mark on cover aligns with specified mark on metal body.

Figure 3-25. On older cars, the well choke spring is adjustable by slackening nut and moving plate with single mark to align with correct mark on other plate.

Figure 3-26. Replacement of sealed choke assembly begins with drilling out rivet heads holding choke cover.

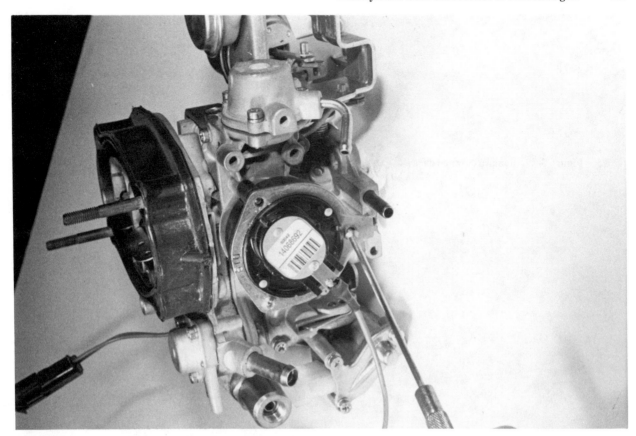

Figure 3-27. Dig out rivet head residue with pick.

Figure 3-28. Remove choke cover as shown.

Figure 3-29. Remove cover adapter.

Figure 3-30. Unthread rivet studs from housing with locking pliers.

Figure 3-31. If necessary, clean stud holes with tap.

Figure 3-32. Refit cover; don't forget to install any hardware removed, such as this linkage sleeve.

Figure 3-33. Install new cover with screws included in service kit. They thread into the rivet stud holes.

able. Remove it and if you see a locknut holding plates with marks (see fig. 3-25), slacken the nut and align the single mark on one plate with the center of the marks on the other. If they're already aligned, reset up to two lines toward "R" (for rich mixture) to correct a hard-starting problem. Or replace the well assembly.

Note: Well assemblies are not adjustable on cars built since the early 1970s.

Choke Vacuum Break. When you first start a cold engine, the choke vacuum piston or diaphragm must pull the choke open just a little bit, ⅛-inch or so, to admit enough air to keep the engine running. If the choke opens too much, the fuel mixture will be leaned out and the engine will stall. If the choke isn't open enough, the mixture will be too rich, and the engine will stall. If you have a cold engine stalling problem, check the opening.

To determine if the opening is correct, start a cold engine with the air cleaner cover off and insert a drill bit of the specified size (reference manuals will list the size for your car and carburetor) between choke plate and the wall of the carburetor barrel (see fig. 3-34). If the drill bit can't fit, the opening is too small; if it slides in and out easily, the opening is too big. Shut the engine and make an

Figure 3-34. When inserting specified drill between choke plate and carburetor barrel when cold engine is first started, drill should move in and out with some drag.

Figure 3-35. Protractor gauge for GM carburetors adheres magnetically to choke plate.

Figure 3-36. Air bleed holes on vacuum diaphragm are taped over and vacuum is applied with manual vacuum pump as shown. Angle of choke plate is compared with specifications.

adjustment. Late-model GM carburetors carry a specification for the angle of the choke plate rather than a drill bit opening. To measure the angle you need a special protractor-type tool with a magnetic base that adheres to the choke plate (see figs. 3-35 and 3-36). The following adjustment arrangements are used:

A link with a V-bend or a U-bend. Remove the link and spread it at the U to decrease the opening; close it up to enlarge the opening. Make small changes in the U-bend and allow the engine to cool between adjustments.

An adjusting screw. Turn the screw to change the opening. On some carburetors the screw is secured with a sealer

123

Figure 3-37. Heat the adjustment screw with a soldering gun to loosen sealer.

and won't turn. Apply heat with a soldering gun (see fig. 3-37) to loosen the sealer before turning the screw.

Adjustment with Engine Off. Because you have to make an adjustment and check, adjust and check, etc., it's better to do the job with the engine off, and on the majority of cars which have external diaphragms, you can. Obtain a vacuum pump-gauge (see fig. 3-38), an inexpensive tool with many other uses on the car. Disconnect the vacuum hose at the diaphragm, attach the hose from the pump-gauge, and operate the trigger handle to obtain 18 inches of vacuum. The choke plate will be drawn open and you can measure the gap between plate and carburetor barrel wall with the drill bit. If adjustments are necessary, you can make them over and over until you get the gap just right, without having to wait each time for the engine to cool off.

If the choke is not pulled open, the diaphragm unit could be defective. However, more likely it has an air bleed, and if you look carefully with a magnifying glass

Figure 3-38. Illustration shows use of vacuum pump-gauge for choke vacuum break adjustment. Pump is applying pressure to vacuum diaphragm with engine cold, while break is checked with drill bit. This type has adjusting screw, which is being turned so that drill bit moves between choke plate and carburetor barrel with light-to-moderate drag.

you should find it and be able to cover it with a piece of tape for the adjustment procedure. Air bleeds that delay the operation of a diaphragm unit are very common on GM cars and on at least one unit in any system where two diaphragm units are used. If a diaphragm unit does happen to fail and not pull open, you'll see no movement of the unit's link when the engine is started, and typically the exhaust will blow black smoke until the engine is warm.

Choke Heat Tube. On many chokes, the exhaust manifold may supply the heat for the thermostatic coil by means of an insulated tube from manifold to carburetor housing. If, when cleaning the choke housing with solvent, you notice a large accumulation of gummy deposits, you can't stop with the cleaning. The problem is that exhaust gas is getting into the housing and depositing there. Reason: The heat tube plugs into what seems like a hole in the exhaust manifold, but actually there's a sealed tube in the manifold that you can't see. If exhaust heat cracks that sealed tube, exhaust gases can leak into it and then into the insulated tube to the carburetor housing.

The cure is a special service kit. There are several

Figure 3-39. Here is one replacement for a heat tube that is broken inside the exhaust manifold. Above, the new heat tube retainer is held to the exhaust manifold by a clamp. The heat tube itself, covered with fiberglass cloth insulation, is run up to the choke housing. Below, you can see it threaded onto the choke housing fitting.

Figure 3-40. If necessary, flare the choke housing end of the heat tube. The nut should be in place before the flaring tool is used, for once you flare the end you may not be able to get the nut on from the other end.

types, but the easiest for a weekend mechanic is a design that clamps to the exterior of the exhaust manifold. Just remove the old heat tube and drive a plug into the hole (the plug is furnished with the service kit). Then attach a half-cylindrical retainer to a suitable location on the manifold, using a large worm-drive hose clamp (this clamp can be opened to install; it doesn't have to fit over an open neck, as do other clamps). Insert a replacement heat tube (covered with fiberglass cloth provided) into the edge of the retainer (where there's a suitable size hole), then carefully bend the heat tube and attach to the carburetor housing (see fig. 3-39).

Note: On many cars the carburetor retaining nut and a tiny piece of hardware called a ferrule are all you need, and they're in the kit. If, however, your car has the tubing flared at the carburetor end, you must install the nut and flare the end of the tube with a flaring kit (see fig. 3-40). If you don't have a flaring kit, leave the job to a professional.

Choke Heaters

The chokes on most late-model carburetors contain an electric heater.

The heater may be built into the choke housing cover.

This type is typically a special, almost electronic type, capable of providing a variable amount of heat depending on ambient temperatures. The wiring may be routed through an oil pressure switch or something similar, so current does not flow to the heater until the engine is running. When the engine starts, probe the terminal on the choke housing with a grounded 12-volt test light, and it should go on. If it does not, there is a break in the wiring circuit to the choke, and unless you have some experience in this area and a wiring diagram, leave the job to a professional.

If there is current to the choke housing, yet the choke is very slow to open, gas mileage will be poor. If the choke is not open in two miles, except in subzero weather, there apparently is a problem with the heater. On older cars the choke cover can be removed after taking out retaining screws. On later model cars, the choke cover is riveted in place and the rivet heads must be drilled out and a kit with special screws or studs and nuts installed to replace the rivets.

Rear-drive Chrysler products with well-type chokes may have a heater to assist choke opening. In this case, trace the wire from the well assembly and it will come to a thermostatic switch, generally bolted to an engine top

Figure 3-41. Test Chrysler rear-drive cars' electric choke switch with ohmmeter on both terminals as shown. There should be an infinite ohms reading when it's cold, a zero ohms reading when it's warm.

Figure 3-42. Test electric choke switch with 12-volt test light as shown, grounded and probing the terminal for the wire to the well choke (cold engine just started and idling). The light should not go on. When the engine is warm or ambient temperatures are high, the light should go on.

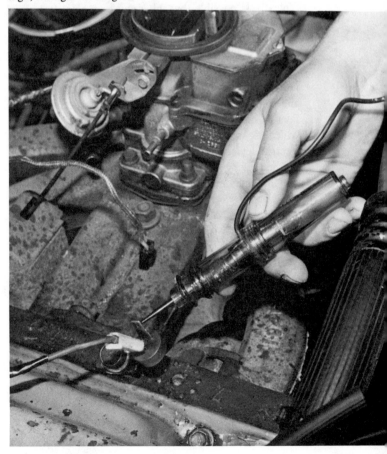

cover. This switch has two terminals, and at low ambient temperatures, it should be closed. At higher temperatures, it should be open. The simplest ways to check are with an ohmmeter connected to the two terminals (car's wiring temporarily disconnected), or with a 12-volt test light (see figs. 3-41 and 3-42). With the ohmmeter, there should be a zero ohms reading at high temperature (or a warm engine). There should be an infinite ohms reading (maximum resistance) when it's cold out (low 50s Fahrenheit or under). With the test light grounded, probe the terminal with the wire to the well choke. The light should not go on if it's cold; it should go on if it's warm.

Idle Speed Adjustments—Carburetor Engines

Whenever you perform a tuneup on a car you should set the idle speed to factory specifications. These are usually listed on a decal under the hood. The adjustment must be made with the engine fully warmed up.

Note: On many 1980 Cadillacs and a wide variety of General Motors cars of other makes since 1981, idle

Figure 3-43. Illustration shows idle and fast idle speed screws on a two-barrel carburetor.

FAST IDLE CAM

FAST IDLE SCREW

IDLE SPEED SCREW

speed is controlled automatically by the engine computer, which drives a DC motor with a plunger against the throttle linkage. Do not try to adjust idle speed on an engine where the computer controls it. A basic adjustment typically is possible, but this requires special technique and tools and an error could be costly. If idle speed is incorrect, leave the job to a professional unless you are experienced, have a factory service manual, and are willing to buy the special tools (sold in auto parts stores). Few idle speed adjustments should be needed on most 1980 and some 1981 VWs with a digital electronic idle stabilizer or on 1981 American Motors six-cylinder engines, which use an electronic control unit to operate a vacuum-electric device that regulates idle speed.

The factory-specified idle speed is a compromise that provides maximum smoothness with resistance to stall, while at the same time minimizing fuel consumption and the "creeping" tendency of a car with an automatic transmission. To do the job you need a tachometer and a screwdriver or small wrench.

First, locate the idle speed adjuster and understand how it works. If it is an adjusting screw, it should bear against the throttle linkage on American cars (on some European carburetors it does not, and you should check your owner's manual for details). If there are two adjusting screws on the carburetor linkage (see fig. 3-43), one is for "fast-idle," a higher idle speed for when the engine is cold. That screw bears against a stepped part called the fast-idle cam, or against a link that bears against the fast-idle cam. It is the other screw you want.

If there is no other screw, there may be a solenoid, an electromagnetic switch with a plunger. When you turn on

the ignition the solenoid is energized and ejects its plunger to bear against the throttle linkage. When you turn off the ignition the plunger retracts, allowing the throttle to close more completely. This minimizes a problem in many cars called "afterrun" or "dieseling," in which the engine continues to run briefly after the ignition key is turned off. Many late-model cars have solenoids, and there are several types. Here's what you may find:

Solenoid with plunger that has a square or hex-shaped tip. See figure 3-44. To increase idle speed, you put a wrench on the hex or square and turn counterclockwise to partly unscrew the plunger from the solenoid.

Solenoid on adjustable carriage. See figure 3-45. The solenoid moves toward you (increasing idle speed) or away from you (decreasing it) as you turn the carriage adjusting screw.

Solenoid plunger bearing against adjusting screw. In this case (see fig. 3-46), you turn the adjusting screw, which is on the throttle linkage.

Solenoid plunger adjuster on other side of solenoid. See figure 3-47. The adjuster is a rod with a hex or square tip on the side opposite to the plunger.

Entire solenoid body is adjustable, plus internal adjuster in back of solenoid. This design is found on many General Motors cars. The basic adjustment is made by turning the entire solenoid body (you may have to disconnect a wire from the solenoid to avoid twisting it) and the adjustment is fine-tuned by turning an internal adjuster. See figures 3-48, 3-49, and 3-50.

You may find more than one likely adjuster, such as both a solenoid and a screw. In this case, you must find out

Figure 3-44. This solenoid plunger has a hex-head tip. Put wrench on tip and turn to increase or decrease plunger length to adjust idle speed.

Figure 3-45. This solenoid is on a movable carriage that is reset by turning the spring-loaded carriage adjusting screw as shown.

Figure 3-46. There's no adjustment on this solenoid. Instead, the solenoid plunger bears up against an adjusting screw on the throttle.

Figure 3-47. This solenoid has an adjuster on the end opposite to that of the plunger.

Figure 3-48. This solenoid is like a gigantic adjusting screw. To adjust your idle speed, turn the entire solenoid body in (against the spring pressure).

Figure 3-49. Back view of the solenoid shows the hex for wrench, to permit easy tuning of the solenoid body. Wire has been disconnected from solenoid to avoid twisting it.

Figure 3-50. Allen wrench is inserted through hole into back of solenoid, to turn internal adjuster in order to fine-tune idle speed.

if the solenoid has another purpose, namely to raise the idle speed to prevent stalling when the air conditioning is turned on.

To check, have a helper start the engine, hold down the gas pedal about an inch, and turn on the air conditioning. If the solenoid is wired into the air conditioning circuit you'll see the plunger extend only after the AC is turned on.

Note: The gas pedal must be held down a bit or the plunger may not extend. The solenoid has only enough energy to hold the plunger in the extended position, not to push the throttle open.

If the solenoid plunger does respond only to the air conditioning switch, to headlights turned on, or to blower fan when set to high speed, it is not used to set the basic idle speed. You should, however, check its operation after setting idle speed to make sure that idle speed is maintained (or rises slightly) when the air conditioning (or whatever else triggers it) is turned on.

Setting Idle Speed. Connect your tachometer to an electrical ground and to the negative terminal (marked with a minus sign or "CB") of the ignition coil. On cars with electronic ignition, see figures 2-45 and 2-46. On engines

with computers, a "secondary tachometer," which clips to a spark plug wire, is the most practical type to use.

Start the engine and compare the tachometer reading with specifications, which usually appear on an underhood tuneup decal. Normally, the underhood decal requires that the engine be fully warmed up. It may stipulate other conditions too, and these must be met.

If the reading is lower or higher than specifications, do one of the following:

Turn the adjustment screw on the linkage.

Turn the carriage screw, plunger, or rear adjuster on solenoids so equipped.

On solenoids of the type shown in figures 3-48, 3-49, and 3-50, turn the internal Allen adjuster with a 1/8-inch Allen wrench clockwise until the adjuster comes to a stop (don't force it past the stop). Then turn the entire solenoid body (disconnect wire if necessary) with a wrench on the hex in back until idle speed is 100 to 150 r.p.m. above specifications. Finally, back out the internal Allen adjuster to reduce idle speed to specifications.

After each turn of the idle speed adjuster, have a helper step on the gas pedal for an instant. This will pull the throttle linkage away from the solenoid and allow the plunger to extend. Wait 10 to 15 seconds for the engine speed reading to stabilize before attempting another adjustment.

Note: The idle speed specifications given, even if it doesn't say so, are plus or minus 50 r.p.m., so don't struggle beyond what is necessary.

Low Idle. On some tuneup decals there will be a specification for an engine speed called "low" or "slow" idle, in addition to "curb idle." In this case, the solenoid controls curb idle, rather than just acting as a speedup for the air conditioning, and there is a "low idle" screw somewhere at the throttle linkage (except for the type with internal Allen adjuster, in which case the solenoid body itself serves this purpose). To check low idle, disconnect the wire from the solenoid, and if low idle is not within specifications, turn the throttle linkage screw (or readjust the solenoid with the internal adjuster) to set it.

Idle Fuel Mixture Adjustment. The fuel mixture is designed into the carburetor and in some cars is controlled electronically. On older cars, however, there still is one adjustment remaining: the idle mixture. This is the mixture that bypasses the throttle to keep the engine fueled when you have your foot off the gas pedal. Years ago you could turn the mixture screws (one for a one-barrel, two for a two- or four-barrel carburetor) a fair amount. With emission controls came the limiter, a plastic cap (see fig. 3-51) that restricted the amount you could turn the screw. On the newest cars (since 1979 on most cars) there is no mixture adjustment (see fig. 3-52).

Figure 3-51. Screwdriver is turning plastic limiter on idle mixture screw. The limiter has a tab that permits only a modest amount of mixture adjustment.

PLUGS COVER
MIXTURE SCREWS

Figure 3-52. Current-model cars have mixture screws preset at factory and sealed by plugs, as shown.

In any case, don't look for a mixture adjustment to cure a real performance problem, for once you step on the gas pedal the idle passages have little effect, and above 25 mph usually none at all.

If the idle is rough, however, a mixture adjustment may help. If your state has periodic motor vehicle inspection with an emissions check, however, rough idle may be the price of passing inspection.

To determine if your car has adjustable mixture screws, look for them at the base of the carburetor, and if you see little screws with springs around them, not threaded into the linkage but into the carburetor itself, they're the mixture screws. Refer to figure 3-51, which shows the typical screw with its limiter cap.

Turning clockwise leans out the mixture; turning counterclockwise richens it.

You should not have to adjust the mixture periodically. When an engine suffers from lean fuel mixtures, the usual reasons are leaking vacuum hose connections. Check these hoses and look for cracks on the hose ends; if you find them, trim off any hardened hose end and refit carefully. Or there may be a leaking gasket at the base of the carburetor or intake manifold. To find out, squirt oil into the gasket joint all around, with the engine idling, and if the idle speed goes up (the oil provides a temporary seal), the gasket is leaking.

ELECTRONICALLY CONTROLLED CARBURETORS

Although the electronically controlled carburetor requires no regular service, you should check all vacuum hose and electric wire connections from the carburetor to the solenoid vacuum valve (if used) and to the computer and oxygen sensor as part of a tuneup.

The oxygen sensor itself (see fig. 3-53) should be replaced in accordance with manufacturer's recommendations. Remove the electrical connector and take out the sensor with a wrench.

Although the electronic system controls the fuel mixture, the range in which it operates is relatively narrow. If it malfunctions it will affect exhaust emissions and performance, but there should be no effect on starting and basic running of the engine.

Figure 3-53. Oxygen sensor is threaded into exhaust pipe. To replace it, remove electrical connector and unscrew it with a wrench (such as a special deep socket and ratchet).

Troubleshooting

The computer system that controls the carburetor is covered by the 5-year, 50,000-mile warranty, but if that has expired, you probably will want to do some basic troubleshooting. Even if it is within warranty, you may have trouble getting free service unless you are aware of what's wrong and can exert your rights.

Check for trouble codes as explained at the end of chapter 2, and if any apply to the carburetor or oxygen sensor, you can consider servicing them on your own, particularly checking the oxygen sensor wire and replacing the sensor.

Note: The oxygen sensor may malfunction without producing a trouble code. Inexpensive testers to check the sensor are available in auto parts stores and may be considered a handy addition to the weekend mechanic's equipment. On cars since 1988, oxygen sensors are covered by the 5-50 warranty.

The mixture control solenoid on most cars may produce performance problems even without setting a failure code. To check, remove the solenoid (held by a few screws) and inspect the tip (see figs. 3-54 and 3-55). If the O-ring is deteriorated or if there is an accumulation of gum, that can affect carburetor operation. The solenoid is not inexpensive, and there are low-cost repair kits to service the most common problems.

Figure 3-54. Remove screws holding mixture control solenoid from carburetor.

Figure 3-55. Lift out solenoid and inspect tip, particularly checking for damaged rubber O-ring.

Figure 3-56. On some cars, mixture control solenoid dwell connector is at the solenoid wiring. Attach tach-dwellmeter positive wire lead to connector and ground the negative wire lead. Follow service manual procedures for solenoid dwell test.

You also may wish to check solenoid dwell (see fig. 3-56). If it fails to vary around the 30-degree mark with the engine warmed up and running (check the factory service manual for the exact procedure), a fuel mixture adjustment may be necessary. Because late-model carburetors have sealed mixture adjustments, you will have to drill or chisel out a cover plug for access. Therefore, you should not attempt this procedure unless you have followed the factory service manual's checkout procedure and made certain the adjustment will help.

Some Fords have been equipped with the Microprocessor Control Unit (MCU) computer. This was not covered in chapter 2 because it does not routinely control spark timing advance, although it may have a feature (in conjunction with the electronic ignition unit) to retard spark timing advance when the engine is knocking.

To determine if your 1981-on MCU system is apparently sound, activate the self-test, as follows:

1. Locate a six-wire connector on the passenger's side of the engine compartment (see fig. 3-57).
2. Connect a voltmeter positive lead to the battery starter terminal, and the voltmeter negative lead into No. 4 terminal. Connect a jumper wire from No. 5 to No. 2 terminal.
3. Turn on the ignition and you should get a code 11 (voltmeter needle pulses to the middle of the scale, pause, then another pulse). If you get this, the system passes the engine-off test.
4. Run the engine, four-cylinders at 2,500 to 2,800 r.p.m., V-8s at idle. When you get two needle pulses on a four or four pulses on a V-8, the self-diagnosis is underway.
5. On V-8s there is a device called a knock sensor (fig. 3-58) that tells the electronic ignition unit to retard the ignition timing when the engine has started to knock (ping, etc.) You must trigger this sensor on V-8s for proper operation of the self-diagnosis feature. Immediately tap vigorously on the intake manifold very close to the knock sensor (not on it), using a long bar and perhaps a hammer. If you don't do this promptly, or if the knock sensor is bad, you'll get a code 25 (two needle pulses, pause, then five needle pulses).

Figure 3-57. If you have a 1981 Ford product with Microprocessor Control Unit (MCU) computer, locate the six-wire connector on the passenger's side of the engine compartment. Connect the voltmeter positive lead to the battery starter terminal and the negative lead to the No. 4 terminal of the connector (numbering applies to the unwired side). Then connect a jumper wire from No. 5 to No. 2 (or to an electrical ground).

Figure 3-58. This is a Ford V-8 knock sensor on intake manifold.

The self-test then will continue automatically. After about a minute, you should see a code 11 if the computer system is operating properly. If you see other codes, the system needs attention (it's warranted for 4 years or 50,000 miles, so leave the work to the dealer).

The four-cylinder computer will give out only one trouble code. If there are more faults, you must fix the one shown, then repeat the test in order to get any other, again just one at a time. On the V-8, all fault codes will be shown, and the sequence will be repeated once.

Because the MCU self-test relies on needle pulses, you can only use a voltmeter with a needle and dial, not a digital type.

American Motors cars also use the MCU computer, but it's a bit different than the Ford setup. There was no self-test procedure in 1980. There is a self-test on 1981–1982 cars, wired to a dashboard Check Engine light. If a failure occurs, the light goes on and pulses out a trouble code (it stops pulsing after the code has been repeated four times). Any number of trouble codes could be pulsed when you are driving the car.

Self-tests and trouble codes ended on AM cars when the Renault Alliance was introduced in 1983. Trouble

codes on all engine control computers are not always indicative of precise problems. In many cases, the code only indicates a trouble area, and it is necessary to follow a manual checkout procedure to pinpoint the failure. The manual checkout is always based on the use of routine service instruments, such as voltmeter, tachometer, test lamp, vacuum gauge, etc.

Although Chrysler products with carburetors do not have a self-test, you can make a rough check of computer control of ignition timing by starting the engine cold and letting it warm up. As the engine gets warm, the timing should retard. This test will require an adjustable timing light, as the initial readings will be off the timing marks indicator scale.

If you still have the car after the 5-year, 50,000-mile warranty on the computer system has expired, obtain a service ("shop") manual for your car to get the manual checkout procedure, both for cars with self-diagnosis and those Chrysler products without it. Checkout without special equipment also is possible on Chrysler and AMC systems, following a service manual procedure. See figure 3-59 for a depiction of a pre-1981 GM underdash computer.

ECM

"CHECK ENGINE" LIGHT

"IGN"

FUSE PANEL

TROUBLE CODE
"TEST" CONNECTOR
(WHT/BLK WIRE)

LONG TERM MEMORY CONNECTOR
(ORANGE WIRE)

Figure 3-59. This cutaway drawing of a GM dashboard shows a pre-1981 computer with on-board diagnosis. The white and black wire *at the left* is grounded to produce a trouble code on the Check Engine light. The orange wire *at right* is connected to the car battery to keep any trouble code in the computer's memory if the ignition is shut off.

Air Cleaner Service

Unless the engine has an adequate source of clean air it will not run very well for very long. Virtually all modern cars have a pleated paper air filter under a cover in the air cleaner housing. Just remove the cover wingnut or spring clips, lift off the cover, and there's the filter element. If it's dirty on the outside, or has gone 2 years or 25,000 miles, replace it (see fig. 3-20).

Some cars have a filter element enclosed in a sealed canister, so you can't see the condition of the paper. The recommended replacement interval is 5 years or 50,000 miles, but few make it that long. If the engine runs smoother with the filter off (test very briefly, for a minute or two, to prevent excessive dirt from getting in), replace the sealed canister (see fig. 3-60). Or replace every 2 years or 25,000 miles to be sure.

Figure 3-60. This is a sealed canister air cleaner, viewed from the underside. You can peer in from the intake or through the circular opening, but you won't be able to tell if the element is clean or dirty.

Installing a Fuel Inlet Fitting or Rebuilt Carburetor

If a carburetor is leaking at the fuel inlet fitting, and tightening the fitting doesn't cure the leak, you don't have to replace the carburetor in many cases. Repair fittings are available for popular American carburetors, and installing them is not difficult (see figs. 3-61 to 3-67).

If you must replace the carburetor, you should know that rebuilt carburetors are available for most cars, although the feedback type with mixture control solenoid may be difficult to obtain. If you can't get a factory rebuilt from a reputable firm such as Arrow or Champion, try to find a reputable local rebuilder who will service your carburetor. Or perhaps you can obtain one from a wrecking yard.

Figure 3-61. Use two wrenches, one on each fitting, to loosen the fuel line fitting.

Figure 3-62. Unthread carburetor fuel fitting next.

Figure 3-63. Remove fitting and anything in it, such as filter and spring.

Figure 3-64. Coat repair fitting with grease, then thread in with wrench. Repair fitting will cut deeper threads and grease will catch metallic particles. Remove repair fitting and carefully wipe threaded area with rag to remove metallic residue, as shown.

Figure 3-65. Reinstall repair fitting, this time with filter and spring. Don't forget sealing gasket too. Tighten in place.

Figure 3-66. If fuel line will not thread into repair fitting, often because of differences in length, install the adapter fitting as shown, and using two wrenches, tighten in place. Cut off the fuel line fitting (shown removed).

Figure 3-67. Use a short piece of fuel hose to bridge the gap and clamp the hose at each end. The job is done.

Installing a replacement carburetor is not a difficult job, but you must keep track of a lot of little fasteners and how parts fit on and linkages go together. Making simple sketches is useful, particularly if there will be any delay in installing the replacement carburetor (which would give you the time to forget). If you are buying a rebuilt, keep the old carburetor until you have installed the new, as you will find that you must transfer some parts from one to the other, such as the choke vacuum diaphragm unit. If possible, use vacuum hose identifiers, which are color-coded male plugs for the hoses and matching female plugs for the vacuum hose necks. If you do not have these, wrap numbered tape (same number on the hose and neck) for correct reconnections. Refer to figures 3-68 to 3-75, which show carburetor removal. Installation of a replacement carburetor is the reverse of that procedure.

Figure 3-68. Begin carburetor removal by disconnecting fuel line, using two wrenches as shown.

Figure 3-69. Disconnect vacuum lines and install identifiers on hose and neck, or wrap each with numbered tape.

Figure 3-70. If there is external choke linkage, disconnect it. Tape the tiny clip shown being disconnected to the external link, so it won't get lost.

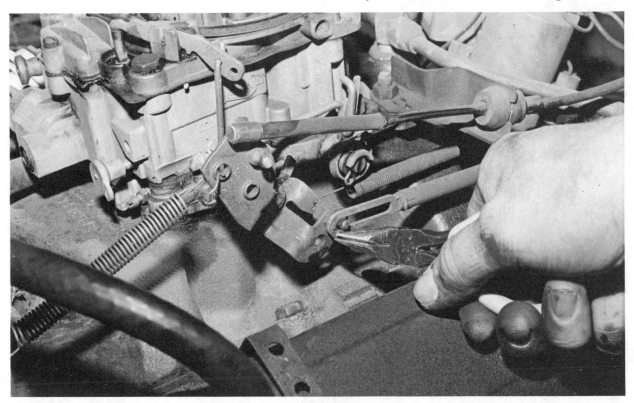

Figure 3-71. This automatic transmission link to the carburetor is held by a tiny C-shaped clip that can be pulled out with needlenose pliers as shown. Tape the clip to the transmission link so it won't get lost and you'll know what it's for.

Figure 3-72. Gas pedal link on this carburetor goes into a spring-loaded ball socket. The joint can be pried apart with a screwdriver as shown.

Figure 3-73. Remove the bolts or nuts holding the carburetor to its base.

Figure 3-74. Lift up the carburetor. Replace the gasket underneath.

Figure 3-75. After installing the replacement carburetor, tighten all retaining nuts and bolts securely to specifications, using a torque wrench if possible.

FUEL PUMPS

The mechanical pump contains a diaphragm with spring-loaded discs that cover and uncover ports inside. One port is connected to a line from the gas tank; the other is connected to the line to the carburetor bowl. The diaphragm is flexed up and down to produce the pumping action. Operating the diaphragm is a spring-loaded arm that is pushed by a lobe on a shaft (called the camshaft) inside the engine. When the arm is pushed in, the diaphragm is flexed downward, drawing in fuel from the tank. The spring then retracts the arm and the diaphragm and the fuel is pushed up to the carburetor (see figures 3-76 and 3-77).

The electric fuel pump is either a diaphragm device operated by a set of contact points (much like the breaker points in an ignition system) or a motorized device with the motor operating a turbine, piston, etc.

The exact method of internal operation of a fuel pump is not important, for the typical fuel pump is sealed. If it doesn't work, you replace it.

A defective pump may be responsible for starting failure, engine misfire, or weak performance.

Testing the Pump

First check to see if fuel is getting to the carburetor. Remove the air cleaner cover, push open the choke plate with your finger, have a helper pump the gas pedal, and look for squirts into the carburetor barrel (from the carburetor's accelerator pump). If there is no fuel squirting from the carburetor, the problem likely is that no fuel is being delivered.

To test the fuel pump itself, disconnect the fuel line from the carburetor and aim the end into a quart container (see fig. 3-78). Have a helper start the engine and run it on the fuel in the carburetor bowl. A healthy pump should deliver a stream of fuel amounting to a pint in 30 seconds on a V-8, 45 seconds on a 4- or 6-cylinder engine. If the engine does not start, just crank it for 30 seconds. The amount of fuel collected in the container should be close to what you'd get with the engine running at idle.

If the pump is not delivering, or delivering much too little, there are four possibilities:

Clogged fuel filter. To check, remove the filter as explained in the previous section and repeat the test. With the in-line type, place the filter aside and position

Figure 3-76. Exterior view of a mechanical fuel pump. Pump's inlet fitting is at *lower right,* outlet is *at left. At upper right* you can see part of the spring-loaded arm, also called an "actuating lever."

Figure 3-77. This drawing shows how the pump works. As eccentric lobe on camshaft turns, it pushes on actuating lever that flexes the diaphragm. When the diaphragm flexes down, it creates a vacuum that draws open the inlet valve and pulls fuel from the gas tank. The camshaft turns, relaxing pressure on the lever, so the diaphragm is pushed back. This creates pressure against the fuel, which pushes open the outlet valve and flows up a piece of tubing to the carburetor.

Figure 3-78. Fuel line is disconnected from the carburetor, and hose is installed over the end of the line. Other end of hose then is aimed into quart container (a clean, empty oil can in this case) or fitted to pressure gauge, as shown above, and the engine is cranked. Amount of fuel discharged into container is measured and compared with specifications.

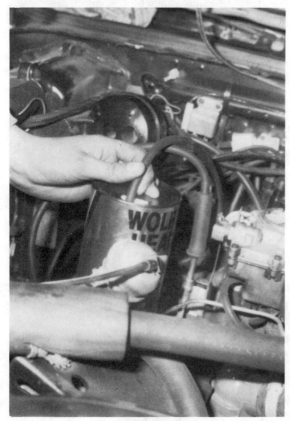

the container at the end of the section of fuel line from the pump.

Restricted fuel line. Visually inspect the fuel line from pump to carburetor, looking for kinks in flexible hose sections and dents in steel sections. Next, jack up the car, support it on stands (see chapter 5), and follow the line back to the tank to check for kinks or dents. A kink may be eliminated by repositioning the line slightly, particularly in the area of a retaining clip. A dent can only be corrected either by replacing the line or by cutting out the dented section with a tubing cutter and installing a piece of flexible fuel line hose which is secured with hose clamps. If you attempt this job on a line between a mechanical pump and rear gas tank, you should jack up the front of the car as high as possible, so as little fuel as possible will flow out of the cut fuel line while you're working. Install a pan underneath to catch the fuel after you cut the line.

On electric pumps, a problem in the electrical circuitry. The problem could be a bad fuse, a defective electrical ground at the pump, a poor connection at the pump, or on some cars a defective oil pressure sensor (the sensor feeds current to the pump so that the pump operates only when the engine is running, not just when the ignition is on).

First, check for a defective fuse. On some cars there is a second fused circuit that operates the pump when the engine is cranking. If your car starts easily you might never know it failed unless the car runs out of gas, in which case it won't restart unless the circuit is repaired or the engine is started by pouring some gasoline directly into the carburetor.

If the problem is not a defective fuse, go to the pump and look for a black wire that is simply screwed down to the car body. The screw-down point could be anywhere, including in the trunk compartment. This is the electrical ground, and if it's loose or corroded the pump won't work. Clean and tighten.

Other problems, including replacement of a defective electric pump, require experience to check and should be left to a professional mechanic.

A defective fuel pump. If this final possibility seems to be it, you can double-check using a vacuum gauge with a pressure section on the dial (most vacuum gauges except the pump-gauge have a pressure section). Fit the gauge hose over the carburetor end of the fuel line and have a helper crank or run the engine (see fig. 3-78). The reading you get should be compared with factory specifications. In the absence of specifications, look for a reading of at least $2\frac{1}{2}$ p.s.i. with the engine running at idle.

Replacing a Mechanical Pump

Most electric fuel pumps, unless they are located in the engine compartment (and the typical one is in the gas tank), require special tools to replace. Therefore, this section is limited to mechanical pumps bolted to the engine.

First, disconnect the fuel lines from the pump. If they are metal, disconnect them with two wrenches, as for a fuel line at the carburetor (see fig. 3-79).

Next, remove the pump mounting bolts or nuts with a ratchet and socket, or with whatever wrench will fit in if a socket won't (see fig. 3-80).

Figure 3-79. Use two wrenches to disconnect fuel line from pump. One wrench holds the pump fitting while other slackens fuel line nut.

Figure 3-80. Once fuel lines are disconnected, remove the pump mounting bolts, as shown.

Figure 3-81. Here's the fuel pump being removed from the engine. Notice the actuating lever. In this case, the flexible fuel hose was left in place. The pump is being brought to a convenient working position, where the hose will be disconnected.

Pull the pump (see fig. 3-81) and scrape any gasket residue from the engine.

Apply a thin film of nonhardening gasket sealer to the replacement pump's gasket surface only. The sealer is sold in small tubes in auto supply stores. Position the gasket on the pump, and the sealer will hold it in place.

Refit the pump to the engine.

Note: On many General Motors engines, particularly Chevrolet, the camshaft does not push on the arm directly. Instead, there is a plunger between them. The camshaft pushes on the plunger, which pushes on the rod. When you take out the old pump, the plunger drops down. You have to push it back up and hold it there so you can install the new pump with the diaphragm arm under it. It doesn't sound hard, but there's no room for your fingers. Special tools are available, but here are two other solutions:

1. First, reach in with your fingers and smear some grease on the plunger; then push it up. The grease will hold it there long enough to get the pump in if you work fast.
2. Push the plunger up with your finger and hold it up with a piece of stiff wire (such as a paper clip) bent

into an L-shape. As you hold it up with the wire, slip in the pump, and just as you're ready to seat the pump into bolt-on position, yank out the wire.

Install the bolts or nuts, starting them by hand, then tightening with a wrench. Reconnect the fuel lines and the job is done.

Note: On some cars the location of one of the fuel line fittings on the pump is such that with the pump in place you will struggle to reconnect. If you see this problem (perhaps you encountered a similar one when disconnecting), make the reconnection before you install the pump.

If your carbureted engine is hard to restart after a highway run in hot weather, it may be suffering from "vapor lock" occurring as the fuel pump and lines absorb heat with the engine off. The car makers often have a fix for the problem on a late-model car, so check with the dealer or factory zone office first. If there is nothing, and you are sure you have vapor lock (you can tell by checking fuel pump pressure—it will be zero), you can install an electric fuel pump.

The electric fuel pump mounts near the gas tank, far from the hot engine compartment, and you can further help the situation by repositioning the fuel line in the engine compartment to provide more clearance from the hot exhaust manifold and other hot engine parts.

A typical electric pump installation is shown in figures 3-82 to 3-86. The fuel pump must be wired to a source of ignition current at the fusebox. To locate one, with a grounded 12-volt test light, probe the output side of the fuses (right sides) and find an electrical accessory terminal that turns on the test light only when the ignition switch is in the "On" or "Run" position. Run the wire along an existing wiring harness to the rear of the car, taping it in place at various points.

Figure 3-82. Electric fuel pump installation begins with finding a suitable location for the pump, near the gas tank, in an area where a frame rail protects it from stone damage. If the only suitable area is open, a metal shield should be installed around the pump to protect it. Measure the width of the pump (with fuel line fittings installed), add a couple of inches to the total and cut out the total length from a section of fuel line with a tubing cutter.

Figure 3-83. Drill holes and mount the fuel pump as shown.

Figure 3-84. Install the fuel pump fittings, which are made to accept rubber hoses.

Figure 3-85. Install rubber hoses to join the pump to the cut ends of fuel line, then secure with clamps as shown. In the passenger compartment, disconnect the fuel lines from the pump (if the kit includes a blanking plate, remove the pump and install the blanking plate over the opening on the engine). Cut the fuel line fittings that connected to the pump, install a connector hose, and secure with hose clamps.

Figure 3-86. Run a wire from a source of ignition current at the fuse box. In this case the wire is passed through a hole in a frame rail. To insure that the wire is not cut, it should be generously wrapped with electrical tape for an area of several inches each side of the hole, and the hole should be filled with rubber paste to further retard movement of the wire. Then the electrical connector should be crimped to the bared end of the wire and attached to the electrical terminal on the pump.

FUEL INJECTION

In a carburetor, inrushing air draws fuel droplets out of a nozzle and carries them into the intake manifold, and from there into the cylinders. Fuel injection is a much more precise system, even when compared with electronically regulated carburetors, because the amount of fuel can be more precisely controlled, and in most designs it can be sprayed in even amounts very close to the cylinders.

If the control is electronic, it often is a computer, the same one that regulates spark timing on some cars. If the control is hydraulic, it may be modified to include some solenoids (electromagnetic switches) for further regulation by a master computer. See "Computer Spark Advance" in chapter 2.

Three fuel injection systems are in widest use:

An electronically controlled system with electrically operated injectors, one for each cylinder. The injectors are located just outside the intake ports of the cylinders. Electronic, electrical, and mechanical sensors for engine and ambient temperature, engine speed, throttle position, etc., tell a computer how much fuel the engine needs, and the computer then supplies current to the injectors for an appropriate length of time. The longer the computer energizes the injectors, the more fuel they spray into the intake ports (see fig. 3-87).

A hydraulically operated system with mechanical injectors, one for each cylinder. This is used on many imported cars. A flap in the air intake (see fig. 3-88) moves inward as airflow into the engine increases. As it does, it pushes up on a valve that regulates fuel flow to the injectors. The higher the valve rises, the greater is the fuel flow. As the engine warms up, however, it needs less fuel. To regulate the flow, fuel under pressure is also fed to the top of this valve. When the engine is cold and maximum fuel flow is required, this fuel pressure is bled off, so the valve rises. As the engine warms up, the bleeding of the fuel pressure is stopped, so it pushes down harder on the valve, preventing it from rising so much, thereby reducing the fuel flow to the injectors. The injectors themselves are like shower heads with a tiny check valve that prevents spraying until there is a minimum amount of pressure.

A throttle body fuel injection design. This has a provision to inject fuel only at one point—the center of the intake manifold. It is built into a module that replaces the carburetor. However, it has a barrel or two barrels with throttle plates, just like a carburetor. Hence the name.

In the most popular design, there are one or two electrical fuel injectors in the throttle body, and they are activated and deactivated by the engine control computer. This is far less expensive than an injector at each cylinder, and although perhaps not as effective, it is simpler and more reliable than the complex carburetors needed on modern cars.

Precise Mixture Control

These systems provide very precise fuel mixture control, which is important if the car is to meet exhaust emission standards.

In many of these systems, the computer receives signals from an oxygen sensor threaded into the exhaust manifold. Oxygen in the exhaust is an indicator of the fuel mixture going through the injection system, so if necessary the computer can richen or lean out the mixture as required for low emissions. The oxygen sensor arrangement was introduced on cars built for sale in California, which has very strict emissions regulations of its own. With this device, the mixture can be controlled so precisely that a special catalytic converter can be used, one that controls all major air pollutants. As explained earlier in this chapter, some carburetor fuel systems also have oxygen sensor electronic controls. The electronic control may be a computer or a simple on-off switching unit. In most cases since 1981, the control is a computer.

Fuel Injection Service

Although major fuel injection service is a job for a professional, a weekend mechanic can perform the only required maintenance—replacement of the fuel filter—do some basic troubleshooting, and if necessary replace a defective fuel injector. When it malfunctions, the fuel injection system can make the car hard or impossible to start, or cause it to misfire. After the inspection of wiring connections described earlier, look for a blown fuse.

On a car with an injector for each cylinder, failure of one injector is obviously more likely just to cause hard starting and rough operation than a complete failure to start. On a throttle body system with one or two injectors, an injector failure is likely to make the car impossible to start, although the injector also may function but spray fuel in an erratic pattern, which affects performance (see fig. 3-89).

Gums that form when the engine is off from components in the gasoline may coat fuel injectors and affect their spray pattern, causing poor performance. This problem, which may occur on systems with an injector at each cylinder, can be prevented by using gasolines with detergent or by pouring a detergent additive into the gas tank with every other fillup.

Injectors may leak fuel when the engine is off, and if this occurs, either of two problems is possible if you attempt to restart within a short period after shutdown:
1. The fuel vaporizes and there is not enough fuel for immediate starting.

Figure 3-87. *At top* is a schematic of an electronic fuel injection system, with an injector at each cylinder, shows how the electronic control module (engine computer) receives signals from the ignition switch, vehicle speed sensor, air conditioning compressor, temperature sensor, crank sensor (to indicate piston position), detonation (knock) sensor, O_2 (oxygen) sensor, throttle position sensor, the hot film mass air flow sensor (an electronic sensor that tells the computer how much air is flowing to the cylinders), and a tach (engine speed) signal from a distributorless ignition system. The computer uses this information to run a motor that moves the throttle to set idle speed and triggers the fuel injectors for the appropriate length of time. B. *At bottom* is a throttle body fuel injection system. It also is wired to the engine computer and there are similiar sensors used. In this case, idle speed is regulated by a motor that moves a valve in an airflow passage with the throttle closed, and there is only one injector (or in some cases two injectors), which is on top of the intake manifold, instead of at the end of each manifold branch, close to the cylinders.

Figure 3-88. Here's a hydraulically-operated system with an intake airflap (called an air sensor). Instead of signaling a computer, however, it has an arm that pushes on a cylindrical valve in a component called the fuel distributor. The greater the air flow, the further the arm pushes the valve, and the greater the fuel flow to the injectors. A control pressure regulator controls the fuel mixture, leaning it out as the engine warms up. Notice that it is connected by tubing to the fuel distributor on top of the valve. When the engine is cold, the regulator is open, allowing fuel pressure to bleed off back to the gas tank. The valve, therefore, moves in accordance with the push from the intake air flap arm. As the engine warms up, however, the regulator closes partially, so that much of the fuel pressure remains on top of the valve, tending to push it down. This downward pressure (opposing the upward push of the air flap arm) reduces the fuel flow through the cylindrical valve, leaning out the fuel mixture. The injectors are very similar to shower heads in that they spray continuously so long as there is adequate pressure in the fuel line. As in the electronic system, the auxiliary air regulator admits additional air for cold driveaway. The fuel accumulator is a spring-loaded valve device that insures a solid column of fuel under pressure in the system at all times. The thermo-time switch is a temperature-sensitive switch that operates the cold-start valve—an injector much like the type in the electronic system that supplies extra fuel when the engine is started at very low temperatures.

FUEL PRESSURE REGULATOR

SCHRADER VALVE

AIR FLOW

ELECTROMECHANICAL FUEL INJECTOR

FUEL SUPPLY FROM PUMP

FUEL RETURN TO TANK

THROTTLE PLATE

Figure 3-89. This is a Ford throttle body fuel injection unit. The Schrader valve is on the top of the unit itself. The Cadillac system is similar, but has the Schrader valve in the fuel line to the throttle body unit and operates at much lower pressure.

2. The fuel "floods" the engine, and it does not start easily. One or two injectors leaking is more likely to be a problem on cars with throttle body systems, as the percentages on a non-throttle-body multi-injection system mean that most injectors will function normally.

Before you try, however, you should understand that the injection system is basically reliable, and you first should look to other items, such as the ignition system, for a solution to a performance or starting problem. If the engine cranks well and there is a good spark, then you can look at the fuel system, and even then, consider first these routine inspection items.

Routine Inspection

On all fuel injection systems, you should check to make sure that no lines are kinked or dented and that all electrical connections are secure. With electronic systems, the computer ground is important. It may be a wire secured to the engine or through the computer mounting screws. A loose ground wire or loose and/or corroded computer mounting screws can cause a variety of problems.

Checking for Fuel. There are various fuel delivery checks you can make if the engine won't start, depending on the system. With the electronic system used on many gasoline engines with an injector at each cylinder, you can remove a cap from the fuel tubing loop on the engine and expose a tire-type valve (see fig. 3-90). With the engine cranking, just depress the valve tip (keep a rag handy to catch spillage), and if fuel squirts out you know there's fuel coming up to the system. On imports that use a similar system, there is no tire-type valve, so for the same check you must disconnect a flexible fuel hose.

Many electronic systems, particularly some throttle body designs, have no tire-type valve or flexible hose, and you must disconnect a fuel line fitting. Before you disconnect any fuel line—flexible or not—to check pump pressure, you must relieve fuel pump pressure. The safest way to do this is to get under the car at the rear and disconnect the wiring from the gas tank (the wiring will include that for the pump). Then check the effect by cranking the engine. If it starts and quickly stalls, the pressure is relieved.

Caution: Many fuse boxes have a fuse labeled for the fuel pump, and under the hood of some GM cars is an in-

Figure 3-90. Remove cap as shown to expose tire-type valve on fuel tubing of injector-per-cylinder electronic fuel injection system. If valve needle is depressed with engine cranking (or in many cases, merely with ignition on), fuel under pressure should squirt out.

line fuse for the pump circuit. However, removing this will not do, as there is a separate circuit through the oil pressure sending unit on most systems, and when the engine is cranked, the sending unit may close and complete the fuel pump circuit, allowing pressure to build up.

When the fuel line is disconnected, you can't just turn on the ignition or you'll get a highly pressurized stream of gasoline. You should aim the end of the line into an empty container, have a helper quickly turn on the ignition, and see if there's a stream. However, a more meaningful check on any system is with a pressure gauge. Some systems operate at about 40 p.s.i., so a gauge that reads to at least 100 p.s.i. should be used. Others operate at about 9 to 10 p.s.i., so you should use a gauge that reads to at least 15 p.s.i. for those.

There are many gauges available for checking fuel pressure, but clearly you must have a setup that includes adapters that connect to your car. If there's a tire-type valve, you want one that threads onto that. If it doesn't, you need an alternative setup. OTC Tools sells pressure gauges with a large assortment of adapters that have worked on every car I've tried them on.

Turn off the ignition and the gauge pressure reading should hold within a few p.s.i. (10 to 15 percent) of the original reading. If the pressure reading gradually drops further, there is internal leakage, probably at the components in the gas tank—a job for a professional.

Throttle Body System. If pressure is normal with the gauge on the end of the line (system with no tire-type valve), recheck with the gauge also connected to the throttle body. Use fittings; or use fittings, hoses, and clamps to form a "T" setup, so the gauge remains in place while fuel flows through to the injector and pressure regulator. If pressure now drops, the regulator is defective or the injector is leaking (check injector as described later).

If the pressure regulator fuel return line is a hose, you can confirm a defect by pinching the hose with pliers—if the pressure reading rises, the regulator problem is confirmed. If there is a metal return line, you can disconnect and plug it with a screw, and if the pressure rises, this also confirms a regulator problem.

Replacement of a throttle body injector (described later) or pressure regulator are jobs an experienced weekend mechanic can perform.

If there is no fuel up to the tubing, look for a kinked fuel line between the engine and the gas tank, and check the in-tank electric pump. General procedures for this service are covered in the previous section of this chapter on fuel pumps. Also note that on some models the fuel filter is located between an electric fuel pump near (not in) the tank and the tank itself. In this case, check for a plugged fuel filter, and in very cold weather, for one in which moisture has frozen.

If there is fuel to the engine and the pressure is low, yet there is no kinked line or throttle body pressure regulator fault, that indicates a plugged filter or a problem with the in-tank fuel pump assembly. You can bypass a suspect filter by removing it, substituting a piece of hose clamped in place, and retesting. However, a problem with an in-tank pump is a job that should be left to a professional. If the pump is external, disconnect the inlet line from the tank and test the pump by attaching a separate line submerged in a container of gasoline. If the pressure remains low, change the pump.

To check the fuel injectors on an electronic system, follow the procedure outlined in the following sections.

Throttle Body System. Disconnect all spark plug wires and rest them against a metal part of the engine so the engine won't start (do this even if you are checking a no-start problem). Remove the air cleaner cover and look at the injector(s). Have a helper crank the engine, and if no fuel squirts out of the injector(s), the problem could be

Figure 3-91. Wiring connector easily unplugs from fuel injector for testing.

Figure 3-92. Replacement of this injector (after fuel pressure is relieved) begins with removal of the pressure regulator screws. The ones here are Torx screws.

Figure 3-93. The pressure regulator is lifted out.

either in the injector(s) or in the harness wiring. Unplug the wiring connector (see fig. 3-91) from the injector(s) and connect a test light across the terminals of the connector. Have your helper crank the engine again and the light should flash, perhaps dimly. If it does, the injector apparently is faulty. Refer to figures 3-92 to 3-94 for a typical throttle body injector replacement procedure.

Note: An inexpensive special test light for fuel injectors, called a noid light, plugs into the wiring connector and is easy to use. It is available from auto parts stores.

Figure 3-94. Injector then is pried up and out. New one is pushed into place and remainder of job is reversal of removal procedure.

Injector at Every Cylinder. Using a stethoscope, listen to each injector with the engine running (see fig. 3-95). The injectors sound like sewing machines when working normally, and all should sound about the same. If one injector makes no sound or an unusual sound, and the engine has been performing poorly (including rough operation), that apparently is the bad one. As with the throttle body system, check the injector's wiring connector with a test light. To change a defective injector, relieve system pressure, unplug the injector(s) wiring, disconnect the "rail" (tubing that holds the injectors), pull out the defective one, and insert the replacement. You must be very careful to align the injectors and seat them properly (they have a rubber O-ring seal that must do its job). If an injector is cocked, fuel may leak at one end and air may get in at the other (if air leaks into the manifold, the engine will race when you start it).

Note: If you cannot reach the injectors for testing with a stethoscope—a common problem on some cars—the only way to check them is with the engine off (so you can remove the intake manifold for access), using an electronic pressure drop tester (see fig. 3-96). This tester, which connects to the injector wiring terminals, permits you to pulse the injector and, with the pressure gauge

connected to the tire-type valve, watch the fuel pressure drop in the system. If the pressure drop is very uneven, or if one injector fails to show a drop, you have isolated a defective one. The tester is not overly expensive, so an experienced weekend mechanic may consider it. Some engine control computers have a provision for checking for a malfunctioning injector, and at this time the one on some Ford engines can check for a weak one.

Throttle Body Fuel Injection. If the throttle body has two injectors and neither sprays fuel (take off the air cleaner cover and look, but disconnect the ignition so the engine won't start), there apparently is a wiring or computer problem, as it is unlikely that both injectors would fail at about the same time. If one injector sprays and the other doesn't, switch the wiring connectors and see if the same injector fails to spray. If it does, replace the injector.

You easily can check for leaking injectors on a throttle body system as a cause of hard restarting when the engine is hot. Just stuff a rag under the injector tip, unplug the wiring connector, and crank the engine. Or let the engine sit in the hot sun for 10 to 15 minutes. Remove the rag, and if it's wet with fuel the injector is defective and should be replaced.

Figure 3-95. Stethoscope can be used to determine if fuel injectors are triggering.

Figure 3-96. If injectors cannot be reached for stethescope testing with engine running, a pressure drop test is another possibility. Fuel pressure gauge is attached to a tire-type valve on fuel line, and the electronic tester shown is connected directly to the injector (its wiring connector removed). With ignition on to pressurize system, tester pulses the injector and pressure drop is noted on the gauge. All injectors should provide equal drop if they are good.

On the hydraulic fuel injection (called K-Jetronic) you can check both for fuel going into the fuel distributor (disconnect the line at the distributor as in fig. 3-97) and either connect a gauge or see if fuel spurts out. To test for fuel at the injectors, proceed as follows:

1. Pull an injector out of its bore and aim it into a jar.
2. Gain access to the airflow sensor by removing the duct (see fig. 3-98).
3. Disconnect any wiring at the airflow sensor housing (see fig. 3-99) and the back of the alternator. Locate the fusebox under the dashboard. On pre-1981 models, you will see a line of metal boxes (switching devices called relays) above the fuses. One has a fuse attached to its exterior; this is the fuel pump relay. Unplug it. With a jumper wire, bridge terminals L-13 and L-14 (they are at 12 and 6 o'clock and numbered) in the underdash panel. Starting in 1981, the cars have the small spade-type fuses and the relays are installed in the fuse box. The relay terminals in the fuse box, however, are not numbered, but the ones you must bridge with a jumper wire again are those at 12 and 6 o'clock (see fig. 3-100). On late models, including the Fox, wiring may differ. Refer to a wiring manual.

4. With pliers, grasp the center of the airflow sensor and move it. You should see fuel spray from the injector into the jaw (see fig. 3-101).

Note: Stop quickly, or the other cylinders may be filled with fuel and hydraulically lock up. If fuel is going into the fuel distributor but not going to the injectors, check injector tubing for kinks, and if it's not kinked, the problem is in the fuel distributor, which is replaced on an exchange basis.

With injector-type throttle body fuel injection, begin by looking for a fuel spray from the injectors as the engine is cranked (air cleaner cover must be off, and in some cases the entire air cleaner housing should be removed for easier viewing). On the Chrysler Imperial system, have a helper turn on the ignition as you look for a single squirt from the spray bars.

If you don't see the spray as the engine is cranked, or you don't see the single squirt from the Chrysler spray bars, locate a Schrader (tire-type) valve in the fuel line near the throttle body on GM and Chrysler cars, or on the throttle body of Ford products (see fig. 3-89). Press the Schrader valve pin while the engine is being cranked, and you should get a strong squirt of fuel (keep a rag handy to

Figure 3-97. Pressure gauge can be used to check hydraulic fuel injection system. You can connect a standard gauge into fuel distributor inlet line (from pump, accumulator, and filter) and so check pressure into fuel distributor, then connect the gauge between fuel distributor and line to control pressure regulator, warm up the engine, and see if control pressure drops to specifications. Or you can use the special gauge with shutoff valve, as shown, connected between the fuel distributor and the line to the control pressure regulator, and with this one connection make both tests.

Figure 3-98. To check the injectors, begin by removing the air duct over the intake air flap as shown.

Figure 3-99. Disconnect the wiring connector on the air distributor next to the air flap as shown. Also disconnect wiring from the alternator.

FUEL PUMP RELAY TERMINALS

Figure 3-100. As of 1981, the fuel pump relay is plugged into the new fusebox, shown in this photo. When bypassing, remove it and connect across the terminals at 12 and 6 o'clock with a jumper wire. VW recommends use of a jumper wire with an 8-amp fuse, which can be made from an in-line fuse holder—sold at auto parts stores—and a pair of alligator clips.

Figure 3-101. Pull an injector out of its bore, aim it into a beaker as shown, and with fuel pump relay bypasses as explained in this chapter, pull on the intake air flap with needlenose pliers as shown (or with a magnet). Fuel should spray from injector into beaker. Pull on flap only long enough to confirm fuel spray, for other injectors also are spraying, and if you do this too long the cylinder could fill with fuel. That could result in engine damage if you try to crank the engine under such conditions.

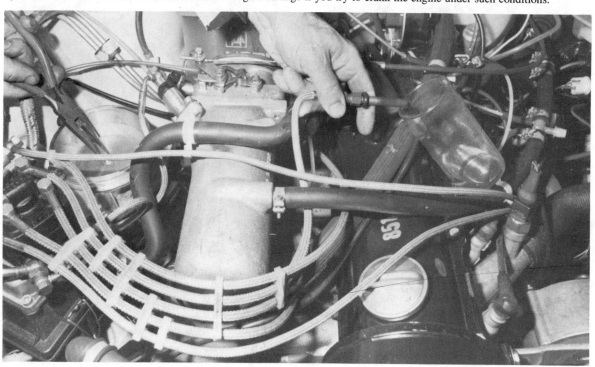

catch the fuel). If you get a strong squirt of fuel from the Schrader valve, check the fuel filter (remove and install a piece of fuel line hose in its place, then repeat the Schrader valve test). If the filter passes, the problem is in the throttle body, a job for a professional. If there still is no fuel to the Schrader valve, check for a kinked fuel hose or dented fuel line. Also inspect for loose or corroded electrical connections at the fuel pump that project from the intank pump.

On 1982 GM cars with throttle body injection, there's no Schrader. If fuel doesn't spray from the injector (with the engine cranking), disconnect the fuel line to check pump action.

Fuel Filter

Change the fuel filter at the intervals specified by the car manufacturer. On cars in which the filter is located in an inconvenient place, use fuel-line antifreeze regularly in cold weather to minimize the possibility of a moisture freezeup that might be physically difficult to correct.

Air Intake

Even more so than on carburetor systems, air leaks can cause performance and starting problems. Check tightness of the nuts or bolts holding the intake air distributor to the engine as part of a tuneup.

A clean air filter, as with a carburetor system, also is important. Refer to "Carburetor Service," earlier in this chapter, for details.

TURBOCHARGERS

The turbocharger, or turbine-drive supercharger, is a common method used to provide power on demand for a small engine. With it, the small engine develops normal fuel economy in easy driving. When you mash the gas

Figure 3-102. Here's how the exhaust turbocharger works. Exhaust gas flows from cylinders into the turbine chamber, spinning the turbine, and then flows out to the exhaust pipe. The turbine is on the same shaft as a compressor wheel, in a chamber between the carburetor and intake manifold. As the compressor spins it pulls an extra amount of air-fuel mixture and forces it into the cylinders, so they produce more power.

pedal, the turbocharger cuts in and gives you the extra power you want.

The turbocharger provides the extra power because it is a form of compressor. Its paddlewheel-like design draws in extra air-fuel mixture from the carburetor and forces it into the intake manifold and through that into the cylinders. More air-fuel mixture in the cylinders means more to burn, and so more performance.

The power to drive the turbocharger is provided by a turbine-like fan on the same shaft, but separated from the intake air-fuel system (see fig. 3-102). This turbine fan is in a chamber that is part of the exhaust system. The harder you step on the gas pedal, the faster the engine runs, so the greater is the exhaust gas flow. Exhaust gases flowing through the turbine chamber spin the turbine before flowing into the exhaust piping. The exhaust gases were heading that way anyway, so the power to operate the turbocharger is essentially free.

There is a limit to how much air-fuel mixture the cylinders can accept before engine loads increase beyond the safe limit. When the engine starts to knock, severe damage can result.

To keep the power boost within safe limits, two controls are used: a waste gate and a spark timing retard system.

Waste Gate on the Turbocharger. See figure 3-103. When the pressure in the intake manifold reaches a certain level, it operates a diaphragm connected by a rod to a part called the waste gate, which is a type of valve. The diaphragm rod pulls the waste gate open and exhaust gases bypass the turbine chamber and go straight to the exhaust piping. In 1981 General Motors used a special type of waste gate control diaphragm, using vacuum in the plenum (a chamber between the carburetor and the compressor wheel of the turbocharger, as shown in fig. 3-102). The vacuum holds the diaphragm and therefore keeps the waste gate open during idle and part throttle, to reduce exhaust back pressure and thereby improve performance and fuel economy. At medium throttle, plenum vacuum drops and the diaphragm springs force the waste gate closed, allowing turbocharger power boost to build. At full throttle, the exhaust back pressure builds up and forces the waste gate open to prevent excessive power boost. On most late-model cars with a turbo, the engine

Figure 3-103. The waste gate is a valve that opens automatically to prevent the exhaust-driven turbine from turning so fast that it causes excessive power boost from the compressor. In this design, when the pressure of air-fuel mixture in the intake manifold exceeds specifications, the pressure (transmitted by a hose) pushes on a diaphragm unit that operates a rod that opens the waste gate, allowing the exhaust gases to bypass the turbine.

Figure 3-104. The knock sensor, an electromechanical accelerometer, is threaded into intake manifold as shown.

computer controls the waste gate. The computer operates a solenoid valve to regulate air pressure to the waste gate. The computer receives data on engine r.p.m., barometric and manifold pressure, and spark advance and can make instantaneous adjustments if necessary for best performance and safe operation for the engine.

The waste gate opens only enough to keep the intake manifold pressures within specifications; the engine still might knock if ambient temperatures and humidity levels are unfavorable. To prevent knock under certain conditions when the turbo is in action, the spark advance on many engines is set back (retarded) by an electronic control unit or the engine control computer. It is signaled by a knock sensor threaded into the intake manifold or mounted on the side of the engine (see fig. 3-104). When the engine just starts to knock, this electronic sensor "reads" a change in engine vibration and signals the electronic control unit. Depending on the strength of the knock signal, the control unit retards the spark a certain number of degrees, up to a maximum of 12.

Turbocharger Service

On many late models, the computer can monitor turbo boost pressure and provide a trouble code if there is a gross malfunction. However, a manual test of the turbo can be useful in spotting moderate problems.

To check out the turbocharger, first go to the waste gate diaphragm and apply calibrated air pressure (see fig. 3-105). When you apply 7 to 10 p.s.i., the diaphragm rod should move. If it doesn't, have the system checked immediately, for the engine might be severely damaged in high-speed use.

If you have the plenum-vacuum-controlled waste gate diaphragm used only on 1981 General Motors cars (you can tell by the fact that there's just one hose on the diaphragm and it goes to the plenum), do not make this test. Instead, apply 20 inches of vacuum with a manual vacuum pump (engine off), and you should see the diaphragm link move.

To test the knock sensor system (a method that will work even on many nonturbo cars that have knock sensors), connect a tachometer or a timing light (aim the light at the marks). Run the engine at 2,000 r.p.m. and have a helper repeatedly rap the intake manifold next to the knock sensor with a rod as shown in figure 3-106. You should see engine speed drop 300 to 500 r.p.m. or spark timing retard. (Perhaps 20 seconds after you stop rapping, the timing and r.p.m. will return to normal.) If you don't get the timing retard or engine r.p.m. drop, then shut off

Figure 3-105. To check manifold-pressure-controlled waste gate operation, disconnect diaphragm unit hose from intake manifold and connect to a hose tee (available from auto parts stores). To the other two necks of the tee, connect a vacuum-pressure gauge and a bicycle pump. Apply specified pressure with bicycle pump and you should see diaphragm rod move. If you can't apply sufficient pressure with the single stroke of the pump, install a tire valve in the hose between the tee and the pump, which will permit you to pump as necessary to build up pressure.

Figure 3-106. To check ignition for a reduction in ignition timing advance, connect tachometer or timing light, run engine at fast idle (2,000 r.p.m.), and repeatedly whack the intake manifold next to the knock sensor with a socket extension rod or similar bar. You should see engine speed drop 300 to 500 r.p.m., or the ignition timing retard.

the engine, disconnect the wire from the knock sensor, and hook up an ohmmeter (with one lead to the sensor terminal and the other lead to the electrical ground). Compare the reading with specifications. If it is outside these limits, you should replace the knock sensor. If the reading is acceptable, have a professional check out the system.

Note: The design of some knock sensors is such that they cannot be triggered by the tapping method. This is part of an attempt to make them resistant to false-triggering, which can affect engine performance. VW sensors are an example of this kind of knock sensor design.

Oil and Filter Change Interval

The turbocharger turbine wheel spins very fast, and so it must be lubricated well to survive. Oil, supplied by a line from the engine, handles the lubrication problem, but some exhaust heat contamination of engine oil results. The useful life of the engine oil in a turbocharged engine is shorter than in a conventional, or "normally aspirated," engine. The factory-recommended oil-and-filter-change interval is much more frequent with turbocharging, and you should observe that interval carefully. A 2,000- to 2,500-mile oil-and-filter-change interval is a good practice, even on water-cooled turbos, which are in wide use today.

4 AIR POLLUTION CONTROLS

The modern automobile is equipped with a wide variety of systems designed to reduce air pollution. Many are built into the engine, but others are external and (except for the catalytic converter) should be checked and serviced as part of tuneup. Although it is widely believed that all pollution controls reduce performance, many of the external ones either have no effect, or their malfunction can hurt performance. In any case, they are the law, and good citizenship calls for keeping them functional.

Although some checks and services are explained in this chapter, you should know that emission control systems (except Positive Crankcase Ventilation) are warranted for 5 years or 50,000 miles, whichever comes first. Therefore, if a system seems to be malfunctioning and is still under warranty, take the car to the dealer for free service.

The key parts of the emission control system are the catalytic converter and the feedback fuel control system. Pre-1981 cars had only a single catalytic converter, which is a housing with a catalyst, a device that promotes a reaction in the exhaust gas to reduce formation of two air pollutants (unburned gasoline droplets called "hydrocarbons," and carbon monoxide). The third major pollutant, oxides of nitrogen, was controlled almost entirely for many years by Exhaust Gas Recirculation, a system by which metered amounts of burned gases were fed back into the cylinders to reduce peak temperatures at which the oxides formed.

Emission regulations were stiffened, and to meet them a second catalyst was introduced—the "three-way," which controls all three emissions. However, for it to work properly the engine must burn a precise air-fuel mixture, and for this to happen, electronics must continuously adjust the mixture, a system called "feedback carburetion" or "feedback fuel injection." The oxygen sensor in the exhaust, covered in previous chapters, is used to sense oxygen content, usually a good indicator of the air-fuel mixture burned.

Although some cars use only one catalyst, a three-way, many have two—first a three-way, then a catalyst that reduces only hydrocarbons and carbon monoxide (called an "oxidation catalyst"). A few cars have a small oxidation catalyst ahead of the main one, to activate earlier (so the car can pass emission regulations). Some cars have dual exhausts, and a second oxidation catalyst for the second set of pipes.

Catalytic converter(s) require no maintenance, but if the engine is misfueled (leaded gasoline used instead of unleaded), they become plugged, and poor performance results. The converters also are subject to damage if their part of the exhaust system is deeply dented. Once the converters are out of warranty, if you find they are malfunctioning (if the car fails an emissions test because of them), you can install lower-cost replacements, available from auto parts stores.

In addition to reducing emissions, other emission controls help engine operation, if given maintenance and service. They are:

Positive Crankcase Ventilation. If this malfunctions, it can cause oil leaks all over the engine, and rough idle.

Thermostatic air cleaner. If this is defective, it can cause hesitation, stalling, and loss of power.

Exhaust gas recirculation. When this misbehaves, the engine may stall, hesitate, run rough, and suffer from knock and ping.

Fuel vapor control. Malfunctions can affect hot engine starting and cause fuel odor.

Air pump. If defective, it may cause backfire in the exhaust.

These are the areas that a weekend mechanic can check and service for air pollution controls.

172

Positive Crankcase Ventilation

The crankcase of your engine, where the crankshaft churns through a bath of oil, is contaminated by fumes from unburned gasoline that slip past the sealing rings on the pistons. These fumes can build up pressures that could ruin oil seals, so they must be purged. On older cars they were allowed to escape into the atmosphere, but on all cars made since the early 1960s they are recirculated back into the cylinders for burning with a system (see fig. 4-1) called Positive Crankcase Ventilation (PCV). If this system plugs, not only can oil seals be damaged, but the engine may idle poorly and stall.

The key to the system is a flow control valve—called the PCV valve—that sits in a rubber grommet in the cylinder head cover on most cars (see fig. 4-2). On others it is spliced into a hose or threaded into a hole that goes through the intake manifold into the engine.

The PCV valve is attached by a hose to the base of the carburetor, where engine vacuum draws up fumes from the crankcase to the top of the engine, through the valve, and into the intake manifold. Here fumes combine with the fuel mixture already there and flow into the cylinders for burning.

The PCV valve regulates the flow. When the engine is idling and can accommodate very little additional fuel, the valve is nearly closed. As the engine speed increases, engine vacuum drops and a spring inside the valve pushes a plunger, allowing the increased flow that the engine can now tolerate.

The drawing out of crankcase fumes creates a light vacuum in the crankcase. This is filled by fresh air. The air may go into the rocker cover through an oil fill cap with a filter built in, or come from the carburetor air cleaner. In the latter case, the air cleaner housing has a small additional filter, for crankcase air, built in.

A few cars do not have a PCV valve. Rather, they have a hose neck with a calibrated orifice through which vapors flow.

Figure 4-1. Schematic of positive crankcase ventilation system. PCV valve draws crankcase fumes up into engine top chamber, through valve into carburetor. Fresh air enters through air filter, then flows into crankcase to help purge fumes.

Figure 4-2. The PCV valve sits in a rubber grommet in the engine top cover. It has been pulled out so you can see what it looks like.

Checking the System

Unlike other pollution control systems, maintenance of the PCV (if required at over 5 years or 50,000 miles) is the owner's responsibility, so here's how.

To check the operation of the PCV system, first disconnect the PCV valve from the engine top cover or from the hose that connects it to the cover or other part of the engine. Then shake the valve, and you should hear a jiggling noise, indicating that the valve parts inside are not stuck.

Run the engine at idle and feel the end of the valve with your finger (see fig. 4-3). If you feel a vacuum, the valve and the hose that connect it to the carburetor base are functional. As you put your finger over the end of the valve, you should feel and hear the internal parts of the valve move. If the valve fails the jiggle or movement test just described, it should be replaced. If you don't feel vacuum on the second test, check the hose to which the valve is connected for kinks or plugging, and if it is okay, replace the valve. In any case, change the valve at least every 2 years or 24,000 miles, but never exceed the car maker's recommendations.

Finally, check the fresh air filter. If it is the type built into the oil fill cap, clean it in solvent. It may be so dirty, however, that a solvent soaking won't help, in which case it should be replaced. If the filter is built into the air cleaner housing, inspect it, and if it's dirty remove the retainer clip and change it (see fig. 4-4).

Figure 4-3. Feeling end of PCV valve for vacuum.

Figure 4-4. Removing fresh air filter from air cleaner housing. When the clip is removed as shown, the entire filter assembly can be removed. Or you may be able to simply remove filter from the assembly and install a replacement.

VACUUM DIAPHRAGM

SENSOR

AIR CONTROL VALVE

AIR HEATED BY MANIFOLD

COLD AIR ENTERS

HEATED AIR ENTERS CARBURETOR

Figure 4-5. Schematic of thermostatic air cleaner. The vacuum diaphragm operates flap in air cleaner. The diaphragm is connected by hose to the temperature sensor, which is connected by another hose to vacuum source at the base of the carburetor or on intake manifold. When the engine is cold, the sensor passes vacuum from carburetor or manifold to diaphragm to operate flap. When engine is warm, sensor bleeds off vacuum to atmosphere, and spring in diaphragm assembly pivots flap to close off hot air duct.

THERMOSTATIC AIR CLEANER

The thermostatic air cleaner is a temperature-controlled flap device that provides preheated air for the carburetor during engine warmup. If the valve does not provide the warm air, the cold engine will stumble and stall. If it fails to shut off when the engine is warm, the air to the carburetor will be overheated, and warm engine performance will be affected. Refer to figure 4-5.

How It Works

The air cleaner housing has an inlet neck—called the snorkel—with a duct that connects to the exterior of the exhaust manifold. This is the source of warm air. When the engine is warm, the duct is covered, and cool air comes in through the opening in the front of the snorkel.

The control device is a simple flap valve. When the engine is cold, it covers the front of the snorkel, blocking the cold air and allowing the engine to draw in warm air from the exhaust manifold duct. As the engine warms up, the flap pivots and starts to block off the air duct and permit airflow through the front of the snorkel. Finally, when the engine is fully warm, the flap closes off the warm air duct completely, and only cool air can enter, through the front of the snorkel.

Operating the flap on the most common—vacuum-controlled—system is a spring-loaded diaphragm device connected through a temperature sensor (inside the air cleaner) to a source of engine vacuum at the carburetor base.

The temperature sensor (see fig. 4-6) is a "bleeding" device. When the engine is cold, it passes all the vacuum

from the engine through to the diaphragm device on the snorkel. As the engine warms up, the sensor starts to open and allows some of the vacuum to bleed off into the atmosphere. Less vacuum stays at the diaphragm device and so it exerts less pull on the flap. A spring on the diaphragm moves a link connected to the flap to the warm air duct. Finally, when the engine is warm, all vacuum supplied to the diaphragm is bled off and the flap closes the warm air duct completely.

Figure 4-6. With air cleaner cover off and filter element out, you can see the thermostatic sensor.

SENSOR

Note: Some cars have different systems. Typically, they have thermostats that directly move the flap. Some GM cars (such as older Chevettes with one-barrel carburetors) have a thermostatic coil spring, much like that in an automatic choke, that coils up tight when it's cold and pivots the flap to block off the intake air snorkel. As the engine warms up, the heat causes the coil to unwind and pivots the flap to open the intake air snorkel. Many older Ford products have a thermostat with a link that connects to the flap, which does basically the same thing.

Testing the System

To check out the system, start the engine when cold and probe the snorkel with your finger if the snorkel is a short one and with a screwdriver if your finger can't reach. The opening should be blocked by the flap. Recheck when the engine is warm and the snorkel should be open. On some cars (see fig. 4-7) you may have to disconnect a cold air duct for access to the flap.

If the flap is stuck in the heat-off position with the engine cold, disconnect the vacuum hose from the diaphragm device and feel for vacuum. If there is vacuum, the diaphragm is defective and must be replaced. If there is no vacuum, check the hose connections at the carburetor base and the underside of the air cleaner (see fig. 4-8)

and if they are good, and the hoses are not kinked, check the sensor by placing a finger over the vacuum bleed neck (see fig. 4-9). If the system now works, the sensor is defective.

If the flap is stuck in the heat-on position with the engine warm, disconnect the vacuum hose from the diaphragm device and check to see if the flap now closes. If it does, replace the temperature sensor, which is apparently not allowing the vacuum to bleed off.

Note: Some new cars have a second, solenoid-operated flap in the snorkel which closes when the engine is off to keep vapors from getting into the atmosphere. Do not confuse this with the thermostatic air cleaner. This second flap should be partly opened by the solenoid when the ignition is turned on (otherwise the engine will not breathe).

Replacement of parts in the vacuum-operated system is an obvious procedure.

If your car has one of the self-contained thermostatic controls also used, you may have to replace the entire snorkel assembly. If a Ford thermostat is available as a detail part, thread it into its mounting bracket to the same depth as the old thermostat. Check operation of the flap after installation and readjust the thermostat on its bracket if necessary (see fig. 4-10).

Figure 4-7. With part of air cleaner snorkel disconnected from cold air duct, you can see this flap clearly.

Figure 4-8. Checking hose connections to sensor on the underside of the air cleaner.

Figure 4-9. Placing finger over vacuum bleed neck. If system now works, sensor is defective. Some systems may not have this type of bleed, but in any case there will be some type of opening through which vacuum can bleed off.

Figure 4-10. Many Fords have used this type of thermostatic air cleaner, in which all movement of the hot air flap is by the thermostat. There is a vacuum diaphragm attachment unit in the bottom but its function is to pull down the flap, opening the cold air snorkel for acceleration. If the thermostat is defective, note the depth it is threaded into the bracket and install a replacement to the same depth. You may find, however, that only a replacement snorkel with the thermostat already installed is available, in which case the precision adjustment isn't necessary.

EXHAUST GAS RECIRCULATION

The exhaust gas recirculation (EGR) system allows a calibrated amount of exhaust gas to enter the intake manifold, where it combines with the air-fuel mixture from the carburetor. The exhaust gas is a contaminant, and it lowers the temperature of the fuel mixture when it burns in the cylinders. This doesn't help gas mileage, but the lower temperatures do reduce the air pollutant called "oxides of nitrogen" (see fig. 4-11).

The heart of the system is the exhaust gas recirculation

valve, a diaphragm unit controlled by engine vacuum or (on 1978 to 1980 Ford 302 V-8s with Electronic Engine Control I) air pressure supplied by the air pump, another pollution control system. The valve is a flow control device that regulates the amount of exhaust gas that can get into the engine. Most cars with EGR have additional controls to modulate and limit the operation of the valve, but these are so complex that their service is best left to a professional.

You should check the EGR to make sure it is functioning, for these reasons: A malfunctioning system contributes to air pollution; on some cars, the vacuum systems

Figure 4-11. Schematic of exhaust gas recirculation system. When carburetor vacuum is applied to the diaphragm inside the valve, it pulls up on the valve, allowing exhaust gas to flow into intake manifold. On many cars, there is more than the simple hose shown between carburetor signal port (the vacuum source) and the EGR valve. Special sensors and time-temperature delay hardware may be used to tailor exhaust flow more precisely.

are so carefully balanced that loss of EGR under some circumstances could affect engine performance; and if the valve operates when it shouldn't (such as when engine is cold and in low ambient temperature) the engine will perform poorly. Too little exhaust gas recirculation can cause the engine to knock. Too much at idle can cause rough idle.

On many engines with computer control, the EGR system is controlled by the computer. If you do not get the EGR motion that is described next, the problem may be in one of the solenoid-controlled valves that regulates the EGR. The computer-controlled system should be left to the car dealer. It is like other emission controls, covered by a 5-year, 50,000-mile warranty.

Checking EGR

First, start the engine from cold, on a cold day, and immediately look at the EGR valve, which is at or near the base of the carburetor. Have a helper hit the gas pedal. The EGR valve stem (see fig. 4-12) should not move. If it does, and you've had cold stalling and other cold performance problems, this could be the reason. Have a mechanic check out the system, for most cars incorporate a cold start delay in the EGR system.

Repeat the test with the engine warm—after the engine has idled for at least a minute. This time the stem should

move. You must wait a full minute, for many cars have warm-restart delays also built into the system.

If you can't see the valve stem on your car, disconnect the hose at the valve. Repeat the test conditions, but this time have your helper hold the gas pedal at part throttle (about one-third down) as you hold your finger over the hose end. You should feel vacuum (or on some cars air pressure). Reconnect the hose, and the engine should slow down just a bit. If you're not sure, connect a tachometer to the engine (see chapter 2). EGR valves need exhaust backpressure to operate, often more than is produced with the test outlined. To build up some backpressure, restrict the exhaust pipe. One way is to partly drive in a suitably sized socket wrench. Another is to take a food can of suitable diameter, cut off both ends, fit it partly over the end of the exhaust pipe, and clamp it in place. Then, with pliers mash the open end of the food can, and that will provide a restriction to build up backpressure. Or you can tee a vacuum gauge into the EGR vacuum hose, using a very long auxiliary hose to the gauge, so the gauge can be routed from the engine compartment to the driver's seat. Road-test the car, and at part to medium throttle you should see a vacuum reading on the gauge as you drive. This tells you that vacuum is getting to the valve, not necessarily that the valve is working. To determine if the valve is working when it is inaccessible or does not have an exposed stem, you can remove it and test it off the car

Figure 4-12. The EGR valve stem, to which the screwdriver points, can be visually inspected for movement to check valve operation.

Figure 4-13. This inexpensive EGR tester can check the valve off the car. It requires compressed air to operate.

Figure 4-14. Use a soft hammer to knock deposits off EGR valve system.

with a special EGR valve tester, an inexpensive tool (made by Tomco, Inc., a maker of carburetor repair fittings). Ask an auto parts store to order it for you if it's not in stock (see fig. 4-13).

If the EGR valve does not appear to be functioning, unbolt it from the engine and inspect it. If you see an accumulation of carbon deposits on the inside, wire-brush off the deposits or knock them off with a soft hammer (see fig. 4-14), then check by trying to move the stem with a screwdriver. If the valve seems free, reinstall and check it. If it still doesn't work, the diaphragm is apparently defective and the valve must be replaced.

It is possible to see nothing at the EGR valve, yet it still may leak and allow exhaust gases to get into the intake manifold. This is a common cause of rough idle and hesitation on acceleration from a stop. The simplest way to check for a leaking valve is to block it with a metal plate. Unbolt the valve and cut a plate from aluminum roof flashing (see fig. 4-15). Or buy a plate from an auto parts store. Install it in place of the gasket (see fig. 4-16) and test the car. If the rough idle and hesitation go away, replace the EGR valve. Do not try to leave the plate in place, as it will soon burn through.

Note: Dealers can bench-test the EGR valve, and if a dealer is willing and finds the valve is bad, a new one can be installed free under the 5-year, 50,000-mile emission control warranty.

Figure 4-15. A blocking plate for an EGR valve can be cut from aluminum roof flashing as shown and installed in place of the valve gasket.

Figure 4-16. Blocking plate is installed in place of gasket. EGR valve goes back on and when nuts or bolts are installed, the test installation is complete.

FUEL VAPOR CONTROL

The fuel vapor control system (see fig. 4-17) is designed to prevent gasoline vapors in the gas tank and carburetor from evaporating into the atmosphere. The typical system relies on two components:

1. *A charcoal canister.* Charcoal holds the vapors that otherwise could escape, and when the engine starts, they're discharged into the carburetor.

2. *A special gasoline cap.* The gas cap on cars with vapor control is designed to prevent vapors from escaping. If you replace the cap, install only this type, called "pressure-vacuum." A cap with a plain vent will allow vapor to escape. If you install a cap without a vent (made for older cars without this system and with a separate vent), the engine will not draw fuel from the tank and will quickly stop. In some cases, the cap without a vent could result in a vacuum in the tank that might cause the tank to collapse.

Figure 4-17. This schematic shows the fuel vapor control system and the hoses and lines which, in the layout shown, connect in some cases to the ignition distributor vacuum control unit and the Positive Crankcase Ventilation (PCV) system.

181

Checking the System

To check this system, just look for the charcoal canister under the hood by following hoses from the air cleaner or top of the carburetor until you come to it (see fig. 4-18). On some cars the canister is in a fender well with a plastic cover, so if the hose seems to disappear into the sheet metal at a fender well, that's where the canister is located.

Check only the canister under the hood for a foam or fiber filter pad in the end opposite to that of the hoses, and if you find it, replace it once a year or every 12,000 miles (see fig. 4-19). On many cars you can feel for the filter, pull it out with your fingers, and push in a replacement. That filter cleans the fresh air that purges the fumes from the charcoal when the engine is started.

Whatever the system (and many cars do not have a replaceable filter in the canister), check for good hose connections at the canister and the carburetor or air cleaner. If any of the hoses are oil-soaked or cracked, replace them. Only use a hose made for the canister system.

If there is a strong gasoline odor under the hood, disconnect the charcoal canister hoses from the carburetor and check for liquid fuel in them. Reposition them to remove kinks and raise any low spots. If this does not eliminate the odor and the car is covered by the 5-year, 50,000-mile emission control warranty, you may be able to get free service on the system.

Note: The mere existence of fuel in a line does not prove there is a problem, as in a few systems this happens normally. It is a possible concern when there is a gasoline odor.

Maintenance services and the gas cap in the fuel vapor system may not be covered under warranty.

Figure 4-18. This photo shows a typical location for the charcoal canister under the hood. On some cars, however, the canister is hidden behind a fender skirt or built into the air cleaner housing.

Figure 4-19. Removing the fiber filter from bottom of charcoal canister is easily accomplished with the canister removed from the car and inverted.

Air Pump

The air pump has been used on American cars as a pollution control system since 1967. For several years (pre-1981), it was dropped on many cars in favor of the simpler Pulsair, a valve device. It made a comeback in 1981 as most American car makers went to special catalytic converters and needed the higher air output of the pump to meet more stringent emission controls. In these new cars, it may be combined with solenoids wired to the engine control computer, so the air pump output is effectively regulated by the computer. Such systems should be left to the car dealer for service.

The object of the air pump is to supply pressurized air to the exhaust system, where it connects to the engine. This air contains extra oxygen to burn off any gasoline that was not consumed in the cylinders, before it can get into the atmosphere.

On most cars that are equipped with the system, the pump's pressurized air flows through external tubing (called an injection manifold) to the exhaust manifold, where it connects to the cylinders (see fig. 4-20). On a few General Motors engines, there is a single connection to the cylinder head, which has internal passages for the air.

On many older cars with the catalytic converter, the air is injected into a single point in the exhaust system, just before the converter. In this case, the extra air does its job only in the converter.

If a car has a three-way catalyst followed by a two-way (called an oxidation converter), the air pump injects into a point between the two (which typically are combined in a single housing). This way the extra air goes only into the oxidation converter, which can use the extra air to improve efficiency.

The pump system also includes a device called an air bypass (or anti-backfire) valve. During engine deceleration, the throttle is closed and engine vacuum is very high. This tends to pull a very rich fuel mixture into the engine, and as a result the exhaust has a higher-than-normal content of unburned gasoline. If air were injected into the exhaust during deceleration, that gasoline would explode, and the engine would backfire. Letting that gas go into the atmosphere is the only solution, for backfire is unacceptable.

This means that air injection must be stopped, and this is the job of the air bypass valve. When vacuum is very high, signaling deceleration, it operates the air bypass valve and sends the air from the pump to one of three locations:

1. To the atmosphere
2. To the air cleaner
3. Into the carburetor, where it helps lean out the fuel mixture

Because the air pump system, when it malfunctions, can cause backfire (as well as higher emissions), checking it and correcting any defects is a part of tuneup.

The Hardware

The air pump system checkout starts with the belt-driven pump at the front of the engine. Some pumps have a paper air filter connected to a hose. Others have a fanlike centrifugal filter just behind the belt pulley. You can replace the paper air filter yourself, but the fan-type is a job for a professional mechanic.

However, the pump is covered by the emission control warranty; so if the pump fails, you may not have to pay for it. You should know that air pumps are not silent, particularly when new. However, if the pump system is very noisy, and pinching off the air hose from the back of the pump stops the noise, either the pump or a check valve in the system is defective.

Always check the pump drive belt and replace or tighten as required (see fig. 4-21). Refer to chapter 7, which covers drive belt inspection and service. Drive belt and filter service are not covered under warranty.

To determine if the pump is working, disconnect the hose from the pump to the air bypass valve and run the engine at fast idle. You should be able to feel air under pressure at the pump's hose neck. If the valve is bolted directly to the pump, unbolt it for the test.

If you can't, and the belt is adequately tight, the pump is defective and should be replaced.

Follow the thick hose from the pump to the air bypass valve, and then the thick hose from that to another valve just before the injection manifold. This is the check valve (see fig. 4-22) and a V-type engine may have one or two (for each bank). Disconnect the hose from the air bypass valve at the check valve, and run the engine at part throttle (warmed up). You should feel air flow at the hose end (check at both check valves that may be found on a V-type engine).

If there is no air flow, and the air pump checked out satisfactorily, check all hoses that connect to the air bypass valve (at both ends) and if they're not kinked or loose at their ends, the air bypass valve probably is defective. A test procedure is described later.

While the hose is disconnected, look at the check valve, and if you see any exhaust gas leakage, replace the check valve. The leakage can contaminate the air bypass valve and pump.

Now test the air bypass valve. Begin by locating the manifold vacuum hose—a narrow diameter hose that goes (perhaps through little control valves) to the base of the carburetor. With the engine at part throttle, feel around the air bypass valve to determine if air is coming out (it should not be). With a Mityvac manual vacuum pump (a tool sold in auto parts stores), apply 20 inches of vacuum

VACUUM SENSING LINE
FROM INTAKE MANIFOLD

INJECTION TUBES TO EXHAUST PORTS

AIR BYPASS VALVE

MUFFLER

AIR FLOW LINES

AIR PUMP—INLET

CHECK VALVE

Figure 4-20. This schematic of an air pump system shows only a single check valve for a V-8; on many cars there is a separate check valve for each bank of the V-type engine.

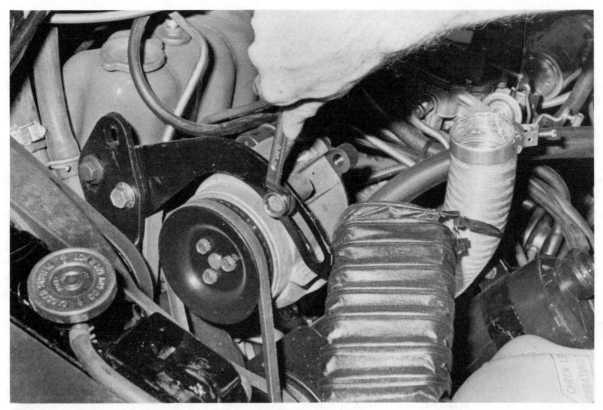

Figure 4-21. Slackening pump bolts prior to adjusting belt tension.

Figure 4-22. The arrow points to check valve, located at the start of the air injection manifold for a V-8 engine.

or more to the manifold vacuum hose neck on the air bypass valve, and air should now vent from the air bypass valve. If the air bypass valve fails this test, it is apparently defective. The air typically vents through a perforated opening in the valve called a muffler. By placing your hand over the valve, you'll feel the air flow.

Finally, shut the engine and manually test the check valves by inserting a Phillips screwdriver and pushing against the valve part inside. You should feel a part move and then spring back into position when you remove the screwdriver. If you can feel no movement, the air will not get into the injection manifold, and the engine may backfire. Replace the check valve.

Upstream-Downstream Controls

The air pump controls on the newest cars are more sophisticated than the type just described. There are two valves, one called the air bypass, the other called the diverter. You should understand that these two terms have previously often been used interchangeably on systems with only one valve.

In the newest system, called "upstream-downstream," the air goes from the pump to the air bypass valve, which either dumps it to the atmosphere or passes it straight through to the diverter valve. The diverter valve has two possible positions: In one it will pass the air into the exhaust manifold, called upstream; in the second it will shift the flow to a position between the two catalysts, called downstream. The downstream air helps the efficiency of the oxidation catalyst only when that catalyst is warmed up; so when the engine is cold, the air goes into the exhaust manifold, where it helps oxidize unburned gasoline. At this time (cold engine), the three-way catalyst also is cold and not functioning, so the extra air in the exhaust manifold does not threaten it. When the engine and the catalytic converter are warm, the airflow shifts. Under certain conditions, such as wide-open-throttle, deceleration, and extended idling, the air bypass valve will vent the air from the pump to the atmosphere.

The air pump system valves may be computer-controlled electrically with solenoid (electromagnetic) valves that regulate vacuum flow from the engine, or directly by electricity, with solenoids in the two air valves. Or the air pump system may be controlled more simply, through a thermostatic valve that regulates vacuum flow to the air control valves.

A simple check of the system can be made with the engine cold and later with the engine warm. Trace the hoses from the control valves and determine which goes to the exhaust manifold and which to the midpoint of the two catalysts in the converter. When the engine is cold, air should go to the exhaust manifold; when it's warm, it should go to the converter when the throttle is cracked open. If you can't feel the airflow by squeezing on the hoses, disconnect the one through which air should be flowing in order to make sure.

Note: When pouring a carbon cleaner into the carburetor, throttle body, or intake air throat to clean out carbon deposits from the engine combustion chambers, the air pump system should be disconnected. Either remove the drive belt or disconnect the air hose from the pump.

Pulsair

Pulsair is a diaphragm device connected by hoses and tubing to the exhaust system at one end (just before the converter) and to the air cleaner or carburetor at the other. The flow of exhaust gases is constantly pulsating, and half the pulses are a light vacuum that draws in air through the valve into the exhaust. There isn't as much air as with a pump, but on some cars the catalyst doesn't need as much, and the very inexpensive valve does the job. To check it, disconnect it from the carb or air cleaner with the engine running, and feel the end for the vacuum pulsations (see fig. 4-23). If you can't feel them, replace the valve.

VACUUM HOSES

Look under the hood of any car and you'll see what looks like a plate of black spaghetti—hoses running from the carburetor all over the place. These are vacuum hoses, and they control many systems, including such nonemission devices as the heater, air conditioning, power brakes, and automatic transmission. You may have trouble telling which hose controls what, but so does a professional mechanic.

Feel each hose for flexibility (see fig. 4-24), and if any is heat-hardened, replace it (really heat-hardened hoses may crack apart as you feel them).

If only the hose's very end is hardened, and there is some slack in the hose, cut off the hard end and reconnect. Flexible vacuum hose will make a more secure, leak-free connection. If a hose is merely loose, push it back on.

TUNEUP CHECKLIST

If you are careful, you will be pleased with the results of your tuneup. If you are not, following is a list of things that you may have omitted or erred in doing:

Did you conduct a compression test? Many skip it because they have the low-cost compression gauges without the hose and can't reach many of the plugs.

Did you use a carbon cleaner or clean the carburetor barrel with solvent? Or did you take a car normally used in slow, short-trip driving for a high-speed highway run? Any of these steps can coat the brand-new

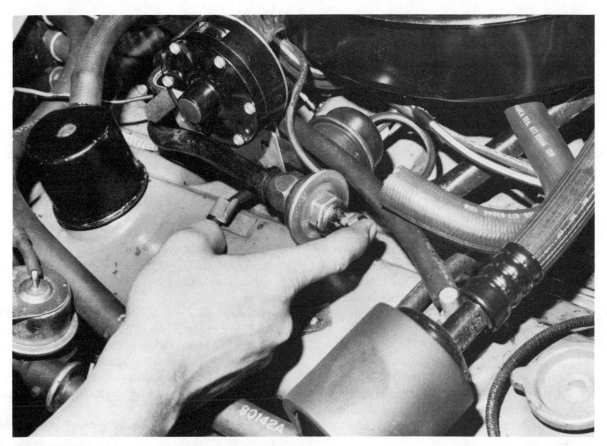

Figure 4-23. Feeling for vacuum pulsations at end of Pulsair valve.

Figure 4-24. Feeling vacuum hoses for flexibility.

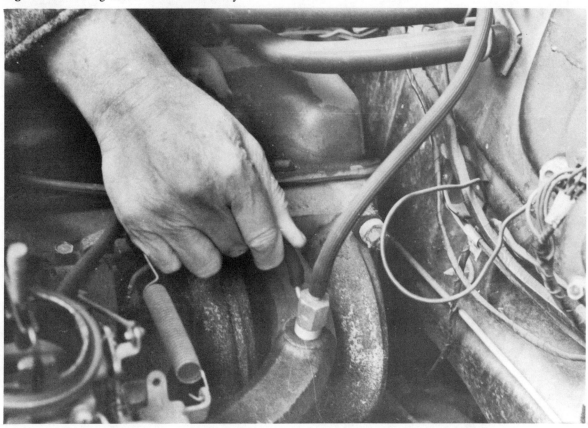

spark plugs with deposits. It's better to do something like this a week before a tuneup, so the deposits coat the old spark plugs.

Did you fail to duplicate the original routing of the spark plug wires? They might now be crossfiring, or one or more may be touching a hot part of the engine and have suffered burned-through insulation.

Did you treat the plug wires roughly? Always pull on the plug wire nipple, never on the wire itself, or you may cause a hairline internal break that eventually causes misfire.

Did you squirt oil onto the distributor wick on a breaker points distributor, or onto the mechanical advance weights of a GM V-8 distributor? The wick should be oiled, but overspray can hit the breaker points and cause them to burn, shortening their life. Any oil on the GM advance weights can get on breaker points, so instead use silicone dielectric grease on their pivot posts.

Did you fail to gap the spark plugs? The gap the factory gave the plugs may not be right for your engine. If it's too small, it may not consistently fire the air-fuel mixtures in many engines. Or if you accidentally rapped the spark plug against the engine during installation, the gap may have closed up and the spark plug won't produce a spark.

Did you pull the old plugs with an inexpensive spark plug wire puller? Many have sharp edges that can cut the plug wire nipple. The cut creates a pathway in which dirt and moisture collect, allowing the high-voltage electricity to wind up in electrical ground, instead of producing a spark in the plug. Wrap the sharp edges of a low-cost puller with plastic electrical tape.

Did you install the plugs with dirty, greasy hands? If enough gets on the plug exterior, it also can provide an easy path to ground for the high-voltage electricity. Keep your hands and the plugs clean.

Did you install a new electronic ignition module on a Ford or GM car and forget to apply silicone dielectric grease to the underside of the module? If you did, it won't last long!

Did you reconnect the air cleaner ductwork? If the hot air duct is off or damaged, the engine will run poorly until warm. If the cold air duct is off, it will lose power after warmup.

Did you move any distributor wiring? If you moved part of a wiring harness as part of underhood work, you must put it back. Many harnesses run to electronic components, and if they are left too close to spark plug wires they can receive unwanted signals from the plug wires, resulting in electromagnetic interference that can affect engine performance.

Did you disconnect any emission controls? Many people think an engine will run better without them, but today's engines are so integrated with the emission controls that they run poorly if any are disconnected.

5 BASIC GAS ENGINE SERVICE

Figure 5-1. To use scissors jack and safety stands, place the jack under a front crossmember. Safety stands are placed under the suspension lower control arms. Once stands are positioned, jack can be lowered and removed, if desired.

Changing the engine oil and replacing the oil filter are basic maintenance services on any gasoline engine (or for that matter, on a diesel). Although service intervals have been extended by the car makers, the more conservative motorist will change both oil and filter at least twice a year on gasoline engines and every 3,000 miles on a diesel. On some gasoline engines with turbochargers, a 2,500-mile interval also is advisable, according to the car makers.

CHANGING ENGINE OIL AND FILTER

Oil and filter service normally is performed underneath the car, so you need a provision for jacking it. There are three possibilities a weekend mechanic may consider:

Drive-on ramps. These are relatively inexpensive and fairly easy to use. You simply drive up on them, or if working at the rear, back the rear wheels up onto them. However, they do not leave the wheels hanging free—a necessity for many repair jobs, such as brakes.

Scissors jack and safety stands. The scissors jack expands like a pair of scissors when you turn a giant screw with a special handle. It takes some time and effort to raise a car with this jack, but its low price makes it suitable for the person who will be doing a limited amount of work on his car. The safety stands are absolutely mandatory with any kind of jack, for a jack itself is not a reliable device for holding up the car, only for raising it (see fig. 5-1).

Hydraulic floor jack and safety stands. The hydraulic floor jack (see fig. 5-2) is the type many professionals use. It has wheels or casters for easy positioning, and with just a few pumps of the handle it has the car up at working height, ready for positioning of the safety stands.

Figure 5-2. Hydraulic floor jack is under front crossmember, and safety stands are under the suspension lower control arms. As with scissors jack, the hydraulic floor type may be lowered and removed after stands are in place, if desired.

Note: Do not confuse this with a plain hydraulic jack. Although there are moderately priced models for weekend mechanics, the hydraulic floor jack still is much more expensive than the plain version, but does a job the plain hydraulic cannot. The plain hydraulic jack has a small jacking pad and its closed height is much too great for underbody jacking.

Where to Jack. On some late-model cars, particularly front-wheel-drive types, there are reinforced pads built into the lightweight bodies, and you should jack only against these pads. Consult your owner's manual for details.

If you have a conventional front-engine rear-drive car, the most suitable jacking points are in the center of the lower control arms of the front suspension (see fig. 5-3) and under the rear axle or the attachment points for the rear springs, if they are the leaf type. A coil-spring rear suspension has control arms (bars from frame to axle); you may jack under them or at their attachments too.

If you wish a front central jacking point on a front-engine rear-drive car, use the crossmember, a boxed section that goes from side to side of the chassis, just under the engine. In the rear, jack under the banjo-shaped part of the rear axle.

Oil Change

Engine oil is drained by removing a plug in the engine's oil pan with a wrench (see fig. 5-4). You should use a wrench that is a perfect fit, rather than an adjustable wrench. If you have a wrench assortment, one will be the correct fit (see fig. 5-5). Or you can purchase a combination oil filter wrench that combines a wrench with all popular sizes for the drain plug and a band wrench for filter removal (see fig. 5-6).

Note: Many new General Motors cars have small-diameter filters, and the combination filter wrench–drain plug wrench will not clamp tightly around them. Obtain a wrench made specifically for the smaller-diameter filter, or get a filter wrench with a cloth strap that will handle any size filter.

The easiest-to-use wrench in many tight quarters is one that fits on the end of the filter (see fig. 5-7). If a filter is nicely accessible, a band wrench (see fig. 5-8) is the easiest. Make sure the wrench you buy will fit the filter you must use; that is, that the metal band is neither too big or too small, or that the end cap type has the shape flutes to match the filter.

Select an oil of high quality, by a reputable refiner; for although there are standards, there is no policing of them.

Figure 5-3. These two photos show underbody jacking and safety stand points. Above is front of vehicle, below is rear. Points marked "S" are for side jacking or support with safety stands. Points marked "J" are for central jacking.

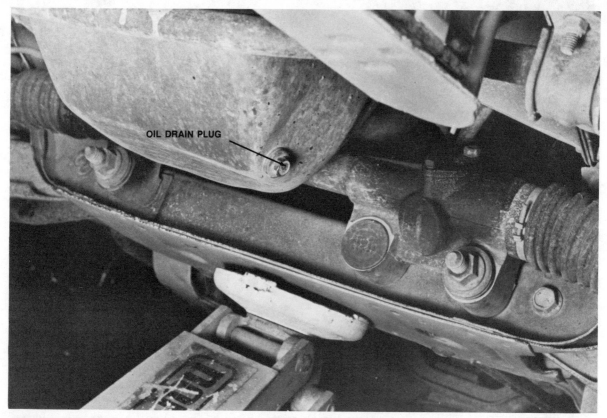

OIL DRAIN PLUG

Figure 5-4. The oil drain plug looks like a bolt threaded into the oil pan at a low point.

Figure 5-5. Removing oil drain plug with a socket wrench.

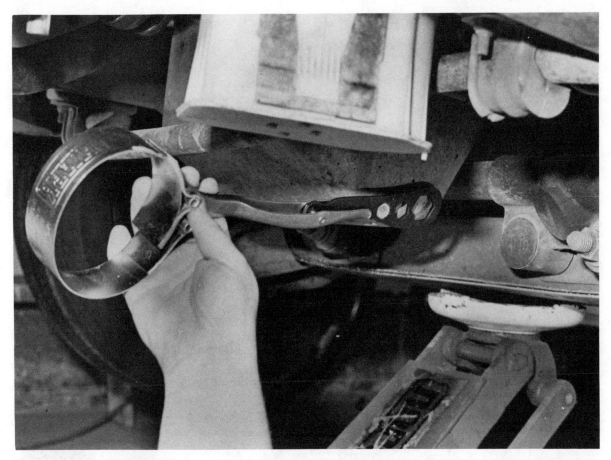

Figure 5-6. Using combination wrench to remove oil drain plug. Notice that drain plug wrench end has three sizes to fit virtually all cars. Oil filter wrench end will fit most (but not all) cars, so check your filter before you buy.

Figure 5-7. Shown are two end-type wrenches. *At left* is the band type; *at right* is a cap type. The cap type is not universal. It must be specified for the make of the filter you are installing; however, it is less likely to damage a new filter, and therefore is preferable.

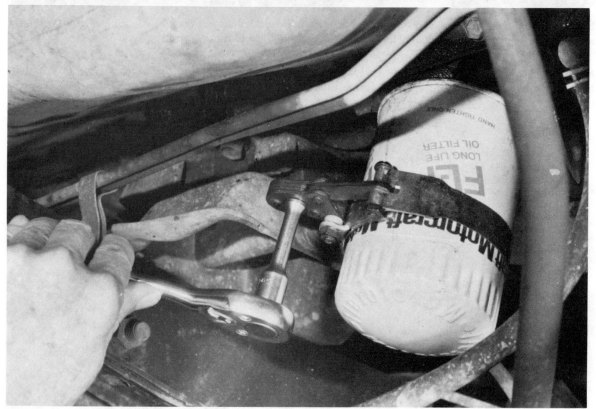

Figure 5-8. *The top photo* shows oil filter wrench with built-in handle. *The bottom photo* shows a filter wrench that accepts an extension and ratchet.

A name-brand oil that is labeled for "Service SE" or "SF" is recommended for gasoline engines; one for "Service CC" is for diesel engines. Use a multi-grade oil (5W-30, 5W-40, Mobile Synthetic 5W-20, 10W-40, 10W-50, etc.) for season-to-season suitability, easier cold starting, and high-temperature suitability. Obtain enough oil to refill the engine—usually about five quarts (some engines need only 2½).

Note: If your engine is seeping oil, a 5W oil may allow more of it to be lost than a heavier grade. The same is true if your engine is burning oil. A synthetic also may not be approved for all diesels; check your owner's manual.

Doing the Job

Start with the engine warm, so the oil will be hot and drain readily. Jack up the car and support on safety stands, or drive onto ramps. Place a drain pan of at least six quarts capacity (eight quarts with motor-home V-8s), under the engine's oil pan, that metal pan at the bottom of the engine. The drain plug looks like a bolt threaded into a low point in the pan and should be obvious.

Note: On Volkswagen Beetles, there is no oil pan as such, and the drain plug is threaded into a small circular metal plate at the center bottom of the engine. If that plate has no drain plug, the entire plate must be unbolted from the engine for the oil to drain out. Procure a new gasket for this plate and replace the old one when you change the oil.

Undo the drain plug. When you're underneath a car, you may become disoriented and attempt to turn the plug the wrong way, so if it seems to be tightening, rethink your position. The advantage of using a ratchet wrench is that you can set it to undo and it will work only in that direction. As soon as the plug is completely loose, remove the wrench, move the drain pan directly underneath, and complete the drain plug removal by hand.

Allow five minutes more for all the oil to drain out, then thread back the plug by hand and complete the tightening with the wrench.

Caution: When you thread back the plug by hand, be sure it is threading normally, not crossthreading. Feel binding? Unthread and start over. If any threads are dirty, clean with a wire brush. Also, don't apply excessive tightening force with the wrench, or you could ruin the threads in the pan or on the drain plug.

Note: Do not discard the washer under the drain plug. If the washer is deteriorated, obtain a replacement. If available, get the washer that has a built-in rubber O-ring for superior sealing.

Finally, if the worst occurs and the plug will not thread back properly, don't panic. There are several types of repair kits for this situation; they're inexpensive and they're sold in most auto parts stores. They come with complete instructions and they're easy to use. The easiest is made by Motormite and has a rubber bushing and a wingnut that you turn to expand the bushing against the drain plug hole. It's available from auto parts stores.

The Oil Filter

When you select an oil filter for your car, be sure to buy one that is both a reputable brand and designed for the service you intend. If you change your oil and filter moderately often (3 or 4 times a year and not exceeding every 6,000 miles) you do not need the so-called 15,000-mile filters. The standard filter will actually do a better job for you. All modern cars have a spin-on oil filter, except VW Beetle. Though the Beetle does not have an oil filter as standard equipment, it may be retrofitted with a kit. If so equipped, the filter also may be a spin-on.

To remove the old filter, just position the filter wrench on it so the wrench band closes up and tightens around the filter as you turn the wrench handle counterclockwise (see fig. 5-8). When the band is tight, continue turning until you loosen the filter. This procedure sounds simpler than it often is, however, because other parts in the engine compartment may prevent easy removal. You may have to reposition the wrench so that there is swing room for the handle with the band tight. Or you may have to move the band along the length of the filter cannister to find a location where there is swing room for the wrench handle.

Once the filter is loose, move the drain pan underneath it and complete the removal by hand. Coat the rubber O-ring of the new filter with a film of clean engine oil (see fig. 5-9), and thread on the filter until you can feel that the rubber O-ring is just touching the engine, then move it one-half to three-quarters of a full turn more. In most cases you will have to use the filter wrench (installed the opposite way so the band closes when you move the handle clockwise) to complete the tightening.

Figure 5-9. Apply some clean engine oil to filter gasket, as shown; then spread it over gasket with your finger.

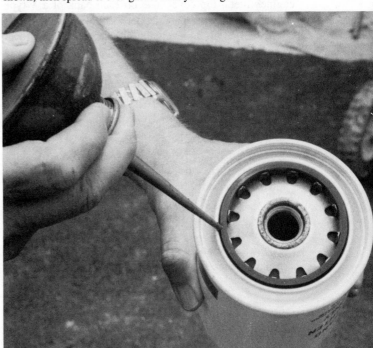

Add fresh oil to the engine through the oil filler neck, until the engine dipstick reads "Full." Start the engine, run it at idle, and check underneath for leaks. If you see any from the oil drain plug or the filter, stop the engine, get underneath, and check tightness of the leaking part. If there are no leaks, let the engine idle for a couple of minutes (the oil filter will fill with oil) and recheck the dipstick. Top off if necessary.

GASKET SERVICE

In mass production, no two flat surfaces mate perfectly. If air, oil, or water must flow between two mating parts, it is customary to use a gasket between them. When the parts are bolted together, the gasket compresses and compensates for minor irregularities in the surface finishes.

Gaskets may be made of cork, fiber, treated paper (actually a form of fiber), synthetic rubber, compositions of these materials, and even soft metal.

Although there are many gaskets on an automobile, this chapter will cover only those that a typical weekend mechanic might attempt to replace. Some weekend mechanics might replace the cylinder head gasket, the one between the cylinder head and engine block, but this is a complex job beyond the scope of this book.

It should be understood that the actual replacement of a gasket is usually a simple job. The problem is to get the part off for access to the gasket. No general book (indeed, even many specific make-of-car factory manuals) can assess the degree of difficulty in removing the part for access. Under the specific gasket headings, however, general comments regarding procedures for handling the most common problems are given.

Oil Sealing

Gaskets that must seal against loss of oil are used on the engine's metal top cover (one on each bank of a V-type engine), engine oil pan, tappet (valve lifter) chamber cover, fuel pump, transmission oil pan, a rear axle cover on some cars, and on engines with a chain- or gear-driven camshaft, the front cover.

Types of gaskets for oil sealing and their advantages and disadvantages are as follows:

Cork. It's very compressible, so if mating surfaces are warped, it does the best job. However, it takes a set and you may have to retighten frequently. It also shrinks when stored in a dry place, is very fragile, and could break if you're trying to install it in tight quarters.

Fiber. It has less compressibility than cork, but doesn't shrink and is somewhat less fragile. It costs a little more than cork.

Cork-fiber. It offers some of the advantages of each material at about the same cost as fiber.

Synthetic rubber. It's much more expensive than cork or fiber, but it won't break and it doesn't shrink. It doesn't have the compressibility of cork or fiber, but it does a reasonable job in this area. Neoprene is the most popular material, and in some cases silicone may be used.

Synthetic rubber paste. This is usually silicone, it extrudes from a toothpaste-like tube, injection tube, or caulking cartridge, and you use it to form a gasket in place. It does a good job of sealing and has great heat resistance. It cures in place, and if it ever breaks when you remove the part for other service, you just have to squeeze out a ribbon of new paste to repair the break.

Note: If you find the tube difficult to use, silicone paste is available in a cartridge that fits into a caulking gun. Silicone rubber paste relies on moisture in the air to cure, and it starts curing the minute it is squeezed from the container.

Anaerobic sealer. This is a fluid sealer, but not nearly as thick as silicone rubber paste. Unlike silicone, it cures in the absence of air, so after you squeeze it from its tube, you can let it stand without the problem of it curing while you attend to other things. However, it cannot seal between surfaces that are not both machined (such as an engine top cover). Anaerobic sealer is suitable for water pumps and thermostat housings, for example.

Synthetic rubber-cork or synthetic rubber-fiber. This type combines cork or fiber with rubber to make a gasket that has the good compressibility of fiber or cork and the unbreakability of synthetic rubber. Price is slightly higher than the plain synthetic rubber type.

Getting to the Gasket

Engine Top Cover. It is also known as rocker or valve cover. At the least, you will have to disconnect a couple of hoses from a pollution control system to get at this, and usually the air cleaner assembly must come off. When removing the air cleaner, note the hose disconnections you must make. Label them with masking tape at both ends so you can correctly reconnect, or you can use color-coded vacuum hose neck identifiers, sold in auto parts stores. In other cases, the fuel line to the carburetor also must be disconnected if it passes over the cover. If the air conditioning compressor bracket interferes, check to see if you can get the cover off without disturbing it. If this isn't possible, work with a helper so one person can hold up the compressor while the other removes the cover. If you are working alone, check to see if you can lay the compressor out of the way without putting any strain on the air conditioning hoses.

If a cover or part sticks after all screws are out, carefully work a putty knife into the gasket joint and gently pry all around.

Note: On late-model General Motors 2.5-liter, 4-cylinder engines, you may need a special tool to avoid breaking the valve cover (see fig. 5-10).

On any engine, be careful not to lose the screw washers, which often are specially shaped to spread load for good oil sealing. Use of ordinary washers may result in oil leaks (see fig. 5-11).

Engine Oil Pan. On some cars you can simply remove the bolts or screws and lower the pan. On others you must unbolt the engine mounts and jack up the engine to gain clearance so the oil pan can slip past a chassis crossmember.

Engine Front Cover. It is also called timing gear or chain cover. Access to this usually requires draining and remov-

Figure 5-10. Late-model GM cars with 2.5-liter, 4-cylinder engines may require a special tool to avoid breaking a stuck engine top cover. The tool is made by Kent-Moore Tools (1-800-345-2243) and is No. J-34144-A.

Figure 5-11. The specially shaped engine top cover washers in this illustration spread the clamping load of the nut for better oil sealing.

ing the radiator and removing the crankshaft pulley assembly (a job that may require use of a plumber's strap wrench to hold the crankshaft pulley, and a puller). The bottom of the cover normally seals against the oil pan gasket, and when you remove the cover you may tear the protruding segment of oil pan gasket. If this happens, get a timing cover gasket kit that includes a replacement for the torn segment. You will not have to drop the oil pan and change its gasket.

Fuel Pump. To remove the fuel pump (mechanical type, on the engine), refer to chapter 3.

Transmission Oil Pan. This is usually wide open; just remove the retaining screws and carefully lower the pan. *Caution:* It's filled with transmission fluid. Also refer to chapter 13.

Rear Axle. On some rear axles (rear-drive cars) there is a cover plate at the rear. To remove, just undo the screws and lift it away. There is seldom any interference of any significance, although it may be necessary to push on a parking brake cable to gain clearance to a particular screw.

Tappet Chamber. The tappet (valve lifter) chamber cover is on the side of an in-line engine and between the banks of a V-type engine. It is rarely easily accessible on the in-line because it's usually blocked by the exhaust system, which must be dropped to get to it. On a V-8, you must remove the intake manifold (see reference later to intake manifold gasket).

Many four-cylinder engines don't have a tappet cover on the side for either of two reasons:
1. The pushrod holes are large enough so the tappets (lifters) can be pulled up through them.
2. The engine has an overhead camshaft and the lifters are in the chamber at the top of the engine.

Servicing the Gasket

Scrape off all residue of the old gasket from both the cover and the mating surface on engine or transmission with a putty knife or scraper. Wire-brush a metal pan or cover if necessary for final cleaning.

Check a cover for warpage by placing against a flat surface and looking at the cover edge. Sheet metal covers, if necessary, can be straightened with a soft hammer, while you hold the gasket surface against a flat block of wood (see fig. 5-12). Check a machined surface, such as a fuel pump or thermostat housing, by laying a machinist's ruler across at various points. Try to slip a .005-inch (.12-mm) feeler gauge underneath (see fig. 5-13). If it doesn't

Figure 5-12. To straighten cocked engine top cover, brace against a flat piece of wood and gently pound back into shape with hammer and wood.

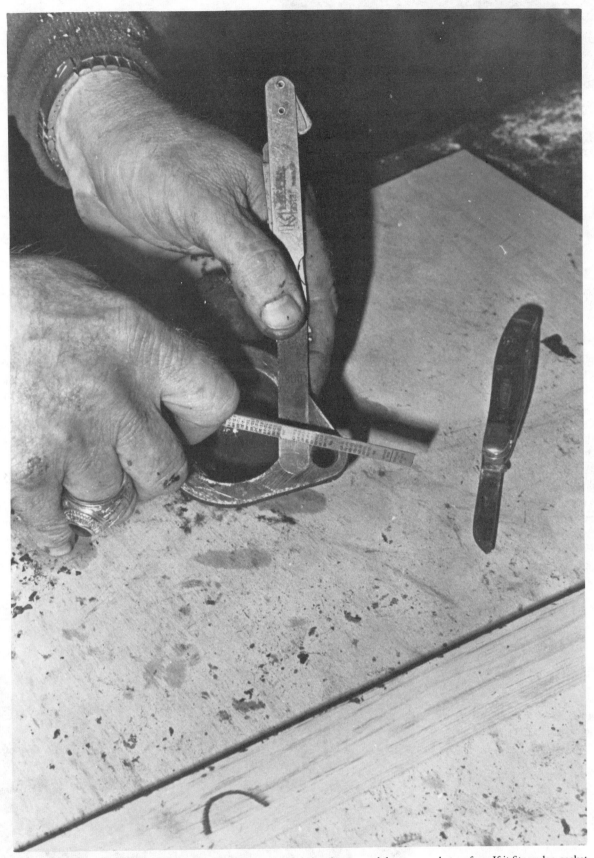

Figure 5-13. Try to slip .005-inch feeler gauge under machinist's ruler pressed down on gasket surface. If it fits under, gasket surface is warped.

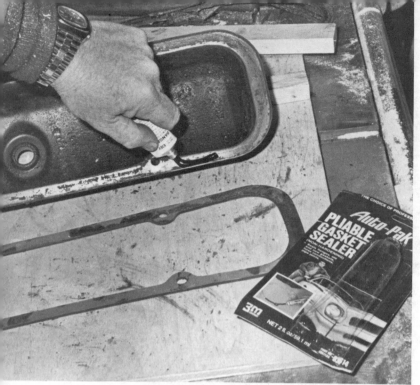

Figure 5-14. When applying ribbon of gasket sealer to cover's gasket surface, spread ribbon with finger until it is a thin coat all around.

fit, warpage is minimal. If it does, try two gaskets and coats of pliable gasket sealer (one on the pump surface, another between the gaskets).

If you're using a preformed gasket, make sure it's a correct fit. Never try to stretch a gasket that seems to be a bit small—it could be the wrong part. If the gasket is cork and seemingly dried out, soak it in a pan of water for half an hour or so and that may restore it to size.

Apply a thin film of pliable gasket sealer to the gasket surface (see fig. 5-14) of the part you removed (never to the engine or transmission), then position the gasket on the coated surface (see fig. 5-15). If you are working with a gasket that has tabs, lock them into the slots in the cover.

Position the plate or part on the engine or transmission gently (to insure the gasket does not shift), then start

threading in the screws, preferably by hand. If clearances are limited, put the screw into a socket with an extension and start the screw in by hand-turning the extension. Either of these techniques is designed to prevent cross-threading.

Once all screws are finger-tight, give them a final tightening with a wrench. If you have a torque wrench, check manufacturer's specifications and tighten the screws accordingly; if not, you must guess, and guessing really is for the experienced, not the beginner.

Always tighten in stages: first finger-tight; then moderately tight; and last, securely tight. With a rectangular part that has many screws, start in the center and work alternately toward each end, as indicated in figure 5-16.

Figure 5-15. Positioning new gasket on sealer-coated gasket surface.

200

Figure 5-16. Typical tightening sequence for bolts or nuts.

Formed-in-place Gaskets

The use of silicone paste to make a formed-in-place gasket is basically similar to installing a preformed gasket. After cleaning the surfaces, extrude a continuous ⅛-inch-diameter bead on the gasket surface of the part you removed, and in addition encircle each bolt hole with a bead about ⅛ inch or more (if the width of the gasket surface permits) from the edge of the hole (see fig. 5-17).

Allow five minutes for the bead to "skin" (cure on the surface), then install and allow 24 hours for the silicone to cure more completely.

The procedure with anaerobic sealer is basically the same. After you have cleaned the gasket surfaces, apply a coat of primer (from an aerosol can) to one surface and allow a couple of minutes for it to dry. Then apply a bead of anaerobic sealer as you would the silicone paste. However, there's no rush to install the part. Allow a half hour after bolting down the part for the sealer to cure.

Just because the factory used a formed-in-place silicone paste gasket doesn't mean you have to. If there is a chance you will smear the bead because of installation difficulty, see if a precut gasket is available for replacement (it often is).

Figure 5-17. *The top photo* demonstrates use of formed-in-place gasket. The proper pattern for spreading is shown *below.*

Water-sealing Gaskets

Water-sealing gaskets are used at the joint between the water pump and the engine, and between the upper radiator hose neck (actually the thermostat housing) and the engine. The radiator cap also has gaskets, but they are not serviceable; if they leak, the cap must be replaced.

The general rules regarding installation of oil-sealing gaskets also apply to those on the water pump and thermostat housing. It is common practice, however, to coat both sides of a water pump gasket with pliable sealer.

Removal Techniques

Upper Radiator Hose Neck (Thermostat Housing). This neck is removed whenever it is necessary to test and/or replace the thermostat. In most cases, just undo two nuts or bolts and lift up the part. If it sticks, pry up gently with a putty knife. Be sure to check this part for warpage, as for a fuel pump (described earlier). If warpage of this part is excessive, you may be able to salvage it by resurfacing with a fine draw file (see fig. 5-18).

Water Pump on Rear-drive Cars. The radiator almost always must come out, to gain working room, if the pump

is conventionally mounted on the front of the engine. In addition, the fan belt and fan should be removed.

Note: When reinstalling, you should tighten the bolts or nuts to factory specifications with a torque wrench if at all possible. As with the thermostat housing, check the gasket surface for warpage. If excessively warped but still functional, try two gaskets and coats of pliable gasket sealer, as described earlier for the fuel pump.

Water Pump on Transverse-engine Front-drive Cars. On these, the job can be very difficult because of limited room between the pump and the right-side sheet metal of the engine compartment. Further, there are specific difficulties. On General Motors 2.8-liter, V-6 engines, the pump and timing cover use the same bolts, and if you remove the pump, the cover could move and antifreeze could get into the engine oil and cause problems. To prevent this, a special bracket (see fig. 5-19) should be installed. The bracket often is included with replacement water pumps by quality parts manufacturers and rebuilders.

On many transverse engine cars the coolant circuit is complex, and there is a pipe from the water pump to the rear of the engine. This pipe has a rubber O-ring seal in the water pump, and this seal should be checked and replaced when the pump is changed.

Figure 5-18. A fine draw file to correct for warpage may be used instead of two gaskets, or in severe cases of warpage, in combination.

POSITION J-29176 AGAINST
TIMING COVER BOSS PRIOR TO
REMOVING WATER PUMP BOLTS.

J-29176

TORQUE MOUNTING BOLT
12 N·m (10 FT. LBS.)

8396

Figure 5-19. Special bracket to hold timing cover during water pump removal on GM V-6 can be ordered from many auto parts stores; or you can make one from bar stock. The engine is widely used in GM cars and was used on some Jeeps.

Some engines have recessed water pumps driven by the camshaft timing belt, including the Ford Escort, GM overhead camshaft 1.8- and 2.0-liter engines, and some Japanese engines. You must disconnect the timing belt to change the pump, a job that requires a service manual and considerable experience.

Air-holding Gaskets

There are three important gaskets that seal in air: between air cleaner housing and carburetor; between carburetor and intake manifold; and between intake manifold and cylinder head. If the gasket between air cleaner and carburetor leaks, dirty air can get into the engine; if either or both of the other two leak, extra air can get in and lean out the air/fuel mixture, causing engine stalling, stumble, etc.

Air Cleaner Housing. Just take off the air cleaner cover and lift the filter housing to check the gasket (if any hoses come off, be sure to reconnect). If it's hardened or dented, replace it.

Carburetor or Throttle Body Base and Intake Manifold. Connect a vacuum gauge to a vacuum neck at the base of the carburetor, and run the engine at idle. If vacuum is normal (18 to 22 inches), the gaskets apparently are sealing. If the reading is low, squirt some oil

along the entire gasket joint as a temporary seal (see fig. 5-20). If the vacuum gauge reading rises, the gasket is leaking. First, try tightening carburetor or manifold nuts or bolts (see fig. 5-21), but if that doesn't cure the vacuum leak, replace the gasket.

To replace a carburetor base gasket, remove the nuts that hold the carb to the intake manifold; if you're lucky, you will be able to lift the carburetor high enough to remove the old gasket and install a new one.

Note: The throttle body or carburetor base gasket may be specially made to resist heat and often is very thick to help isolate the carburetor from heat. Do not fabricate a gasket from sheet cork or other material. If you can't raise the carburetor enough, you must remove it. Look for electrical connectors and vacuum hoses and disconnect as required, taping each connection (and marking the tape) so you can reconnect correctly. It should not normally be necessary to disconnect the linkage from the gas pedal, but if it is, the detachment (which varies from car to car) should be obvious (see chapter 3).

Intake Manifold. Once the throttle body or carburetor is off, remove the intake manifold bolts. On many cars with air conditioning, the AC compressor bracket is connected to the manifold, and this must come off too. In addition, you may find other brackets attached to the engine by the intake manifold bolts.

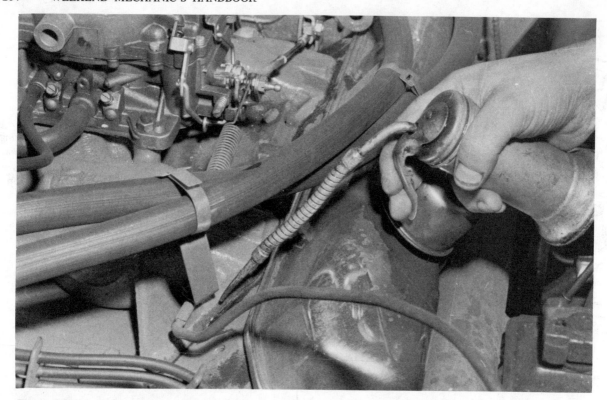

Figure 5-20. Squirting oil along intake manifold gasket joint as a temporary seal. If vacuum gauge reading rises or if engine idle smooths out or increases, the gasket is leaking.

Figure 5-21. Before replacing a leaking intake manifold or carburetor base gasket, try tightening the nuts or bolts as shown.

Important: On some cars the ignition distributor must come out in order to take off the intake manifold. This must be done in a special way, so you can refit the distributor without disturbing ignition timing. Remove the distributor cap and note the exact position of the rotor pointer, as if it were the hour hand on a clock. Also mark the location of the distributor body with a dab of nail polish on the distributor base at the location of the lockbolt.

Remove the lockbolt (see chapter 2) and lift out the distributor. If it sticks, twist it back and forth with an upward motion to free it. When you refit the distributor with a gear on the bottom of the shaft, you will have to "lead" the rotor, for once the gear meshes, the rotor position will change slightly (but slightly off is unacceptable). You will understand this if you do it wrong, for the rotor will not be in exactly the same position as when the distributor was removed. If the bottom of the distributor shaft has a female hex and a gear, proper refitting may take repeated tries until both gear and hex engage properly.

Caution: Never crank the engine with the distributor removed, or you'll never get it back in correctly without professional help.

Once the intake manifold is off, you have access to both the manifold gasket(s)—one on each side of a V-type engine—and the V-8 valve lifter chamber and its cover gasket. Or a single gasket may be used for both.

Like carburetor base gaskets, intake manifold gaskets are specially made for the applications, so never use a homemade. Tighten manifold bolts to factory specifications—in stages with a torque wrench, if possible. Also, use the crisscross tightening pattern for rectangular parts described earlier.

HYDRAULIC LIFTERS

How They Work

The hydraulic lifter has two interrelated purposes:
1. To eliminate shock in the valve train by keeping all parts in constant contact
2. To compensate for wear in the parts

A detailed diagram of how the hydraulic lifter works is shown in figure 5-22.

The lifter is designed so there is a slight leakage—called leakdown—between the plunger and the body. This controlled leakage allows the oil to escape when the engine is shut off for an extended period. Thus, when you first start the engine, the lifters are noisy until they fill up with oil. The plunger spring is a rather mild one, yet if functioning properly it will take up the slack in the valve train during the leakdown process. If there is any sticking of the plunger, either from gums or dirt in the oil, the mild spring will not be able to push it up to compensate for clearances in the valve train.

Frequent oil changes, using the best quality oil, is your best insurance against any and all lifter malfunctions.

Hydraulic Lifter Service

The rhythmic clatter of valve lifters (also called tappets) is a common engine noise. On the modern car with hydraulic lifters the noise should stop after a half minute or so as they fill with engine oil. If they don't fill up, the engine is not only noisy, but there is loss of power and premature

Figure 5-22. The hydraulic lifter. When the valve is closed (camshaft lobe is not pressing on the lifter) there is no pressure on the pushrod (1) so that the lifter plunger spring (2) pushes up the plunger (3); engine oil under pressure from the oil pump enters the lifter through port holes (4) in the lifter body (7), then through a check valve (5) in the lifter into the space (6) below the plunger. When the camshaft turns so the cam lobe is pushing up on the lifter, the check valve (5) closes, making the lifter and plunger (and the oil between them) into one solid part. The lifter then pushes up on the pushrod and rocker to open the valve.

B

ENGINE VALVE OPEN

A

ENGINE VALVE CLOSED

VALVE SPRING

ROCKER

SECTION OF ROCKER SHAFT

VALVE

HYDRAULIC LIFTER

CAMSHAFT

PISTON

Figure 5-23. This is a typical pushrod-type valve train, with the engine block and cylinder head removed for clarity. Hydraulic lifters rest on camshaft lobes, and when the camshaft spins, the lobes force the lifters up. The lifter pushes up the pushrod, which causes the rocker to pivot on its shaft (or on a ball-shaped stud). When the rocker pivots, it pushes down on the valve stem against the pressure of the valve spring. When the camshaft lobe no longer exerts upward pressure on the lifter, the valve spring closes the valve and pushes all the parts back toward the camshaft.

wear of the valve train—the system that opens and closes the valves (see fig. 5-23).

Once the engine is warmed up, hydraulic lifter–caused tapping is a matter for concern, and here's how to check it out.

First, inspect the oil level on the dipstick. If it's too high or too low, air can get into the oil and then into the valve lifters. Adjust the oil level, and if the noise continues, determine if the lifters are really the problem.

Obtain a piece of heater hose about thirty inches long, and hold one end to your ear. With the engine idling, slide the other end along the engine top cover (also called the valve or rocker cover on a V-type engine). If you hear a loud clicking noise through the heater hose, the problem is in the valve system.

Remove the engine top cover (see "Gasket Service" earlier in this chapter). This time, place the end of the hose on the pushrod of the rocker arm. A noisy lifter will sound much louder at its rocker arm than another.

Note: On overhead camshaft engines (which have no pushrods) place the hose end on the lifter side of the rocker. If there is no rocker, place the hose as close to the lifter as possible.

When you find what seems to be the noisy lifter, make these additional tests before condemning it:

For worn valve stem and/or valve guide. With the end of a hammer handle, apply pressure at the side of the valve spring (trying to push against the coils). Repeat at the opposite side. If the noise is reduced, the problem is a worn valve stem and/or valve guide, a repair job for a professional.

Note: Valve guide service can be expensive. If the problem is accompanied by high oil consumption, you may solve the oil consumption problem yourself, as described later in this chapter, with new valve stem seals.

Check for a loose rocker shaft. On some engines the rockers all are on a shaft, and if this shaft is loose, the tapping noise can occur.

Where adjustment can be made. There is a provision for adjustment on some older Ford and Chevrolet V-8 engines. On these engines there is no rocker shaft; rather, the rocker is on a ball-stud and is held by a nut. With the engine idling, back off the nut until there is severe clatter, then turn it down until the clatter is just eliminated, plus one full turn of the wrench (three-quarters of a turn on 1976 to 1977 Chevrolets). This often cures lifter tapping, if tapping is caused by wear in the valve system rather than a defective lifter. If you exhaust the adjustment range, the wear in the system is excessive or the lifter is defective.

Note: During this adjustment oil may squirt out of the rockers and make a mess. You can prevent this by first inserting the end of a large paper clip into the hole (on the pushrod side) and bending the clip over so it holds against the bottom end of the rocker (see figs. 5-24 and 5-25).

On cars without a provision for adjustment. Insert the thickest feeler gauge possible between the rocker arm

Figure 5-24. If oil squirts through the hollow pushrod, then through the hole in the pushrod end of a rocker on a ball-stud, you can minimize the flow by inserting a paper clip as shown. Pull out the open end of the clip, insert into hole, then hook remainder of the clip on the underside of the rocker.

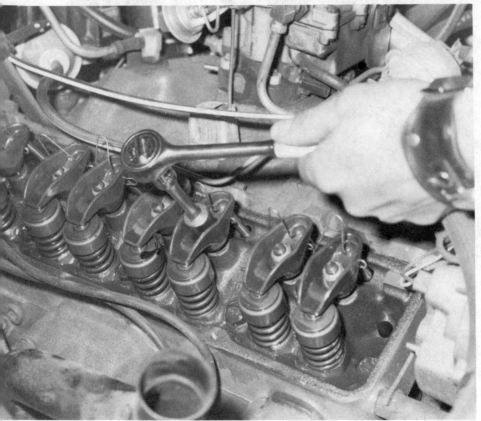

Figure 5-25. With clips in place, oil merely oozes out of rocker hole as you turn the ball-stud nut to adjust clearance in the valve train.

and the valve stem tip with the engine at idle. If the noise goes away and does not come back, the problem is either wear in the valve system, probably in the rocker or valve stem end, or a lifter that is stuck internally. If it's in the rocker, you probably can replace the rocker yourself. If the valve stem tip is the problem, it's a job for a professional.

If the noise comes back almost immediately, the problem is in the valve lifter, which is leaking down, excessively (see "Hydraulic Lifters" and fig. 5-22).

If the problem is an internally sticking lifter, you may be able to get it working again. Drain the oil and change the filter, then refill the crankcase with four quarts of kerosene (or a gum solvent made for lifters that contains kerosene and special chemicals) and one quart of SAE 10W-30 oil.

Run the car for two hours at very low speed—under 25 mph. Then drain the oil-kerosene mixture, change the filter once more, and fill the crankcase with the normal quantity of oil. If you're lucky, the stuck lifter will be free. If it is not, or if the problem is a lifter leaking down excessively, you must replace the lifter. In a professional shop, it is standard practice to replace all lifters when one has failed, on the theory that the others

soon will follow and so will customer complaints. When you do the job yourself, however, you have the option of replacing only the defective one.

Replacing Lifters—Pushrod Engines

On a V-type engine, the access to the lifters is through a cover that is under the intake manifold in the center of the engine (see fig. 5-26). You must disconnect the throttle linkage and remove the carburetor and intake manifold (see "Gasket Service" earlier in this chapter).

On an in-line pushrod engine, there are three possible ways to remove the lifters. Only one will apply to any particular engine. The cylinder head may have to be removed, a job for a professional. The lifters may come out through the pushrod holes, after removing the pushrods. This is a most convenient way, although a special lifter-pulling tool is commonly needed. The Chrysler slant six-cylinder, since 1981, and the General Motors "J" car four-cylinder, since 1982 (Chevrolet Cavalier, etc.), have had hydraulic lifters that can be removed through pushrod holes. Or there are covers on the side of the engine block for access to the lifters. In this case, which is more common, you must remove parts that inter-

Figure 5-26. With intake manifold and engine valley cover (the lifter chamber gasket) removed, you can see pushrods and lifters.

Figure 5-27. Special tools, such as the slide hammer puller shown, simplify removal of stuck hydraulic lifters. After the pushrod is out, insert the bottom of this tool into the top of the stuck lifter. Turn knob at top of tool and jaws at bottom lock against inside wall of lifter.

fere with simple unbolting of the covers, perhaps dropping the exhaust system. The covers have sealing gaskets that probably will require replacement.

Before you go to the trouble of removing these parts, make sure you can get the defective lifter(s) out.

It is possible for the base of a lifter to mushroom, preventing you from removing the lifter even with a spe-

Figure 5-28. Illustration of the lifter pulling tool in use. The T-shaped slide hammer is yanked upward to shock lifter free.

cial puller. Although this is not a common situation, it does mean that it must be pushed out through the bottom. To provide clearance, the camshaft must be removed first, and this is a job for a professional.

There is no simple way to know if a lifter has mushroomed. If you encounter the problem, you'll have to give up and reassemble. Because the possibility is so remote, don't let it stop you from trying the job.

After gaining visual access to the lifters by removing the carburetor and intake manifold or the in-line engine side covers, you must take out the pushrods. On cars with rocker shafts you can sufficiently slacken the bolts that hold the shafts to provide clearance to pivot the rocker, disengage it from the pushrod, and move it aside. If you can do this, lift out the pushrod.

On engines without rocker shafts, slacken the rocker retaining nut sufficiently or remove it entirely, lift up the rocker, and pull out the pushrod. If you remove the rockers completely, keep them in order, so if serviceable they can be refitted to the same position. If you're lucky you can just lift the lifter from its bore. If not, squirt some penetrating solvent between the lifter and the engine block bore and try again. If a lifter is really stuck, obtain a special valve-lifter pulling tool, an inexpensive item available at auto supply stores (see figs. 5-27 and 5-28).

Replacing Lifters—Overhead Camshaft Engines

The typical American overhead camshaft engine has rockers, and the lifters are not under the camshaft. Therefore the camshaft does not have to be removed, in which case lifter replacement would be a job for a professional.

You will, however, need a special compressor for the valve spring so you can compress the spring and remove the rocker, which is under the camshaft and over the lifter. Before attempting to use the tool, crank the engine until the peak of the cam is no longer bearing against the rocker.

Note: Disconnect thin wires from coil or pink wire from General Motors HEI distributor cap flange to prevent engine from starting.

The next section of this chapter, "Curing Oil Burning," shows this type of compressor in use. Various universal models are available in auto supply stores.

Buying New Lifters

Although it is possible to disassemble and clean a stuck lifter with solvent, it is not really the practical approach. Unless you are both very careful and very fortunate, the cleaned lifter will not last very long, so shop around for the best discount and buy new lifters. Before installation, oil the exterior of the new lifter and squirt as much oil as possible through the holes in the body into the interior, or immerse the lifter in a pan of clean engine oil and operate the plunger by pressing down with a pushrod or dowel.

CURING OIL BURING

When your engine starts to burn oil you may psychologically be prepared for a major engine repair. In many cases, however, the problem is caused by something relatively simple.

The first step is to be sure you are burning engine oil, for on many cars with automatic transmissions it is possible for transmission oil to be sucked into the engine through a defective diaphragm device called a modulator (see chapter 13). If the power brakes have failed, it's possible that brake fluid is being sucked in. Or it is possible that the exhaust smoke is caused by a defective fuel system or leakage of coolant. If the smoke is blue-gray, it's oil; black, it's fuel; white, it's coolant. Check the tips of the spark plugs (see fig. 2-97) to help confirm the problem.

If you know it's oil, the next step is to trace the problem. It could be piston rings, a major repair, but much more likely it is one of the following:

Positive crankcase ventilation system. See also chapter 4, "Pollution Controls." If you see oil contaminating the carburetor air filter element, oil may be blowing out of the crankcase because of a defective PCV valve. Also pull the valve out of the engine top cover on cars so equipped and look for a baffle in the top cover. If there is a baffle and it's loose, oil droplets in the chamber below may be bypassing this baffle. In this case they will be drawn into the engine through the PCV valve. Either replace the top cover or have a shop weld the baffle back into position so it prevents oil loss.

Intake manifold. On many cars with V-type engines, the design of the intake manifold is such that a loose or defective intake manifold gasket can readily allow oil from the engine to be drawn into the intake manifold. There is one check you can make: Squirt oil all around the exterior joint of the intake manifold and cylinder head, and if the engine speeds up a bit the gasket is defective (the oil acts as a temporary seal). This test is not a positive check for a defect in the gasket on the oil-sealing inner joint, so the gasket could pass this check and still be defective. You still must keep the gasket under suspicion. One helpful thing to keep in mind is that if the oil consumption has suddenly become severe, the gasket is a likely cause.

Piston rings. Take a compression test (see chapter 2). If the compression readings are lower than specifications, squirt about a tablespoon of oil into a cylinder (see fig. 5-29) and immediately repeat the test. The oil acts as a temporary seal, and if compression readings suddenly jump to normal or above (showing an increase of more than 35 to 40 p.s.i.), the piston rings are suspect. You should understand that piston rings can be worn and still not be responsible for much of the oil consumption, for there is one ring (called the oil ring) that has little to do with sealing compression pressures but does most of the job of sealing against oil consumption. However, if compression rings are badly worn, there is a good chance the oil ring also is deteriorated.

Valve Stem Guides and Seals

On most late-model engines, defective valve stem seals (shields) or worn valve guides are a major cause of oil consumption (see fig. 5-30). The stem of the valve slides in a machined hole—called the guide—in the cylinder head. The seals are little rubber or teflon rings, sometimes shaped like miniature umbrellas, that are placed on the part of the valve stem that protrudes into the chamber under the engine top cover.

If there is excessive wear between valve and guide, accompanied by deterioration of the seal, a lot of oil can flow down the guide into the cylinder, where it is burned. The seal is the more critical item because even if there is a fair amount of wear between stem and guide the oil loss may remain within normal limits if the seal is good.

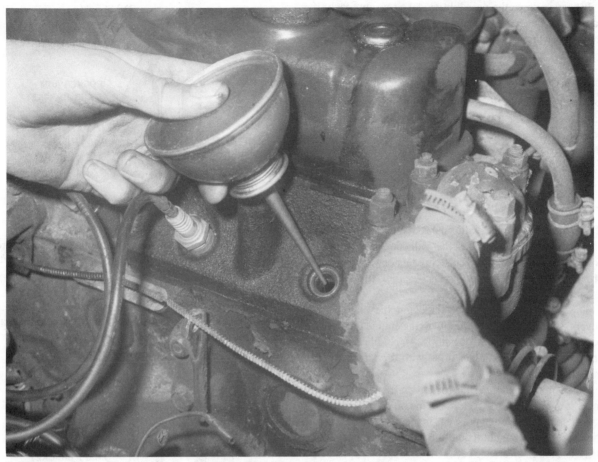

Figure 5-29. Squirt a tablespoon of oil into the cylinder through the spark plug hole, as shown. Even if rings are worn, this will seal the piston temporarily, and if you perform another compression test, the reading should show a significant rise if the rings are the problem.

Figure 5-30. Oil seals (also called shields) are placed over end of valve stem in engine top chamber. The valve spring has been removed for illustrative purposes.

If narrow down the possibilities, take this approach: If compression is acceptable and the engine is an in-line, go straight for the stem seals and valve guides. If the compression is acceptable and the engine is a V-type, go for the possible cause—stem seals or intake manifold gaskets—that is easier to do. If the intake manifold is extremely difficult to remove, do the stem seals first, particularly on a car with 35,000 miles or more on the odometer. At that mileage, there is a reasonably good chance that new stem seals will help, even if the manifold gasket is the major problem.

Pushrod Engines

If you have an engine with pushrods (not an overhead camshaft) you can make a test that will determine if the oil consumption is caused by the stem seals or valve guides, provided the engine is emitting visible smoke through the exhaust.

The procedure consists of removing the engine top covers, shutting off the oil supply to the engine top chamber, and seeing if the smoking stops. An engine can safely be run for about 45 minutes or so with the oil cut off to that chamber.

Here's how: If there is no rocker shaft (that is, if the rockers are on ball-stud pedestals), the oil comes up to the rocker chamber through passages in the pushrods. Loosen the rocker retaining nut (count the number of turns) until there is enough clearance between the rocker and pushrod to insert a little piece of rubber (tire inner-tube thickness) between pushrod and rocker. Tighten down the nut the number of turns you loosened, less two (to compensate for the thickness of the rubber). Do this to all the pushrods and rockers and the oil flow will be stopped.

On Chrysler and some Ford powerplants in rear-drive cars, the rockers are on a shaft that is lubricated through

Figure 5-31. Engine top chamber is lubricated in this design by a passage in the cylinder head. Oil flows up and around the rocker shaft bracket screw shank.

Figure 5-32. To shut off oil flow around the bracket screw shank, insert an O-ring that fits tightly around the shank of the screw, as shown.

Figure 5-33. If oil flows up to rocker shaft through passage, as shown, use a thin shim (about .005 inch) between bracket and cylinder head to shut off the oil flow.

passages in the shaft and in a shaft retaining stand. Remove the rocker-shaft, find the oil supply hole, plug it with a piece of rubber (perhaps a pencil eraser), then reinstall the shaft and tighten the bolts that hold the stand, using a torque wrench, to factory specifications (see figs. 5-31 to 5-33).

Run the engine, and if the smoking stops, the valve guides and/or seals are the problem. Remember to remove the plugs blocking oil flow after the test is completed.

Servicing Stem Seals. You can service valve stem seals by putting special plastic covers (in a low-cost kit called Smoke Stopper, made by Dorman Co. and sold in auto parts stores) over the valve springs (see figs. 5-34 to 5-40). To replace valve stem seals you need a special valve spring compressor that permits compressing the springs

Figure 5-34. Installation of kit begins with removal of valve cover and gaskets, then scraping gasket residue and removing rocker arm assembly. The type shown has the arms on a shaft. On other engines, the rocker arms may be on individual ball-stud pedestals.

Figure 5-35. Clean oil drain holes with a 1/8-inch-thick rod.

Figure 5-36. Place a preslit towel between valve stems to catch excess dirt (vacuum valve chamber with wet-or-dry vacuum if necessary).

Figure 5-37. Clean top of valve retainers with a wire brush as shown. Inspect valve stem tips for signs of mushrooming, and file edge if necessary to restore cylindrical surface.

Figure 5-38. Apply bead of sealant (included in kit) to the top of the valve stem retainers as shown.

Figure 5-39. Install plastic covers into place as shown.

Figure 5-40. Clean rocker arms or rocker arm assembly; then reinstall, following any special instructions included in Smoke Stopper kit.

without removing the cylinder head from the engine. There are many universal designs on the market, most of which are relatively inexpensive.

You also need a method of holding up the valves when you operate the spring compressor. It is possible to do this by stuffing the cylinder with clothes line (through the spark plug hole), but this is a tedious procedure. A better way is to use compressed air through the spark plug hole. Available in most auto parts stores are special adapters (see fig. 5-41) that thread into the spark plug hole and attach to a compressed air line (see fig. 5-42). If you have a paint-spraying compressor or a compressed air tank (an inexpensive item you refill at service stations), you can use the air method.

Figure 5-41. To change stem seals, you must hold up the valves. Remove spark plug and use adapter *at left*, into which you thread a coupler (shown installed); then attach the air line *at right*.

Figure 5-42. With adapter installed and air line connected as shown, compressed air flow will keep the valve up.

Remove the rocker arm shaft of the individual rockers (keep them in order so you can refit them to the places from which they were removed). Thread in the adapter and apply compressed air to hold up the valve.

Note: If you can feel a considerable flow of compressed air escaping through the tailpipe, an exhaust valve is leaking badly; if you can feel the airflow through the carburetor air cleaner, an intake valve is leaking. If engine performance is poor, the engine needs major valve service, a job for a professional.

Follow the instructions with the tool to compress the valve spring (see fig. 5-43). Lift out the two semicircular spring retainer locks (see fig. 5-44). A magnetic tweezers can be used, as shown in figure 5-45. Then carefully release pressure on the spring and remove it.

Note: As with rockers, springs must be refitted to the same place.

Try to rock the valve stem side to side, and if you feel more than just barely perceptible movement, the clearance between the stem and the guide is excessive, and professional service is required. If there is just slight play, the replacement of the stem seals should be sufficient.

When you buy a set of new stem seals, ask the store for the best available, such as the umbrella design or one of the new teflon-and-rubber seals.

Note: If the top of the valve guide has a machined surface, you can install a teflon-and-rubber seal that will retain positively and do a superior job. If it doesn't, you can have a machine shop cut the top of the guide and install this type (see fig. 5-46). However, the cylinder head must be removed for this.

If the seal kit comes with plastic caps, place them on the top of the valve stems, then push the seal onto the stem as far down as it will go (see figs. 5-47 and 5-48). The cap will protect the seal from damage; remove it after the seal is installed. Some seals are very flexible, will not be damaged by the valve stem tip, and no cap is supplied.

Check the valve spring for straightness by placing it against a right angle. If there is more than $1/16$-inch clearance between any coil and the side of the right angle, the spring should be replaced. For balanced performance, change all valve springs.

Position the valve springs (or both springs on some cars) over the stem, then compress. Apply some chassis grease to the half-circle locks, then put them into place on the end of the valve stem (the grease will help keep them in position). Gradually release pressure on the spring, and it will rise, securing the locks to the spring's washer-like retainer.

Repeat this procedure for all valve stems, then refit the

Figure 5-43. With the valve held up, you can use a special valve spring compressor to press down on the spring. The spring compressor shown here is a universal type being used on an overhead camshaft engine. There also are types designed for pushrod engines only; they may be less expensive.

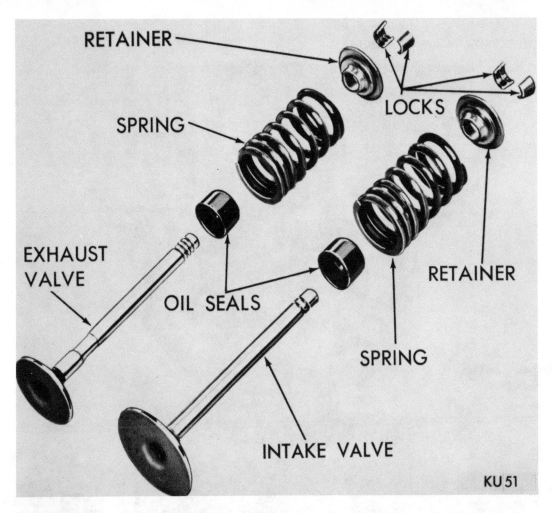

Figure 5-44. Here's an exploded view of the parts. When you press down on the retainer with the compressor, you expose two half-moon locks that fit against the grooves in the top of the valve stem.

Figure 5-45. Top view of a universal valve spring compressor in use, plus magnetic-tip tweezers to withdraw the half-moon locks.

Figure 5-46. If you wish, a machine shop can cut a machined surface on the top of the valve guide as shown, so the guide will accept a premium seal. Or you may be able to rent the tool and do the job yourself. Or even better, your engine may already have the machined surfaces on the guides.

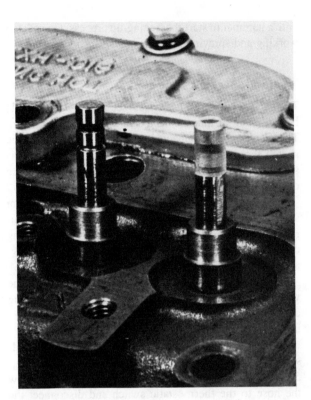

Figure 5-47. A plastic cap installed on valve stems protect new seals.

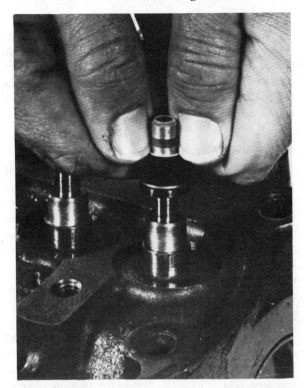

Figure 5-48. A new seal is pushed down over the plastic cap into place on the machined surface of the guide. Then plastic cap is removed and discarded.

rocker shaft and tighten to specifications with a torque wrench, in three relatively even stages (if the specification is 25 lbs.-ft., for example, first tighten all nuts or bolts to about 10, then 20, finally 25). If the rockers are on ball-stud pedestals, tighten to specifications with a torque wrench, unless they are the Ford or Chevrolet adjustable type, in which case you should follow the adjustment procedure described under "Hydraulic Lifter Service," earlier in this chapter.

Overhead Camshaft Engines with Rockers

The basic procedure for overhead camshaft engines with rockers is similar to the pushrod type. First, however, crank the engine until the valve is closed (the cam peak will not be bearing against the valve rocker). Compress the valve spring and remove the rocker, then take out the half-circle retainers and the valve spring, and you'll have access to the seal.

On overhead camshaft engines without rockers, the job requires that the camshaft be removed, so leave it to a professional.

MANIFOLD HEAT CONTROL VALVE SERVICE

As the fuel mixture passes through the carburetor, it enters the intake manifold, a casting with a series of chambers that carries it to the cylinders. When the engine is cold, the fuel in the mixture could condense inside the manifold, and either not get to the cylinders or be improperly distributed to them.

To prevent this, most engines have a provision for heating the intake manifold when the engine is cold. In a few cases, engine coolant runs through passages in the intake manifold, but on many cars there is a device called a manifold heat control valve, or a "heat riser."

The heat riser is actually located in the exhaust manifold. On in-line four- and six-cylinder engines it is a valve that pivots open to allow hot exhaust gas to flow up against the top of the exhaust manifold (the casting that carries the exhaust from the engine to the exhaust system). The top of the exhaust manifold butts up against the bottom of the intake manifold at one point, so the exhaust flow heats the intake manifold.

When the engine is warm the valve closes, stopping the exhaust flow.

On V-type engines there is an exhaust gas passage in the intake manifold (separate from the fuel mixture passages, but close enough to them to transfer heat). In this case, the heat riser opens and exhaust gas is allowed to flow through the intake manifold, warming it up. When the engine is warm, the valve closes and stops the exhaust flow.

There are two types of heat risers, and both should be checked periodically and serviced if necessary. If they stick in the heat-off position, the engine will perform poorly until it warms up. If they stick in the heat-on position, the fuel mixture will be overheated so badly that the engine will starve for fuel, stall out, and have poor high-speed performance.

Valve Locations

The locations of heat risers can vary from car to car, but if you look around the exhaust manifold you should find yours. The one on an in-line engine, if it is used, is always near the point where intake and exhaust manifolds come close together. On a V-type engine you will have to look at the exhaust manifold on each side, and in some cases you will have to jack up the car, support it on safety stands, and look from underneath.

Self-contained Heat Riser

The self-contained heat riser has a thermostatic coil attached (see fig. 5-49). With the engine off and cool, just try to flip it back and forth, holding it at the external counterweight. If it isn't absolutely free in its movement, spray with penetrating solvent, aiming the spray into the joint between the shaft and the bore in the exhaust manifold. If the valve is badly stuck, tap the counterweight

with a hammer to start the freeing-up process. Do not stop working and spraying until the valve flip-flops freely.

Vacuum-operated Type

The vacuum-operated heat riser (see figs. 5-50 and 5-51) has an external link connected to a vacuum diaphragm. The diaphragm is connected by a hose to a thermostatic switch threaded into the engine's water jacket, and this switch has a hose to a source of engine vacuum at the base of the carburetor.

When the engine is cold, the thermostatic vacuum switch is open, and engine vacuum flows from the carburetor base through the switch to the diaphragm, yanking on it. The movement of the diaphragm pulls on the linkage to pivot the valve.

To check this type, start a cold engine as you watch the valve linkage. If it is pulled up, the system is functioning correctly when cold. Recheck when the engine is warmed up; the linkage should not move.

If the linkage fails to move when the engine is cold-started, disconnect the hose from the diaphragm (see fig. 5-52) and feel the end for vacuum. If there is none, follow the hose to the thermostatic switch and disconnect the other end of that hose. Feel for vacuum at the hose neck. None? Disconnect the other hose and feel its end for vacuum. If there is vacuum at this hose but none at the

Figure 5-49. A self-contained manifold heat control valve on a six-cylinder engine.

VACUUM

VACUUM ACTUATOR

SHUT-OFF BLADE

Figure 5-50. This heat riser is controlled by a vacuum actuator (diaphragm unit). The vacuum hose runs to a coolant-temperature-controlled vacuum switch threaded into the engine, and from there to a source of vacuum at the carburetor base or intake manifold. When the coolant is cold, vacuum can pass through the switch to operate the heat riser. When the engine warms up, the coolant temperature switch closes, shutting off the vacuum and allowing a spring in the vacuum actuator to close the shut-off blade.

EXHAUST CROSSOVER

EXHAUST GAS

EXHAUST GAS

VALVE

Figure 5-51. Vacuum-operated-manifold, heat-controlled valve, as actually installed on a V-type engine. In this design, the valve permits exhaust gas flow through a crossover passage in the intake manifold.

Figure 5-52. When pulling off the vacuum hose at the diaphragm unit, feel the end for vacuum when engine is cold and idling.

other hose's neck, replace the thermostatic switch, which is simply unthreaded from the engine with a wrench.

If you find vacuum at the diaphragm hose end, but no diaphragm movement, pull on the diaphragm rod. If it can be pulled (against moderately stiff spring pressure), the diaphragm assembly is defective. Unbolt and replace it. If the rod can't be pulled, the thermostatic valve in the exhaust manifold is sticking. Apply penetrating solvent spray and free it up in the same basic manner as the self-contained type.

If the linkage moves to the heat-on position when you restart a thoroughly warm engine, replace the thermostatic switch.

Electric Heater

On a few carburetor-equipped cars starting in 1981, the heat control valve has been dropped in favor of an electric heater. General Motors builds the heater (a ceramic grid) into the carburetor base gasket. American Motors cars made in 1981 and 1982 have an electric heater that screws into the intake manifold from the underside of the manifold. With both these designs, you should check for current to the electrical connector when the engine is cold and the engine first is started. If you must unplug the electrical connector for any service, be sure to reconnect, or cold-engine operation will be poor.

6 THE DIESEL ENGINE

Figure 6-1. Oldsmobile V-8 diesel, used on many GM cars and some trucks.

HOW IT WORKS

Until fuel supplies became plentiful again in 1983, passenger car diesels were hot sellers. If shortages return as some predict, their popularity could resume. The diesel differs from the gasoline engine in that there is no spark ignition system. Instead, the air/fuel mixture is squeezed even more tightly than in the gasoline engine, building up so much heat that the fuel self-ignites. The compression ratio of a diesel is typically 22:1 or higher, compared with perhaps 8:1 for the gasoline engine today.

As in the gasoline engine, the pistons go up and down in a four-stroke cycle: down on intake, up on compression, down on power, and up on exhaust. During the intake and compression strokes, however, only air is in the cylinder. As the piston approaches the completion of the compression stroke, fuel is sprayed into the cylinder by an injector, and it ignites in the hot air (figs. 6-1 to 6-3).

The diesel engine does not have a throttle plate. When you step on the "gas" pedal, you operate linkage to the pump that supplies fuel to the injectors—one injector for each cylinder. The linkage moves mechanical parts in the pump to increase the amount of fuel injected as the pedal is depressed.

Unlike gasoline, which is rated according to octane, the diesel fuel is rated according to cetane, which is basically the opposite. Octane is resistance to burning (so the gasoline doesn't self-ignite and cause engine knock).

There are two diesel fuels, No. 1 for cold weather, No. 2 for warm. If No. 2 is used in cold weather, it can form wax

224

crystals that can plug fuel lines and prevent fuel flow.

Because the diesel fuel must self-ignite from the heat of compression, starting in cold weather can pose problems because the air entering the engine is cold and there is no spark to get ignition going.

Glow Plugs and Car Battery

All passenger car diesels, therefore, are made with pre-chambers; that is, miniature chambers next to the cylinder that contain glow plugs. It is into these chambers that the fuel is sprayed (see figs. 6-4 and 6-5). The glow plug is a heating element that warms the air so that it will ignite the fuel in cold weather. It takes a lot of current to operate the glow plugs, so in very cold weather when batteries do not perform at their best there is quite a drain on the car battery. Further, it takes a lot more electrical power to crank a diesel because of higher compression. Since the tiny pre-chamber is a lot easier to heat than the complete combustion chamber, it extends the life of the battery besides contributing to smoother performance in the diesel.

The heavy current requirements for cranking and glow

Figure 6-2. The diesel engine cycle. Note that fuel is sprayed into a tiny pre-chamber just above and to the right of the top of the cylinder. This is common design practice for passenger car diesel engines, so that the glow plug, which threads into the pre-chamber, also can be used to ease cold-weather starting.

Figure 6-3. Volkswagen four-cylinder diesel. The gear at the *front right center* is the one that drives the fuel injection pump.

Figure 6-4. When the wiring connector is removed, you can see the end of glow plug projecting from cylinder head.

Figure 6-5. This is a glow plug from a VW diesel, removed from engine.

plugs make it important to be sure the battery terminals are clean and tight, and if the battery is a conventional type, topped off with water.

Note: The early GM diesel V-8s were equipped with two batteries to provide extra current; the VW and later GM diesels have only one battery, but it's a heavy-duty model. If a diesel battery fails, make sure you install a replacement of equal or greater power. In extremely cold climates, install a battery warmer, a device that plugs into household current and keeps the battery at a temperature that will enable it to develop full power. Battery warmers are available at auto parts stores and are easily installed.

Coolant Heaters

Many diesels come with engine coolant heaters as standard or optional equipment to keep the engine warm and help prevent starting problems. If your diesel is not so equipped, install a retrofit kit, available from most auto parts stores. Like the battery warmer, it plugs into household current. Also useful is a fuel heater powered by battery current.

Although the diesel does not have spark plugs, it does require periodic maintenance in addition to battery care. Here are other aspects of diesel maintenance you should know.

Engine Oil and Filter

Use only an oil recommended for diesels. Many gasoline engine oils also are rated for diesel service. Change oil and filter every 3,000 miles or 3 months. The diesel combus-

tion process results in very rapid contamination of engine oil, so the importance of frequent oil change cannot be overemphasized.

Fuel Filter

The diesel fuel injection system is composed of parts made to very precise tolerances. Tiny dirt particles can cause malfunctioning, so fuel filtration is extremely important. The size of the filter used with different diesel engines varies and, therefore, so does the replacement interval. Do not exceed the manufacturer's fuel filter replacement interval. The filter may be a spin-on cannister, serviced much like an engine oil filter (see fig. 6-6), or one with fuel lines threaded on. Use tubing-type open-end wrenches to slacken the fittings on this second type.

Idle Speed

The idle speed adjustment is made to the linkage at the fuel injection pump (see figs. 6-7 and 6-8). Although you simply turn the screw (or slacken the locknut and turn the screw on the VW diesel), there is one problem: You cannot use a standard tachometer because it works off an electric ignition system, and there is none on the diesel. You have these choices:

1. Buy a vibration sensor, which VW sells (see fig. 6-9). It clamps magnetically onto the engine top cover and connects to the car battery and a conventional tachometer. Engine vibration produces a signal proportional to engine speed, and the sensor converts this to an engine speed pulse.

Figure 6-6. Removing spin-on fuel filter from VW diesel.

Figure 6-7. Adjusting idle speed on Olds (GM) diesel. Air cleaner was removed for photograph, but need not be disturbed for adjustment.

Figure 6-8. This is the VW diesel fuel injection pump, with key parts identified. Do not confuse the locknut and adjusting screw for idle speed with the locknut and screw on the other side of pump that is for setting maximum engine speed (necessary only after professional service of the pump). You can tell the idle speed screw by the fact that it touches the accelerator pedal linkage lever when the engine is idling.

Figure 6-9. The VW vibration sensor produces an engine speed signal that works with conventional tachometer.

2. Buy a photoelectric tachometer. Just make a chalk mark on the crankshaft pulley, aim the tachometer at it, and the chalk mark will trigger the tachometer. This probably is the best choice because it also can be used on gasoline engines. In fact, it is one of the few types that will work well on distributorless ignition gasoline engines.

3. Buy an electromagnetic tachometer. The GM diesel has a holder next to the crankshaft pulley, designed for a special probe used to measure ignition timing on the gasoline version of the same engine. The electromagnetic tachometer also comes with a probe (and also measures ignition timing on gasoline engines with the tester). Just shove the probe into the holder and it will read engine speed on the diesel. Although this tachometer is not made for the VW diesel, it also can be used on that engine. The VW engine also is based on a gasoline powerplant, and there is an ignition timing probe hole (at the flywheel end of the engine). You will have to make a bracket to hold the probe in position.

Fuel Stop Solenoid

When you turn the key to shut off a gasoline engine you are cutting off electricity to the ignition system. A diesel, however, doesn't need electricity once it is running, so a special part must be used to stop it—a solenoid (electromagnetic) valve that blocks the fuel flow when you turn off the key (see fig. 6-8).

If that solenoid does not energize when you turn the key to on, the engine won't start. If the solenoid is shorted, the engine won't turn off.

Before you go into any detailed engine inspection for a starting problem, have someone turn the key to on while you feel the solenoid (fig. 6-8), the only part with an electrical connector on the fuel injection pump. If you can't feel or hear a click, and the engine won't start, the odds are the solenoid is defective. It can be unthreaded and replaced without disturbing the injection pump.

If the engine won't shut off, a short circuit in the solenoid wiring is surely the problem. As a temporary measure, disconnect the wire from the solenoid to stop the engine, and disconnect the battery ground cable(s) to prevent battery drain. Reconnect the solenoid wire, then the battery cable when you have to start the engine. Do not try to operate the car this way for longer than is necessary to get the car into a garage for tracing and repair of the short.

Note: Mercedes-Benz diesels have a vacuum-operated shutoff valve. If it fails, however, there is an underhood lever (with the label "Stop") that can be pushed to stop the engine.

Engine Testing

If a diesel starts to misfire, there are three common causes: defective fuel injector, low compression, or water in the fuel.

To test for a defective injector, disconnect the fuel line at the injector, insert a plug, then reconnect the line. Start the engine, and if the engine speed is no different, the plugged injector is the defective one. An injector is either threaded into the pre-chamber (remove with a deep socket) or force-fitted and held with a clamp (remove clamp, then take out injector with a special puller).

Note: This test procedure will detect only an injector that has failed completely. One that is not spraying the correct amount of fuel must be checked on a special tester.

The injector is carefully sealed to prevent loss of compression, and when you take out an injector any seals in the hole or on the injector must be replaced. If you are removing an injector for other engine service, and will be reinstalling it, you also must be particularly careful not to damage the tip.

Whenever you disconnect a fuel line, plug it immediately to keep out dirt.

Compression Testing

It takes a special compression gauge to check a diesel engine, because the higher compression pressures developed are beyond the range of the gasoline engine gauge (500 p.s.i. vs. 250 p.s.i. for the typical gasoline gauge). Further, there is no spark plug hole, so the gauge requires special adapters to thread either into the glow plug holes (GM procedure) or into the injector holes (VW method). If you remove the VW injectors, remember to replace the seal, which can be withdrawn from the injector hole with a magnet (see figs. 6-10 and 6-11).

If a diesel engine compression reading is low, the engine will be hard starting, if it starts at all, and it will perform very poorly.

Water in the Fuel

The problem of water in diesel fuel varies from area to area and service station to service station. All diesels are designed to pass small quantities of water, but substantial amounts can cause both misfire and rusting of fuel injection system components.

Figure 6-10. Using compression gauge with adapter that threads into fuel injector hole (VW). On most other passenger car diesels, the adapter threads into the glow plug hole.

Figure 6-11. After the compression test on VW diesel is complete, remove the seal with magnet as shown.

Different cars have different provisions for the water problem. GM diesels are equipped with a water sensor in the fuel tank that is wired to a dashboard light. Although this system is not on most other cars, it can be retrofitted with a kit available from many parts "jobbers" (parts stores that service professional as well as weekend mechanics). If you have water in the fuel, there's no question about what to do. On early GM diesels, take the car into a service station, put it on a lift and have the water siphoned out of the tank. The basic procedure should be a familiar one to stations that sell diesel fuel (see fig. 6-12). Later GM diesels have a pushbutton water drain arrangement under the hood. Volkswagens have a water drain cock in the base of the fuel filter. Just open the cock and allow the filter to drain until you see no water. Inasmuch as VWs do not have dashboard warning lights, unless you have had one retrofitted, you should periodically open the drain cock in the filter to check.

Figure 6-12. If the dashboard warning light goes on signaling water in the diesel fuel, the tank must be siphoned. Locate the two fuel lines from the tank unit, disconnect the fuel hose from the narrower diameter one, shown in the photo, and attach the siphon to that line.

Figure 6-13. Probing glow plug's master connector, disconnected for check with test lamp. Helper must hold key in test position for this test. Test lamp should light, even for an instant, unless engine is hot.

Checking Glow Plug Circuit

If a diesel engine fails to start only in cold weather, check to see whether current is getting to the glow plugs. Disconnect the wire to a glow plug (see fig. 6-4) or to the master connector if used (see fig. 6-13). Connect a test lamp to the glow plug wire terminal or master connector wire and to ground. Have a helper hold the key in the glow position and the test lamp should light, even if only for an instant.

Note: On most General Motors diesels, a fast-start glow plug system is used, and the current will flow to them for a maximum of 6 seconds (at 0°F). On others, the time ranges from a few seconds at warm temperatures to a maximum of about 60 seconds.

If the test lamp doesn't come on at all, the problem is a defective connection in the circuit up to the glow plugs. You probably will give the job of tracing the wiring problem to a professional, but at least you'll know the basic cause of the starting problem.

7 THE COOLING SYSTEM

HOW IT WORKS

The burning of gasoline (or diesel fuel) in the cylinders produces a tremendous amount of heat, and it is the job of the cooling system to get rid of the excess. On most cars a so-called "water cooling system" is used (see fig. 7-1). A mixture of water and antifreeze—called coolant—is circulated throughout the engine by a pump, called the water pump, and then pushed through a hose (called the upper radiator hose) into the radiator, a finned grouping of tubes that dissipates the heat into the surrounding air.

The coolant at the bottom of the radiator is pulled up into the water pump (through the lower radiator hose), circulated through the engine to pick up heat, and

Figure 7-1 The typical water-type cooling system. Mixture of water and antifreeze is circulated by water pump through engine to pick up heat, then through radiator to dissipate it. The heater core, a miniature radiator, comes into the picture to dissipate heat into the passenger compartment when desired (coolant control valve permits flow when actuated). On many cars the overflow reservoir is used to catch hot coolant that would otherwise be lost.

UPPER RADIATOR HOSE NECK

AIR-CONTROL DOORS

MOTOR

FAN SHROUD

CROSS-FLOW RADIATOR

COOLANT TEMPERATURE SENSOR

THERMOSTATICALLY CONTROLLED POLYPROPYLENE FAN

LOWER RADIATOR HOSE NECK

Figure 7-2. Electric motor drives fan when engine is mounted sideways, as on many front-wheel-drive cars. The coolant temperature sensor in the radiator triggers the motor. The fan shroud directs airflow for maximum fan performance when it is on. The air control doors, a unique feature on this particular design, swing open when the car is moving along at cruise speed, permitting maximum airflow through radiator. In this mode, the coolant temperature may remain low enough to keep fan off, saving power.

235

returned to begin the cycle again.

A fan is used to improve the airflow through the radiator when the car is moving slowly or standing still. On most rear-drive cars the fan is bolted to the front of the water pump, just in back of the radiator, and both pump and fan are turned by a drive belt. Or there may be an electric motor, triggered by a temperature sensor, which operates a fan. This is commonly used if the engine is mounted sideways, as on some front-wheel-drive cars, where it would be difficult to relocate the belt-driven water pump (see fig. 7-2).

The electric fan also is used on some cars where the engine is mounted front-to-rear, because it uses less energy than fully mechanical fans.

HEATER

Not all the heat is dissipated into the atmosphere. During the winter, some of the hot coolant also flows through a small radiator called the heater core. The heater core is located in ductwork in the passenger compartment, along with a small electric fan, called the blower fan. The fan blows air through the core, heating the air, which then flows into the passenger compartment.

THERMOSTAT

The temperature of the coolant is extremely important. If it rises slowly, the engine warms up slowly, and with any real driving experience you know that a cold engine doesn't perform as well as a warm one. The reason is that the engine parts expand with heat and reach optimum size when warm. A warm engine is important for other reasons:

1. When the engine is cold, unburned fuel sneaks past the pistons into the crankcase, diluting the engine oil. When the engine warms up fully, most of these unburned fuel vapors are removed from the oil by the PCV system (see chapter 4). Unless the engine warms up quickly, a car used in short-trip driving may operate with fuel-diluted oil, which is harmful.
2. When the coolant is cold, the heater performance is poor in winter. If the engine runs too hot, that's also harmful, for overheating can cause the engine to stall, and may cause engine damage.

The thermostat has the job of both speeding engine warmup and helping to maintain coolant temperature. It's a little temperature-sensitive valve placed in the top of the engine just beneath the upper radiator hose. It is closed when the engine is cold, so that coolant flow is limited to the engine, where the coolant gets hot rather quickly (see fig. 7-3). When the engine reaches operating temperature, usually 180° to 205° F, the thermostat opens (see fig. 7-4) and allows the coolant to flow through the upper hose into the radiator (see figs. 7-5 and 7-6).

Figure 7-3. With the thermostat closed, coolant flow is limited to the engine, so coolant gets hot quickly.

Figure 7-4. When coolant reaches operating temperature, the thermostat opens.

Figure 7-5. With the thermostat open, coolant flows through upper radiator hose into radiator, then is drawn back into engine through lower radiator hose.

Figure 7-6. Circulation of coolant through engine and radiator is shown. Spinning fan draws air through radiator, coolant dissipates heat through radiator tubes and fins into air.

PRESSURE CAP

Generally, the thermostat can open and close as necessary to maintain temperature in cold weather, although if it's very cold and the engine design is such that it runs cool anyway, it may not. In this case, an ever-so-slight thermostat opening results in a cold-running engine and poor heater performance. In this instance, it may be necessary to put a piece of cardboard in front of the radiator or air conditioning condenser to raise coolant temperatures.

In the summer buildup may be so great that even a wide open thermostat may not prevent the coolant temperature from exceeding 205° F. In fact, on some cars it is not uncommon for temperatures to approach or exceed 250° F in hot weather in heavy traffic. This is particularly true if the air conditioner is on, for the air conditioner rejects the heat it absorbs through a condenser, which is located in front of the radiator on most cars. The double dose of heat (from AC and radiator) reduces the effectiveness of both.

Therefore, the engine must be able to run at very high temperatures without boiling the coolant. The pressure cap is an important contributor to this capability.

The cap contains a spring-loaded valve that limits hot coolant expansion, so pressure is built up in the system.

Coolant under pressure has a higher boiling point, about 2.6° F for each pound of pressure. The typical cap's valve will hold up to 16 p.s.i. before the coolant pressure forces it open. Boiling point of the coolant is raised some 40° F, from 212° to 252° F.

A further improvement in boiling point is provided by antifreeze, which is now required as a year-round coolant. If you have a 50:50 mixture of water and antifreeze, the boiling point is raised about an additional 13° F. With a 70:30 mixture of antifreeze and water (the maximum recommended), the boiling point is raised from 212° to 238° F. Combine these increases with that provided by the pressure cap, and the system may operate at 265° to 278° F without boiling. Never exceed 70 percent antifreeze concentration.

OVERFLOW RESERVOIR

Under severe conditions, or if something is wrong in the system, the coolant may boil, push open the radiator cap valve, and escape. In most late-model cars, it does not flow to the ground, but into a catchpot called an overflow reservoir (see figs. 7-1 and 7-7).

When the engine and coolant cool off, the coolant

Figure 7-7. Close-up look at the coolant overflow system. When coolant gets hot it expands, pushing open the pressure valve in the radiator cap. Coolant flows into recovery bottle (reservoir) and when the engine cools down, coolant contracts. Vacuum in cooling system then draws coolant from reservoir back into radiator to automatically top it off again.

Dodge

RADIATOR PRESSURE CAP

RADIATOR

OVERFLOW

COOLANT RECOVERY BOTTLE

contracts, creating an empty space in the top of the radiator. This empty space is not filled with air, so it is a vacuum. With the conventional system (no overflow reservoir), a second valve in the radiator cap opens and admits air. With an overflow reservoir, air cannot normally enter. Instead, the vacuum draws in coolant from the reservoir and the radiator is automatically topped off once more.

OTHER CONNECTIONS

On some cars the cooling system serves additional functions. By running hoses (usually joined into the heater hose connections), coolant can be used to warm up the carburetor's automatic choke, to warm the air-fuel mixture in the engine's intake manifold, and to cool exhaust gases before they are used for the exhaust gas recirculation system (see "Pollution Controls," chapter 1).

COOLANT SYSTEM SERVICE

To minimize the chance of overheating in summer or freezeup and poor heater performance in cold weather, you should give your cooling system annual service. This consists of checking the radiator cap, hoses, hose connections, drive belt, radiator and fan, and changing the antifreeze.

Changing the Antifreeze

Remove the radiator cap (press down and twist counterclockwise until you come to a stop, then press down again and twist some more). If the coolant is dirty, the system should be cleaned. Pour in a container of cooling system chemical, flush, and drive the car per the instructions given.

Next, flush out the system. There are many ways this can be done (see figs. 7-8 to 7-10), but the simplest is with a flushing tee kit, available at a very low price from almost any auto supply store or discount house auto department. The tee, which is installed in the heater inlet hose, accepts a connection from a garden hose, and turns cooling system flushing into a five-minute job.

First, locate the heater inlet hose, which is the one connected to the top of the engine, not to the water pump (watch out, for on some engines the inlet hose connection is very close to the water pump). Just cut the hose at some convenient point, push the necks of the tee into each cut end, then secure with the hose clamps provided (see figs. 7-11 and 7-12).

Figure 7-8. Here's the first step in a system flushing procedure that can be performed without special tools or a flushing tee kit. Just remove radiator cap and open petcock (see fig. 7-16) or remove drain plug at bottom of radiator. Collect draining coolant in bucket and look at it. If it's very dirty, this flushing procedure should be discontinued, for it is too mild. Instead, use the flushing tee method described in this chapter. If coolant is not extremely dirty, continue with this method.

HEATER-HIGH

REPLACE CAP

CLOSE

Figure 7-9. Close petcock or refit drain plug and fill the system with water through the radiator fill neck. Reinstall the radiator cap (making sure it's on all the way). Start engine, turn heater control to maximum, and drive the car for 7 to 10 miles. Stop the engine.

Figure 7-10. Remove the radiator cap, open the petcock (or remove drain plug) and allow the radiator to drain once more. Then repeat the step shown in fig. 7-9. If you do this four times, 94 percent of the old coolant will be removed; five times, and 97 percent of the old coolant will be removed.

OPEN CAP

COOLANT

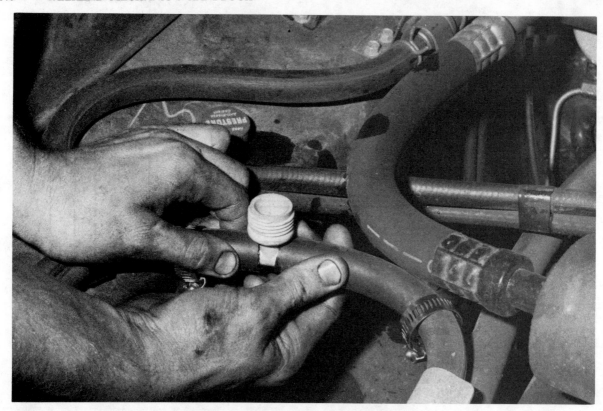

Figure 7-11. Install flushing tee in heater inlet hose, which has been cut in two with a razor blade.

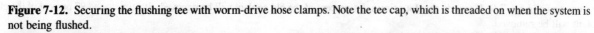

Figure 7-12. Securing the flushing tee with worm-drive hose clamps. Note the tee cap, which is threaded on when the system is not being flushed.

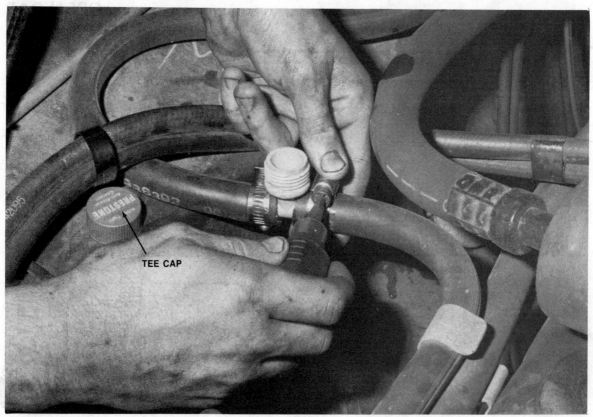

TEE CAP

Connect the garden hose, using the double-female adapter provided (see fig. 7-13). Remove the radiator cap and press the water deflector into place, then aim it forward (see fig. 7-14). Start the engine, turn the heater to high, then open the water bibcock. The water will flow through the tee into the heater inlet hose, through the heater, into the engine, through the lower radiator hose, and up the radiator and out (see fig. 7-15). When the water runs clean for two minutes, shut the engine and the water bibcock.

Note: If the radiator is a crossflow (tubes run horizontally) as on most U.S. late models, leave the radiator cap in place. Disconnect the upper radiator hose from the engine and aim it away from the engine and fan. Water will run out of this hose, and when it runs clean for two minutes, shut the engine and bibcock.

Figure 7-13. Connecting garden hose to tee, using double-female adapter supplied with tee kit.

Figure 7-14. Water deflector pressed into radiator cap neck and aimed forward.

HEATER INLET HOSE

DEFLECTOR HOSE

THERMOSTAT IN PLACE SPECIAL TEE

HEATER

RADIATOR

HEATER-OUTLET HOSE TO PUMP

BLOCK

TEMPERATURE CONTROL

WATER PUMP

FLOW DIAGRAM

Figure 7-15. Illustration shows how water from hose flows through tee and heater hose, into engine and heater core, then up radiator and out the fill neck through the deflector.

ANTIFREEZE REQUIREMENTS

Check manufacturer's specifications, usually in your owner's manual, for cooling system capacity. Fifty to 70 percent of that number should be antifreeze. Example: If capacity is 16 quarts, minimum is 8 quarts of antifreeze, and maximum is 11 quarts.

If a 70 percent concentration of antifreeze is exceeded, the boiling point of the coolant starts to rise, the engine runs hotter, and may suffer from knock. This can happen if one merely drains the radiator and adds a couple of gallons of antifreeze every year. As the concentration rises, the freeze point comes up. When there's virtually all antifreeze in the system, the freeze point is only $-8°$ to $-10°$ F.

ADDING ANTIFREEZE

After flushing, the system is filled with water. The typical radiator has a drain cock (see fig. 7-16) or drain plug at the bottom, so begin by draining the radiator. If there is no plug or cock, you must disconnect the lower radiator hose.

On the typical car, only 25 to 40 percent of the coolant will drain out from the radiator. Since a 50 to 70 percent concentration of antifreeze is desirable, just filling the radiator normally is not enough. There are several possible solutions.

Drain Plugs. Most engines have drain plugs threaded into the block. If you can find and remove these plugs, the block will drain. Unfortunately, they usually are rust-frozen in place.

Further, in many cases the design of the system is such that once drained, it is difficult to refill completely because air pockets form. In these cases, the actual coolant content may be low enough to cause overheating and poor heater performance at the same time. Most systems self-bleed the air, so if you check the coolant level after every period of engine operation and add coolant as possible, you should be able to top it off completely in

Figure 7-16. Photo shows drain petcock at bottom of a typical radiator. Turn counterclockwise (grasping by ears with pliers if necessary) to open.

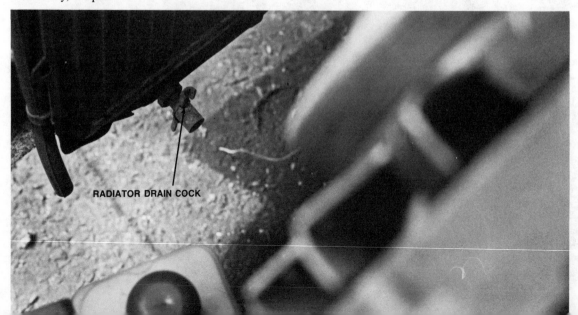

RADIATOR DRAIN COCK

short order. Or if the system has an overflow reservoir, it should be able to suck coolant from it to eventually top off. There are significant exceptions, however, including the Pontiac Fiero and some other GM cars with 2.5-liter, 4-cylinder engines; pre-1987 Ford products with 2.8-liter, V-6 engines; 1987 Ford Taurus and Sable with 2.5-liter, 4-cylinder engines; Chrysler products with 2.2- and 2.5-liter, 4-cylinder engines; Volkswagen Rabbit; and a host of European and Japanese cars. If you wish to drain

the cooling systems on these cars, you must know how to bleed or fill them. Examples follow:

GM Cars 2.5-liter, 4-cylinder engines with special thermostat housing. Remove the cap from the special thermostat housing on the engine (see figs. 7-17 and 7-18) and reach in and pull out the thermostat. Then pour coolant in through the opening. In addition, there is a time-consuming bleeding procedure for the Fiero.

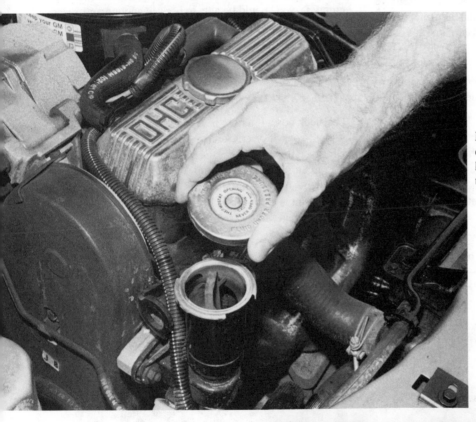

Figure 7-17. On GM 2.5-liter, 4-cylinder engines with the special thermostatic housing, just take off the cap for access to the thermostat.

Figure 7-18. Pull out the thermostat as shown, and fill the system through the opening. Inspect the thermostat O-ring for damage and replace if necessary.

Volkswagen Rabbit. Jack up the front of the car so the radiator is highest, and air will bleed out. This approach can be helpful on many cars where the radiator or other location of the fill neck is not the highest point in the cooling system.

Ford 2.8-liter, V-6 engine. Disconnect upper hose from radiator and pour coolant into engine through hose.

Taurus and Sable 2.5-liter, 4-cylinder engines. Open bleed valve on engine. Many Japanese and European cars also have bleed valves.

Chrysler 2.2- and 2.5-liter, 4-cylinder engines. Remove air bleed plug from top of thermostat housing before pouring coolant into radiator. Fill until coolant runs out of air and bleed plug hole.

Look carefully. You may find a cooling system air bleed on an increasing number of cars. In 1988, some applications of the GM 2.8-liter V-6, plus the Premier 3.0-liter V-6, joined the list.

Running the Engine. Disconnect the heater outlet hose (the one to the water pump) and plug the hose neck on the water pump with a cork or rubber plug. Run the engine (heater on high). Water will flow from the hose and you will be able to pour in additional antifreeze to fill the system.

Flushing Tee. If you have a flushing tee, just leave it uncapped with the engine running and the heater on high, and some water will flow out.

Note: With either of the previous two methods, some antifreeze may mix with the water and flow out too, but the amount lost should be small. As soon as you have all the antifreeze in, stop the engine and cap the tee. Or remove the plug and reconnect the heater hose immediately.

Overflow Reservoir. If you have an overflow reservoir, empty it; you should be able to pour in enough antifreeze to do the job. In time, the antifreeze in the reservoir will mix with the water in the engine.

HOSES AND CONNECTIONS

Feel each hose. If a hose is very soft, unusually hard, or if it is oil-soaked or cracked by heat, it should be replaced. One hose that should be given a *very* careful inspection is the radiator bypass hose, a little one used on many cars. It permits coolant to circulate through the engine when the thermostat is closed, and because of its location it is very prone to heat failure (see fig. 7-19).

Figure 7-19. Radiator bypass hose on engine. This little hose is subject to high engine-compartment heat, so it is prone to failure.

RADIATOR BYPASS HOSE

Replacing a Hose

To replace a radiator hose, begin by removing the hose clamp (see figs. 7-20 and 7-21). If the clamp is corroded and won't loosen, cut it apart with a circular saw on a small hobby grinder (being careful not to cut through the hose into the hose neck).

Caution: Don't try to pry the clamp apart with a screwdriver against the radiator hose neck, for you might dam-age the neck and face an expensive repair. If necessary, cut the hose off at the neck, make longitudinal slits around the circumference of the hose remainder (on both sides of the clamp), and pull the cut sections out (they normally will tear through under the clamp). Soon you'll have clearance to remove the clamp.

Note: If you have spring clamps, obtain hose clamp pliers to compress them.

Wire-brush rust and dirt from the hose neck (see fig.

Figure 7-20. Loosening retaining screw on band-type hose clamp.

Figure 7-21. Once hose clamp, regardless of type, is loosened and out of the way, gently pry between hose and neck with screwdriver to free up hose.

Figure 7-22. Wire-brushing hose neck to remove rust, corrosion, and dirt is necessary.

7-22) and then fit the new hose into place. Install worm-drive hose clamps (which can be installed with the hose already in place). These tighten with a screwdriver and will be easy to remove, even years later. Center the clamp on the hose section that is on the neck.

Radiator Bypass Hose

Replacing a radiator bypass hose (see fig. 7-23) is a similar operation, except that the hose may be physically difficult to install because of tight quarters. To reduce future replacements, obtain a premium hose made of silicone rubber. It should last the life of the car.

Heater Hoses

On most cars the heater hoses are readily accessible at both ends. If they are not accessible at the heater end (because the heater core is hidden in underdash ductwork), a simple solution is to feel the entire length of each hose. You usually will find that the hose is in good condition until it is close to the engine. Just cut the damaged section off and use a flushing tee as a connector between

the good, old section and a brand-new section to the engine.

OVERHEATING

Any engine will overheat in severe enough conditions, such as heavy traffic operation or operating a heavily loaded car in mountainous or hilly areas, particularly with the AC on.

Top off the radiator with coolant as required, then check the problem when you're home. If the overheating occurs under milder conditions, and the system has recently been flushed and filled with enough antifreeze, the system should be checked.

Caution: When you overheat, let the engine cool before removing the radiator cap.

Leaks. If there are any obvious leaks, they must be corrected. Look hard. You might find something as simple as a loose hose connection.

Radiator. Is the front of the radiator obstructed by leaves, bugs, dirt, or other debris? Clean it off with a soap or

Figure 7-23. Removing a bypass hose. Note that this particular hose was held by a spring clamp.

Figure 7-24. Pen points to outer gasket of radiator cap on car with overflow reservoir. If outer gasket is deteriorated, air may be drawn in, instead of coolant from reservoir, when the engine cools down.

detergent-water solution and a soft brush if necessary. On AC-equipped cars, check the front of the AC condenser, the radiator-like part in front of the radiator.

Could the coolant level have been low? Even a healthy cooling system loses some coolant, and if you neglect it the level will drop. If the system has an overflow reservoir, it should automatically top off when it cools. If it doesn't, the problem is a defective gasket in the radiator cap that allows air to leak in instead of coolant being sucked in (see fig. 7-24). Replace the cap.

Could the antifreeze protection level have dropped severely? If you have been topping off with water for some time, the dilution of the antifreeze lowers the concentration and the boiling point. Obtain an inexpensive hydrometer and check the freeze protection (see fig. 7-25). If the freeze protection is very low (above 10° F), the boil-over protection also is cut, so that in moderately severe operation overheating can result.

Perhaps the radiator is plugged.

If a car overheats in highway operation but not in low-

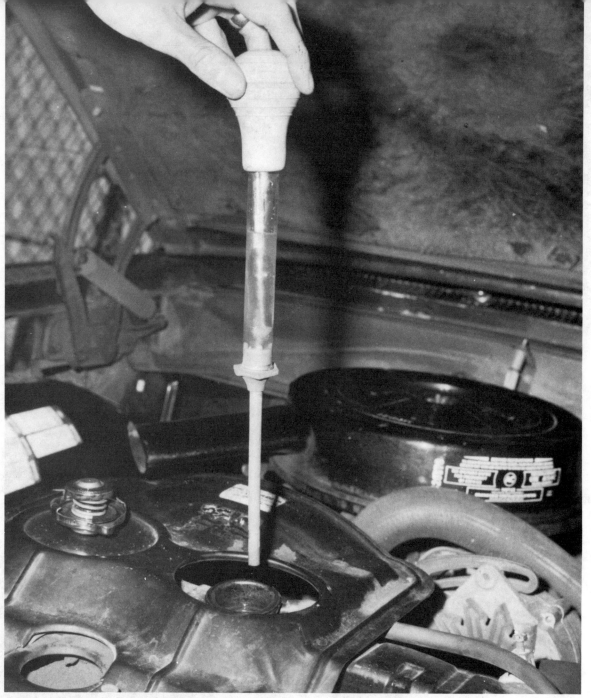

Figure 7-25. Checking antifreeze protection level with hydrometer. Small sample is drawn into tool with syringe top. Marked float indicates protection level at the surface of the coolant.

speed use, a plugged radiator is indicated. You may be able to look in through the radiator or hose necks and see if the ends of the tubes are covered with white corrosion. Or take out the radiator and have a radiator shop test it for proper coolant flow rate. The shop also can clean it out if necessary. Or if you do see the white corrosion, clean it out with a special premium cleaner designed for the purpose and sold in auto parts stores.

Removing the radiator is an obvious job on most cars. Disconnect the radiator hoses—the automatic transmission cooler lines on cars so equipped, the shroud if used. On transverse engine cars, also remove the electric fan assembly. Take out the nuts or bolts that hold the radiator at the top, and lift it out.

Thermostat. If the thermostat is stuck closed, the engine normally will overheat very quickly, perhaps in the first mile or so of driving on a hot day. Remove the thermostat as follows:

1. Drain the radiator into a pan (if the coolant is clean and suitable for re-use).
2. Remove the bolts or nuts holding the thermostat housing, the part to which the upper radiator hose connects on the engine (see fig. 7-26).

248

Figure 7-26. Removing the bolts that hold thermostat housing to engine. Although upper radiator hose has been removed, this normally is not necessary unless hose is being replaced too.

Figure 7-27. Thermostat housing is lifted off, and there's the thermostat underneath. Just lift it up and out after noting its position for correct installation of the existing stat or a replacement. *Note:* On some engines the thermostat is in a housing itself.

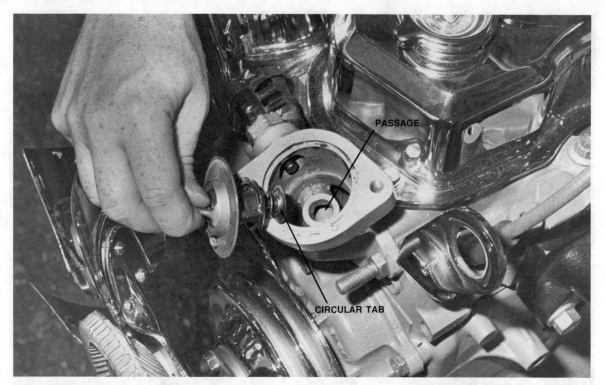

Figure 7-28. This thermostat has a circular tab projecting from the bottom to seal off the water passage in the center. When replacing this thermostat, be sure the new one also has the tab to close off a passage to the coolant-heated intake manifold. If the passage is not closed off in very hot weather, the fuel mixture in the intake manifold will be overheated, and poor engine performance will result.

Note: On some VW or Audi models, the thermostat is accessible after removing a lower radiator hose housing from the bottom of the water pump. On some cars, such as the Ford Escort/Lynx, the thermostat must be twisted out to remove, and in to install. If the thermostat alignment in its housing and duplicate (or in some cases a water passage) will not line up properly, overheating results.

3. Lift up the thermostat housing and remove the thermostat. Note which way it faces so you can reinstall correctly (see fig. 7-27 and 7-28).

4. Suspend the thermostat in a pot of water on a stove, holding it with a piece of wire. When the water starts to boil, the thermostat should be open. If you're not sure what part is moving on the thermostat, douse it with cold water and see if anything moves. Whatever moves should also move the opposite way when the thermostat is in the hot water. If nothing happens, the thermostat is stuck and should be replaced.

Some thermostats have an accessible valve. Wedge a .002-inch or thinner feeler gauge between valve and seat (see fig. 7-29) and suspend the stat by the feeler gauge in the pot of water. When the valve opens, the stat will drop off the end of the feeler. Just read the temperature at which this occurs. This is a more precise test, and you can compare the temperature with

the temperature stamped on the thermostat itself (you may have to convert the number, as many thermostats are stamped with metric Celsius temperatures).

5. With a putty knife, scrape off gasket residue from the engine and/or thermostat housing mating surface. Put the new gasket in place, then install the thermostat (new or old as required), and refit the thermostat housing and the bolts or nuts. Tighten the nuts or bolts gradually in a crisscross fashion.

On those GM 2.5-liter, 4-cylinder engines with the special thermostat housing, just remove the cap and pull out the thermostat. Never take off the housing unless it is necessary for another reason, as it distorts during installation at the factory and is unlikely to seal properly during reinstallation. If you must take it off, you will have to buy a new thermostat housing made specifically for service.

Radiator Cap. If the cap fails to hold pressure, coolant will flow out. With an overflow reservoir it won't be lost, but the coolant level of a hot engine could drop so low that the engine still will overheat.

The cap may not hold pressure for one of two reasons:

1. There is dirt or rust in the radiator neck, on the surface against which the cap's rubber seal seats. Clean the neck with a rag (see fig. 7-30).

Figure 7-29. The thermostat should drop off the feeler gauge when water reaches the temperature stamped on the thermostat housing.

Figure 7-30. Cleaning radiator fill neck. Any dirt, rust, etc. on the sealing surface inside (about an inch or so from the top of the neck) can prevent the radiator cap from seating properly.

2. The cap's valve is malfunctioning. Have a shop pressure-test it for you or obtain a low-cost weekend mechanic's pressure tester, which connects to the overflow tube on the radiator (see fig. 7-31). A defective cap is one of the most common causes of coolant loss and overheating.

Drive Belt. A loose drive belt causes poor water pump and fan operation. Press down on the belt midway between water pump–fan and alternator pulleys, and if it deflects more than ¾ inch it should be adjusted as explained later in this chapter.

Fan. Watch a mechanical fan (the type bolted to the engine) spin as you view the engine from the side. If it seems to wobble, the fan, or the pulley on which it is mounted, is apparently defective. On cars with clutch fans (see fig. 7-32) try to spin the fan by hand. If it spins freely (five or more revolutions with a single, forceful flip) it should be replaced. You may, after you have some experience, be able to replace it yourself.

Other Causes. There are many other causes of overheating, such as internal engine leakage and defective water pump. If the problem is not traced to something covered in this chapter, it probably is a job for a professional.

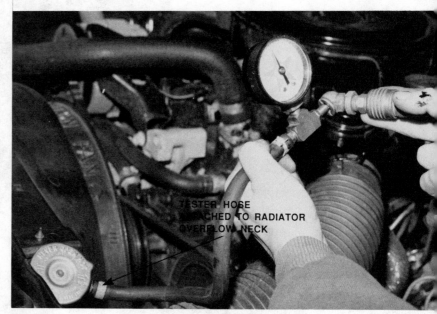

COMPRESSED AIR SUPPLY HOSE

TESTER HOSE ATTACHED TO RADIATOR OVERFLOW NECK

Figure 7-31. A. *At left* is professional-type pressure tester being used to check cap. B. *At right* is low-cost weekend mechanic's pressure tester, being used to test both a cap and the radiator.

Figure 7-32. The finned circular disc in front of fan is the fan clutch.

DRIVE BELT SERVICE

The typical engine may have as many as four drive belts wrapped around the pulleys of different accessories at the front of the engine. Belts drive the alternator, water pump–fan, power steering pump, antipollution air pump, and air conditioning compressor.

The problem is obvious if a belt snaps. In many cases, however, the belt is deteriorated from use, poor adjustment, or oil and road film splashed onto it.

To check a belt, look for oil soaking (if you find it, replace the belt). Twist the belt over on its side and look for glazing or cracks in the sidewall. If you find any, replace the belt. It's a lot easier to replace a belt at home than on the road. If a belt is an inner one (meaning other belts must come off first), home is the only place to be.

The ribbed belt is in wider use. On this type, look for missing sections of ribbed area ½ inch or longer, and replace the belt if found.

Removing a Belt

To remove a belt you must release tension on it, and there are many ways a belt may be tensioned.

The simplest and most common is that one of the accessories around which it wraps has a bolt passing through an elongated slot in a bracket (see fig. 7-33). Just slacken this bolt and one other mounting bolt, push the accessory in toward the engine to remove tension by using a pry bar, and then take off the belt.

Figure 7-33. The most common drive-belt adjustment is as shown at this alternator. You slacken two bolts or nuts, one of which passes through the elongated slot, then apply and hold tension with pry bar as shown, while tightening bolt also as shown. Complete job by tightening the accessory's other mounting bolt.

The belt may be tensioned by a jackscrew (see fig. 7-34) or stud adjuster (see fig. 7-35). Loosen the lock-bolt(s) on the jackscrew adjuster, then turn the jackscrew; or loosen the locknuts on the stud adjuster, then turn the stud nut until the belt is loose enough for removal.

On VW Beetles, the generator pulley is actually a two-piece design. Place a screwdriver in the slot in the pulley to brace it, and remove the pulley nut with a wrench. Pull off the pulley's outer half, and the belt can be easily removed (see figs. 7-36 and 7-37).

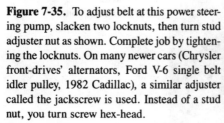

Figure 7-34. This screw-type belt adjuster, similar to the stud adjuster used on Ford power steering pumps (Fig. 7-35), is found on Chrysler 1981 front-wheel-drive cars, including Omni-Horizon. Just loosen the lockbolt and turn the adjusting screw.

Figure 7-35. To adjust belt at this power steering pump, slacken two locknuts, then turn stud adjuster nut as shown. Complete job by tightening the locknuts. On many newer cars (Chrysler front-drives' alternators, Ford V-6 single belt idler pulley, 1982 Cadillac), a similar adjuster called the jackscrew is used. Instead of a stud nut, you turn screw hex-head.

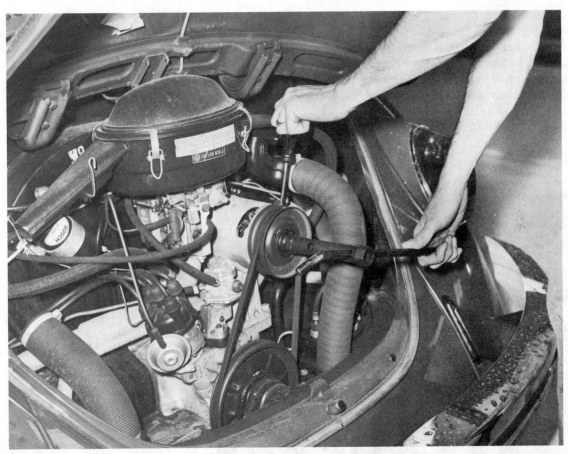

Figure 7-36. VW Beetle uses the split pulley arrangement. Install screwdriver in pulley slot to hold pulley, then use wrench to remove pulley nut.

Figure 7-37. After removing nut, take off washer as shown, then pull off the outer half of the pulley. Tension is adjusted by installing or removing washers between the pulley halves. Spare washers are stored as shown.

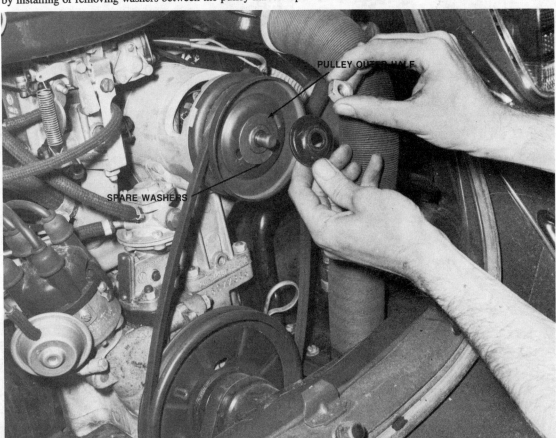

There may be an idler pulley. This is a pulley that does nothing but guide the belt and is adjustable to control tension. The idler pulley is commonly held by a locknut, and when the locknut is loosened you can pivot the pulley to adjust the tension (see fig. 7-38). Often there is a hex or a partial hex surface on the pulley stud, so that you can put a wrench on it to move the pulley to remove tension so it is possible to take off the belt. The wrench also is used as a

tensioning lever for tightening the new belt. Or the accessory bracket may have a square hole for a ratchet drive, so you can use the racket as a pry bar (see fig. 7-39).

With the one-belt, spring-loaded idler pulley there is just the special ribbed belt. Use a pry bar on the spring lever to release tension (see fig. 7-40); or use a ratchet, a square hole, or a ratchet with a socket on the spring lever or on the pulley to release tension.

Figure 7-38. Shown is Chrysler 2.2-liter, 4-cylinder. To adjust idler pulley (for air conditioning belt), loosen lockbolt in slot and pivot bolt, apply force with ratchet and socket on welded hex, and when tension is right, tighten lockbolt.

Figure 7-39. Square hole in power steering bracket accepts square drive from ratchet for belt tensioning.

INSERT PRY BAR HERE

Figure 7-40. Single belt wraps around all accessories on this Ford engine. Insert pry bar into spring tang and yank to release tension on belt. Note that most pulleys are grooved to mate with ribs on one side of belt. Some Olds-built GM diesels also have this self-tensioning spring.

Belt Selection

When you buy a new belt, be very careful to get the right one. If your belt has cogs (see fig. 7-41) or ribs, the replacement also must have them. Also, the width of the belt must duplicate the original. If you get a belt that's too wide, it will not fit completely into the V-groove of the pulley. Inasmuch as the V-belt transfers power from its sides to the sides of the pulley, this contact is extremely important. If you get a belt that's too narrow, it will fit all the way down into the pulley, make poor side-to-side contact, and the bottom of the belt may be damaged by contact with the V-groove.

In most cases, you will be asking the counterman at a parts store for the new belt. Because of performance problems that could result from the incorrect belt, double-check his selection for width and type. If your belt is snapped, you can't check overall circumference, but if it isn't, you can make an approximate comparison. The new belt should be no larger and preferably slightly smaller in circumference (the old belt may be larger because it has stretched in use). If you can't get the right belt, don't settle for one that the counterman "thinks" may do the job. Shop around and get what you need.

Emergency Belt

If you have an emergency situation, a special belt kit is available as a temporary replacement. You just wrap it around the pulleys, cut it to size, then attach the cut ends with a special crimp-together fitting.

Installing the Belt

Make sure the belt is neatly fitted into all the appropriate pulley grooves. On many engines it is all too easy to put a belt into a wrong pulley, particularly on the front of the crankshaft, which may have several pulley grooves.

Draw the belt tight with your hand at the adjustable pulley; then, if possible, slip the belt onto the adjustable pulley by hand. Can't do it? Try slipping a large screwdriver under the belt and very gently prying it over the pulley edge into the groove.

Don't pry hard, or belt damage can result. Push in harder on the accessory, or try another brand of belt (belts are "compromises" to fit as many cars as possible, and in addition there are tolerances in belt length).

If the belt is twisted, you can align it without dislodging it from the groove. Once you have some general automo-

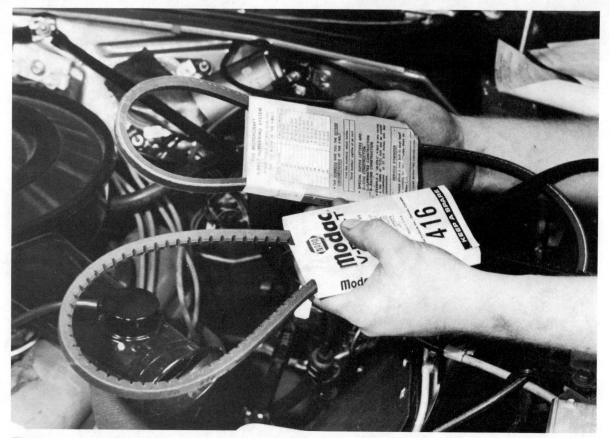

Figure 7-41. Some belts have cogs. The cogs help the belt operate at sharp angles, so if the original is cogged, the replacement should be too.

tive experience, you can crank the engine in very short bursts with the screwdriver under the belt and braced on the pulley edge. The belt will literally jump onto the pulley if you do it right.

Caution: This technique takes "touch." The ignition system must be disconnected (see chapter 2) to prevent the engine from starting, and the cranking bursts must be very brief.

Note: These instructions do not apply to the VW Beetle or to one-belt systems. See pages 260 and 261 for instructions for installing and tensioning the belt for the VW Beetle and one-belt systems.

Tensioning the Belt

Once the belt is on all pulleys it must be adjusted for correct tension. The most accurate way to measure tension is with a special gauge that hooks on the belt as shown or rests on the top surface (see fig. 7-42). The gauge may be used both while setting tension or for post-adjustment checks.

With the elongated slot adjustment, exert force on the accessory to pivot it outward to apply tension, then tighten the nut or bolt to secure the adjustment. Finally, tighten the other accessory mounting bolt.

Important note: How you exert force is extremely important. If the part is stamped steel or aluminum with fins, use of a pry bar may cause damage. On most power steering pumps, for example, there is a special pry bracket with a square hole (see fig. 7-39) so you can insert a ratchet with a long handle (or a pipe over the shank to extend the working length). Just insert the square drive end of the ratchet into the hole and gently pull on the wrench handle to tension the belt.

If the ratchet will not fit into the working area, check with an auto supply store to see if you can get a special thin bar with a square drive for belt adjustment. Or see if you can reach the square hole (or a hex-head as in fig. 7-43) from the rear, using a long extension rod with the ratchet.

On some cars there is a hole in the accessory's mounting bracket (see fig. 7-44) for a pry bar. By inserting it in the hole provided, you are sure of prying against a safe location.

If there is no provision, and you are concerned, you can obtain a special strap wrench that locks safely around the

Figure 7-42. Belt tension gauge hooks onto belt to measure tension. The reading is compared with factory specifications. Shown are two belt tension gauges. At left is a standard type that may be a tight fit in some engine compartments. At right is a compact gauge, which is much less expensive.

Figure 7-43. The hex-head on back side of power steering pump bracket accepts a socket. A wrench (in this case a torque wrench) with a long extension permits the socket to reach the hex-head. For this particular adjustment, the car manufacturer provides torque specifications—hence the use of the torque wrench—in addition to belt tension specifications.

Figure 7-44. The finger points to hole in alternator bracket. Insert pry bar in this hole and it will be positioned correctly for tensioning belt.

accessory, so you can pull on the wrench shank to apply tension.

Idler Pulley. If there is an idler pulley adjustment there is some method provided for moving the pulley, usually with a wrench on the pulley's stud shaft.

VW Beetle Belt Adjustment

With the VW Beetle, just slip the belt around the crankshaft pulley (and the AC compressor if installed), holding it up to the pulley half remaining on the generator. Adjusting belt tension is a cut-and-try operation, and it is done simultaneously with the reinstallation of the outer pulley half. You must select a number of washers (extras are stored on the generator armature shaft, held in place by the pulley nut against the outside face of the outer pulley half).

A practical approach is to use the number of washers you found between the pulley halves as a starting point. Assemble the pulley, store the extra washers on the shaft, then thread on the nut. Put the screwdriver in place to brace the pulley and then tighten the nut with a wrench. Check belt deflection by pressing down with a finger midway between generator and crankshaft pulley (see fig.

7-45), and if it is more than a half-inch, remove a washer or two, reassemble, and check belt deflection again. Removing washers from between the pulley halves reduces the distance between them and causes the belt to ride higher in the groove, increasing tension. If tension is too great (little or no deflection), or if you can't assemble and tighten the pulley halves, insert washers between them to reduce tension.

Note: Some VW Rabbit (and other European designs) have air conditioning compressors that use a similar arrangement. That is, the pulley comes apart and shims are moved.

Retightening

All drive belts stretch in use. Most of the belt stretch occurs in the first 15 to 20 minutes of operation, so after a brief test drive be sure to recheck tension and readjust if necessary.

One-belt Systems

With the one-belt system, the spring-loaded idler pulley automatically sets and maintains correct tension. Once

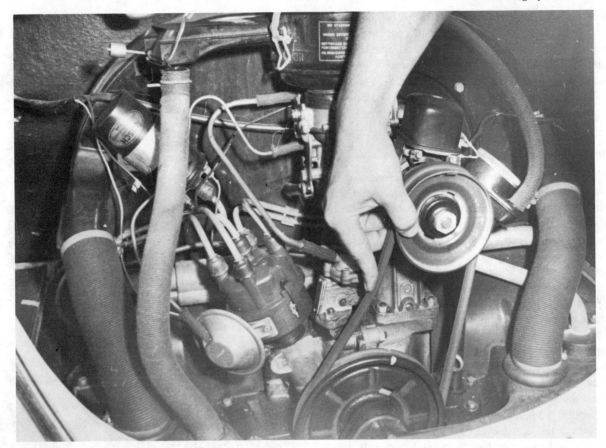

Figure 7-45. On the VW Beetle, check belt tension by pressing down with your finger midway between pulleys.

you have the belt wrapped around all other pulleys, use the pry bar in the spring tang or a ratchet wrench in a square hole provided (set ratchet to loosen) to move the idler to the no-tension position (see fig. 7-46). Slip the belt around the idler pulley and then release tension on the pry bar. The idler pulley will spring back.

Note: Take care to insure that the belt fits properly into the grooves on the pulley itself on those pulleys that accept the ribbed side of the belt. There are belts with different numbers of ribs. Make sure you have the correct belt.

HEATERS

Heaters are heat exchangers just like radiators, but they are small and have smaller coolant passages, which can plug more easily. The flushing tee arrangement reverse-flushes the rest of the system, which can dislodge dirt without disturbing the heater core. You can reverse-flush the heater this way: Disconnect the hoses from the heater hose necks at the firewall (rear wall of the engine compartment). Attach auxiliary hoses, aiming the hose you attached to the heater inlet neck (the one with the hose that

Figure 7-46. A pry bar in the spring tang is used to release tension on the belt, permitting it to be disengaged from the idler pulley. Note the serpentine route of the belt, with its smooth top side against the idler pulley and also against the water pump pulley. Both these pulleys, therefore, are not grooved.

does not lead back to the water pump) downward and away from the engine. Force the end of a garden hose into the heater outlet neck (you will need an adjustable tapered nozzle). Turn on the water and let it backflow out the heater inlet. When the water runs clean, you are done.

Note: If the water coming out is just a trickle, the heater is plugged and requires professional service.

Heater Performance

If heater performance is poor, the usual reason is a defective thermostat, one that is opening too much, too early. Remove the thermostat, test it, and replace it if necessary. Some engines dissipate heat so quickly in winter they tend to run cool even with a good thermostat. In that case, you may find that taping a piece of cardboard in front of the radiator or air conditioning condenser is the only way to build up coolant temperatures for satisfactory heater performance.

There are other reasons for poor heater operation. One is failure of the temperature lever to properly operate a flap door in the underdash heater case. If the lever is very stiff to operate, or if it moves with absolutely no resistance, the flap door may not be moving. Have a professional check this out.

Another is a plugged heater. Warm up the engine fully, disconnect the heater outlet hose from the heater neck, turn on the heater, and look for a solid stream. If there's only a trickle of coolant flowing, the heater is plugged and should be serviced professionally. If you make this test, shut the engine off quickly, so it doesn't lose all coolant and overheat.

Or on some cars, the heater valve may not be opening. Look for a valve (see fig. 7-47) in the heater inlet hose, and if there is one, turn the temperature lever to "Hot" and feel the hose on both sides of the valve with the engine warmed up. If the hose is hot on one side but not on the other, the valve isn't opening. If it has a cable attached to it, see if the cable moves a shaft on the valve, while a helper operates the temperature lever. A loose cable attachment may permit the cable to operate without opening the valve, and that should be visually obvious. If it has a vacuum hose, as is more common, disconnect the vacuum hose, and if you feel vacuum at the end (engine running, lever set to "Hot"), the dashboard control is defective. If you feel no vacuum, the valve apparently is stuck and should be replaced.

RADIATOR ELECTRIC FANS

The radiator fan normally is triggered by coolant temperature or turning on the air conditioning (unless the air conditioning condenser is alongside the radiator rather than in front of it and has its own electric fan). If the fan

Figure 7-47. Shown is a vacuum-operated heater valve. Disconnect vacuum hose as shown and feel end of hose for vacuum.

comes on immediately (or within several minutes) after turning on the AC, but not with the AC off, or clearly too late to prevent an overheat, the problem is almost always a defective temperature switch (on engine computer-controlled systems, a computer problem is a remote possibility).

If the fan does not come on at all, check for a blown fuse. If the fuse is good, unplug the wiring connector at the fan motor (see fig. 7-2). Connect one terminal from the motor side of the connector to the battery positive terminal, the other to the battery negative, using jumper wires. If the fan does not run, replace it. If it does, the problem either is in the fan relay (used on almost all systems) or the temperature switch (threaded into an engine coolant passage to sense coolant temperature) that triggers the relay. Or on some cars, the engine control computer (getting a signal from its temperature sensor) triggers the fan relay. See figure 7-48.

You will need a factory service manual with the locations of electrical components (along with a wiring diagram) to find the switch and the relay. With that

Figure 7-48. This is a typical wiring schematic diagram for a simple single-speed electric fan. When the temperature switch closes, an electromagnetic coil in the relay is energized, pulling the relay arm closed, and completing a circuit from the main current feed to the output wire terminal to the fan motor. Also, when air conditioning is turned on, the fan relay also is energized, turning on the fan. The diagram *at left* is for a V-6 engine, *at right* for a four cylinder.

information, you can test a system that is not controlled by the engine computer (as on many imports and some Chrysler and GM cars) as follows: To test the relay, unplug the wiring connector from the temperature switch. If it has a single wire connector, ground the connector terminal with a jumper wire, and if the fan now runs (ignition on), replace the temperature switch. If it doesn't, go to the relay, unplug the wiring connector, and bypass the relay with a jumper wire from the thick wire current feed terminal to the output wire terminal on the wiring connector. If the fan now runs, replace the relay.

On Chrysler and GM cars with the engine computer controlling the fan, unplug the wiring connector. Ground it on GM (unplugging is sufficient on Chrysler), and start the engine. If the fan starts almost immediately, the temperature switch is defective if the fan comes on too late to prevent overheating. If the fan doesn't come on at all, test the fan motor separately, and if it fails, replace it; if it passes, the relay apparently is defective.

Some Japanese cars work differently. When you unplug the temperature switch, the relay should spring closed and turn on the fan (ignition on). Keep this in mind, and check the possibility before concluding there is a problem.

Other cars either have no relay or have a temperature switch threaded into the radiator, that provides no electrical ground. Therefore, the switch and its wiring connector have two terminals. Unplug the wiring connector and connect a jumper wire across its two terminals, and if the fan now runs, replace the switch. If it doesn't, go to the relay.

Note: If a temperature switch on the engine has two terminals (except late-model Chrysler products), it may have two separate functions (it really could be two switches in one), so don't connect the jumper wire across the terminals. Refer to the wiring diagram to determine which terminal is for the fan, and ground that wiring connector terminal only.

Late-model Fords have an electronic fan controller, so if the fan motor passes the test, suspect the controller, which is located under the dashboard. A detailed checkout, however, should be left to a professional, unless you can read and interpret wiring diagrams.

8 EXHAUST SYSTEM SERVICE

Exhaust System Components are expensive, but if you inspect the system periodically (see fig. 8-1) and make small repairs when they are first required, you can reduce expensive replacements to a minimum.

Jack up the car and support it with safety stands at front and rear; if you only have a pair of ramps, raise one end at a time. Inspect the muffler and the piping very carefully, looking for:

1. Deep dents (more than one-quarter of the way in, such as one-half inch into a two-inch diameter pipe) that could cause restrictions preventing the engine from developing normal power, particularly at cruising speeds.
2. Holes or cracks anywhere in the pipes or muffler (see fig. 8-2). Feel the top of piping and muffler for holes or cracks you might not be able to see.

Figure 8-1. This is a typical exhaust system with a catalytic converter, which is the cannister at the left. Note the detail illustration of the converter joint, with the exhaust pipe designed for a tight seal. The cannister at the rear is the muffler.

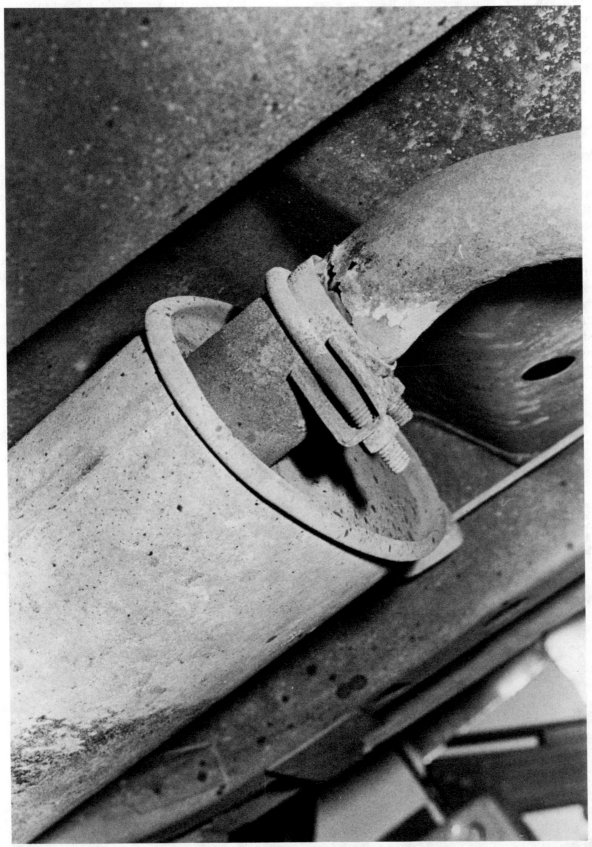

Figure 8-2. Check the entire exhaust system for breaks and dents. Note the break in the pipe just forward of the muffler in this illustration.

Next, look at the clamps and hangers. If any are broken, rusted away, or (in the case of hangers) the rubber support is cracked or broken, replacement should be made. If you don't, the exhaust system may come apart or fail, and you'll face a major expense.

EXHAUST SYSTEM SERVICE

Dents

If you find a dent in a catalytic converter, perhaps only the bottom cover need be replaced on many cars. Although this is a job for the car dealer (special equipment is required), it is far less costly than a new converter.

Note: The bottom cover is not replaceable on all cars; check with your dealer.

If there are dents in piping or muffler, you can check to determine if they are causing a severe restriction by using a vacuum gauge. Remove a vacuum hose at the base of the carburetor or intake manifold (see fig. 8-3), plug the hose end with a pencil, and connect the gauge hose to the carburetor neck. Run the engine at idle, and then have a helper hit the gas pedal. If the vacuum gauge reading drops to 0 and rises to a number that is less than normal 16 to 22 inches, the exhaust is restricted.

Note: For this test on late-model cars, disconnect the vacuum hose from the EGR (exhaust gas recirculation) valve and plug the hose end. Operation of the valve could give inaccurate results.

This vacuum gauge test is a useful one for checking for exhaust restrictions even if there are no dents, but there is a loss of power at cruising speeds. Two other possible causes of exhaust restrictions are: plugged muffler or collapsed inner wall of a laminated (two-wall) exhaust pipe. This design is used on many cars to eliminate exhaust ringing noises. However, heat and cold can cause the inner wall to collapse, while the outer wall remains intact.

To determine where a restriction is located, you must disconnect the exhaust at different points and recheck engine vacuum. Once you make a disconnection that results in normal vacuum readings, you know the part you disconnected is plugged. Begin at the front of the muffler, then move forward, toward the front of the car. This is possible only if the system is bolted together. Generally a plugged catalytic converter is the most likely possibility on late models.

Figure 8-3. A vacuum gauge test can tell you if the exhaust system is restricted.

Figure 8-4. Foil patch covers hole in exhaust, then bandage is wrapped over foil and wired into place. Bandage cures from exhaust heat and wire can be removed.

Holes

If a hole in a muffler is no more than about two inches in diameter, it can normally be patched. The same is true for a hole up to $\frac{1}{2}$ inch in a 2-inch diameter pipe, provided that the opening is not at or very close to a clamp joint, or at a sharp bend in the pipe.

Patches are not approved by motor vehicle inspection laws in all states, so check before you buy. The most popular types of patches are the fiberglass bandages treated with high-temperature resin.

With any type, you place a piece of foil (provided in the kit) against the hole as a flame guard, then wrap the bandage around it and secure the bandage with wire (see fig. 8-4). After a day of driving, the patch will cure and the wire can be removed.

Pinholes

If an entire section is dotted with pinholes, a bandage patch on the muffler and a repair section (discussed next) on the pipe are the best approaches. When you have only a few isolated pinholes, however, you can repair them with patching putty. Just sand away the rust around the hole and smear on a coat of putty, working it into the hole. It will heat-cure as you drive.

Dents and Major Breaks

When a section of pipe is deeply dented, badly rusted through, or open right next to a clamp joint, you can't patch it. If the defective pipe section is straight or has a curve you can match up, a repair pipe section is the way to go (see fig. 8-5). These repair sections come in many sizes and lengths, so check with a parts store to see if you can get what you need for repair. If the bad section is only a couple of inches long, you may get by with just an exhaust pipe connector, a very inexpensive part that joins two pieces of pipe.

Figure 8-5. If piping is good except in one area, pipe repair of the section is the most economical choice. This long pipe is a typical section. Short pipes are connectors that can be used for repair if dent or break is very small, and to connect pipes of the same or different sizes.

Installing a repair section begins with cutting out the damaged part of the old pipe. You may be able to do this with a hacksaw, or if clearances are limited, you may have to rent an exhaust pipe cutter (see fig. 8-6). If you don't get a clean cut, file the pipe end. If the pipe end is misshaped or there is a slight variation in pipe sizes that prevents a smooth, slide-in fit, rent a pipe expander to flare out the pipe end for a good connection (see fig. 8-7). Just insert the expander into the end and turn the forcing screw with a wrench. Do not overexpand, or the repair pipe section won't fit over it. Sand any rust off the end of the pipe ends

(see fig. 8-8), and file the edges if necessary to remove burrs.

You'll need two clamps the right size for the pipe. Choose premium clamps if you can get them, for they will seal better. If you can't, buy a container of exhaust pipe sealer (a special putty) and apply a thin coat to each cut pipe end before you install the repair pipe and the clamps.

Fit the repair section into place and install a clamp at each end. Aim the clamp so the U-bolt ends face in a direction that permits easy tightening, but not directly downward.

Figure 8-6. Exhaust pipe cutter makes a clean cut and works well in tight quarters.

Figure 8-7. Pipe expander flares out a pipe end or muffler neck if necessary for a good connection.

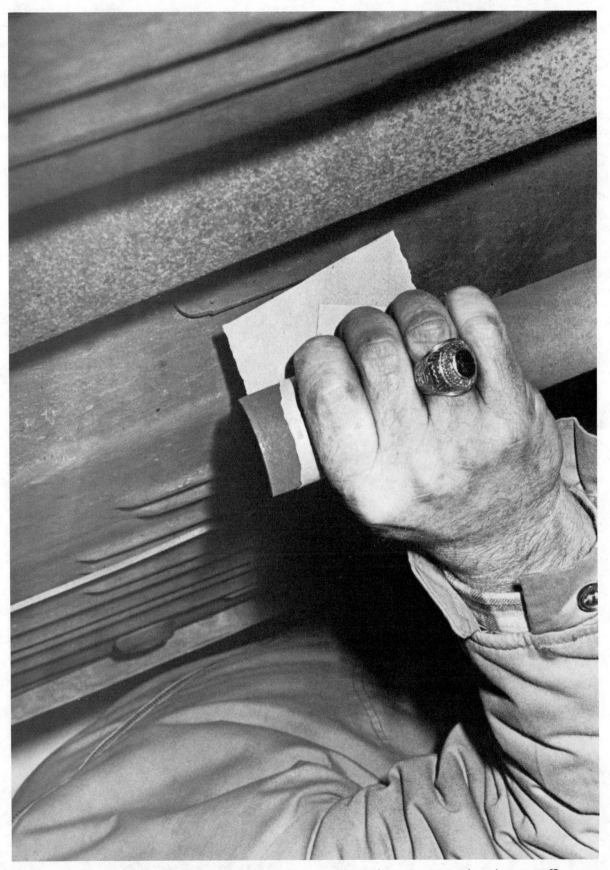

Figure 8-8. Sand rust off old pipe end as shown before inserting into a new pipe, connector, repair sections, or muffler.

New Pipe

If you can't get a repair section, buy a complete new pipe (the cost still will be lower than if you took the car into a repair shop). In most cases, the pipe from the engine will be in good condition for some distance from the engine, so you don't really have to replace the whole thing, just the section that includes the deteriorated part.

Begin by cutting the old pipe at a point where it's good and straight. Next, remove the deteriorated portion from the muffler. Then remove the clamp holding the pipe to the muffler. Spray a rusty clamp with penetrating oil, then loosen with a wrench and remove. If the clamp refuses to budge, cut it apart with a hacksaw and discard.

Separate the muffler from the pipe. This can be easier said than done. If the pipe won't come out of the muffler neck, cut if off nearby and clamp vise-type locking pliers to a protrusion. Whack the pliers with a hammer (see fig. 8-9). If the pipe is really stuck, obtain a muffler chisel and drive it in between the pipe and the muffler neck (see fig. 8-10). Use a pipe expander to reshape the muffler neck.

Once you have the damaged section of old pipe

removed, line up the new pipe at the muffler and measure carefully. The object is to cut the new pipe so that when you install the new section in the muffler, the other end of the new section will line up (to within less than an inch) of the old, still good section. Store the unused new section in case the old ever does fail.

Bridge the two sections with an exhaust connector (see figs. 8-11 and 8-12), a short pipe that fits over both ends of the exhaust pipe, new and old. Clean and expand the old pipe end if necessary. Clamp the connector at both ends, and the repair is complete. If you're using standard clamps, apply a film of exhaust sealer putty to each cut pipe end before positioning the connector.

Figure 8-10. Using muffler chisel to cut stuck piece of pipe in muffler. After cutting, the piece may be removable with ordinary pliers or with vise pliers and hammer.

Figure 8-9. Using vise-type locking pliers and hammer to remove stuck piece of pipe from a muffler.

Figure 8-11. Lining up old pipe and repair section. *Note:* Exhaust connector is on old pipe.

Figure 8-12. The connector is slid over joint between new and old pipe, and clamps are tightened to secure the joint.

Welded System

If the exhaust system is welded to the muffler, you cannot cut the old pipe off at the muffler. If the pipe is good in the area of the muffler, cut as far forward of it as possible. If it isn't, the muffler must also be replaced as explained later in this chapter. Cut just past the weld (the replacement pipe will be sized to compensate).

Laminated Pipe

If your problem is a collapsed inner wall of a laminated or two-wall pipe, replace with a single wall pipe (the exhaust ringing will go away as the exhaust soot coats the inside of the pipe) or obtain a laminated pipe with vents in the outer wall. It should be far more resistant to the problem.

Replacing Hangers

The mounting of exhaust hangers should be obvious when you're looking underneath. If any are rusted out or have rotted or cracked rubber, you realize that immediate replacement could save expensive parts.

New universal pipe hangers come in several varieties, most of them cheap and short-lived (see fig. 8-13). If you look hard, however, you can get high-quality hangers that can work at a substantial horizontal angle (up to 45°) and can swivel to any horizontal angle (see fig. 8-14). This makes installation easy when, as is common, parts do not align perfectly.

To remove a defective hanger, begin by spraying the upper end (where the bolt holds it to the body) with penetrating oil, then remove. If penetrating oil also will free up the lower end where it clamps to the exhaust system, that's a plus. If that doesn't work, cut it apart with a hacksaw.

Note: If you have an import with a rubber doughnut-shaped hanger, replace only with a quality brand, which will be made of high-temperature rubber. If necessary for good alignment, bend the doughnut retaining tangs on the body, not on the exhaust system.

Some late-model American cars (primarily front-drives) have hangers similar to the import car doughnut. They have rubber sections that are push-fits on rods that are built into hanger brackets (see fig. 8-15). To remove, just pull them off or pry them off with a screwdriver.

Figure 8-13. Exhaust hanger shown is inexpensive, but its life is limited if it must work at anything but a very slight angle.

Figure 8-14. This premium exhaust hanger has an end that can be turned 360 degrees and heavy-duty straps in rubber section, so it will hold even at severe angles.

Figure 8-15. Some American cars have exhaust hangers somewhat similar to the European rubber doughnuts. The one shown has a rubber segment that fits on tubular necks that extend from the upper and lower metal sections of the hanger. Just pull or pry off the rubber segment when disconnecting the exhaust system.

Figure 8-16. This is a heavy-duty clamp with a welded saddle and nuts and threaded U-bolt that also will take a lot of torque. Heavy-duty clamps cost a little more, but may take some shopping around to find.

Replacing Clamps

If available, use a heavy-duty clamp (see fig. 8-16) for all installations. If the pipe is heavy (close to the catalytic converter), you must use a heavy-duty clamp, as a cheap one will not hold. If necessary, buy the heavy-duty clamp from the car dealer.

Replacing Muffler and Tailpipe

Replacing the muffler and tailpipe is the most common exhaust system job, and it's well within the ability of a weekend mechanic. If you're using jack and stands, jack up the car and place the safety stands under reinforced (box) sections of the chassis, rather than under the usual locations on the suspension or rear axle. This will permit the suspension to drop, and there will be more working clearance for you.

Begin by removing the clamp that holds the muffler to the exhaust pipe. Next, spray the joint with penetrating solvent, then knock the muffler off the exhaust pipe with a hammer. Disconnect the rear hanger from the tailpipe, and if possible remove muffler and tailpipe together. If underbody clearances make this impossible, you have two choices: salvage or disposal. If the tailpipe is salvageable, spray the joint with penetrating oil and try to knock the muffler forward, off the rear joint. If the tailpipe is to be replaced, just cut it with a hacksaw at any convenient point.

If the system is welded at the exhaust pipe–muffler joint, cut the exhaust pipe where it tapers down to single thickness, a few inches from the muffler (that's where the muffler neck ends, but because of the welding, the neck is obviously not a separate part). Many replacement mufflers have a slightly longer inlet neck to compensate for the fact that part of the pipe was cut. If the one you obtain does not, also buy an exhaust connector that is sized at one end to fit into the muffler and at the other end to fit over the exhaust pipe. Every joint between pipes must be clamped, so if you use a connector you'll need two clamps.

Note: The new muffler will almost invariably be a "consolidated" design. That is, it will fit many cars, and therefore it will come with adapters and adapter pipes. Follow the instructions very carefully and use a ruler or tape measure to be sure the length of the assembly exactly matches that of the old muffler. Or if the system is welded, make sure the new muffler is even longer to fit over the pipe ends properly.

The best procedure for installing the new parts depends on the shape of the tailpipe. If it's long and curved and you couldn't pull out the old parts together, install the tailpipe first, just letting it hang over the rear axle. Next, fit the muffler to the exhaust pipe. If necessary, prepare the exhaust pipe by sanding the cut end, flaring if required, and coating with a film of exhaust sealer. Install but do not tighten the clamps. Then install the tailpipe on the rear muffler neck, and fit the clamps but do not tighten.

Install the hanger(s) and connect them to the exhaust system. If necessary to reduce the working angle of the hanger, rotate the muffler and/or tailpipe. It's important to have some clearance between the exhaust system parts and the body, suspension, brake lines, etc., so try to duplicate the original positions as closely as possible. When you think it looks safe, tighten everything only enough to hold it in place. Lower the car to the ground, get underneath, and recheck to see if everything is clear. If not, turn muffler and tailpipe as required to get the clearances. Only then should you give everything a final tightening.

9 THE ELECTRICAL SYSTEM

The electrical system of the automobile is direct current (DC), compared with the alternating current (AC) used in the house. The automobile does have an AC generator (alternator), but the current, in order to be used, is changed to DC by electronic components called diodes. The battery charger which plugs into household current also is an AC device, but it too has electronic components that convert the current to DC to charge the battery.

The DC circuit is basically very simple. A wire is connected to a source of current at one end and run to the current "consumer" (bulb, motor, radio, etc.) at the other. The source of all current is the battery, and you undoubtedly have noticed that it has two posts or terminals, one marked positive, one marked negative. The positive post is the source, but as a practical matter current can be picked up anywhere in the wiring that is in some way directly connected to the battery. For example, the battery positive post is connected to the starter, and from the starter there is often a wire that goes into a multiple connector. Any of the wires that emerge from that connector are also "hot"; that is, they can carry current because they are in some form of metal-to-metal contact with a wire from the battery. In many cases, "hot" wires go into fuseboxes or into switches, which when closed will complete circuits and make additional wires capable of carrying current. For example, when you turn on the ignition key you complete a circuit to the ignition system, and when you turn it still further, you complete a circuit to the starter solenoid and the engine cranks.

In order to flow, current must have a complete path from the source and back to the source. When there is such a complete path, it is called a "circuit" (see chapter 2, fig. 2-1).

ELECTRICAL CIRCUITS

In the automobile we use the metal car body, chassis, and engine as if it were one big wire, in a system called the electrical ground. The car battery's second post or terminal is connected by cable to either the body, engine, or both (if not both, there is a separate cable elsewhere to connect body and engine).

Everywhere else, the circuit back to the battery is completed by grounding to the car body or engine. This is commonly done in either of two ways:
1. A wire is connected to the body or engine.
2. The part itself is made of metal, and when it is held to the body or engine by mounting screws, the mounting screws provide the ground, through the metal part (see fig. 2-2). Inside the metal part there is a physical connection, either by wire or by a metal tab, from the current consumer. As an example, a light bulb has a socket that is made in part of metal. When you install the bulb, the metal retainer for the glass is in contact with the metal part of the socket, and the socket itself is in metal-to-metal contact with the car body.

The Switch

The switch (see fig. 2-3) is nothing more than a mechanical break in a piece of wire. When we want to, we connect a metal tab to both ends of the break, and the wire is now "complete." The closing of a switch may join ends of a hot wire or a ground wire. When you press the horn button, for example, you are completing a ground circuit.

What Goes Wrong

Two things can happen to a circuit: It can break, forming an open circuit, or it can short out.

Open Circuit. A switch is a form of open circuit. When you operate the switch, you close, or complete, the circuit. That's normal. When a wire breaks or a wiring terminal becomes so severely corroded that current won't pass through, an open circuit also is created, but this one can't be closed, and the part to which the wiring is connected won't work. If the wire goes into a harness or is otherwise inaccessible, the actual break in the wire may be difficult if not practically impossible to find. Finding the break is not important, for once the existence of the break becomes obvious, a mechanic runs a new wire (outside the harness) to correct the problem. A corroded wiring terminal may be wire-brushed clean to correct a problem, or it may be cut off and a new terminal attached. Auto parts stores sell replacement terminals that can be attached to a wire with a pair of pliers.

Short Circuit. Electricity takes the path of least resistance, and the only way to force the electricity to go into a part and do some work (such as light a bulb or operate a motor) is to hold it in the wire until it reaches the part. Holding in the electricity is the job of that plastic covering, the insulation. If the insulation is cut or otherwise damaged, the electricity may be able to find an easier path through the insulation break to an electrical ground, such as a metal part of the car body or engine, for example; and although the circuit to ground is complete, it ends short of the part the electricity is supposed to operate (see fig. 9-1).

Because there is little resistance to the flow of electricity through a break in insulation, and because the electricity may flow even when all switches are turned off, the electricity flow will be very substantial and the battery will often quickly run down.

In some cases you may lift the hood and see smouldering insulation at the break. You may be able to cure the problem in such an obvious situation. Disconnect the battery ground cable and tape over the insulation break with plastic electrical tape. If the wire itself is damaged, cut away the damaged section and splice in a replacement, using crimp-together connectors sold at auto parts stores.

HOW TO BUY A BATTERY

The battery (see fig. 9-2) is the storage unit of the car's electrical system. It accepts electrical energy from the charging system (the alternator) and converts it into the chemical energy it is designed to store. When you turn the key to crank the engine or turn on the radio or other electrical accessory, it converts that chemical energy back into electricity and transmits it through cables to the part that needs it.

If you cut apart a battery, you'd find a series of plates (made of lead and a stiffening alloy, such as antimony,

Figure 9-1. This is a short circuit. If the wiring insulation breaks and the bare wire touches against the car body, electricity can get to ground without going through the bulb. Although the bulb does not light, electricity is consumed.

Figure 9-2. Cutaway view of a battery showing the plates.

calcium, and in some cases strontium) bathed in an acid solution. Actually, there are groups of plates, each group called a "cell" and providing two volts (the measurement of electrical pressure). Put 3 cells together and you have a 6-volt battery; put 6 together and you have a 12-volt battery. All batteries of the same voltage are not the same. One significant difference is in the amount of amps—electric current—they can supply.

The internal details of battery construction might be helpful if you could cut apart a battery before you bought it, but you can't, so instead you should concern yourself only with the battery ratings and any external features.

Rating Battery Performance

Amp-hour Capacity. The amp-hour rating of a battery tells you how long it can survive a slow discharge, such as if you left the car with the dashboard lights on. A battery that can last 20 hours with a 2.5 amp discharge is given a rating of 50 amp-hours. If that battery supplied 5 amps, the rating would be 100 amp-hours. Generally, the higher the amp-hour rating, the greater is the power available under more severe conditions. "Generally" is not "always"; therefore, the following two ratings are probably more significant to you.

Zero Cold Rating. The number of amps the battery can deliver for 30 seconds during cranking at 0° F without going dead.

The rule of thumb for buying a battery used to be to get one with cranking amps equal to the number of cubic inches. That is, if you have a 300-cubic-inch engine, get a battery with 300 cranking amps. This still is valid for large V-8s used in moderate climates (few days in the 0° F range).

However, there are many more small three-, four-, and six-cylinder engines today, and it's been found that the number of cranking amps on them may actually be higher than on big V-8s. The design of the intake manifolds often is such that the engine must crank at relatively high speed for starting. The minimum voltage necessary to operate electronic fuel injectors also may raise the capacity requirements of the battery.

Further, cars are being kept longer, and as a battery ages, it loses its ability to get up to full charge. So if you are in a cold area, get a battery at least equal to what was supplied as original equipment. In a milder area, you can safely go one size smaller. In a severely cold area, where temperatures commonly dip below 0° F, consider a battery one capacity size larger. The references to sizes smaller or larger depend on the battery manufacturer. Generally, the capacity differences will be under 100 cranking amps for batteries under 500 cranking amps; they may be greater for higher-capacity batteries.

If you live in an extremely cold area, you may be able to get the −20° F cold rating, which is the number of amps the battery can deliver for cranking at 20° F. Use that number as a basis for comparison if available.

Reserve Capacity. This tells you how long a fully charged battery can provide a fairly substantial amount of current—25 amps—if you have a sudden charging system failure, such as a snapped drive belt, or alternator, or regulator malfunction. The amount of current is an estimate of what it would take to run the ignition system, headlamps, wipers, and heater, and gives you an idea if you can limp the car home when the charging system warning light goes on or the ammeter suddenly shows discharge. An hour rating is an acceptable figure.

Battery Maintenance

You can buy a conventional battery, a low-maintenance type, or a so-called "no-maintenance" battery.

The low-maintenance type is the kind you see advertised as "normally never needs water during the warranty period." This is a battery designed for low water usage, having a large water capacity, so it just might make it without water. This type does have some sort of cell cap so you can add water if necessary, and it is a good idea to check the water level at least once a year.

The no-maintenance type has a smooth top and no provision for water additions. Though not guaranteed for life, it is guaranteed for some given amount of time. Some of the no-maintenance batteries have a charge indicator built into the top.

Note: These batteries are not really sealed (there are hard-to-see vents built into the sides), so don't tip them over during any removal for underhood service, or you may lose some water you can't put back in.

The standard battery is just what you have known all these years. It needs water additions at least once every few months. If you have a smaller car, particularly with a four-cylinder engine, it is probably all the battery you will need for starting, which is your primary consideration. Its lower price makes it a good investment, even if it carries only a modest warranty, such as 24 months.

Fewer standard batteries are available today, and some of the larger manufacturers offer none for the passenger car markets.

Side-terminal vs. Top-post Battery

If your car comes with a side-terminal battery instead of the conventional top posts, you may feel you have to get the same thing as a replacement. You do not! If your best buy is one with top posts, that's what you should get, for adapters are readily available at auto parts stores and are very inexpensive. However, be sure that the battery can be secured properly. Many batteries are designed for clamping at the bottom edge on one side (see fig. 9-3). Adapting this type to a top hold-down arrangement is impractical and would probably eliminate any saving on the price of the battery. However, a battery designed for bottom-edge clamping typically can also be installed with a top hold-

Figure 9-3. If a battery is designed for bottom clamping with bracket as shown, so should replacement, as adapting for a top hold-down will eat up any saving on a battery without the correct shape.

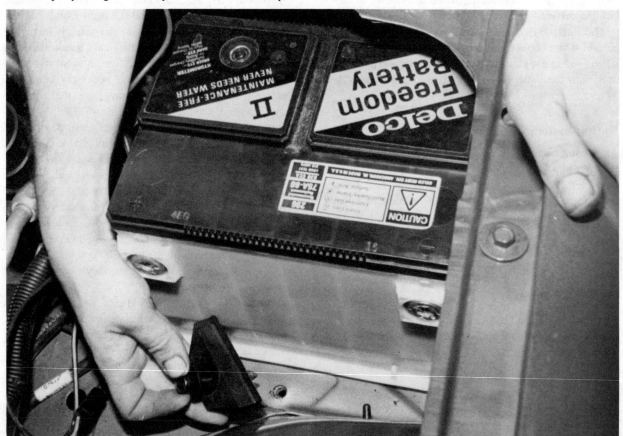

down. The top-post design has one important advantage you also should consider: It's a lot easier to use for jump-starting and for connecting a charger or test equipment.

Note: If you are buying booster cables, be sure to get the premium type designed for both top-post and side-terminal batteries. The type for top-post only, which has alligator jaw terminals, may not make good enough contact with the side terminal for full transfer of current. Or you can obtain a charging adapter that fits between the positive side terminal and its cable to provide a large surface for the alligator jaw.

Battery Warranties

There are many types of battery warranties, and you should read them carefully and understand them before you buy.

Lifetime. This means that the seller will replace the battery if it fails, unless that failure is caused by an electrical problem in your car, for as long as you own that car. The words "you own" and "that car" are important. You can't transfer the warranty when you sell the car, and you can't transfer the battery to a new car. The price for such a battery with such a warranty is measurably higher, so unless you have every intention of keeping your car for many years, it really doesn't pay. The battery is a top-line design, but there's nothing "lifetime" about its construction. The seller is betting that most people will sell the car before the battery dies, and the extra charge covers the cost of servicing those who don't.

Simple pro rata. A pro rata warranty means that if a battery with a 36-month warranty fails at 18 months, you get a new one at half the current price. There also is a free replacement clause in the deal, usually limited to the first 30 days or 3 months, or sometimes even 6 months.

Initial free replacement, then pro rata. The free replacement is for a longer period, often up to 18 months; then it's pro rata. This is a good bet if you're planning to keep the car for about a year and a half, for it costs very little more than simple pro rata. You should understand that once you're past the 18 months free replacement, you're instantly into pro rata that includes that period. For example, you have a 48-month battery warranty with 18 months free replacement. The battery fails at 19 months. You must pay $^{19}/_{48}$ths of the cost of a replacement, not for just one month of use.

When looking for a new battery, consider what you need to start the car, reserve capacity (particularly if you drive a lot on roads without service facilities), price, and warranty. Maintenance characteristics are not significant, because all battery cables loosen from road shock and periodic attention is required, even if water additions are reduced. Look for the best overall value, but don't buy more or less than you really need. Just because a huge-capacity battery with a long warranty is on sale for $20 off the regular price doesn't mean it's worth buying. It may still be $10 more than you really need for the little four-cylinder car you plan to dump in a year.

Used Batteries

If you are planning to sell your car very shortly, you can take a small gamble and save big money by buying a used battery from a wrecking yard. A good battery from a late-model wreck should last for a good long time, and it will probably cost as little as one-fourth the price of a new one. Reconditioned batteries are available in some areas of the country, but quality of battery reconditioning is very uneven, so you are taking a chance unless the local rebuilder has a good reputation.

Battery Service

Batteries require care, particularly for winter starting A battery at 0° F develops only 40 percent of the power it would (in the same state of charge) at 80° F.

If your battery is a conventional type, periodically check the water level and add water as required. It is not necessary to use distilled water unless the tap water in your area is unusually hard.

Exterior Cleaning. Clean the top of a conventional battery with a solution of baking soda and water (one tablespoon baking soda to an eight-ounce glass of water) whenever it is dirty.

If the battery hold-down bracket is corroded away, or if it has loosened, the battery may vibrate as the car moves down the road. This vibration could crack it and allow fluid to lead out. The battery then would be ruined. Wire-brush corrosion off the bracket, coat it with corrosion-resistant paint, then tighten securely. If the corrosion is severe, replace the hold-down.

State of Charge. The state of charge of the battery is extremely important in cold weather. A substantially discharged battery could freeze internally and crack apart. If the battery is a no-maintenance type without fill caps but has an external indicator, you can make an easy visual inspection. If it is the conventional type, you can check its condition with a hydrometer or an electronic tester.

The hydrometer is a glass device with a float built in. Just remove a cell cap, draw out a small sample with the syringe top, and read the float at the surface line of the fluid. If it is below 1.220 (see temperature correction chart, fig. 9-4), the battery needs a recharge. If there is a difference between high and low readings of more than .025, the low cell is defective and the battery must be replaced.

Figure 9-4. Temperature correction chart for battery hydrometer readings. If you have a reading of 1.220 and the battery temperature is 80° F, you make no change. If it's 100° you add 8 to raise the number to 1.228.

The sealed-top battery may have a built-in hydrometer (see fig. 9-5). This design is often misinterpreted. Here is what the appearance of the plastic circle in the top of the battery means:

Green. A green dot or any green appearance means the battery can be tested, such as with a voltmeter. It does not mean the battery is good. The hydrometer goes into just one cell, and if another cell is bad, the battery won't work properly even though the green dot is there.

Dark (green dot not visible). If there's a cranking problem, it may be caused by a defect in the electrical system, including the charging system, and the battery. Check these too.

Yellow or clear. This has often been interpreted to mean the battery should be replaced. Actually, it means that the battery may not be in great shape, but may well be able to continue in service. If, however, there is a cranking problem that can't be obviously traced to bad cables or a defective starter, replace the battery.

If these sound a bit fuzzy, you must understand that the sealed-top battery can only be checked accurately with equipment the weekend mechanic will not find to be cost-effective. If you have a battery with removable caps, however, you can test it with a low-cost electronic tester.

With the electronic tester, you simply insert the probes into adjacent cell holes, and the tester should light. If it does not, the cell is low. If all cells are low, try a recharge. If only one is low, the cell is apparently defective.

The simplest way to test a "sealed-top" battery (or any other) is to use a digital voltmeter across the two terminals. The reading should be 12.65 to 12.80 volts (surprisingly, a reading of just 12.0 volts indicates serious undercharge, even though the nominal rating of the battery is 12 volts). If the battery has just been charged, the reading could be noticeably higher than 12.65 to 12.80, so crank the engine for 10 seconds (with the ignition disconnected so the engine won't start) to remove the surface charge that raises the reading (see fig. 9-6).

Recharge. To recharge a battery you need a charger that plugs into household current. A small charger (maximum 10 amps) will do the job, given enough time, and inasmuch as slow recharging is best for the battery, even very small chargers are not necessarily a bad investment. A 24- to 48-hour recharge with a 4-amp charger, for example, will do just fine.

If after a slow recharge all cells do not read in the normal range, replace the battery.

Note: All recharging should be done with the caps off, cells topped off with water, and adequate ventilation.

Cleaning Cable Terminals. One of the best things you can do for a battery is clean and tighten the cable terminals and the battery posts. Connections that are clean and

Figure 9-5. This sealed-top battery has a temperature-compensated hydrometer built through the top into one cell.

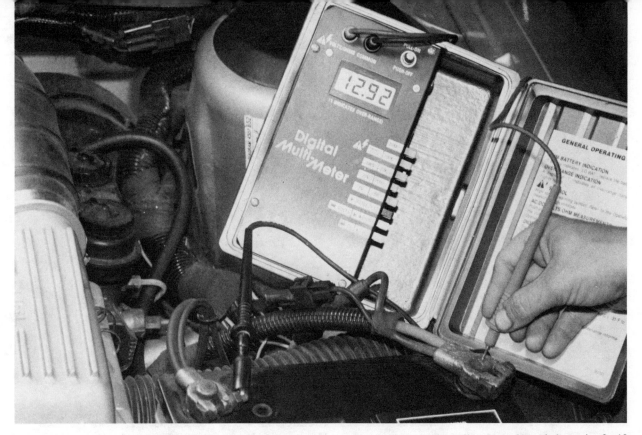

Figure 9-6. This battery produced a reading of over 12.9 volts after recharge. Do not use this reading. Instead, crank the engine for 10 minutes and recheck.

tight will permit easier current flow and make cold weather starting much more feasible.

Removing Cables on Top-post Batteries. Slacken the nut that secures the cable terminal to the battery and twist it back and forth with an upward motion. If the terminal is stuck, tap it back and forth with a hammer to free it up. Still having trouble? Don't try prying or yanking, or you could ruin the battery post and the battery. Buy a terminal puller, an inexpensive tool that makes cable terminal removal safe and easy (see fig. 9-7). With a wire brush, clean corrosion from the inside and outside of the cable terminal and the entire surface of the post (see figs. 9-8 and 9-9). Refit the cable terminal and tighten securely. Spray the connection with a rust-preventive lubricant and the job is done.

Figure 9-7. Using terminal puller on top-post battery.

Figure 9-8. Using a wire brush to clean inside of battery cable terminal. Also clean exterior of terminal.

Figure 9-9. Using a wire brush to clean the battery post.

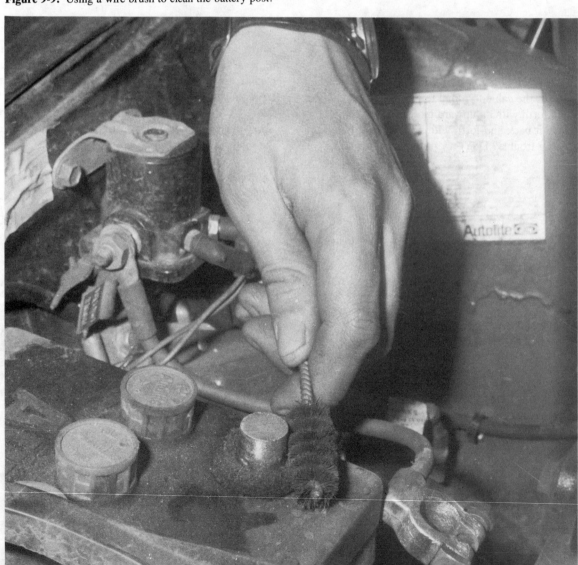

If the cable terminal is distorted and will not tighten properly, buy a new terminal, cut off the old with a hacksaw, and install the replacement (see fig. 9-10) on the cable (attachment is an obvious procedure). This is much easier than replacing an entire cable, particularly the cable that goes to the starter motor.

Side-terminal Batteries. Although these are less susceptible to corrosion, the smaller contact surface between the cable and the battery terminals means that even a small amount of corrosion, perhaps not even visible to the naked eye, can prevent a car from starting. Remove the retaining screw, separate the cable and battery terminals, wire-brush the contact surfaces carefully (see fig. 9-11), and then refit and tighten. Although this type of terminal has a very long life, if necessary it also can be cut off the cable, and a replacement can be installed.

Figure 9-10. If a battery cable terminal is corroded, cut it off, bare the end of the wire, and fit a replacement terminal. The bared wire goes between the plate (part with two screws) and the base of the terminal.

Figure 9-11. Clean the disc contact surfaces on cable terminal and battery with a wire brush.

ALTERNATORS AND GENERATORS

Charging System Service

The alternator or AC generator is the heart of the charging system. Driven by a belt from the engine crankshaft, it converts the mechanical energy of rotation into AC current. The automobile uses direct current (DC), so the AC is passed through electronic check valves—called diodes—which convert the AC to DC. The DC current then flows through cables to operate the electrical system and recharge the battery.

To control the output of the alternator, a device called a voltage regulator is used. On most cars the regulator is an electronic device, in many cases built into the back of the alternator. On older cars it is a mechanical device with contact points that close to permit current flow and open when the battery is charged and no current is needed. In actual practice, the points vibrate open and closed so fast that you can't even see that it is happening. With an electronic regulator there are no moving parts, and tran-sistors electronically open and close the circuit from the alternator.

Two things can happen to the charging system: It can produce too much current or too little. If it produces too much, the battery will overcharge and water will "gas" out of the battery. If it produces too little, the battery will run down, and in the extreme case (no current at all) the car won't start or will stop running once the battery is dead.

If your battery runs dry very often, overcharge is the likely cause. The easiest way to check this is with an electrical evaluator, a tester sold at auto supply stores (see figs. 9-12 and 9-13). You use it right at the battery or alternator and simple lights (actually voltage-sensitive, light-emitting diodes—LEDs) tell you whether the system is charging normally, overcharging, or undercharging. Or you can use a voltmeter. With the engine and all electrical accessories and lights off, check the voltage across the battery terminals (and it should be at full charge). Start the engine and raise r.p.m. to 1,500. The voltage should rise up to (but not more than) 2 volts. Allow several minutes for the reading to hit its peak.

If the reading does not go up, the system is undercharg-

Figure 9-12. Here, a pencil-type charging system tester is used at the battery.

Figure 9-13. This tester is easily connected at the alternator. For most tests, no disconnections of car wiring at the alternator are necessary.

ing; if it goes up by more than 2, it is overcharging. If the reading increases by up to 2 volts, make this next test: Turn on the heater or air conditioning and set the blower speed to "High." Turn on the headlights to high beam. Raise engine r.p.m. to 2,000, and the voltage reading should be at least a half volt above the original engine-off reading. (That is, if it were 12.7 with the engine off, it should be at least 13.2 volts.) If the voltage increase is too low, this is an indication of undercharge. You can make this test with an analog (needle-and-dial) voltmeter.

Overcharge. Overcharge is normally caused by a defective regulator, and the cure is to replace it. If your car does not have a separate regulator, you often must replace the alternator. Both cases and their solutions are explained later.

Undercharge or No Charge. The more common problem is that the alternator does not keep the battery fully charged or does not provide any charge at all.

1. Check the drive belt. A snapped belt will result in no charge. A slipping belt will result in undercharge. See chapter 7 for details on belt service.
2. If the car has a separate voltage regulator, the problem may be caused by a defective electrical ground. The

ground is provided by the regulator mounting screws, which thread into the body. As a simple test, connect a jumper wire (a piece of wire with an alligator clip at each end) from one of the mounting screws to another suitable grounding point, such as a metal screw on the engine. If the charging system now operates properly, remove both mounting screws, wire-brush the threads, reinstall, and tighten securely. If brushing the threads doesn't work, make up a grounding wire from a piece of wire and a pair of crimp-on terminals (see fig. 9-14).

Alternator Output Test

If the problem is not in the regulator ground or drive belt, it is either in the alternator or regulator. To make a suitable test, you will need an ammeter. Proceed as follows:

1. Disconnect the battery ground cable, the one that is bolted to the car body and/or engine block (see fig. 9-15).
2. Disconnect the wire from the armature terminal (also called the battery terminal) on the back of the alternator (the correct terminal is the one with the thicker wire and may have A, ARM, B, or BAT embossed

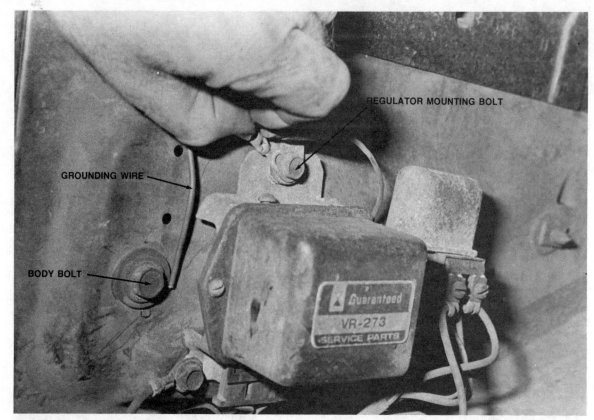

Figure 9-14. Installing regulator grounding wire. Although this step is rarely necessary, it may solve a problem if the regulator mounting bolts are not providing a good electrical ground.

Figure 9-15. Disconnecting battery ground cable from engine. *Note:* Most ground cables are either also grounded to the body, or are split into two wires, one that grounds at the engine, the other at the body.

Figure 9-16. Field and armature wires are disconnected from alternator, and jumper wire is connected to the alternator's armature and field terminals. The test instrument used is a combination ammeter-voltmeter that has only a single wire lead with a "shunt tab" for ammeter, instead of positive and negative wire leads for an ammeter-only instrument.

next to it). Connect the wire from the ammeter positive terminal to the alternator terminal, and the wire from the ammeter negative terminal to the wire you disconnected. If you have a combination amp-voltmeter, the ammeter section likely has just a single lead with a rectangular tab—called a shunt—at the end. The shunt tab is shaped so that one end goes on the alternator armature terminal and the other attaches to the wire you disconnected from that terminal. Make these connections, then move the meter switch to the "Amps" position.

3. Disconnect the thin wire from the field terminal (marked F or FLD on the alternator) and connect a

jumper wire from the armature terminal to the field terminal (see fig. 9-16). On cars whose alternators have built-in regulators, ground out the regulator with a screwdriver or special tool inserted into the hole in the back of the alternator (see fig. 9-17). Reconnect the battery ground cable. Turn on all accessories.

4. Start the engine, rev it for an instant, and the ammeter reading should reach or exceed the rated output, which is a minimum of 35 amps on smaller cars. Shut the engine down immediately and turn off accessories.

If the alternator output is not satisfactory, replace the alternator. If output is normal, replace the voltage regulator (on those with an external type).

Figure 9-17. Inserting screwdriver into hole in back of Delco (GM) alternator with built-in regulator. When the screwdriver tip comes into contact with tab, lean the shank of the screwdriver against the alternator body. Regulator is now eliminated from charging circuit, so if ammeter output now is normal, your problem is the regulator.

Replacing the Alternator

Replacing an alternator is a simple procedure. Begin by disconnecting the battery ground cable and any wiring at the back of the alternator.

The typical alternator is held by two bolts, one of which passes through an adjusting bracket. Loosen both bolts (see figs. 9-18 and 9-19), then pivot the alternator in toward the engine and disconnect the drive belt from the pulley (see fig. 9-20). Remove both bolts and lift out the alternator (see fig. 9-21).

Obtain a factory rebuilt alternator (using your old one as an exchange unit) from a parts store that serves professional mechanics. You could get a new alternator, but the price will be at least three times higher, with a long wait for delivery.

Install the rebuilt alternator with both mounting bolts but do not tighten. Engage the drive belt (make sure it is properly installed on all pulleys, not just the alternator one); adjust drive belt tension as explained in chapter 7.

Connect wiring at the back of the alternator, and refit the battery ground cable.

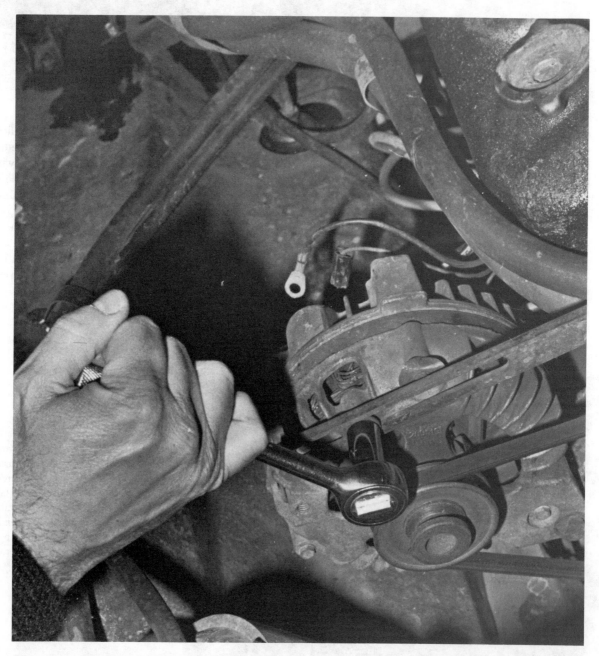

Figure 9-18. Loosening alternator mounting bolt that passes through slot in adjusting bracket. Remove this bolt.

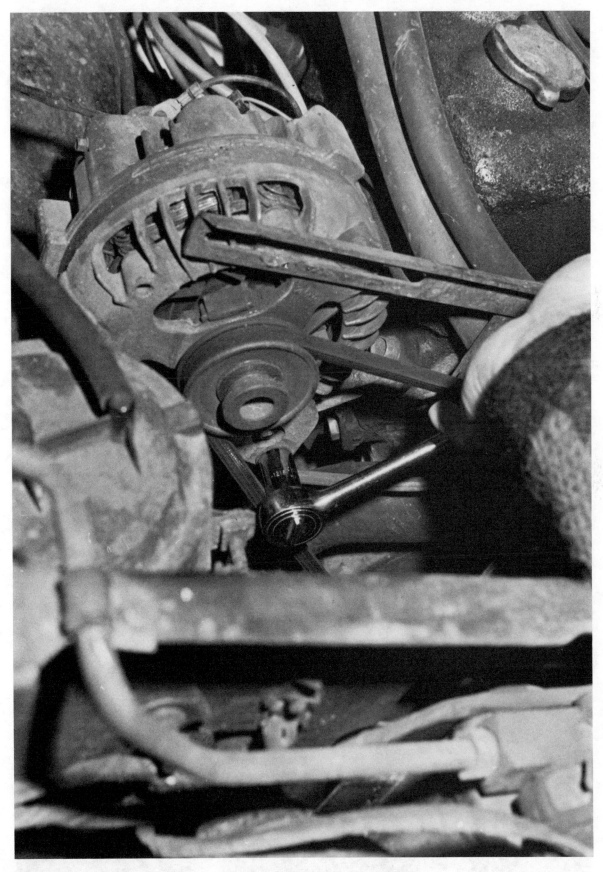

Figure 9-19. Loosening second alternator mounting bolt. Remove this bolt, too.

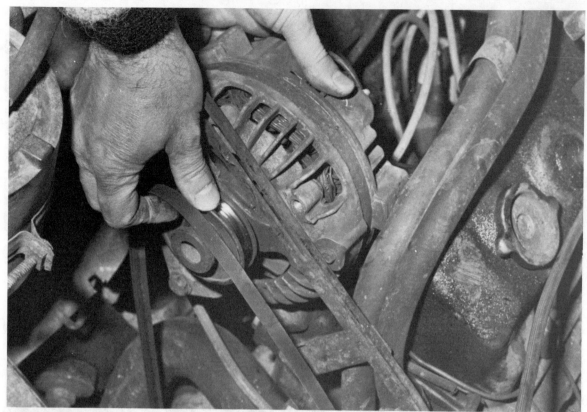

Figure 9-20. With both mounting bolts out and wiring disconnected from back of alternator, slip belt off the pulley.

Figure 9-21. Lifting alternator out of the car. Installation is the reverse of removal, plus drive belt tension adjustment.

Replacing the Regulator

If the alternator passes the output test, your problem is a defective regulator. To replace, simply disconnect the battery ground cable and the electrical connector at the regulator. Remove the regulator mounting screws and install a new regulator and the screws. Reattach the regulator electrical connector and then reconnect the battery ground cable.

On alternators with built-in regulators, either obtain a rebuilt or take the alternator to an auto electrical repair shop for disassembly and installation of a new regulator.

STARTER

When you turn the key to crank the engine, what you are actually doing is completing a circuit from the battery to an electric motor and an electromagnet switch on top of the motor.

When this switch (called the solenoid) receives current, it closes, pushing a fork or lever. The fork or lever moves a little gear—the pinion—on the end of the motor shaft into engagement with another gear—the ring—on the engine's flywheel (see figs. 9-22 to 9-24).

Figure 9-22. This is a schematic of the starting circuit. When key is turned, it closes a switch that completes a circuit from the battery to a second switch (actually called a solenoid or relay). When the solenoid or relay is energized, it closes and completes a second circuit (capable of carrying more current) from battery to solenoid or relay to the cranking (starter) motor. The starter spins a little gear that turns the large gear on the engine flywheel.

Figure 9-23. Cutaway view of a solenoid-type starter motor. When the solenoid is actuated, it not only supplies current to the starter motor but also moves a shift fork that pushes the pinion gear forward into mesh with the engine flywheel gear.

FLYWHEEL RING GEAR

STARTER MOTOR

Figure 9-24. A rear view of the engine with transmission removed shows flywheel and starter motor.

The solenoid serves a second purpose. When it closes, it completes a thick wire circuit (thick wire carries more current) from the battery to the motor portion of the starter.

As the motor's shaft turns, the little pinion gear turns the big flywheel ring gear, and that's what starts the crankshaft and all other parts of the engine into motion.

When the engine finally runs on its own, the flywheel spins so comparatively fast (even at idle speed) that its gear tries to drive the little gear on the starter. If this were allowed to happen, the starter would quickly be damaged.

To prevent this, a two-section device called an overrunning clutch is used. When power is supplied by the starter, the front half of the overrunning clutch locks onto the rear half and the power of the starting motor is transferred to the little gear. When the little gear is running faster than the starter (because the flywheel is spinning it), the front half of the overrunning clutch automatically disengages from the rear half. All this action takes place in an instant, because once the engine starts the normal driver releases the key. Immediately, the starter solenoid disengages and the little pinion gear retracts from the ring gear on the flywheel.

You can visually identify this starter by the solenoid on top (see fig. 9-25) and by the two wire connections, a thin wire to trigger the solenoid and a thick one to carry current for the starter motor.

Other Starters. In another popular design, the overrunning clutch is used, but instead of a solenoid another type

of electromagnet is used to move the fork that pushes the little pinion gear into mesh with the flywheel ring gear.

This type has only a single electrical connection to the starter. With this design, widely used on Ford and American Motors products, there is a device called a relay mounted close to the battery. When you turn the key you actually complete a circuit to the relay, which is another form of electromagnetic switch. The relay closes and completes a circuit from the battery to the starter motor (see fig. 9-26).

Ford and AMC also use a solenoid starter on some

Figure 9-25. External view of starter motor with solenoid atop it.

SOLENOID

STARTER MOTOR

292

BATTERY

SOLENOID LINK

STARTER SOLENOID

STARTER RELAY

S

R

TO IGNITION COIL

STARTER

START SWITCH AND SAFETY SWITCHES IN CLOSED POSITION

IGNITION TERMINAL

SAFETY SWITCH TERMINAL

STARTER RELAY

STARTER WITH RELAY

FROM BATTERY

TO SAFETY SWITCH

#31

FROM IGNITION SWITCH

TO STARTER SOLENOID

Figure 9-26. *At the top,* schematic illustration shows a typical Ford starter circuit (A). *Below* is a Ford-American Motors-type relay (B), and *at the bottom* is a Chrysler relay (C). In the Ford-AM arrangement, ignition switch current flows to the relay when the ignition key switch is closed, and when the clutch is depressed or automatic transmission is in neutral or park (so the safety switch is closed), the relay circuit is complete and a heavy amount of current flows from the battery through the relay to the starter solenoid (a solenoid is not used on all Ford starters). On Chrysler products, the closing of the relay completes a light current circuit to the starter solenoid, closing the solenoid so the heavy current flow can go from battery through solenoid to the starter.

293

models, but with the relay. In this case, the relay closes and completes a circuit from the battery to the starter motor terminal on the solenoid. A metal link connects from this terminal to the solenoid terminal to simultaneously activate the solenoid.

Most Chrysler cars also use a starter relay, although it differs from the Ford-AMC type (as explained later). See fig. 9-26.

Starter Problems

The only function of the starter is to crank the engine. If the engine cranks reasonably well (as a driver, the normal sound should be familiar to you), any failure to start is not the fault of the starter.

The following may or may not be starter problems:

Engine cranks very slowly. This could be the starter, a weak battery, corroded connections at the battery, poor cable connections at the starter or the battery ground on the engine, very thick engine oil, or a defective engine.

Starter spins but the engine does not crank. If you hear a fast whirring noise from the starter, but not the familiar sound of the engine cranking, the starter is either not in engagement with the ring gear or the overrunning clutch is not holding. Replace the starter.

Engine does not crank at all. This could be a starter problem, but might also be caused by a dead battery, poor cable connections, or a defective neutral safety or clutch switch. On all cars with automatic transmission, a neutral safety switch is installed to prevent cranking the engine in anything but neutral or park positions. If this switch is maladjusted or fails, the starting circuit is not complete. Many manual-transmission cars have a switch on the clutch linkage so the engine will crank only if the clutch pedal is fully depressed. If this switch is maladjusted or fails, the effect is the same as a neutral safety switch problem on an automatic.

Erratic and/or noisy cranking. If you get unusual noises and erratic cranking, the problem might be in the starter, or a ring gear may be loose on the flywheel (so that it turns but the engine doesn't crank or cranks erratically).

Troubleshooting Techniques

Slow or No Cranking. If the battery and cable connections are good, check the starter current draw with an induction ammeter, an inexpensive little tester that clips onto the battery cable to the starter (see fig. 9-27). If the current draw is more than 150 to 300 amps in warm weather, and up to 375 in cold weather, it is excessive (exception is the diesel engine, typical normal draw on diesels can approach 600 amps in −20° F).

High Current Draw. High current draw may be caused by very thick engine oil. Do you have a sludged-up engine from poor oil change practice? Do you have a couple of cans of engine oil thickening additive in the crankcase? Or could the engine itself be the problem?

The problem also can occur in hot weather, after a run at highway speed. When you turn off the engine, the cooling system also shuts off and dissipates a lot of heat, thinning out any oil on the cylinder walls. The oil then flows off the walls, and when the engine next is cranked, the small amount of oil that remains results in increased engine friction, raising starter current draw and causing the engine to crank slowly. Use a heavier oil (such as 15W-50) if you encounter this problem in summer.

Remove the starter (as explained later) to check it out. With the starter removed, test it with a good battery and jumper cables. Connect one booster-type jumper cable from the starter frame to the battery ground post, and another from the battery starter terminal to the thick wire terminal on the starter or solenoid. Have an assistant help you hold the starter in place, or even better, secure it in a vise for safety, and connect a thin jumper wire from the thick starter terminal to the solenoid's S terminal. The starter should energize, and you should see the pinion gear move forward and spin enthusiastically. If it hangs up, or if the starter turns sluggishly or not at all, replace the starter.

If the starter spins well outside the car but not when installed on the engine, the problem is caused by either:
1. Excessively thick engine oil.
2. Defective battery cable(s).
3. If a battery other than the one in the car was used for the test, perhaps the battery is the cause.

Test the battery state of charge as described earlier in this chapter. Inspect the cables for corroded terminals, damaged insulation (on the cable to the starter), frayed or broken wires (on an uninsulated ground cable) and loose connections.

Normal Current Draw. If the current draw is normal, remove the starter and look at the pinion and ring gear teeth (you will have to move the flywheel with a screwdriver on the ring gear to see all the teeth). If you see damaged teeth, or if the flywheel ring gear is loose, the transmission must be removed, the flywheel taken off, and a new ring gear pressed on. This is a job for a professional.

No Current Draw. If there is no current draw, the starting circuit is not complete. Check the connections from the battery, and if they are complete, make this basic test on all cars with solenoids on the starter: Run a jumper wire from the battery to the solenoid's S terminal. If the engine cranks, you know that the solenoid, starter, and battery are okay. The problem is in the neutral safety switch (on automatic transmissions), the clutch switch (on some manual transmissions), the key switch, or possibly the relay (on cars with a relay).

If the engine does not have a solenoid on top of the starter, such as Ford and AMC cars with the relay, a similar test can be made.

Starter Relay (Ford, Chrysler, AMC). If your car is one with a starter relay, it makes a good starting point simply because it's normally quite accessible in the engine compartment. Tests at the relay also may pinpoint problems in the key switch and clutch or neutral safety switch.

With the Ford-type relay (see fig. 9-28), disconnect the thin wire and connect a jumper wire from the battery starter terminal to the thin wire terminal of the relay. If the engine now cranks, the problem is in the key switch or the neutral safety-clutch switch or their wiring. Pinpointing the problem any further requires you to locate the neutral safety or clutch switch, remove the wiring connector, and attach a jumper wire across the connector's two terminals. If the engine now cranks with the key, the neutral safety-clutch switch is the problem. If it doesn't, the key switch is at fault.

Figure 9-27. Using an induction ammeter that clips onto the battery starter cable, you'll find the amperage draw is 300 in cool weather, within specifications.

Figure 9-28. Ford-type starter relay.

Note: Ford and some other makes with steering column levers do not have a neutral safety switch (a lock in the column prevents turning the key except when the lever is in neutral or park). Only console shifts have the switch. Clutch and neutral safety switch locations will be discussed later in this section.

If the engine doesn't crank with the jumper wire from the battery to the relay thin-wire terminal, the relay itself is apparently defective. Double-check by connecting a booster cable from one relay thick-wire terminal to the other (these are the battery cable terminals). If the engine now cranks, you have confirmed that the relay is the problem.

If there are two thin-wire terminals, the S terminal is the one you want.

Some AMC cars use the Ford-type relay, and if there is a light blue wire with white tracer, it goes to the neutral safety or clutch switch. To bypass that switch, ground the terminal to which this wire connects, and if the engine now cranks, the neutral safety or clutch switch is the problem. With the other test procedures, you can isolate a key switch or relay problem.

Note: On some Ford-type relays, the second terminal wire carries current to the ignition coil. Do not confuse this with the AMC blue and white wire to the neutral safety or clutch switch.

On Chrysler cars, the starter relay is usually on the driver's side of the firewall (the sheet metal rear of the engine compartment). Run a jumper wire from the battery starter terminal to this relay's I terminal, and if the engine cranks, the key switch is the problem. Connect a jumper wire from the relay G terminal to ground, and if the engine now cranks, the neutral safety or clutch switch is at fault. If the engine still doesn't crank, run a jumper wire from the battery starter terminal to the starter solenoid's S terminal, and if the engine now cranks the relay is defective.

Neutral Safety-clutch Switch Locations.

The clutch switch is usually under the dashboard and is the only switch you will find that bears against the clutch pedal linkage. If it has two wires, disconnect them and join them together with a jumper wire to bypass the switch. If it has only one, connect it to an electrical ground with a jumper.

The neutral safety switch on console floor shifts is typically under the shift lever cover, which may be held by just four to six screws. On steering column cars, if it is used, it is somewhere on the column near the bottom, under the dash or under the hood. It may be distinguished by the fact that it moves when you move the shift lever.

Note: On many cars you can tell if the neutral safety switch is bad without much trouble, for it commonly also operates the backup lights and on some cars the warning light that goes on if you put the car into "Drive" without your belts fastened. Should these indicators fail simul-

taneously, the neutral safety switch is obviously the problem.

If not, look for the switch on the column on GM and older Ford products. It is threaded into the transmission on Chrysler and AMC cars, but can be tested at the easy-to-reach starter relay on those models.

Caution: For safety, only crank the engine when the transmission is in Neutral or Park, even though it would crank in the other positions with the switch bypassed. Have a mechanic replace the switch as quickly as possible.

Key Switch.

If you bypass the neutral safety switch and can't crank the engine after the test procedures outlined earlier, the key switch is suspect. Replacing it usually is a job for a professional, however.

Note: On many cars the switch is not in the key assembly, but at the base of the steering column, operated by a rod from the key lock assembly. On this type, widely used on late models, you can replace it. Consult a service manual for your car to find out how.

Replacing a Starter.

In many cases, the solution comes down to replacing the starter. Whether or not you can replace a starter depends entirely on its physical location. On some cars, starter removal is blocked by other components which must be taken off first. On others, you just remove two or three bolts (see fig. 9-29) and lift the starter out. You will have to look at the starter and its location and decide if you can do the job.

On all but a few cars, the car must be jacked up and the starter removed from underneath.

Always begin with the battery ground cable disconnected. Next, disconnect wiring at the starter, then

Figure 9-29. Remove mounting bolts and disconnect wires to starter to remove it. Battery ground cable should be disconnected first.

remove the bolts and take out the starter for testing and/or replacement. You will undoubtedly select a rebuilt starter because of its much lower cost and easier availability. Have it bench-tested before installation.

Note: As with any auto electrical work on cars with engine computers, disconnecting the battery may result in a drop in performance for up to several hours of engine operation after reconnection, as the computer "relearns" some aspects of its operations. Low-cost adapters that use a 9-volt battery at the cigarette lighter are available to prevent this.

HORN SERVICE

Horns are prone to any one of three problems; they won't blow, they won't stop, or when they blow the sound is weak. Correcting these faults is usually something a weekend mechanic can handle.

You will be able to do a job on the horn circuit much more easily if you become familiar with it before something goes wrong. Learn it now, beginning with the basic operation (see fig. 9-30). There are two types of horn circuits in popular use.

On the most common horns (GM, Chrysler, American Motors, and some Ford), the current circuit is from the fusebox to a type of electromagnetic switch called a relay. The circuit cannot be completed to the horn itself until the relay is electrically grounded, which is done by the horn switch in the car. When you press the horn button, you complete the circuit by providing an electrical ground for the relay.

The current then flows through the relay to the horn, a spring-loaded diaphragm device operated by a pair of electrical contact points that are part of another electromagnet.

The contact points are normally closed, and when current flows through them an electromagnet is formed that pulls them apart, breaking the circuit. The diaphragm

spring then pulls them back together and the electromagnet is again formed. This happens many times per second, and each time the diaphragm flexes it makes a sound. A cone-shaped metal section of the horn amplifies the sounds, which occur so fast that they seem like a single, continuous sound. Some Fords have a nonrelay circuit that works this way: There is a current feed wire to the horn switch on the steering column, and a second wire from the switch to the horn which is grounded by its mounting bolt. When the switch is operated, current flows through the switch to the wire to the horn, sounding it.

Component Locations

To check out a horn circuit you should know where the components are located. You can find your horn (if you do this when it works) by having someone press the button while you trace the noise. Or you can just look under the hood at the front of the engine compartment.

The horn relay is usually, but not always, plugged into the fusebox or is taped to the wiring harness somewhere near the box. If you are foresighted enough to check it out before it goes bad, just disconnect the wire from the horn and have someone press the horn button. You'll hear a click, which is the operation of the relay. Just trace it to a little metal can—the relay.

The horn button can be built into the steering wheel or a multipurpose stalk switch on the steering column.

Troubleshooting Horn Problems

Horn Won't Stop Blowing. This is a maddening problem because you've got all that noise. First, disconnect the battery ground cable so you can collect your thoughts. Next, disconnect the horn and reconnect the battery cable, so although the horn won't work you can do some testing.

First, press the horn button, and if you don't hear the relay click the problem is a stuck relay or a defective horn button.

You can determine which it is by having a helper disconnect the battery ground cable, then reconnect it as you listen at the relay. If you hear the relay click when the cable is touched to the battery post, the problem is a stuck horn button. If you don't, the problem is a stuck relay. If you wish, you can double-check as follows:

Remove the relay and test it alone at the battery with jumper wires (you'll need two). Connect the relay terminal marked B or 1 to the battery starter terminal, the one marked S or 3 to an electrical ground. You should hear the relay click. If you don't, replace it.

If the relay tests good, the problem is in the horn button. On the rim-blow type, the cure is to replace the steering wheel, but that's too expensive. Just get to the wire from the relay's S or 3 terminal and clip it off near the relay. Splice on a new piece of wire and run it along the steering column

Figure 9-30. Typical horn circuit with relay. When you press the horn button, you complete an electrical ground for the horn relay. Current then flows through the relay to the horn, which is electrically grounded by its mounting bolt.

to a replacement horn switch, which clamps onto the top of the steering column jacket. Run a second wire from the auxiliary horn switch to a suitable electrical ground, such as a metal screw into a metal part under the dashboard.

Other horn buttons may be replaced less expensively, or you could just remove the button section from the wheel and look for a bent tang making contact and causing the problem. That's something you might fix with a screwdriver. If you can't figure out how to fix the switch, you can, as with the rim-blow type, just run a new switch.

Note: When splicing in a new piece of wire, use a crimp-together electrical connector, available at auto supply stores, and cover the connection with plastic electrical tape.

Horn Won't Blow. This could be caused by a poor horn ground (see fig. 9-31), defective horn switch, bad relay, or defective horn. To check the horn itself, just disconnect the wire and run a jumper wire from the horn terminal to the battery starter terminal. If the horn now blows, it is good.

Next, with the horn still disconnected, push the horn button and listen for a click. If you don't hear one, remove the relay for testing at the battery, and if it doesn't click there, replace the relay.

Finally, if the relay is good, you're back to a horn button problem.

Horn Sounds Weak. This problem is caused by the horn. You could just unbolt the horn and install a replacement,

but you might also be able to make an adjustment. Look at the horn and you'll see a locknut and adjusting screw, or a self-locking adjusting screw (see fig. 9-32). With everything connected, turn the screw counterclockwise until the horn just stops blowing, then clockwise until it has a clear sound. Don't make adjustments with the horn blowing, but blow between adjustments to check.

Intermittent Operation. Like intermittent problems of any kind, an intermittent horn problem can be impossible to trace when the horn is working. You must test when it is not.

Wiring Problems. The test procedures all are based on component problems rather than wiring difficulties, for wiring problems with a horn circuit are comparatively less common. If you find that the horn and relay are good, but the horn doesn't blow, it is possible that the problem is not in the horn button, but in the wire from the relay to the button. There could be either an internal break in the wire (causing no-blow) or bared insulation short-circuiting against the steering column (causing continuous blow). Installing the accessory horn button that clamps to the steering column will also handle this problem, just as if the horn button were the cause. You might try snaking a new wire up to the horn button and through the steering column jacket, but his may not be a simple job. Occasionally, a weak-sounding horn problem may be traced to a poor wiring connection at the horn terminal.

Figure 9-31. To check for a poor horn ground, attach jumper wire to horn body and press against a body bolt as shown. Have a helper press the horn button on the steering wheel, and if the horn now works, the ground is the problem. Remove the horn mounting bolt (which provides the ground), clean the threads, reinstall, and tighten.

Figure 9-32. Typical horn with adjusting screw. This type has hex-head adjuster; others have locknut and screw slot adjuster.

AUTOMOTIVE LAMPS

Your car has many lamps: for parking, directional signals, stop indicators, dashboard and other interior convenience, and of course the headlamps. Replacing them is work you can do at a substantial savings, for the price of bulbs is much lower at the discount house than from the garage or service station.

Headlamps

You can replace headlamps without disturbing the aim. First, make sure the problem is a defective headlamp. If a single headlamp works either on high or low beam (but not both), the problem is likely in the headlamp itself. If both headlamps work on one beam but not the other, the problem is likely in the wiring of the headlamp switch or the dimmer switch. On four-lamp systems, a simultaneous failure of two headlamps (high or low beam) is statistically unlikely; if they don't work, suspect a switch or wiring problem.

Replacement Procedure. The exact method of getting to the headlamp varies from car to car, but usually it's obvious. In most cases there is a molding or chrome ring held by screws or force-fit into place (see fig. 9-33). Once you remove it, look carefully at how the headlamp is held: You'll see a metal ring held by three screws; those and only those screws should be touched (see figs. 9-34 and 9-35). There are two other screws (spring-loaded, which do not go through the ring) that control headlamp aim.

If the metal retaining ring screws are tight, don't force them. Spray them with penetrating solvent until they can be worked loose. Remove the ring, and then disconnect the headlamp from the electrical connector in back (see fig. 9-36). Install the new headlamp, making sure you have the correct side up (or headlamp aim will be completely distorted). Most headlamps have a number somewhere on the lens, to make positioning easy.

Figure 9-33. Removing headlamp molding after taking out retaining screws.

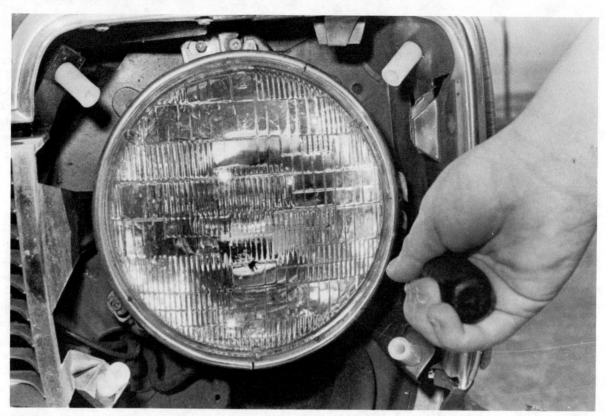

Figure 9-34. Removing the screws that hold the headlamp retaining ring. Do not confuse retaining screws with headlamp adjusting screws or you will disturb the headlamp aim.

Figure 9-35. With retaining screws removed, the ring can be withdrawn as shown.

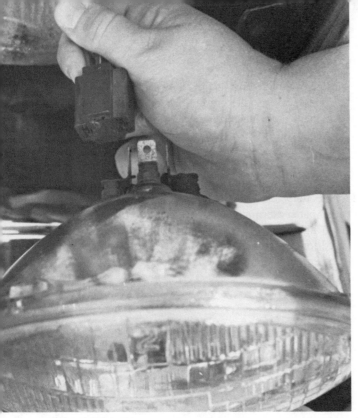

Figure 9-36. Disconnecting wiring plug at back of headlamp.

Figure 9-37. Access to "aerodynamic" quartz-halogen headlamp bulb on this car begins with removal of plastic retaining screws from housing.

Figure 9-38. Move headlamp housing forward and bulb unscrews from back easily.

If your car has quartz-halogen headlamps with a replaceable bulb, there is an obvious procedure for access to the bulb (see figs. 9-37 and 9-38).

Caution: When you install a new bulb, do not touch its glass envelope with your fingers, or its life may be considerably shortened.

Headlamp Aim. Headlamp aim can be set accurately only with headlamp aimers, and the cost of even the least expensive portable type is probably more than you want to spend. If you have a private house with a driveway, however, you can maintain the aim of your headlamps (immediately after they have been set professionally) with this simple procedure:

Place your car at the foot of the driveway, about 25 feet from the garage door. Turn on the headlamps and mark the center of the beams on the garage door. If your driveway slopes too sharply, park your car just outside the garage door and use the inside wall of your garage instead. Mark the location of your car exactly, either by paint marks, an embedded stake, etc., so you can put your car in the same position at any time.

If your headlamp beam is ever below your marks on the garage door or wall, turn the top adjusting screw clockwise (to raise the beam); above the marks, turn it counterclockwise (to lower it). If the beam is to one side or the other, turn the side adjusting screw to bring it back into alignment.

Note: Low-cost aimers are now available. They cover

only vertical aim, but this is usually all that needs resetting. These aimers are made by the manufacturer of the leading professional type.

Exterior Lamps

Most exterior lamps are easily accessible, either from the back (just untwist the bulb or socket and remove) or after removing the front cover lens held by a couple of screws (see figs. 9-39 and 9-40).

To remove the typical exterior bulb, push it in slightly, then twist, and it will release and spring up. If there isn't enough of the glass protruding to get a good grip, buy an inexpensive bulb removal kit—a set of sleeves that fit over the glass, and usually prevent damage (see fig. 9-41). If you do break the glass, use needlenose pliers to grasp the broken filament in the base, push down, and twist to release (see fig. 9-42).

If the filament of the old bulb appears to be good, test the bulb before buying a replacement. Just set the base on one battery terminal, then run a jumper wire from the other battery terminal to the metal side of the bulb. If the bulb lights, it is good. With two-filament bulbs (those used for headlamps or both stop and tail lighting), both filaments should light (see fig. 9-43).

Figure 9-39. Gaining access to exterior bulb by removing front lens held by screws.

Figure 9-40. Gaining access to exterior bulb by prying out entire socket-lens assembly, which is held by spring clips in rectangular holes.

Figure 9-41. Using plastic holder to remove bulb.

Figure 9-42. Using needlenose pliers (jaws wrapped with masking tape to improve grip) to remove base of broken bulb.

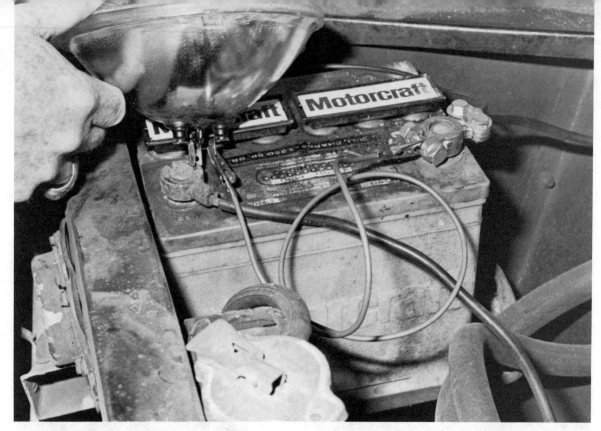

Figure 9-43. Checking out headlamp at car battery. *Note:* one electrical prong of headlamp rests on battery post, while a jumper wire connects from another prong to other battery post. Other car bulbs can be checked in a similar manner. However, you should understand that the other car bulbs are wired to the yellow metal side, so the jumper wire should be touched against this side while the base of the bulb is on the battery post.

Figure 9-44. Wire-brushing corrosion from bulb socket.

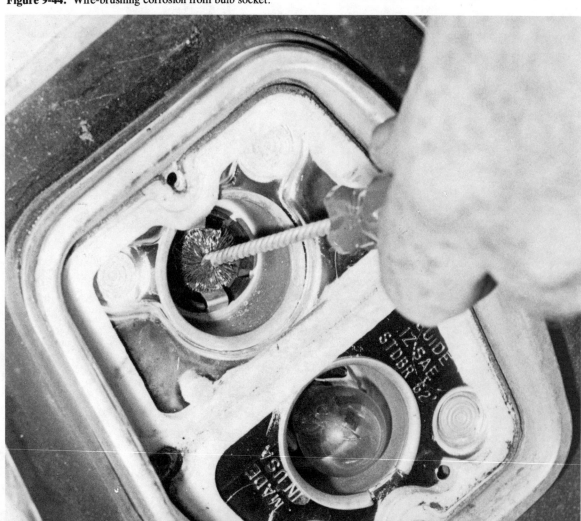

Socket Service. If the inside of the socket is physically good (that is, no broken spring contact), just wire-brush it (see fig. 9-44) and spray with penetrating oil to clear out any corrosion. See broken contacts? Replace the socket.

If the bulb still doesn't work in the socket, a wiring problem apparently exists, and that is a job for a professional mechanic.

In almost all cases, however, the problem is in the bulb or the socket.

Installing a Bulb. The exterior "bayonet" bulb has protruding tangs on the side that engage slots in the socket. On many bulbs, the tangs and slots are at different heights, and you must aim the bulb into the socket correctly to engage them when you push down and twist to seat the bulb.

Interior Bulbs

The dome light and the dashboard bulbs are the ones common to all cars, and in most cases they are easy to install if you know how.

Dome Light. Removing the lens is the only tricky part of dome light service. The lens is held somewhat differently on every car, but if you don't see anything obvious, try pushing in on the lens and twisting it, first one way, then the other, and it may release and drop out, giving you access to the bulb. If the lens is not flexible and there are no screws, it must be pried out (see fig. 9-45).

Dashboard Lights. The dash lights may be reachable from behind the gauges. See if you can fit your hand up in there and remove the bulb. Some twist out and others pull out; all you can do is feel your way around and try both techniques.

If access from the back is difficult, the odds are one of the following:

1. The gauge cluster comes out after removal of a few screws and perhaps unplugging the speedometer cable (see fig. 9-46).
2. The dashboard is front-service. You remove cover bezels held by easily accessible screws, and you then can remove any gauge or switch from the front (see fig. 9-47).

Figure 9-45. Dome light lens isn't flexible and there are no retaining screws, so it must come out by prying with screwdriver as shown. Be careful not to damage headliner.

Figure 9-46. This gauge cluster comes out after removing four external screws, pulling forward, then reaching in back to disconnect electrical connector and speedometer cable. On some cars you may have to disconnect cable before you can pull cluster forward. On others the cable housing may be caged and you can pull the cluster forward without a cable disconnection.

Figure 9-47. This is a front-service dashboard. Cover bezels and moldings are unscrewed and removed, and everything—including bulbs—is accessible.

3. The bulbs are front-service, just remove the cover bezels.
4. The bulbs are accessible after removing a speaker grille from the top of the dash.
5. The lights are fiberoptic, that is, special fibers carry light from an accessible location where the bulb is placed to an inaccessible one. One bulb may light many runs of optical fibers. Check with your dealer service department on this one, if none of the other options pan out.

10 AIR CONDITIONING SERVICE AND REPAIR

Although many air conditioning repairs require special equipment and training, most aspects of routine maintenance—including simple recharging with refrigerant gas—is work that the weekend mechanic can do. All you need are some inexpensive tools and a basic understanding of the system and some of its components.

How It Works

There are three basic components in the automotive air conditioning system: an evaporator, a compressor, and a condenser (see fig. 10-1). They are connected by hoses and form a closed system (not open to the air) that is filled with a gas called Refrigerant 12 (Freon is its most popular trade name). Refrigerant 12 has the unique characteristic of boiling at −21.7° F at normal atmospheric pressure.

The compressor is a pump that circulates the refrigerant gas through the system.

As a liquid, Freon flows into the evaporator, a part that resembles a tiny radiator, located in the air conditioning ductwork (in the passenger compartment or at the rear of the engine compartment). In the duct it absorbs heat from the surrounding air and boils, turning into a gas once more. This is much like a pot of water on the stove. It absorbs heat from the stove and at 212° F turns to a gas (steam). The change from liquid to gas is the way many fluids absorb heat.

Inasmuch as cold is the absence of heat, the air in the

Figure 10-1. This is the air conditioning system on a late-model GM or Ford product. The compressor circulates the refrigerant, called Freon, first compressing it (which raises its temperature and pressure) and sending it to the condenser, which is in front of the radiator. Here it is cooled, and it turns from a high-pressure gas to a high-pressure liquid. It flows from the condenser to the orifice tube, which meters it into the evaporator. In the evaporator it vaporizes to absorb heat and flows through into the accumulator, where any liquid is trapped. From the accumulator it goes into the compressor inlet, where the cycle begins again. A pressure-sensitive switch, typically mounted in the accumulator, controls the cycling of the compressor's electro-magnetic switch.

ductwork becomes cold. A fan called the blower then blows this cold air into the passenger compartment.

The heated Freon (now a gas) is drawn from the evaporator by the compressor, which compresses it and pushes it into the condenser, that finned radiator-like part in front of the cooling system radiator. Here the airflow through the condenser cools the refrigerant gas and turns it into a liquid. It then flows as a liquid to the evaporator to continue the cooling operation.

The air conditioning system has many control valves, switches, and other parts, but for routine service the only ones that you need to understand are described in the following sections.

Cycling Clutch Switch. The output of most air conditioning systems is controlled by turning on and off the electromagnetic clutch on the front of the compressor, and the control is performed by this switch. On many cars it has a tube clamped to a refrigerant gas line to sense temperature; on late-model GM and Ford products, it has a pressure-sensitive switch threaded into the system so it responds to refrigerant gas pressure. There is a precise relationship between refrigerant gas pressure and temperature, so a pressure switch also can be calibrated to perform temperature control functions. The switch may cycle the compressor on and off automatically several times per minutes. This is in addition to the on/off operation when you move the dashboard controls.

Suction Throttling Valve. This automatically controls the output of the air conditioning system on older cars (it was dropped because it was one of the least fuel-efficient choices). Systems with this valve (also called a POA valve), do not have a cycling clutch switch. Instead, they measure the Freon pressure at one point in the system and either open or close to control Freon flow.

Orifice Tube or Expansion Valve. This is the dividing line between liquid Freon from the condenser and gas in the evaporator. It meters the amount of liquid Freon so it turns to a gas as it flows into the evaporator to absorb heat. The orifice tube is a calibrated opening. The expansion valve is a valve that is opened or closed, commonly triggered by a temperature-sensing tube clamped to a refrigerant line, like some cycling clutch switches.

Accumulator. This is a liquid trap for Freon that does not vaporize in the evaporator (to prevent it from reaching the compressor, where it could cause internal damage). The accumulator, which contains a desiccant to absorb moisture (which is very harmful to the inside of air conditioning lines) is primarily on systems where a cycling clutch and orifice tube are used.

Receiver-Dryer. This is a liquid storage device (as opposed to a trap) used on systems with expansion valves. Where used, the system does not usually have an accu-

mulator, and the desiccant is in the receiver, hence the name receiver-dryer (see fig 10-2). A few older American Motors cars did not use a desiccant (rather the system

Figure 10-2. This is a receiver-dryer that includes air conditioning control valves. It is called a VIR, for valves-in-receiver. This particular one, unlike most, contains a moisture indicator to show if there is any free moisture (not held by the desiccant) in the system.

Figure 10-3. The little window the finger points to is a sight glass. It enables you to see if refrigerant gas is circulating in the system. Most newer cars do not have it, however.

contained alcohol to prevent moisture inside from freezing), and so the part was merely called a receiver. On many cars the receiver has a tiny window (see fig. 10-3) so you can actually see into the sealed refrigeration system. How this is used is explained later in this chapter.

AC Sections

The air conditioning system is divided into two sections: the high-pressure side and the low-pressure side. The compressor separates the sections, with the compressor inlet (where the gas is drawn from the evaporator) being the low-pressure side, and the compressor outlet (where the gas is compressed and pushed into the condenser) being the high-pressure side.

The evaporator and the line connecting it to the compressor inlet, therefore, constitute the low-pressure section. The line from the compressor outlet through the condenser and up to the evaporator inlet (at the expansion valve or orifice tube) is the high-pressure side.

Checking the System

If your air conditioning system is not performing properly, all you want to know is if the problem is one you can correct, or if it's something that requires professional service.

First, check the front of the condenser. If it's plugged with road film, bugs, leaves, or other debris, it can't cool the refrigerant gas. Clean it with a pail of household detergent and water and a soft brush.

Next, check the compressor drive belt. If it's loose or so badly deteriorated that it's slipping on the pulley, performance also will be poor. Adjust the belt if necessary (see chapter 7).

Finally, sit in the car, run the engine at fast idle, and turn on the system. Within five minutes you should feel cold air. If it's a very humid day, the air won't be as cold as on a dry day, but that's normal. If the AC performance only seems poor because the blower won't go up to high speed, that's an electrical problem (check for a blown fuse before taking the job to a shop). If the AC works normally for 10 to 15 minutes, then starts blowing warm air, the problem is moisture in the system. The sealed system must be discharged and moisture vacuumed out of the system using a special pump. This is a job for a professional shop.

Note: Most GM cars built before 1977 have a fuse called a thermal limiter under the hood in wiring near the compressor. This fuse is supposed to blow only when refrigerant has been lost, but may blow when the system is otherwise good. A new thermal limiter is cheap, so if the system fails completely, buy a new one and see if it cures the problem. With the new one in your hand you should have no trouble locating the fuse holder and installing it.

If the AC performance is just very weak, however, the likely cause is loss of refrigerant gas. No seal is perfect, and within a few years most systems need some additional refrigerant.

Begin by checking the system pressure at the test valves with the gauge.

TEST VALVES

The pressures developed to the high- and low-pressure sides of the system are important indicators of what is happening inside. To permit measurement of these pressures, all auto air conditioning systems have valves to which pressure gauges can be connected. There normally is one for the high-pressure side and one for the low, although many older Chrysler cars have a second valve on the low-pressure side.

Note: Some cars have only one valve, typically on the high-pressure side. This can pose problems in testing and adding Freon to the system.

Professional mechanics use somewhat elaborate gauge sets to measure pressure, but you can find out all you need to know with an inexpensive tire-type air conditioning gauge (see fig. 10-4).

Finding the Test Valves

When looking for them, start at the compressor. With one exception, they resemble tire valves (including the thread-on cap). On many cars they are on the compressor itself or in the connecting lines very close to it.

Chrysler Cars. On most older rear-drive cars the high-pressure test valve is on a cylindrical can (called a muffler) in a line very close to the compressor (see fig. 10-5), and the low-pressure test valve is on the compressor. If you see two valves on the compressor, the one you want is NOT on a flat plate held by eight bolts. It is the one next to the tubing line that goes to the condenser or receiver-dryer.

General Motors Cars. On cars with a receiver-dryer that includes the expansion valve (and another valve), you'll find the low-pressure valve at the top and the high-pressure one at midpoint on the cylinder (see fig. 10-6).

On cars with an accumulator (see fig. 10-7), the low-pressure valve is on the accumulator; the high-pressure one is on a line that is physically nearby.

On older models with standard air conditioning, both valves are on the compressor. On older models with automatic temperature control systems, the high-pressure valve is at the expansion valve (just follow the line from the receiver-dryer until you come to it). The low-pressure valve is at a part called the POA valve (just follow the low-

Figure 10-4. This inexpensive pressure gauge, much like a tire gauge, permits you to check pressure inside the air conditioning system. It may not work on the low pressure side of late-model GM cars. If it doesn't, you will need an adapter.

Figure 10-5. Fingers point to pressure test points on a Chrysler air conditioning system. *At left* is the low-pressure point into which refrigerant may be added. *At right* is the high-pressure point with its cap removed and placed *just to the left.*

pressure line—the thicker hose—from the compressor until you come to it).

Ford Products. Older (1970s) models of this car line can present the most difficult problems for the novice, for there are three possibilities:

1. The high-pressure valve is close to the compressor, in the line that goes to the condenser; the low-pressure is in the line close to a part called the suction throttling valve (just follow the low-pressure line—the thicker hose—from the compressor until you come to it: see fig. 10-1).

   Caution: There is a valve on the suction throttling valve that will resemble the one for testing. It is used for testing, but it's not the one you want.

2. Both test valves are in the lines very close to the compressor. The low-pressure one is in the thicker hose.

3. There are two valves on the compressor (see fig. 10-8); however, they are manually controlled, rather than the tire-type. You cannot use the tire-type gauge on these valves, but instead must have a professional gauge set. Further, the ports for adding refrigerant gas are not made for use with the kits packaged for use by weekend mechanics. Leave the service on this design to a professional. This manual valve arrangement also is used on American Motors cars, including most domestic-built Renaults (Alliance and Encore).

A single test valve is often encountered on rear-drive late-model Ford cars, an occasional GM car, and the Eagle Premier.

311

Figure 10-6. This illustration shows location of pressure test points on General Motors VIR system.

LOW PRESSURE GAUGE FITTING

VIR UNIT

HIGH PRESSURE GAUGE FITTING

VIR INLET LINE

Figure 10-7. Fingers point to pressure test points on General Motors system with accumulator (the cylindrical can *at left*). Low-pressure point is on accumulator; high-pressure point is on narrow-diameter air conditioning hose.

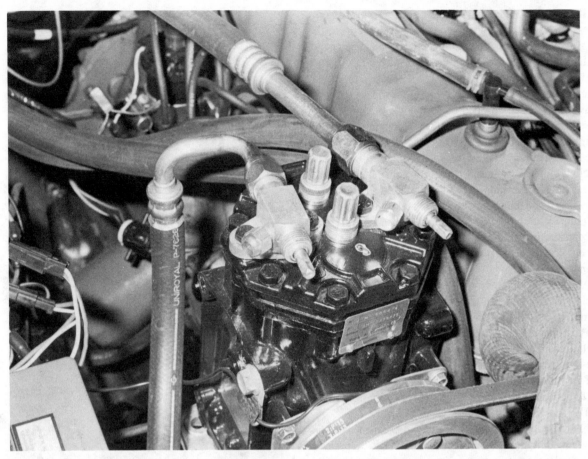

Figure 10-8. Air conditioning with manual valves as shown should be left to professional with special equipment.

DETERMINING NEED

To determine if your system requires additional refrigerant gas, check the sight glass on systems so equipped. Run the engine and turn on the AC. You should see slight bubbling in the glass. If bubbling does not stop after five minutes, additional refrigerant gas is necessary.

If the compressor clutch does not engage, you cannot make an inspection for bubbling. One of the following may have happened:

The Freon level may be so low that a safety cutout switch has opened to prevent compressor operation. This is done because on most systems the compressor is lubricated by oil mixed in with the Freon, and without an adequate amount of Freon, the compressor would fail. On older GM cars (and on some European cars with GM-type systems), the compressor clutch circuit is controlled by a thermostatic switch on the back of the compressor, and when that switch signals a low Freon level, it completes a circuit through a special type of fuse called a thermal limiter, and the limiter blows. You can't see if the limiter has blown, but if you remove it, connect a jumper wire across terminals B and C or the wiring connector. Turn on the AC, and if the compressor clutch now engages, you have confirmed the problem. Start the engine and immediately (and quickly) check pressures with the gauge. If they are very low, add Freon. If they are normal, the limiter has inadvertently blown. Just replace it (it's an inexpensive part) and system operation will be restored.

There may be an electrical problem somewhere in the clutch circuit. Modern compressor clutch circuits are complex and require a wiring diagram to troubleshoot, along with extensive experience with automotive wiring. There is one exception: failure of the cycling clutch switch. Unplug the wiring connector from the switch and connect a jumper wire across the connector terminals. Turn on the AC. If the clutch engages, the switch is defective. Replacement is covered later in this chapter.

If you see no bubbling at the start or as the unit continues to operate, and there is absolutely no cooling, the system probably has lost all its gas charge from leakage. The leak that allows the refrigerant to be lost relatively quickly also is enough to admit moisture, so the best procedure is to get the system vacuum-pumped and recharged by a professional.

If your car does not have a sight glass, locate the high-pressure test valve, run the engine and AC, remove the cap, and take a pressure reading with the tire-type gauge.

If the system is low on Freon, the clutch will cycle on and off rapidly, and the bubbling will occur so often that you can't make a reasonable check (this is the reason sight glasses have been dropped on so many systems). In this case, add Freon and check system pressures after the compressor clutch is engaged, as follows: After five minutes of operation, unplug the wiring connector from the cycling clutch switch and connect a jumper wire across the connector terminals; this will keep the compressor clutch engaged for a pressure check (make it after a couple of minutes of compressor operation). Once pressures are acceptable, inspect the sight glass and it should be clear except for the period when the clutch cycles off and then on.

Note: Some clutch systems are designed to cycle more rapidly than others, so fast cycling itself is not always a symptom of a low Freon level.

Pressure readings are dependent on many factors, including humidity, and it is possible to get a normal high-pressure reading even if something is wrong. However, see if you get a reading of more than 120 p.s.i., and preferably closer to 170 to 210 p.s.i. on a warm-to-hot day (70° F and above).

Next, remove the cap on the low-pressure valve and take a reading there. Normal pressure is 15 to 30 p.s.i. If both readings are very low, and there is effectively no real cooling from the system, inspect the expansion valve exterior. If it's frosted at the inlet, see a professional. If not, adding Freon should do the job if there are no leaks of significance in the system.

If there is no low-pressure test valve, a special adapter can be installed on systems with an accumulator and a pressure-sensitive cycling clutch switch. Only a professional may have the resources for this, so if necessary, have a pro install it, and pay to leave it in place.

CHECKING FOR LEAKS

Before you add refrigerant gas, you can check for leaks in the system in any of these ways:

Brush a soap-and-water solution around each hose connection. If you see bubbling, you've found a leak. Tighten the connection with wrenches and repeat the test. If you stop the leak, you can proceed to add refrigerant to the system. If you can't eliminate a leak by normal tightening, the hose must be replaced and the system completely vacuum-pumped and recharged. A new receiver-dryer also may be necessary. See a professional.

Use a leak detector. The propane leak detector is the only inexpensive type (electronic types are the pro's choice).

Figure 10-9. When the search hose of a propane detector encounters a Freon gas leak, the propane flame changes color. Move the search hose all around each connection, particularly at the bottom.

The flame changes color in the presence of a Freon leak (see fig. 10-9). Details on color changes are included with each tester. These leak detectors are far more accurate than soap solution, and will pick up leaks that the soapy water won't.

Look for oil. A light oil deposit indicates a leak (except at the front of the compressor, where seepage is normal). Be careful not to confuse refrigeration system oil with engine oil splatter.

If you find a leak at a line connection, you can try tightening it if it is loose. The typical connection has a rubber O-ring, so it is not necessary to tighten it very much. Overtightening distorts an O-ring and this can cause a joint to leak.

Note: Late-model Ford products and some other cars have spring-lock couplings that cannot be tightened.

ADDING REFRIGERANT GAS

Refrigerant gas comes in 13- to 15-oz. cans. You should always add refrigerant into the low-pressure side of the system using a charging kit, which includes a special tap-valve assembly for the can and a hose. Only use R-12, not R-11 or R-22, in a car. If your car does not have a low-pressure valve, have an adapter installed. Do not attempt to add R-12 through the high pressure valve.

Close the valve on the refrigerant can tap and install the tap onto the can, following the kit manufacturer's instructions. Connect the hose to the can tap valve.

Thread the other end of the hose onto the tire-type valve as finger-tight as you can make it.

Wearing gloves (or using a pair of pliers to keep your hands away), loosen the hose connection at the refrigerant can tap valve to allow some refrigerant gas from the system to purge air from the hose. As soon as the gas pours out (a second or so), tighten the hose connection at the tap valve.

Run the engine at fast idle (2,000 r.p.m.) and turn on the AC. Open the tap valve on the can and the refrigerant gas will flow into the system (see fig. 10-10). Keep your hands wrapped around the can to warm it and the flow of gas will be faster. When you feel the can is empty, close the valve and disconnect the hose from the low-pressure valve.

Note: You will feel the can get very cold as it empties (and the weight also will drop). If the can is very slow to empty (more than 10 minutes), heat it in a pot of water to 120° F (no higher, for it can explode at 125° to 130° F).

Two cans of refrigerant gas normally will restore performance when the problem is a simple loss. Do not, however, attempt refrigerant gas additions as some sort of cure-all when the problem is not clear-cut. A low refrigerant problem usually is obvious, and that's when refrigerant addition will give you results.

Replacing Cycling Clutch Switch

If the switch is threaded into the accumulator, just unplug the wiring connector and unthread the switch with a

Figure 10-10 Installing refrigerant into the low-pressure side of the air conditioning system.

wrench (see fig. 10-11). Behind the switch is a tire-type valve that automatically will close as the switch is unthreaded, so no Freon in the system will be lost.

If the switch has a tube clamped to a refrigeration line, begin by removing the insulating putty over the end of the tube. Then undo the retaining clamp and lift away the tube (see fig. 10-12). Remove the screws that hold the switch and install a replacement in its place. Route the tube (see fig. 10-13) to the mounting point and secure it with the clamp. Cover the clamp and tube end with putty (if the original putty crumbles, cover with plumber's putty—see fig. 10-14).

If the switch tubing goes into a sheath around a refrigeration line, measure the length that goes in, and be sure to insert approximately the same length tubing on the replacement switch. The sheathing should be filled with grease, which serves as an insulator. If it is not, insert the tube and pack the opening with plumber's putty.

Failure to insulate the tubing in either case will affect the operation of the air conditioning.

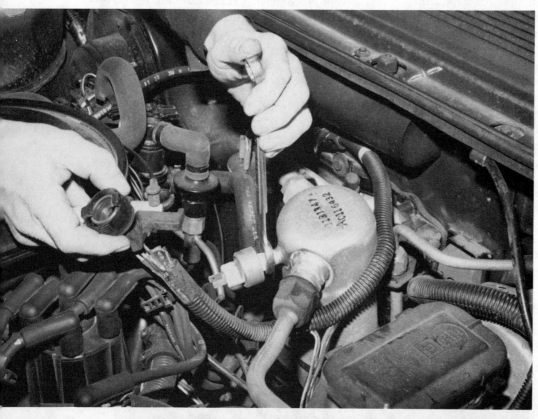

Figure 10-11. After unplugging connector, unthread pressure switch with wrench as shown.

Figure 10-12. Begin thermostatic switch replacement by undoing clamp that holds sensing tube to air conditioning line.

Figure 10-13. Route sensing tube of new switch to line, using gentle bends.

Figure 10-14. After clamping tube to line, cover end with plumber's putty as an insulator.

317

11 THE BRAKE SYSTEM

The braking system on a modern car is actually three systems in one: a hydraulic system that transfers movement of the brake pedal to each wheel; a friction system at each wheel that is actuated by the hydraulics to stop the car; and a mechanical linkage from the parking brake pedal or handle to the friction system.

HOW THE BRAKES WORK

Hydraulic System

When you step on the brake pedal you push a rod that goes into the master cylinder, a fluid-filled (hydraulic) cylinder with pistons. The movement of the rod pushes on the pistons, which push on the fluid.

This movement is transferred through tubing that runs from the master cylinder to each wheel (see figs. 11-1 and 11-2). At the wheel the hydraulic pressure goes to one of these:

A *wheel cylinder* (see fig. 11-3). This is a cylinder with a piston at each end, positioned by a spring between them. Hydraulic pressure pushes the pistons outward to act on the friction mechanism.

A *caliper* (see fig. 11-4). This is like a C-clamp, but instead of a forcing screw, there's a piston in one side. Hydraulic pressure pushes the piston out to apply the friction mechanism.

The fluid used in a braking system is a special formulation that will not boil at the temperatures built up from the heat of friction braking. The hydraulic system should not leak, but over a period of time minor loss of fluid may occur. A reservoir at the top of the master cylinder permits easy addition of fluid (see fig. 11-5). On a new car you should use a top-quality fluid, one with a boiling point of at least 450° F.

Note: The fluid level should drop slightly as the front disc brake shoes are pushed outward to compensate for wear of their friction material. Refer to the following explanation of the friction system.

Friction System

The friction system is what actually brings each wheel to a stop. There are two types in popular use:

Drum Type. In this design the wheel is bolted to a drum, which is shaped somewhat like a jar lid. As the wheel spins, so does the drum. The friction material is called brake lining and it is attached to two half-moon-shaped parts called brake shoes. The wheel cylinder is used in this system, and when its pistons are pushed outward they force the shoes against the inside surface of the drum (see fig. 11-6) bringing the drum (and the wheel) to a stop. When you release the pedal, coil springs retract the shoes (see fig. 11-3).

All drum brake systems must have a provision to adjust the position of the shoes to compensate for wear of the linings. On older cars (and a very few current models), manual adjustment is required. At the top or bottom of the brake, between two shoes, is a threaded adjuster called a star wheel (see fig. 11-3). Turning it one way unthreads it to move the shoes closer to the drum. Turning it the other way threads it in, moving the shoes further from the drum.

On most current cars, the drum brake shoes adjust to compensate for wear automatically, by means of a lever that turns the star wheel (see fig. 11-3) to move the shoes closer to the drum.

Disc Type. The clamp-like caliper is positioned over the edge of a part shaped like a phonograph record, called the disc or rotor (see fig. 11-4). The wheel is bolted to the disc and spins with it. The friction material, as in the drum

DUAL MASTER CYLINDER

REAR WHEEL BRAKES HYDRAULIC CIRCUIT

WARNING LIGHT

WARNING LIGHT PRESSURE SWITCH

FRONT WHEEL BRAKES HYDRAULIC CIRCUIT

Figure 11-1. The hydraulic portion of the braking system. When you step on the pedal, fluid pressure is transferred from the master cylinder through tubing to the front and rear wheel brakes. If there is a failure in either fronts or rears, a warning light pressure switch is activated, but braking still is available from the unaffected pair of brakes.

BRAKE LINES

FRONT CALIPERS

WHEEL CYLINDERS PISTONS AND LINKS

Figure 11-2. Close-up look at a basic hydraulic system. A rod connected to the brake pedal pushes on a piston in the master cylinder. Pressure is transferred through the brake lines to calipers at the front wheel disc brakes and wheel cylinders at the rear wheel drum brakes. The typical caliper is a single-piston clamp that applies friction material parts to the sides of a disc. The typical wheel cylinder has a piston in each end that pushes out against friction material parts called brake shoes.

Figure 11-3. Here's what a drum brake looks like when the drum is removed. The pistons inside the wheel cylinder push out (against retracting springs) to force the shoes with their lining against the drum. To compensate for wear of the friction material a star wheel adjuster is used at the bottom. When the car is braked in reverse, the star wheel is operated automatically by a mechanism that includes an automatic adjusting lever and cable.

system, is called brake lining, and it is attached to a flat steel pad, called the pad or shoe. Although most brake linings are made of asbestos, there is a trend to linings that are made with metallic powder and fibers called "semimetallics" (and to nonmetallic natural and synthetic fibers). The reasons for the switch are that asbestos particles are considered a health hazard, and the semimetallic linings last longer and are more fade-resistant. However, they are more expensive. There are two shoes at each wheel, one in each side of the caliper (on each side of the disc). One shoe rests against the caliper piston; the other is directly opposite and rests against a flange on the caliper.

When hydraulic pressure pushes out the caliper piston, it forces one shoe against the side of the disc. Simultaneously, the caliper slides (along rods or guides) and draws the shoe on the opposite side against that side of the disc. This provides the two-sided clamping action to stop the disc and therefore the wheel.

A few cars over the years have had fixed calipers with one or two pistons on each side of the caliper. In this case, each piston or pair of pistons pushes out a brake shoe.

Parking Brake

The parking brake operates by a mechanical cable-and-linkage setup that applies the rear brakes. If the car has self-adjusting drum brakes or disc brakes (or as do a few imported cars, a linkage and cable that operate the front brakes) the parking brake theoretically needs no attention, since these brakes are inherently self-adjusting and compensate for brake lining wear.

There have been some cars with rear disc brakes that contain a drum-brake parking brake system within the rear discs (pre-1988 Corvettes, for example).

The parking brake cables stretch, and soon you find yourself at the limit of parking brake application, yet the car won't hold. In this case the cable must be shortened, as explained in this chapter.

DISC BRAKE SERVICE

The single piston sliding caliper front disc brakes (see fig. 11-4) have been used on virtually all American cars since 1976, and were used on many imports even earlier. Inas-

FRICTION MATERIAL (LINING)

PISTON

CALIPER

DISC

FRICTION MATERIAL (LINING)

Figure 11-4. This is a phantom view of a single piston disc brake. A friction material shoe is on each side of the disc, covered by the caliper. When the brakes are applied, hydraulic pressure pushes the caliper piston out to force the shoes against the sides of the disc. Because the disc and wheel are bolted together, the wheel comes to a stop when the disc does.

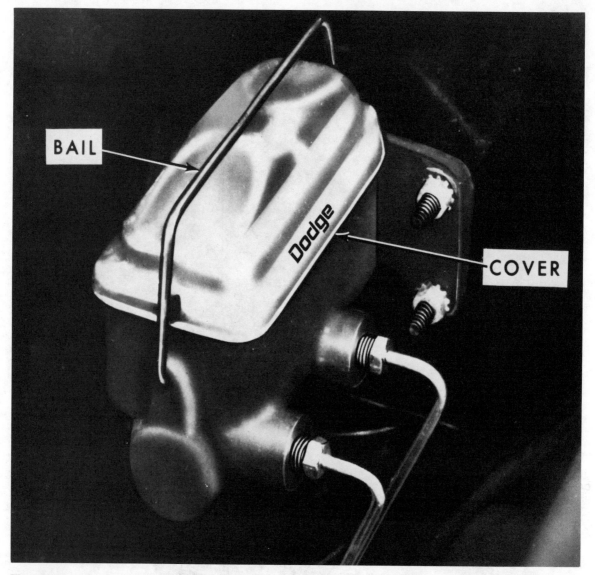

Figure 11-5. Here's a typical master cylinder. When the bail wire is pried away to the side, the cover can be lifted off so the amount of fluid in the master cylinder reservoir can be checked. *At the right* the two brake lines come out of the side. One goes to the front brakes, the other to the rear. The master cylinder itself is also separated into two sections, so no matter where a partial failure occurs the car retains some braking.

much as the front brakes do at least 60 percent of the braking (up to 80 percent on some front-wheel-drive cars), they wear out faster than the rears. It is not uncommon for rear brakes to last more than twice as long as the fronts.

A weekend mechanic can service disc brakes. This isn't a job you should attempt as your first effort, but once you have general experience with tools and have done the routine under-the-hood services there is no reason why you should be afraid. You must be careful, of course, for we're talking about a key safety item, and if you aren't confident, don't attempt it. There is, however, nothing mysterious about the brakes, and many weekend mechanics do routine brake service. Start with simple

shoe replacement on a car that has enjoyed normal brake performance, and if you're careful all will go well.

One thing is in your favor: If you aren't sure about how things go together, just look at the wheel on the other side of the car. It will have a completely assembled mirror-image model.

Brake Inspection

On some cars there is an inspection hole in the side of the caliper, through which you can see one or both brake shoes. If you see that the lining is worn to $1/16$ inch or less, the shoes should be replaced.

Begin by loosening the wheel nuts, then jack up the car

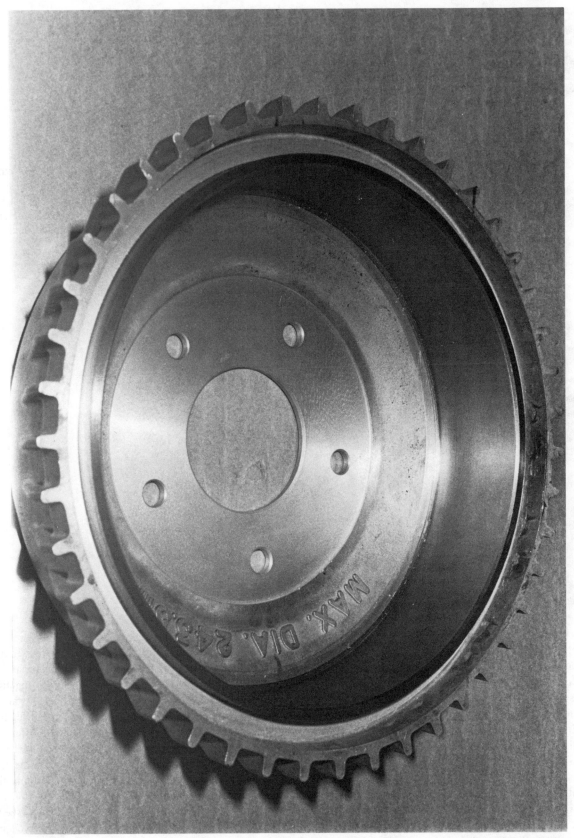

Figure 11-6. This is a typical drum removed from a rear wheel. Notice the smooth inside surface against which the shoes are pushed by the wheel cylinder. Both rear wheel and drum are bolted to the rear axle shaft, so when the drum is stopped by the brakes, so is the rear wheel.

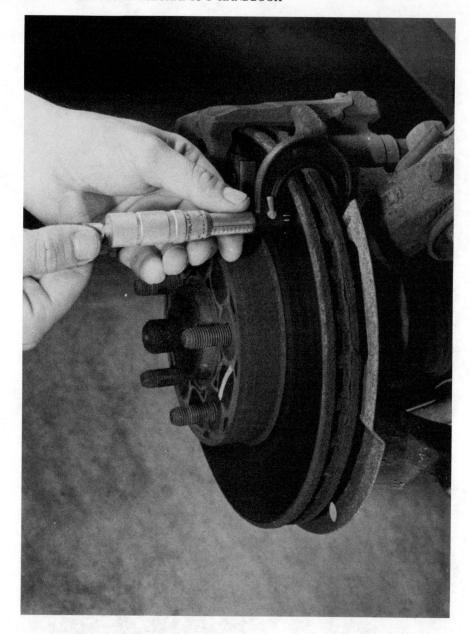

Figure 11-7. Using an outside micrometer on a disc. Measure at several points around the machined surface, and the maximum difference in thickness should be no more than .0007-inch.

(see chapter 5), support on safety stands, and remove the wheels. You'll see the disc and the caliper, which is the hydraulic clamp that forces the shoes against the sides of the disc.

Inspect the disc on both sides. Spin it, and if it wobbles (in-and-out movement called "runout") check wheel bearings (see chapter 12), and if they aren't the problem the disc itself is defective. Inspect the disc for deep scores (deep enough to completely stop a fingernail) as you move your finger along the surface. If you find such scores on the otherwise smooth surface that comes in contact with the brake shoes, the disc must be resurfaced. If the fingernail can glide in and out of the score, it can be ignored. Discs are much more tolerant of scores than drums.

You also should check the disc for minimum thickness, variations in thickness, and "runout" using an outside micrometer you can buy (and often rent). See figure 11-7.

Measure the thickness of the disc (about an inch in from the edge) at four to six equally spaced points around the circumference. The readings should meet the manufacturer's specification for minimum thickness (stamped somewhere on the disc) and they should not differ from each other by more than .0007 inch. If the disc fails the minimum thickness measurement, it must be replaced. If it passes that check, but the difference between the highest and lowest readings on the micrometer is more than .0007 inch, the disc must be resurfaced.

Measuring disc runout calls for a dial indicator (see fig. 11-8)—an inexpensive tool, but still one that you may choose to rent. It also can be used for checking wheel bearings and engine valve guides, so if you're planning to do a lot of weekend mechanic work, consider buying one.

Figure 11-8. Checking a disc for runout (wobble) can be done with a dial indicator. The type shown has a bracket that clamps to the suspension, and it has a link arrangement, so it can be positioned as shown. The little rod that projects from the indicator is brought into contact with side of disc, then the indicator is zeroed and the disc is turned by hand. Runout is shown by changes in readings on dial indicator.

With the dial indicator attached to a fixed point, such as the steering knuckle, position the dial head plunger so it is pushing on the brake shoe contact surface of the disc, as illustrated. Turn the dial until it reads "zero," then turn the disc. If the dial needle moves more than .005 inch, the disc runout is excessive. Try adjusting the wheel bearing nut (see chapter 12) on all cars with adjustable wheel bearings (rear-wheel-drive cars only) and repeat the test. If runout still is excessive the disc must be resurfaced, if possible, or replaced. Removing the disc is discussed later in this chapter.

Preparing to Remove the Caliper

You can gain access to the brake shoes on the modern sliding caliper only after removing the caliper from its mounting over the disc.

If there is any rust on the outside edges of the disc, however, the brake shoes will catch and make removal impossible. Therefore, you must provide clearance by pushing the caliper piston back into its bore. This will allow the brake shoe that bears against it to also come back, and when you remove the caliper there should be lots of room to complete the job.

First, check the brake master cylinder reservoir level (see fig. 11-9). If it's topped off, siphon out some fluid from the larger (front) reservoir, or if you're not sure, both reservoirs. When you push back the piston, fluid will be forced up into the reservoir, and if it's full already it will overflow.

Next, attach a large C-clamp so that it braces against the disc or a protruding part of the brake shoe on one side and against the caliper on the other (see fig. 11-10). Close the clamp and the caliper will be squeezed against the disc, forcing the piston back into its bore. When you can't turn down the clamp any more, the piston should be all the way in. If you can't turn down the clamp at all, the piston is apparently stuck in the bore. Removing it is probably best left to the professional, but if you want to try, the procedure is described in the following section. On a few cars with fixed calipers, you should have little trouble removing the shoes even if the pistons are sticking.

Figure 11-9. Prying bail wire off the top of the master cylinder cover. Cover then is lifted for fluid level inspection. If reservoir is full, siphon off some fluid from each of the two chambers so they won't flood over when disc brake caliper pistons are pushed back.

Figure 11-10. Using C-clamp on caliper to push back the piston. This step will permit easy removal of the caliper from its position over the disc.

Taking Off the Caliper

Most calipers are held to a bracket on the steering knuckle assembly by the rods along which they slide. The rods are secured by some form of fastener at one end, such as a clip, nut, cotter pin, etc., or the rod threads into the caliper bracket on the steering knuckle. Typical fastening arrangements are shown in figures 11-11 to 11-14. Remove the fastener or unthread the rod.

Note: Many bolts have Allen or Torx slots cut into the bolt heads, and these require special wrenches. Although an Allen wrench often can be substituted for a Torx wrench, this frequently is not true on caliper bolts, which are so tight that use of the Allen wrench may damage the Torx slot and turn bolt removal into a major problem. Next, pull the rod itself if necessary, using pliers on the end with the head. Lift the caliper up (see fig. 11-15) and out and secure it to the suspension with coat hanger wire. Do not let the caliper hang free or the brake hose will be strained.

Some cars have guides—called ways—machined into the caliper mounting bracket (see fig. 11-16) instead of rods. On this arrangement, remove the bolt-on part of the lower way (see figs. 11-17 and 11-18), then lift the caliper up and off, and hang it to the suspension. Occasionally, the mounting of the brake hose is such that you must disconnect it from the caliper to get the caliper off. If this is done, plug the end of the hose to minimize fluid loss and entry of air. You will have to bleed air from the brakes at the conclusion of the job.

If you can't force the caliper piston back in, you must first check the edge of the disc circumference for rust, and if there's a rust ridge it must be sanded off. Then remove the caliper from its bracket on the steering knuckle, and pull it away from the disc. If you're lucky, it won't be a hard pull. If you still can't get it off, you must remove the disc and caliper together.

Disc Removal

Once the caliper is off, the front disc can be removed for service, if necessary. On the conventional rear-drive car,

Figure 11-11. If you see that the caliper rods have the "speed nut" type washers on the ends, pry them off with a screwdriver. Install new speed nuts when reassembling.

Figure 11-12. After speed nut is off, pull out rod with pliers as shown.

Figure 11-13. If rod is threaded in, remove with suitable socket and Allen or Torx socket bit extension and ratchet as shown.

Figure 11-14. Perhaps caliper is held by large cotter pin. Straighten the dual ends, and then pull out from the single "head" end with pliers as shown.

Figure 11-15. Lifting caliper and brake shoes off the disc.

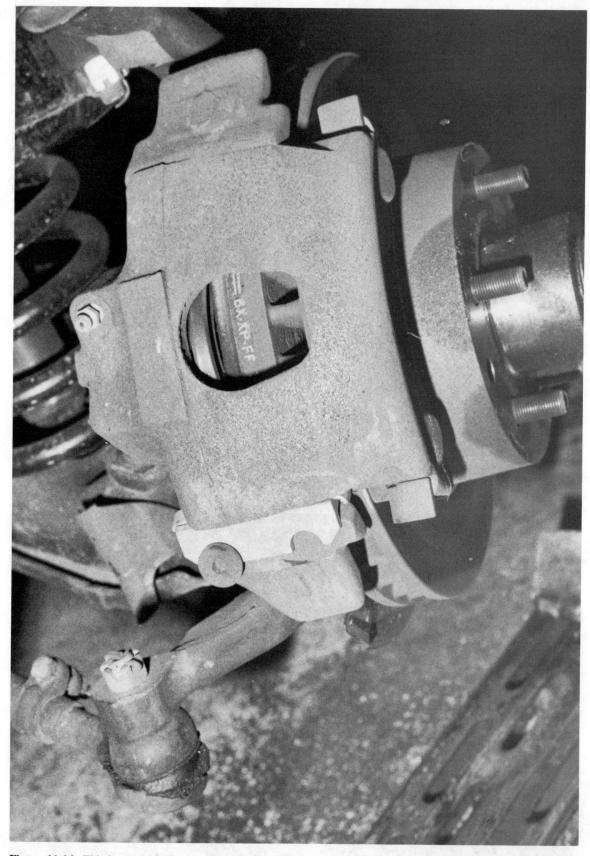

Figure 11-16. This is a machined-way caliper. Guide rails (ways) are machined into the edges of the caliper and the mounting bracket. Bottom of this type is held by bolt. On other types, both top and bottom rail sections unbolt from the caliper bracket.

330

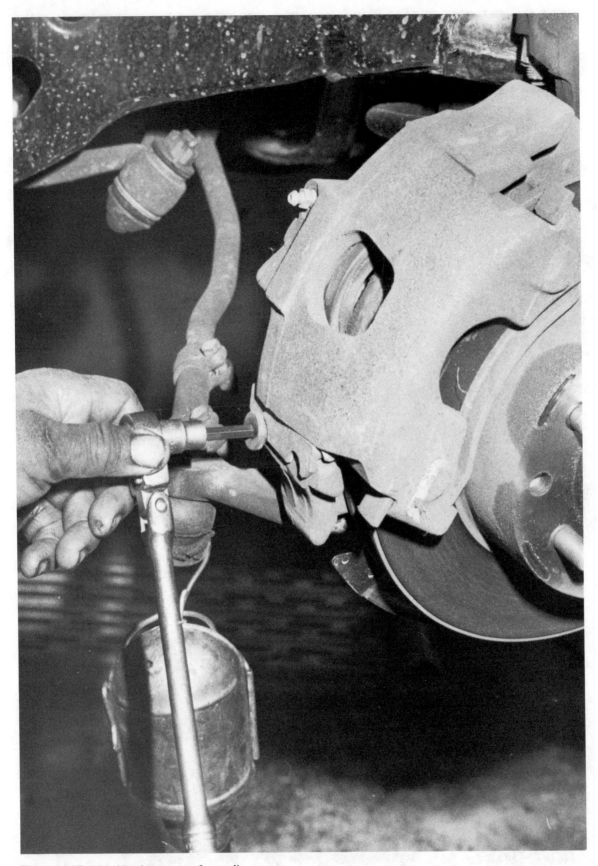

Figure 11-17. Unbolting bottom way from caliper.

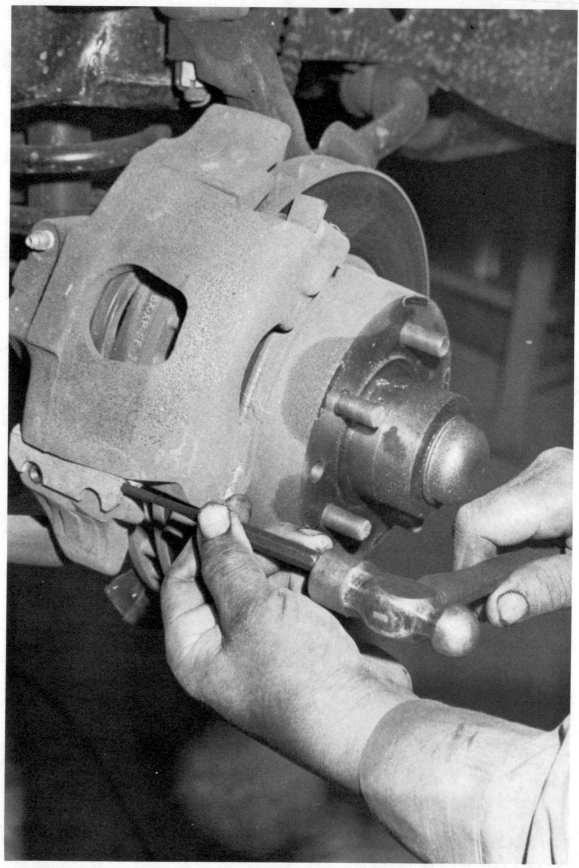

Figure 11-18. Driving out the unbolted way with hammer and punch.

remove the dust cup, wheel bearing nut, and outer wheel bearing, then pull the disc off, as explained in detail in chapter 12. On front-wheel-drive cars, or any cars with sealed front-wheel bearings, the disc simply slides off or unbolts from the hub. Many Japanese cars are exceptions to this, and the only way the disc can be removed on these is with a special puller or by unbolting the suspension and having the disc removed in a large hydraulic press. This should be left to a professional.

Note: Some shops that feature foreign car work have special on-the-car lathes to resurface the discs without removal.

If you are struggling with a caliper stuck on the disc, follow the procedure for disc removal. Disconnect the brake hose at the caliper (and plug the hose end), then take the disc and caliper to an automotive machine shop that has the equipment necessary to separate them. The machine shop also may be able to remove the stuck piston and rebuild the caliper, or at least obtain a rebuilt caliper for you.

When you reinstall a disc after disturbing the wheel bearing adjustment, you must adjust the wheel bearings, unless they are the no-service type. If you disconnected the brake hose, don't forget to reconnect and bleed the brakes, as explained later in this chapter.

Caliper Inspection

Inspect the caliper before proceeding further. If there is fluid seepage or if the dust boot is cut or unseated, odds are that some dirt has gotten in. Have a machine shop disassemble it and replace the piston seal and dust boot for you, or obtain a rebuilt caliper.

If the caliper passes inspection, clean out the inside (keeping clear of the piston and dust boot) with a wire brush. If the piston was not pushed back all the way before removal, complete the job now.

On calipers with machined ways, inspect the ways for rust. If they're rusty, remove the rubber O-rings around them (if used), clean with a wire brush, then refit the O-rings. Smear a film of silicone dielectric grease (available in auto parts stores, perhaps called an "electronic heat sink grease" or "spark plug boot release grease") on the machined ways.

Installing Brake Shoes

In most cases, the disc can remain in place and the caliper will come off with no problem, permitting you to proceed directly to brake shoe replacement. Observe how the old ones fit. For example, one shoe (usually the one that bears against the piston) may have a curved spring that scratches against the disc when the lining is worn down, to alert the driver. If the replacement shoes have such a spring, be sure to install the shoe in the same location (such as against the piston).

The shoe that bears against the piston may be held to the piston by a spring clip. Notice how it fits, so you can correctly install it later (see fig. 11-19).

On most machined-way calipers, the inner shoe (that bears against the piston) does not come off with the caliper. Instead, it remains on the caliper bracket. With the caliper off, it can easily be removed (see fig. 11-20).

In some designs there is a tab on the back of the shoe that engages a slot near the outer circumference of the piston, to keep the shoe in proper alignment. Don't miss this one.

On many cars, particularly General Motors and Chrysler products, the outer shoe (the one that does not bear against the piston) has a projecting ear on the metal back.

Figure 11-19. When removing brake shoe that bears against piston, look for a spring as shown and note how it fits so you can correctly reinstall it.

Figure 11-20. Removing inner shoe left in place when machined-way caliper is out.

Or the shoe may have ears projecting from holes in the caliper. Clinch the ear of this new shoe to the caliper, using large pliers (see figs. 11-21 and 11-22).

Note: This can also be done with the caliper mounted in place, as a final step before installing the wheels. If the shoe ear is too thick for bending with vise pliers as is common on many rear-drive Chrysler products, bend it by tapping with a hammer, so it is a force fit, and holds the shoe in place (see fig. 11-23). If the shoe won't fit on with moderate force, clamp it on using old shoes as supports and a C-clamp.

To prevent brake squeak, many discs have silencer pads that bear against the back of the shoe. If yours do not, obtain a tube of paste rubber silencer and apply it to the backs of the new shoes before installation, following the manufacturer's instructions.

Figure 11-21. Clinching ear of new outboard shoe with pliers, a procedure typically required on General Motor cars.

Figure 11-22. If the shoe ears project through the caliper as shown, use the following procedure to clinch them: After mounting the calipers, have a helper apply the brake pedal firmly three times, then release. Pry up on the outboard shoe with a large screwdriver reacting against the hat section of the disc as shown in the photo on the left. While prying, have the helper apply moderate force on the pedal. Then, with a one-pound ball-peen hammer resting on the tab as shown in the photo on the right, hammer on the back of the ball-peen with a brass hammer until the ear is bent at a 45-degree angle. If you do not have a brass hammer, use a brass drift between the ball-peen and a second, larger ball-peen.

Figure 11-23. Tapping ear of outboard shoe with a hammer with shoe braced on a steel bar, so that shoe is a force fit on the outboard side of the caliper. If the shoe ear is too tight to simply push into place, clamp it on, using old shoes between the clamp and caliper and shoe.

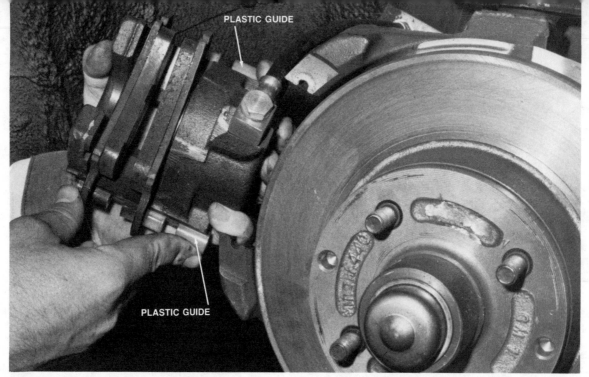

Figure 11-24. Plastic guides or rubber bushings should be replaced when doing a brake job. Also, lubricate with silicone spray before installation of the rods.

Caliper Slide Rods' Bushings and Guides

If the caliper slides along rods through rubber bushings or plastic guides in the caliper (see fig. 11-24), replace the bushings or guides in which they move. Before installing the rods spray the inner surfaces of the guide or bushings with an aerosol silicone lubricant.

On some cars with the rod arrangement you will think you need three hands to hold the caliper, position the plastic guides, and start the rods. It really can be done with only two, however.

Always use new retainers for the rods if they are not the thread-in type.

Machined-ways Caliper

The shoe that bears against the caliper piston on the machined-ways arrangement fits onto the bracket, and the caliper (with the other shoe in it) is installed afterward.

Put the brake shoe that bears against the piston onto the bracket, where it will hold in place. Then install the caliper (with the other shoe attached inside) on the bracket. To prevent the possibility of the shoe's metal back damaging the piston dust boot, insert a thin piece of cardboard in the caliper and hold it against the piston as you refit the caliper (see fig. 11-25). Once the edge of the brake shoe has cleared the piston, pull out the piece of

Figure 11-25. Notice piece of cardboard in caliper. It is on the inboard side against the piston to protect the piston, on a machined-ways caliper, from damage by the inboard shoe, which is put into place first.

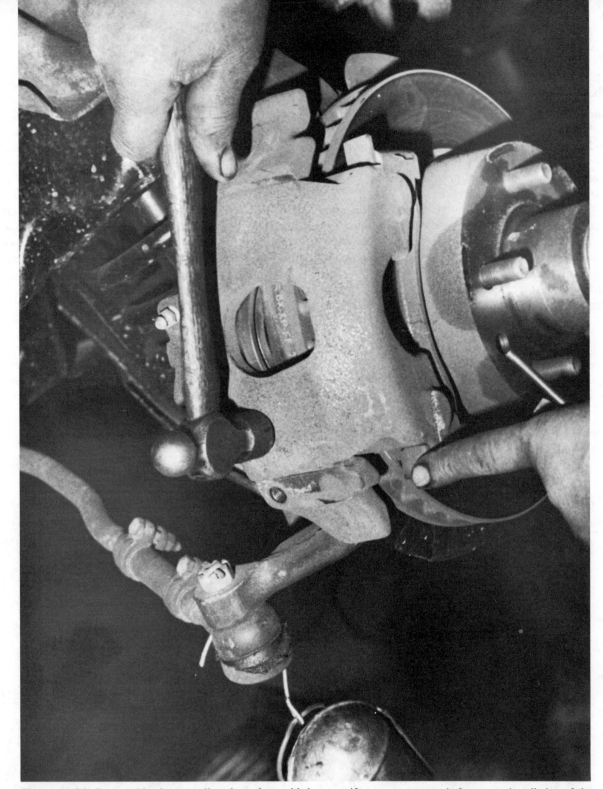

Figure 11-26. Tap machined-ways caliper into place with hammer if necessary to seat it for proper installation of the removable way.

cardboard. Set the caliper in position on the bracket and then bolt on the removable part of the lower way.

Note: Tap caliper with hammer if necessary to seat it for installation of the lower way (see fig. 11-26).

Install the wheels and tighten the lugnuts.

Note: On pre-1979 Olds Toronado and Cadillac Eldorado, the lugnuts must be very tight—130 lbs.-ft. With any front-wheel-drive car it's a good idea to check

specifications and use a torque wrench to be sure.

Note: If the caliper was disconnected from the brake line, bleed the system of air as described later in this chapter.

Initial braking may be slightly erratic. Break in the brakes by driving the car at 30 to 40 mph and making moderate stops every half mile. After about ten stops under these conditions the brake action should be normal.

Fixed Caliper Disc Brakes

Some older cars and more recent versions of the Chevrolet Corvette, have a fixed caliper disc brake system (see figs. 11-27 and 11-28). In this arrangement, the caliper does not move. Rather, there is a piston on each side, or two pistons on each side, that push each brake shoe into the sides of the disc.

You do not have to remove the caliper to change the brake shoes on most of these systems. First, inspect and measure the disc. If it requires service or replacement, leave the job to a professional. If the disc is okay, take off the wheel, remove a retainer (held by a spring clip, cotter pin, etc.) from the caliper outer end, then remove the shoe retaining rods (see fig. 11-29). Now you can pull out the

shoes with vise-type locking pliers or a screwdriver (see fig. 11-30). As with the sliding caliper system, if the master cylinder reservoir is full, siphon some fluid from the reservoir to prevent overflow when you push back the pistons. Once the shoes are out, insert a flat piece of steel against the piston and insert a prying tool (such as a heavy-duty screwdriver) between the steel plate and the disc to force the piston back into the caliper.

Note: Do not grind off friction material from an old disc brake shoe to provide a prying surface, as the friction material dust, if asbestos, can be hazardous to your health. Pry with the screwdrivers to force the piston back into the caliper bore (see fig. 11-31). Repeat the procedure for the other side. Now there's clearance to install the new shoes with their full-thickness lining.

Figure 11-27. This is a typical fixed caliper disc brake. When splash shield is removed, the brake shoes can be pulled from the side of the caliper. Therefore it is not necessary to disturb the caliper for simple replacement of brake shoes.

EXTERNAL TRANSFER TUBE

CALIPER SPLASH SHIELD

CALIPER ASSEMBLY

HUB AND ROTOR ASSEMBLY

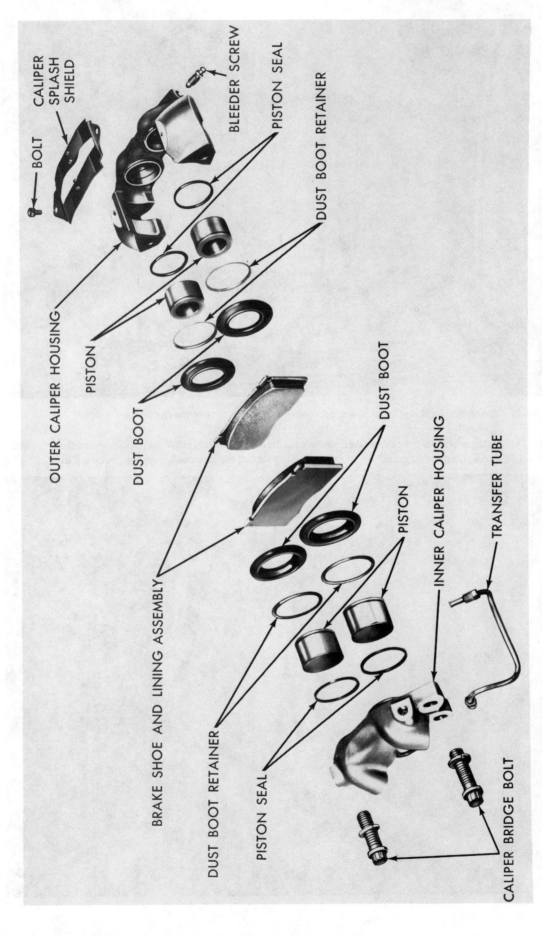

Figure 11-28. Disassembled view of the typical four-piston fixed caliper. Some imported cars with fixed calipers have only a single piston on each side.

339

Figure 11-29. The splash shield is off, and now the retaining rods are being removed from a fixed caliper.

Figure 11-30. On this particular fixed caliper there are holes in the brake shoe steel plates, so you can pry out the shoes with a screwdriver as shown. On other fixed calipers you may have to yank out the shoes with vise-type locking pliers.

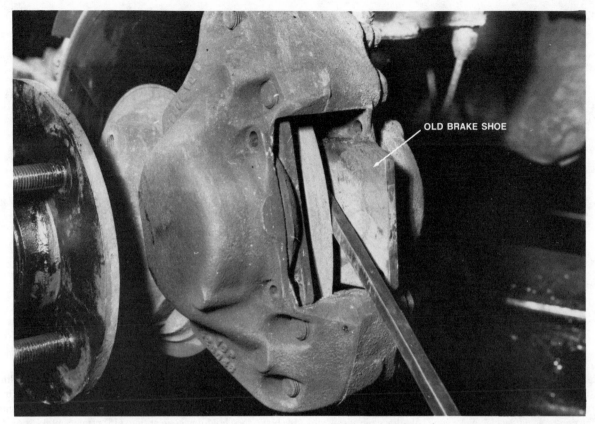

OLD BRAKE SHOE

Figure 11-31. Once the old shoes are out of the fixed caliper, grind off the lining remaining on one of them and reinsert as shown. With the lining ground off, there is clearance to insert a screwdriver between the shoe and the disc as shown, to pry and so push back the pistons.

REAR DISC BRAKES

The only difference in servicing rear disc brakes is the way in which the piston is pushed back.

DRUM BRAKE SERVICE

As with disc brakes, drum brake service should only be attempted after you have had experience with simpler services and have a good familiarity with use of tools. Also as with disc brakes, you can disassemble at one wheel with the knowledge that there is an assembled mirror-image version of what you are taking apart on the other side of the car.

Your first brake job should be simple replacement of worn brake shoes, and this is something that is within the ability of the weekend mechanic. The only special equipment requirement may be a tool that is used to remove and reinstall brake shoe springs.

The drum brakes on virtually all cars are self-adjusting, but there are some exceptions, as explained later in this chapter. Before beginning, study figures 11-3, 11-32 and 11-33 carefully, so the parts will look familiar when you see them.

Front Drum Brakes

All late-model cars have front disc brakes, but if you have an older car, it may have front drum brakes instead of discs.

For access to the brake shoes, begin by removing the hub caps or wheel covers, then jack up the car (see chapter 5) and support it on safety stands.

Remove the dust cap in the center of the wheel, then the wheel bearing nut and outer wheel bearing, and finally the brake drum and wheel assembly. This service procedure is described in chapter 12 under "Wheel Bearing Service."

If the brake drum won't slide off, it apparently is binding on the brake shoes (or on a rear-drive car on the axle flange—see procedure explained later). You must, therefore, back off the brake shoes from the drum, working through an access slot in the backing plate (see fig. 11-34), the steel plate to which the brake shoes are attached. Pry out the plastic or rubber plug in this slot, then look inside with a penlight and you'll see what figure 11-35 is all about. Insert a thin screwdriver to push away the lever, then insert another screwdriver or an inexpensive tool called a brake spoon into the slot to engage the slots between the teeth or the shoe adjuster (star wheel). In most cases you lift the handle of the spoon upward to back

Figure 11-32. Disassembled view of a rear drum brake. Parts are: (1) backing plate; (2) wheel cylinder dust cover; (3) wheel cylinder piston; (4) wheel cylinder piston cup seal; (5) wheel cylinder body; (6) brake shoe hold-down pin; (7) antirattle spring; (8) parking brake strut; (9) parking brake lever; (10) brake shoe return spring; (11) brake shoe automatic adjusting cable; (12) brake shoe automatic adjusting cable guide; (13) brake shoe hold-down pin spring cup; (14) brake shoe hold-down pin spring; (15) primary brake shoe; (16) brake shoe automatic adjusting lever spring; (17) brake shoe star wheel adjuster; (18) secondary brake shoe; (19) spring; (20) brake shoe automatic adjusting lever; (21) over-center-travel assembly part of automatic adjuster.

Figure 11-33. This is a leading-trailing shoe-type rear drum brake. Notice that the star wheel is not at the bottom, but just above the midpoint. This particular type does not have an automatic adjuster.

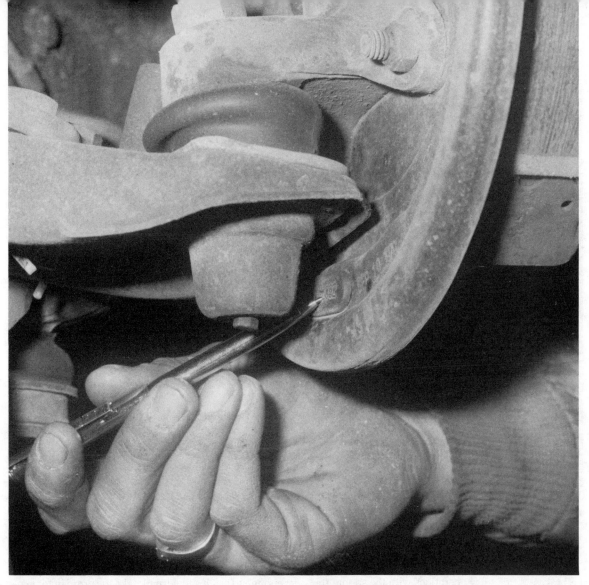

Figure 11-34. Pen points to rubber plug in the inboard side of the brake backing plate. Pry out the plug for access to brake shoe star wheel adjuster if necessary, to back off the brake shoes in order to remove the drum.

RUBBER PLUG
REMOVED

SELF-ADJUSTING
LEVER

STAR WHEEL

MOVE HANDLE UPWARD
TO RETRACT BRAKE SHOES

Figure 11-35. Retracting brake shoes with drum on are shown in this illustration. A thin screwdriver is used to push away the automatic adjusting lever and brake spoon is used to turn star wheel. A screwdriver can be used instead of a spoon.

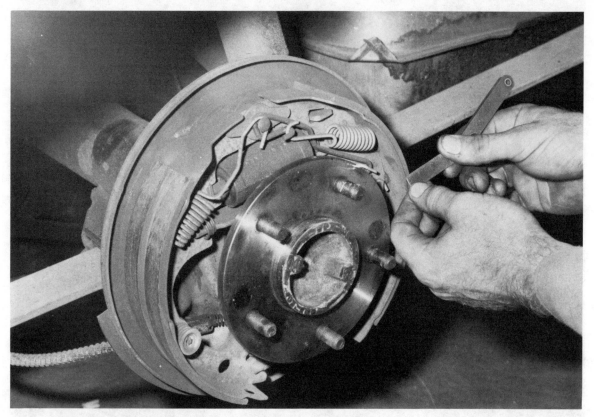

Figure 11-36. Measuring thickness of brake lining with ruler. The ruler shown is one that is included with a set of feeler gauges and has very small gradations.

off the brakes. After a few operations with the spoon, the drum should be free. There are other arrangements and procedures used to back off the brake shoes which are explained later in this chapter.

You now have access to the front brake shoes (see fig. 11-3). If the linings on the brake shoes are worn down to $\frac{1}{16}$ inch at their thinnest point (see fig. 11-36), the shoes should be replaced. If the linings are held to the shoes by rivets, the $\frac{1}{16}$-inch thickness should be above the heads of the rivets.

The normal wear pattern of the linings is somewhat greater in the center. If you see an irregular wear pattern, such as tapered from inboard toward outboard side, or very thin at one or both ends, the shoes and/or drums are warped. You will automatically replace the shoes and you also should take the drum into an automotive machine shop for measurement and resurfacing if necessary.

Note: If one drum needs resurfacing, have the one on the opposite side resurfaced too, and have the shop fit new shoes with oversize linings to match. The machine shop is typically an adjunct to an auto parts store, so this is normally no problem.

Also check the drum's brake shoe contact surface with your finger (see fig. 11-37). If there are any scores deep

enough to catch a fingernail, take the drum in for resurfacing—and take the opposite side drum too.

Look for any cracks in the drum, and if you find any that go through, replace the drum. Drums are not inexpensive, so consider a used one from a wrecking yard.

Replacing the Shoes

Begin by removing the brake shoe return springs (also called retracting springs as in fig. 11-38). Then disengage the self-adjusting mechanism, the method for which depends on the type.

If it's a simple cable type, just remove the connecting spring from the lever to the primary shoe, then disconnect the cable.

If there is a cable with an overtravel assembly (designed to prevent overadjustment of the brakes under abnormal conditions) as shown in fig. 11-32, begin by sliding the eye of the cable off the anchor at the top, then remove the cable from the shoe. Next, disconnect the cable from the opposite end of the adjuster lever and rotate the adjuster lever clockwise. You'll be able to disengage it from its retaining pin and a connecting spring.

Figure 11-37. Feeling brake drum surface with finger. If there are scratches on which a fingernail hangs, the drum must be resurfaced.

With a lever-type self-adjuster, just remove the two springs between the lever and the secondary shoe and the wirelike actuating link that connects to the anchor pin at the top and the lever at the bottom. You'll then be able to take out the lever itself.

Other self-adjusting lever mechanisms also are used, but no matter what the individual design the method of removal should be reasonably obvious. If there are springs connected to the lever, the usual procedure is to take them off, then disengage the lever and any other links.

Important caution: On many cars the brake shoe return springs for primary and secondary shoes are not the same, although they are visually very close. Be careful not to confuse them. In fact, to be sure you don't get mixed up, tape the springs to a piece of cardboard, in the same relative position as on the car. Then double-check yourself by referring to the wheel assembly on the opposite side, keeping in mind that a primary shoe spring on the driver's side is on your left as you face it, but on the passenger's side it's on your right, and vice versa for the secondary springs.

Hold-down springs. The brake shoes are held in the center by little spring-loaded hold-down assemblies. You can

remove them with the special tool by just pushing in on the top retainer and turning 90 degrees, which will turn the retainer so that the head of a through pin will pass through the key slot in the retainer (see fig. 11-39). Without this special tool, you can do the job by pressing down on the retainer with needle-nose pliers and using the plier jaws to grasp and turn the head of the retainer pin.

Finally, spread the shoes away from the wheel cylinder and lift them out with the star wheel and connecting spring at the bottom still attached (see fig. 11-40).

Star wheel. The star wheel is the adjuster. As you will be able to see with the drum off, the movement of the self-adjusting lever rotates just the star wheel, unthreading it to push out the brake shoes closer to the drum to compensate for lining wear. When you reached in with two thin screwdrivers (or an awl and screwdriver) to back off the shoes, what you did was thread down the star wheel, and the return springs pulled them away from the drum surface.

If any of the teeth on the star wheel are damaged, the star wheel must be replaced. If you try to reuse it, the self-adjusting lever may simply ride over damaged teeth and not turn the star wheel.

PRIMARY SHOE
RETURN
SPRING

SPECIAL TOOL
(REMOVING AND
INSTALLING)

TAB OF
ANTI-RATTLE
SPRING

SECONDARY
SHOE RETURN
SPRING

ADJUSTER
CABLE

LEVER
SPRING

ADJUSTER
SPRING

ADJUSTING
LEVER

NU243A

Figure 11-38. Removing brake shoe return springs with special tool, an inexpensive item available in most auto parts stores. Other types of special tools, including a form of pliers, also are available for this job. The tool is shown at the anchor end of the return spring on a rear drum brake, but the principle is the same for front and rear drum brakes of this type. *Note*: This tool cannot be used on General Motors transverse-engine front-drive cars because there is no anchor pin against which the tool can react. Instead, there is a riveted-in-place shoe rest at the top. To remove and reinstall the springs without a struggle, use a special tool with a hook attached. The special tool, sold in auto parts stores, reacts against a rivet head, as the hook pulls on the spring *(see illustration at bottom)*.

Figure 11-39. Using the special tool to disengage the retainer from the shoe hold-down pin.

Figure 11-40. Spreading the brake shoes apart from the anchor and wheel cylinder to remove them from the wheel. *Caution:* If the innards of the wheel cylinder start to come out, stop immediately and wrap wire around them and the wheel cylinder body to prevent this. Or you can obtain special spring clips from an auto parts store to hold the wheel cylinder together.

Figure 11-41. Unthread the two sections of the star wheel adjuster and lubricate the threads with penetrating solvent, then thread them together and apart as often as necessary to work the solvent in. Stop when the parts thread absolutely freely.

Even if the star wheel teeth are in good condition, unthread the assembly and spray the threads with penetrating lubricant. Then thread it together and unthread it several times to work in the lube (see fig. 11-41).

Backing plate. Clean with solvent and wipe off the outboard side of the brake backing plate. If there are any raised platforms on the backing plate, lube them with a thin film of silicone grease.

Wheel cylinder. The wheel cylinder is the terminal of the hydraulic system. Inspect it by gently prying back the dust covers at each side with a thin screwdriver. If you see any evidence of brake fluid leakage, you must replace the wheel cylinder. If the dust boots are cut or heat-cracked, replace them. Refer to "Brake Hydraulic System," later in this chapter.

Note: A beginner who might not wish to tackle replacement of a defective wheel cylinder should make the inspection before removal of the shoes (see fig. 11-42).

Reassembly with new shoes. Before you leave for the parts

Figure 11-42. The wheel cylinder dust cover can be pried away gently as shown, to check for fluid seepage. If there is none, the cylinder may be assumed to be in good condition. This can be done with brake shoes off, or before you start the job (as illustrated), when everything is in place.

store to exchange your old brake shoes for replacements, check the shoes for any dowel pins or guides for the self-adjusting mechanism and parking brake linkage. On many shoes they are removable parts (unbolt or knock out with a hammer and punch) that must be installed on the replacement shoes.

When you buy new brake shoes, ask the parts supply store for its premium line. It may cost three times the price of the cheap line, but you get exactly what you pay for. The better lining will not only last a lot longer but will provide better stopping for its entire life, and it will be quieter.

You may be offered a choice of riveted vs. bonded linings. At one time mechanics always took the riveted because the bonding agents were of inconsistent quality and sometimes there was separation of lining and shoe. This is not a problem today. The bonded lining will last longer because it can be worn down almost to the shoe, whereas the riveted lining must be changed when it is close to the tops of the rivet heads. However, bonded shoes may be noisier (squeak) than the riveted type.

If the brake springs have a bluish tinge (indicating they were overheated) or if the springs were not replaced at the last brake job, get a new set now. It's an inexpensive purchase that adds a measure of security to the job.

Reassembly of the brake parts is basically the reverse of disassembly. Work with clean hands and a clean backing plate to prevent grease from getting on the linings. If any grease does, lift up the glob with a putty knife and sand down the lining to remove any that got into the surface.

A simple starting point is to install the shoes with the hold-down assemblies, then insert the star wheel adjuster and connecting spring at the bottom. Add the self-adjusting mechanism and springs, and finally the shoe return springs. Be very careful (wear safety glasses) when installing stiff springs such as the shoe returns. If one slips off the tool it might cause injury.

Note: The star wheel adjuster should be threaded all the way in.

Refit the brake drum and wheel assembly, and the wheel bearing and adjusting nut, and adjust the bearings as explained in chapter 12.

Caution: The self-adjusting drum brakes adjust only when the car is braked while moving in reverse. Do not back the car up until you are assured the road is clear, then brake gently the first few times, taking it as easy as possible on the brakes for the first 50 miles or so to give the linings a chance to wear in.

Rear Drum Brakes—Rear-drive Cars

Although there are similarities in the service of front and rear drum brakes, there also are important differences.

Perhaps the most important is getting off the drum. Loosen the wheel lugnuts on the ground, then jack up the car (see chapter 5), support it on safety stands, and remove the wheels.

Look at the studs and see if there are any tiny clips on them, to hold the drum. If there are, pry them off with a screwdriver and discard. Or if there is a screw holding the drum, remove it.

Try to pull the drum straight off. If it is stuck, turn the drum slowly and listen for a scraping noise. Have trouble turning the drum and hear a scraping noise? Well, there is some resistance to turning a rear drum because you're also turning a shaft and gears in the rear axle, but if there's real binding and a scraping noise the brake shoes are probably in contact with the drum. Back them off as described earlier for front drum brakes. If there is no slot in the backing plate for access, look for a lanced area in the drum or backing plate and knock it in with a hammer and punch to obtain an opening. Turn the drum until the opening in the drum is aligned with the star wheel, hook onto the self-adjusting lever with stiff wire, and turn the star wheel with a screwdriver or brake spoon.

Note: This opening must be sealed; plugs are available at auto supply stores. Discard the lanced piece after removing the drum.

If there is no access slot or lanced area for a star wheel, look for what appear to be hex-head bolts on the brake backing plate, near the outer circumference (where the shoes are located). These hex-heads operate cam adjusters for the brake shoes. Turn them all the way until they stop, one at a time. Then spin the brake drum, and if it spins, the shoe is backed off. If it is locked, turn the hex-head all the way in the opposite direction, and the shoe will be backed off (see figs. 11-43 and 11-44).

If there's no scraping noise or unusual resistance when turning the drum, the problem is that it's stuck to the axle shaft hub. You have four possible approaches:

1. Douse the joint between the hub and the big hole in the center of the drum with penetrating solvent. Also douse the joints between the lugnut studs and the drum. Allow the solvent to soak in and pry with big screwdrivers (180 degrees apart) between the brake drum and the backing plate. It may take several treatments over several hours to free up the drum (see fig. 11-45).

2. You can use a brake drum puller. In combination with penetrating solvent treatments this should pull even the most stubborn drum. The puller is an inexpensive item that will easily justify its existence, but if you don't want to buy you probably can rent one. The puller shown in figure 11-46 is typical and easy to use. The jaws grasp the edges of the drum, and you turn down the forcing screw with a T-handle (the forcing screw pushes against the axle shaft hub while the jaws pull out on the drum).

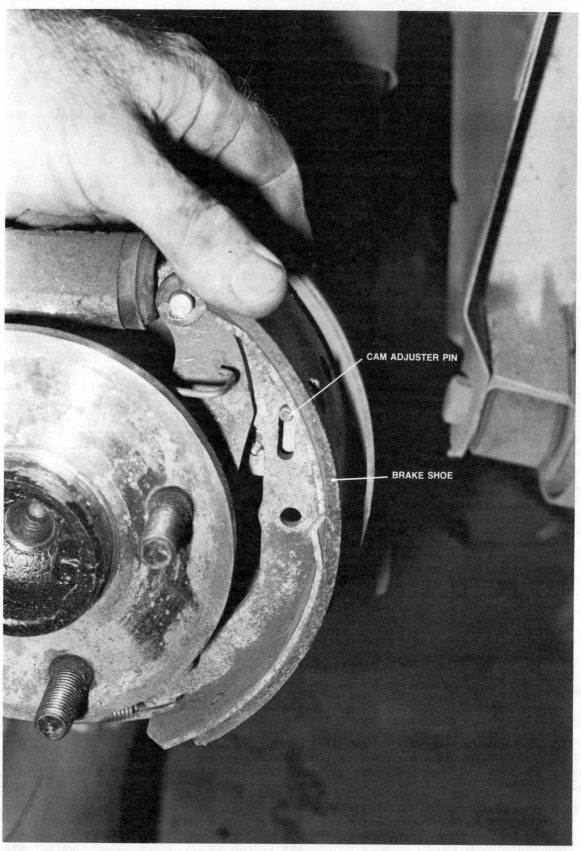

CAM ADJUSTER PIN

BRAKE SHOE

Figure 11-43. Some self-adjusting drum brake systems do not use the star wheel. This one (from an older Chevette) has a cam adjuster with a pin that operates in a slot in the brake shoe.

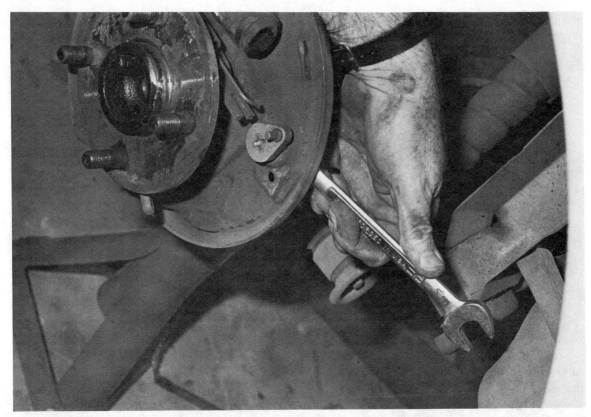

Figure 11-44. With brake shoes removed you can see the cam adjuster and pin. Turning a hex-head on the inboard side of brake backing plate with a wrench spreads or retracts the shoes.

Figure 11-45. Spraying penetrating solvent around center hub and stud holes may free up stuck drum.

SPRAY HERE

Figure 11-46. Special brake drum puller available in auto supply stores can be used to pull drums when solvent treatment doesn't work. Jaws grip against inboard edge of drum while forcing screw is turned down against axle shaft hub.

3. On cast-iron drums you can apply heat from a propane torch around the areas where the binding exists (stud and hub holes in the drum). Heat causes the holes to expand and break the rust bond.

   Note: Do not use heat to break a corrosion bond on an aluminum drum. If in doubt, put a magnet to the drum's exterior surface. It will not be drawn to aluminum.

   Caution: Work in a well-ventilated area when using a torch at the rear, and aim the flame away from the gas tank. Gas fumes and flame are an explosive combination.

4. On some imports, push in a brake hydraulic pressure regulator lever (see fig. 11-47).

Shoe Replacement. Once you have the drum off, you can proceed to disassemble the brake as you would a front brake, with these exceptions:

The rear brake also serves as the parking brake. A set of cables and levers from the parking brake handle or pedal operates the rear brakes mechanically, to hold the car for parking. You therefore must disconnect the parking brake from the secondary brake shoe.

A typical arrangement is a clip (possibly with a spring washer) holding a lever to a brake shoe. The lever is hooked onto the parking brake cable (see fig. 11-48). Disengaging the parking brake lever from the shoe is usually obvious, such as by prying out the spring clip with a screwdriver (see fig. 11-49).

If the lever is held to the shoe by a pin, you may have to remove that pin from the old shoe and install it on the new one.

Note: On some cars it's easier to disconnect the cable from the lever, remove the lever with the shoe, then separate.

On some rear brake systems the two shoes are the same. If you might re-use the brake shoes, you should mark one of them so you can reinstall in the same position.

On some rear drum brakes, a single return spring is used for both shoes. Limited clearances and the shape of the spring make the standard brake spring tools unusable. Instead, do the job with needlenose pliers and be prepared for a bit of a struggle, particularly on reinstallation. It may be helpful to have an assistant. While you stretch the spring to align the hook with the eye in the shoe, the assistant can push on the hook with a screwdriver or punch to force it into the eye.

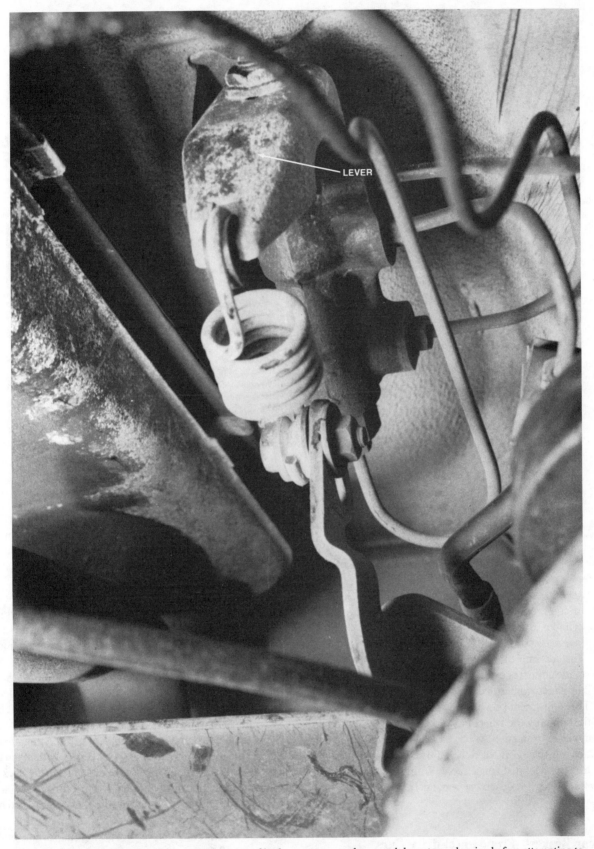

Figure 11-47. If you have an import with this type of brake pressure regulator, push lever toward spring before attempting to remove the drum.

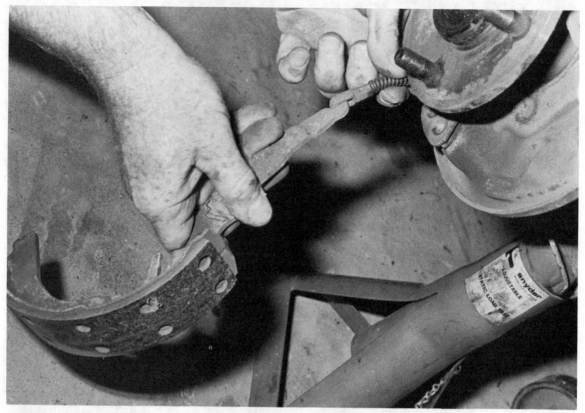

Figure 11-48. Parking brake lever from brake shoe is hooked to parking brake cable. Just disengage this type with brake shoe removed.

Manual Adjustment Brakes

Not all cars have self-adjusting drum brakes. If your owner's manual lists rear brakes for periodic adjustment, look for one of the following:

1. *Access hole in backing plate and a star wheel adjuster.* In some cases it is at the top, just under the wheel cylinder. See figure 11-33.
2. *Hex-head bolts for cam adjusters on the backing plate.* They resemble the arrangement for the cam-type automatic adjusters explained earlier, but only bear against the shoes, rather than have a pin fitted into them.

The adjustment procedure is simple: Turn the adjuster while spinning the wheel forward by hand (car jacked up and on safety stands). As soon as the wheel starts to drag noticeably, back off (turn the adjuster the opposite way) until the wheel just spins freely. With two adjusters (one for each shoe), set each one separately.

Rear Brakes—Front-wheel-drive Cars

The rear brakes on front-wheel-drive cars somewhat resemble the front drum brakes on older cars. You remove the wheel, but then it's a matter of removing the wheel bearing dust cap, wheel bearing nut and outer bearing, and pulling off the drum to gain access to the brake shoes. On some newer models, the wheel bearings are not adjustable, so the drum unbolts from the assembly that holds the wheel bearings.

Although most rear drum brakes on front-drive cars have star wheels accessible through a hole in the backing plate, there are exceptions. A significant one, introduced in 1980 on VW Rabbits, is a tapered-wedge arrangement (see fig. 11-50). To retract the shoes on this model, you must remove the wheel and turn the brake drum so that a lugbolt hole aligns with the bottom of the wedge. Then insert a screwdriver and pry up on the wedge, against the pressure of its spring. As you do, the stronger spring between the two shoes will compress, retracting them.

On still other cars, such as Ford Escort with standard rear drum brakes, remove the access plug from the back of the brake backing plate, insert a thin screwdriver, and twist it to disengage a toothed quadrant from a toothed pin (see fig. 11-51).

Note: Whenever you are working on drum brake designs with a single spring, you cannot use a brake spring tool to lever it back on. Instead follow the procedure previously noted for drum brakes on rear-drive cars.

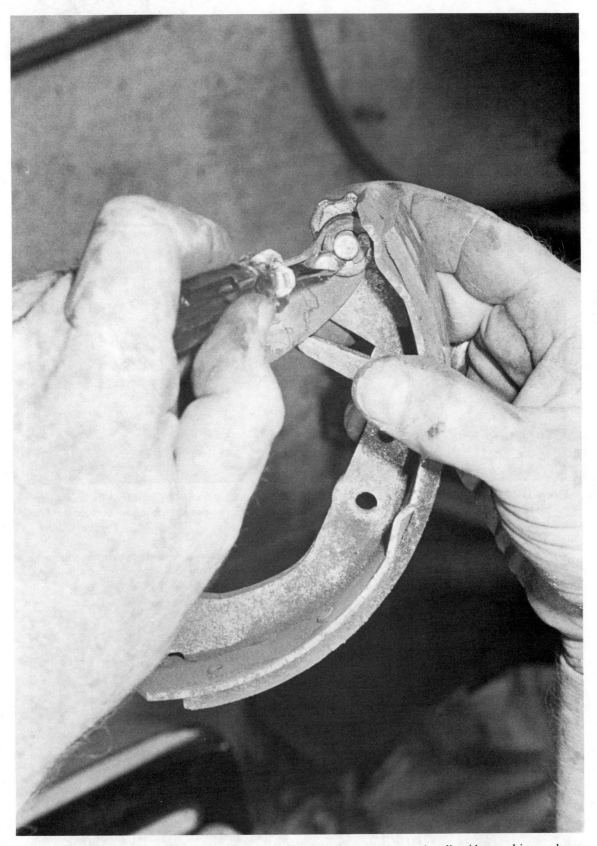

Figure 11-49. To separate this old brake shoe from the parking brake lever, pry away spring clip with screwdriver as shown.

Figure 11-50. As of 1980, the drum brakes (rear) on VWs are an unusual self-adjusting design. As the linings wear, the tapered wedge is pulled down by a spring to hold the shoes partly out, so much of the free space between the shoes and drum is taken up.

Figure 11-51. This is a standard rear drum brake on the Ford Escort. If necessary to remove a stuck drum, remove the dust cover and reach in through the hole in the backing plate with a thin screwdriver until it makes contact with the pin. Apply pressure, and the adjuster quadrant will disengage and release the adjustment.

BRAKE HYDRAULIC SYSTEM

The hydraulic system transfers foot pressure on the brake pedal to operate the friction mechanism at each wheel to stop the car, as explained at the start of this chapter.

The master cylinder, the heart of the system, often fails by leaking internally. If the brake pedal slowly sinks to the floor under steady foot pressure (engine running with power brakes) and there is no fluid loss at the master cylinder reservoir or the wheels, the master cylinder apparently is defective.

If your brake warning light comes on, it means there has been a failure at one or more wheels. The failure could be in either the hydraulic or friction systems.

To check the hydraulic portion, remove the master cylinder reservoir cover (see fig. 11-9) and see if you have lost fluid. A small drop in the fluid level is normal on cars with disc brakes, but if the level is quite low, there is a leak in the system.

Inspect brake hoses and tubing connections from the master cylinder while a helper presses down on the pedal. If you can't find a leak, remove the brake drums and then the disc calipers, as explained in earlier segments of this chapter, to inspect for leakage.

A leaking wheel cylinder or caliper or a defective master cylinder should be replaced. You might be able to rebuild, but this is an operation requiring some experience and therefore not recommended for a beginning weekend mechanic. Inexpensive rebuilt components are readily available from auto parts stores.

Note: Whenever you do any work on the brake system that involves draining old fluid, discard that fluid, even if it is visually clean. Brake fluid attracts moisture in the air and this lowers the boiling point of the fluid, which reduces its effectiveness. As explained earlier, buy only a high-quality brake fluid, with a boiling point of 450° F or higher. Keep the fluid container tightly capped when not in use, to prevent the fluid inside from attracting moisture.

Caution: Do not use a silicon-type brake fluid in a system that has held a conventional fluid.

Replacing Calipers

Remove the caliper as explained earlier in this chapter, then disconnect the brake line at the caliper with a wrench. Plug the end of the brake line with a rubber eraser or something similar to minimize fluid loss and entry of air. Squirt brake fluid slowly into the replacement caliper to displace as much air as possible, then reconnect to the brake line. Reinstall the caliper and complete the job by bleeding the brakes, as explained later in this section.

Replacing Wheel Cylinders

Most wheel cylinders are held by bolts, accessible either from the inboard or outboard side of the brake backing plate. First disconnect the brake line to the cylinder, working at the inboard side of the backing plate with a wrench. Plug the end of the line to minimize air entry and loss of fluid. Remove the drum, take out the bolts, and withdraw the wheel cylinder. If you see no bolts, look for a circular locking retainer on the inboard side (on some older General Motors cars). To remove it, insert awls or pins of 1/8-inch diameter or less into the access slots between the wheel cylinder and the retainer's lock tabs. Bend both tabs away with the tools, at the same time, until the tabs spring over the wheel cylinder and release it. See figure 11-52.

Installation of a wheel cylinder is basically the reverse of removal. You must complete the job by bleeding the brakes.

Bleeding the Brakes

There are many methods of bleeding the brakes, and many special tools. There are two ways particularly suitable for weekend mechanics.

Begin by making sure the bleeder valve can be loosened, using a tight-fitting wrench (but do not open it). Then slip a long piece of rubber hose of a diameter that is a tight fit onto the brake bleeder valve nipple (see fig. 11-53) and submerge the free end into a glass jar containing clean brake fluid.

Note: Some brake bleeder valves are recessed and difficult to reach with an ordinary wrench. If those on your car fit this description (particularly on rear drum brakes), check at the local auto parts store for a specially shaped wrench for the job. K-D and Cal-Van tool lines may have what you need.

If the car is equipped with antilock brakes, disconnect the battery cable and apply the brakes moderately at least 20 times to exhaust hydraulic pressure in the system.

Following the car maker's recommended sequence, have a helper depress the pedal slowly once and hold it down. Loosen the bleeder valve one full turn and allow air bubbles in the fluid to escape into the jar. Tighten the valve and let the helper slowly release the pedal. Wait 15 seconds and repeat this procedure. You may have to do this a dozen or more times until all air is removed. If the manufacturer's sequence is not available, begin at the valve that is farthest from the master cylinder, then go to the other valve on the same circuit. If there is one circuit for left rear, right front and another for right rear, left front, begin at the right rear, then do the left front, then the left rear and finally the right front. If it's a front-rear split system, do the right rear, left rear, right front and left front. Common exceptions to this recommended sequence are General Motors front-drive compacts and subcompacts (right rear, left front, left rear, right front), AMC four-wheel-drives and Honda Accord (left front, right rear, right front and left rear), air-cooled Volkswagens

Figure 11-52. Prying out retainer for wheel cylinder on some cars. Working from inboard side of brake backing plate, insert awls or pins with $\frac{1}{8}$-inch diameter or less into access slots between wheel cylinder and retainer locking tabs. Bend both tabs away simultaneously until the tabs spring over the wheel cylinder shoulder. When installing a new wheel cylinder, use a new retainer. Hold the wheel cylinder against the backing plate by inserting a block between the wheel cylinder and the axle flange. Install the new retainer over the wheel cylinder, lining up the tabs with the wheel cylinder tab grooves, then drive the retainer into place (snapped under the abutment) with a $1\frac{1}{8}$-inch socket and a long extension (10 inches). If there is limited clearance and/or you do not have a suitable socket for installation, you can obtain an inexpensive tool from an auto parts store for this job. The caliper-like tool spreads the tangs of the clip for easy removal and installation. *See below.*

Figure 11-53. To prepare for bleeding, attach a tight-fitting hose to the bleeder valve nipple and submerge the free end in a glass jar containing clean brake fluid. Or use the special tool at right.

(right front, left front, right rear, left rear), and Chevy Corvette and most Toyota Corollas (left rear, right rear, left front and right front). The left side is the driver's side of the car. If, however, you have only introduced some air into one wheel brake, such as when a caliper or wheel cylinder is replaced, you may start at that wheel. After bleeding out the specific amount of fluid, you normally will also have removed all the air in it too.

Check your work by hitting the brake pedal. If it's firm,

all air is out. If necessary, repeat the process until the pedal is firm.

Manual Bleeding. This requires a helper and a special clip for the stem of a part called the metering valve (on cars with front discs, rear drums only). Just follow the brake lines from the front wheels until they come to a junction block. Have a helper hit the brake pedal and you should see a dowel-like stem either eject or move into the junction block, which is really the valve assembly.

Figure 11-54. Special clip on metering valve stem holds it in open position so brakes can be bled. Other makes require a tool that holds the valve stem in. To determine which you have, locate the stem and see if it can be pushed in, or if it's already in and could only come out.

If the stem is ejected when the brake pedal is depressed, you must hold it out. If it goes in, you must keep it in. Inexpensive special clips for this purpose (see fig. 11-54) are available from auto supply stores.

Note: If you have your helper pump the pedal hard, the special clip need not be used.

You'll also need a hose that fits tightly over the bleeder valve nipple and a clear glass jar. Fill the jar halfway with brake fluid, force the hose end onto the bleeder valve nipple, and submerge the other hose end into the jar of fluid.

Have a helper pump the brake pedal, then hold steady pressure down on it. Open the brake bleeder valve with a wrench. The helper's foot will push the pedal to the floor. He must not lift his foot yet. As the pedal goes to the floor, fluid will be expelled through the hose into the jar, and with this fluid are trapped air bubbles.

Close the valve. Now the helper can lift his foot and pump the pedal once more, then hold it down. Open the valve again and watch the fluid in the jar. If there are air bubbles, you must close the valve and have the helper pump again, then hold down on the pedal. If there are no air bubbles, close the valve and have him test the pedal for firmness. You normally will save the pedal test for when you have bled all four wheels.

Note: Top off the master cylinder reservoir after bleeding at a wheel.

Remove the metering valve clip when you are done. If you encounter trouble getting air from a rear brake, this procedure may help on some cars, particularly Chrysler products: Crack a front bleeder screw open and apply the brakes. The warning light valve will shift (and the warning light will come on and stay on), but any entrapped air should now come out with bleeding at the rear wheels. Bleed the front brakes, then apply the brakes with moderate force, and the warning switch valve will recenter and the light will go out.

Note: Normally, it will take three or four pedal-pumping sequences at each wheel to get rid of all the trapped air.

Stuck Bleeder Valve

If the bleeder valve is frozen and cannot be loosened with a tight-fitting box wrench or ratchet and socket, spray the fitting joint with penetrating solvent and whack the handle of the wrench with a hammer. If that doesn't work, and bleeding is absolutely necessary, you must remove the wheel cylinder or caliper and have the old bleeder valve drilled out and a replacement installed. Kits for this job are available at many auto supply stores, but installation really isn't a job for a weekend mechanic. The machine shop of an auto parts store, however, can handle it for you.

Brake Master Cylinder

The brake master cylinder is normally long-lived, but eventually the seals inside deteriorate and fail to hold hydraulic pressure. When this happens, as explained earlier in this chapter, the pedal sinks slowly to the floor under foot pressure, making the problem obvious.

The typical brake master cylinder is held by two to four nuts or bolts and is readily accessible at the firewall (rear sheet metal surface of the engine compartment) on the driver's side. Just undo the tubing connections (then plug the tubing ends to minimize air entry and loss of fluid). Undo the nuts or bolts and withdraw the master cylinder.

If your car has power brakes, make sure the replacement you buy is for power brakes.

Cars with antilock brakes may pose special problems. Refer to a factory service ("shop") manual.

Bleeding the Master Cylinder

The brake master cylinder must be bled before installation to remove most of the air inside. Attempting to bleed it by working at the wheels alone could take a long time and still not be successful.

You can bleed either off or on the car. To bleed on the car, install the master cylinder on the car and tighten the bolts but do not connect the brake lines. To bleed off the car, mount the master cylinder in a vise and obtain a wooden dowel to use as an out-of-car manually operated pushrod.

Obtain a master cylinder bleeding kit, which consists of flexible tubing and fittings to connect to the tubing connections on the component (see fig. 11-55). Aim the flexible tubing into the master cylinder reservoir, which should be filled to the halfway mark with clean brake fluid.

Operate the master cylinder by pushing in and releasing the dowel as shown, or have a helper pump the brake pedal. When air bubbles stop forming in the reservoirs, the master cylinder bleeding is complete. Connect the lines from the wheel brakes and check the pedal for firmness. Some final, minor bleeding at the wheels may be necesary.

If the car has disc brakes or is a 1973 to 1976 Chrysler, Dodge, or Plymouth with drums, there is a minor complication. When you release pressure on the wooden dowel or the brake pedal, brake fluid will be drawn back into the tube, and it will just move forward in the tube when you do apply pressure.

Therefore, pinch the hoses before you release pressure on the dowel or brake pedal to prevent this. Let go when you have pressure applied.

Note: You may be able to obtain brake master cylinders that are "self-bleeding." This type has special plastic outlet fittings installed (see figs. 11-56 and 11-57) that eliminate the need to pinch the hoses. The special outlet fittings also may be obtained in a master cylinder bleeding tool kit, available in auto parts stores, made by Thexton Manufacturing Co., Minneapolis, MN.

Figure 11-55. Bleeding kit made up of tubes (plus fittings that thread into master cylinder) and a dowel. With master cylinder in vise and reservoirs full, pump dowel until there are no more air bubbles from tubing into reservoirs.

POSI-CHEK HOSE CLIP AND BLEEDER HOSE

POSI-CHEK VALVES
with built-in residual check valves

Figure 11-56. This master cylinder comes with special bleeding kit that does the job with the master cylinder on the car if desired. Special fittings and flexible hose combine to operate as check valves, simplifying the bleeding process.

Figure 11-57. This master cylinder bleeder kit is similar to the one in the previous photo, except that is has tapered fittings secured by screw clamps, so it fits all makes.

BALANCER

TURNBUCKLE

Figure 11-58. This parking brake has a turnbuckle adjuster to compensate for cable stretch. Just turn the turnbuckle and cable slack is taken up.

Parking Brakes

Because the parking brake is just a mechanical linkage to the rear brakes, it normally needs no special attention. It is common, however, for the parking brake cables to stretch, and so require adjustment to shorten them.

All parking brake cable arrangements have some provision, usually a type of turnbuckle arrangement, to shorten the operating length of the cables to compensate for stretch (see figs. 11-58 and 11-59).

The normal location for the adjustment is near the equalizer, a bracketlike part at which the cable from the passenger compartment lever and the cables to the rear brakes meet. This is under the car in most cases, but if you can't find it underneath and you have a console-type parking brake, lift the console and you'll probably find it there (see fig. 11-60).

Usually there is a locknut and an adjusting nut. Loosen the locknut and turn the adjuster, which will pull on the rear cables. Give the adjusting nut a couple of turns,

Figure 11-59. These are two typical brake cable arrangements in which turning the adjusting nut takes up cable slack.

CONNECTOR

RELEASE CABLE

ADJUSTOR ROD

ADJUSTING AND LOCKNUT

ADJUSTING AND LOCKNUT

CONNECTOR

ADJUSTER ROD

Figure 11-60. This cable adjuster is under the console. With this type you slacken a locknut, turn the adjusting nut to take up slack, and then tighten the locknut.

Figure 11-61. Add-on adjuster removes slack from brake cable if car's adjuster is rust-frozen or has used up its adjustment range. Cable is fitted under hook and when nut is turned it pulls cable down into adjuster, reducing slack. A locknut then is turned against the adjusting nut.

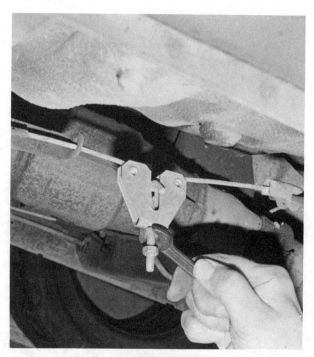

tighten the locknut, and try the parking brake lever. It should catch on about the fifth notch or after a few inches of movement. If it locks up almost immediately, the adjustment is too tight. Back off a turn or two and recheck.

It should be reasonably obvious which way to turn the adjusting nut to shorten the effective length of the cables (normally clockwise), but if it isn't, a bit of trial-and-error will soon demonstrate the proper direction.

If the car's adjuster is rust-frozen, as often happens (or has to be turned to use up all its adjustment range), install an add-on adjuster to any convenient point along the brake cable near the adjuster (see fig. 11-61). As you turn the add-on adjuster, it will take up free play in the cable. In severe situations, you may have to use two or even three add-on adjusters to compensate for all the cable stretch.

POWER BRAKES

The power brake on most cars is a large vacuum diaphragm device that uses engine vacuum to reduce the pedal pressures (see fig. 11-62). If the diaphragm unit fails, the pedal pressures required to stop the car increase dramatically, beyond those required for a car without power brakes. In some cases, failure also can allow engine vacuum to suck brake fluid from the master cylinder through the vacuum diaphragm into the intake manifold. Of course, a hard pedal also may be caused by defects in the friction and hydraulic systems, so check first.

A power assist defect may be in the unit or in the vacuum supply. Disconnect the vacuum hose at the power unit (see fig. 11-63) and feel the end for vacuum (and any telltale sign of brake fluid). If the vacuum is weak, check the hose for kinking. If the vacuum is good, disconnect the hose at the intake manifold and test vacuum at the source with a vacuum gauge. Normal manifold vacuum at idle is 16 to 22 inches. If noticeably lower, the engine requires service.

If you have normal vacuum to the power brake unit and a hard pedal, the problem may be in the vacuum valve or its retaining grommet (see fig. 11-64). If you can get a replacement valve and grommet, try it before condemning the complete power unit. If the valve and grommet are not the problem or are not available, the only cure is to change the power brake unit

Note: Unless you are an experienced weekend mechanic who has done most other brake work, leave replacement to a professional.

Note: A rebuilt power brake unit is your most economical choice (and may be all that's available). However, it typically comes with a new master cylinder, as rebuilders attempt to "insure" a successful job this way.

The replacement procedure on most cars is normally straightforward. Disconnect the power brake pushrod from the brake pedal, then unbolt the master cylinder from the power brake and the power brake from the firewall. You should be able to pull the master cylinder forward far enough to remove the power brake unit.

When you obtain a replacement (normally a rebuilt), check to determine if the power brake pushrod length has been correctly preset. On some units it is preset at the rebuilder; on others the pushrod is adjustable and a gauge with instructions is (or should be) included in the package.

HYDRO-BOOST

On some cars the power brake unit is not vacuum-operated, but is an additional hydraulic unit operated by pressurized fluid from the power steering pump. If the drive belt is loose or fails, or the pump reservoir fluid level is low, the system will not operate properly. In addition, most antilock brake systems have hydraulic-assist, provided by an electric pump. Failures in this system are usually indicated by a dashboard warning light.

Figure 11-62. This is a typical power brake arrangement. Linkage from brake pedal operates diaphragm assembly. Check valve at top is connected by a hose to the engine's intake manifold, a source of vacuum.

CHECK VALVE

PUSH ROD

LINKAGE

BOOT

TANDEM MASTER CYLINDER

POWER BRAKES

Figure 11-63. Disconnecting hose from check valve and feeling for vacuum with engine idling.

Figure 11-64. Check valve can be pulled out of grommet in power brake unit for replacement, as shown.

12 BASIC SUSPENSION MAINTENANCE

The suspension supports the body and chassis as the car rolls down the road. Many different types of automobile suspension systems are used, but they all have certain things in common.

At the front, the suspension is combined with the steering mechanism. Each wheel is mounted on a spindle that is part of the steering knuckle. The knuckle has upper and lower mounting points.

In an upper-lower control arm suspension (see fig. 12-1), there are two A-shaped arms attached to the chassis by a hinge bolt at the wide end, and to the steering knuckle by a little swivel called a ball joint at the tip end. In between the arms is a coil spring and a shock absorber.

When the wheel hits a road irregularity, the spring-loaded arms rise, the spring flexes to absorb the road shock, and the shock absorber dampens the spring movement to smooth out the ride. The shock absorber, as you can now see, really doesn't absorb shocks—the spring does that. The shock just stops the spring from oscillating, to keep the wheels on the road.

A common variation on this design is the placement of the coil spring between the upper arm and the body (see fig. 12-2).

Still another arrangement is the use of a torsion bar instead of a coil spring. The torsion bar is a spring in the form of a rod, and it twists to absorb road shock. It is commonly attached to the lower control arm at one end and to the chassis at the other—either to the rear of the control arm, or transversely, toward the center of the car at the front (see fig. 12-3).

Figure 12-1. Typical upper-lower control arm suspension, with coil spring between them and shock absorber inside the coils.

Figure 12-2. In this upper-lower control arm suspension, coil spring is between upper control arm and the body. Shock is also inside the coils.

Figure 12-3. This is a torsion bar suspension, in which the springs are bars that twist to absorb road shock. In this type, some spring sag can be taken up by turning height adjustment bolts.

HEIGHT ADJUSTMENT BOLT

ANTI-SWAY BAR

TORSION BARS

COIL SPRINGS
SHOCK ABSORBERS
LOWER CONTROL ARM

CROSS
MEMBER

STEERING KNUCKLE

Figure 12-4. This is the most common type of strut suspension, in which the coil spring and shock absorber are combined into a single assembly, eliminating the upper control arm and upper ball joint.

SUSPENSION BASICS

Strut Suspension

The use of two control arms is an effective design, but the upper arm takes up space that could otherwise be used to enlarge the engine compartment—valuable real estate in today's smaller cars. The strut suspension (see fig. 12-4) therefore is very widely used on many cars today.

The strut is a shock absorber to which the upper part of the steering knuckle is clamped (so one ball joint is eliminated at each side).

The steering knuckle swivel is permitted in this case by

the ball joint at the lower control arm and the strut upper mounting, which typically includes a bearing assembly.

In most cases, the spring is a coil and it is mounted directly on the strut. However, the spring also may be coil-mounted separately (see fig. 12-5) or may even be a torsion bar.

Steering

When you turn the steering wheel you are turning a shaft, at the end of which is a gear. This gear meshes with another in the steering gear box, and through an arrangement of shafts and links it turns the steering knuckle at each front wheel one way or the other (see figs. 12-6 and 12-7).

Figure 12-5. Although the arrangement shown, with the coil spring separate from the strut, is from the front suspension of a Ford rear-drive car, it is used primarily as part of an independent rear suspension of some front-drive cars.

Figure 12-6. When you turn the steering wheel in a recirculating ball-nut steering gear at the top, you operate a steering shaft that turns the cross shaft to move the pitman arm in one direction or another. The pitman arm is attached to the steering linkage, shown underneath. The tie-rod end at each end is attached to the steering knuckle, a member that includes the wheel spindle on which the wheel is mounted. The idler arm is a swivel brace for the linkage. The steering damper is a type of shock absorber used on a few cars.

RACK & PINION STEERING ASSEMBLY

STEERING COLUMN

SEAL ASSEMBLY

STEERING
KNUCKLE

BUSHING

PIN

SLEEVE

SHAFT ASSEMBLY

PINION GEAR (IN HOUSING)

RACK
(IN HOUSING)

CROSS MEMBER

VIEW AA

KEY NO.	PART NAME
1 —	HOUSING, RACK & PINION
2 —	BEARING ASSY, ROLLER
3 —	PINION ASSY, BEARING &
4 —	RING, RETAINING
5 —	SEAL, STEERING PINION
6 —	ADAPTER, SEAL
7 —	BOLT, PINCH
8 —	FLANGE ASSY, COUPLING & STRG.
9 —	BEARING, RACK
10 —	SPRING, ADJUSTER
11 —	PLUG, ADJUSTER
12 —	NUT, ADJUSTER PLUG LOCK
13 —	RING, SHOCK DAMPENER
14 —	ROD ASSY, INNER TIE
15 —	CLAMP, BOOT
16 —	BOOT, RACK & PINION
17 —	NUT, HEX. JAM
18 —	ROD ASSY, OUTER TIE
19 —	FITTING, LUBRICATION
20 —	SEAL, TIE ROD
21 —	NUT, HEX LOCK
22 —	PIN, COTTER
23 —	GROMMET, MOUNTING (LT)
24 —	GROMMET, MOUNTING (RT)
25 —	BUSHING, RACK
26 —	RING, BUSHING RETAINING
27 —	RACK, STEERING

Figure 12-7. This is a rack-and-pinion steering mechanism, used on most late-model cars, particularly front-drives. Turning the steering wheel operates the pinion, a gear at the end of the steering gear shaft. The pinion meshes with the rack, a rod that has gear teeth cut into it. Tie-rods attach to the rack at one end and the steering knuckle at the other.

Suspension Geometry

If you could measure the distance between the front wheels using precision equipment, you would find that the wheels are slightly closer at the forward than at the rear end—they toe-in slightly. You also would find that the wheels do not hang straight up and down, but tip in slightly at either the top or bottom, depending on the suspension design. Further, you would find that the steering knuckle is not perfectly vertical—that the top mounting (at the upper control arm or strut) is not in a vertical line with the bottom ball joint.

All these differences are called "suspension geometry" or "wheel alignment," and if the slight angles are wrong the car handling is affected. The fact that the front wheels are closer to each other (by perhaps an eighth of an inch) at the forward end is called toe-in. The slight tip-in of the wheels at top or bottom is called camber, and the steering knuckle inclination is called caster. On many cars, all three are adjustable, but special measuring equipment is required, so the job should be left to a professional.

Note: On many U.S. and European cars, only caster is fixed and both camber and toe-in can be reset. As manufacturing tolerances tighten, however, a trend (started by the Japanese) toward fixed camber may be occurring. If camber adjustment proves necessary to compensate for wear in the suspension, there are kits and special tools to permit it to be made. However, their use should be left to a professional.

Rear Suspension

There are three basic types of rear suspension: nonindependent, semi-independent, and fully independent. If you look at the front wheels, you will notice that each wheel can rise and drop independently of the other. This is called independent suspension, and it helps ride and handling.

In a conventional front-engine, rear-wheel-drive car, there is less advantage to having the rear wheels rise and fall independently, and because independent suspension costs more it is not used. There is a rear axle assembly, with shafts to each wheel, and the whole thing is held to the chassis and body by coil or leaf springs (see fig. 12-8) and shock absorbers.

If the engine is in the rear, or if the car has front wheel drive, the actions of the rear suspension are more critical, and either semi- or fully independent suspension is used.

The semi-independent type has a shock and coil spring (perhaps combined as in the strut suspension), and the two rear wheels are connected by a bar or beam that is really a torsion bar (see fig. 12-9). Therefore, although the wheels are connected they are virtually independent of each other. Each end of that torsion bar or beam can twist to let one wheel respond to road irregularities. Because the two wheels are connected by the torsion bar, the term semi-independent is used.

In the fully independent suspension, there is a separate control arm (just one, at the bottom for each wheel), plus a spring and shock absorber for each wheel, as in figure 12-10.

Figure 12-8. This is a typical rear suspension of a car with front-engine-rear-drive. Although leaf springs are used in this design, coil springs are also a common choice.

SHOCK ABSORBERS

COIL SPRINGS

TRAILING ARM

CROSS MEMBER

STUB AXLE

Figure 12-9. This is a popular type of semi-independent rear suspension, as used on a front-wheel-drive car. The crossmember actually is a form of torsion bar. Therefore, if one wheel hits a road irregularity, it can transfer the shock to the crossmember, which will twist to absorb it while not causing the other wheel to lift. The crossmember mounts to steel members called trailing arms that also hold the stub axle on which the wheel is installed.

Figure 12-10. This is a fully independent rear suspension. Each control arm is separately hinged to the chassis, so if one wheel hits a bump or pothole, the other wheel does not also respond.

CONTROL ARM

CHASSIS

SHOCK ABSORBER

CONTROL ARM

REAR DRIVE VS. FRONT WHEEL DRIVE

Many cars are of the front-wheel-drive type, including an increasing number of American models. Big boosts to the FWD concept came in 1978 when Chrysler introduced the Omni and Horizon, and in 1979 when General Motors converted the 1980 Chevy Citation and its other compacts to the system, joining the luxury Toronado, Eldorado, and Riviera. In 1981 came the Chrysler "K" cars (Reliant and Aries) and the Ford Escort and Lynx. Next on the scene were the GM "J" cars (Chevy Cavalier, etc.)

In a conventional rear-drive car (see fig. 12-11) the engine is in front, followed by the transmission. A long shaft, called the propeller shaft, is next in line (it's under the hump in the middle of the passenger compartment), and at the rear it connects to the rear axle, which houses a little gearbox called the differential. The differential turns the power around 90 degrees (from front-to-rear to rear-to-sides). From the rear axle it is transferred into solid shafts (called axle shafts), on which the rear wheels are mounted. The rear wheels receive the power and force the car to move; the front wheels are just along for the ride.

On a front-wheel-drive car, the rear wheels are the ones along for the ride. Power from the engine goes into a combination transmission-differential that transfers it through shafts to the front wheels. There's no propeller shaft and just a minor exhaust pipe hump in the passenger compartment. Although some FWD cars have the engine and transmission-differential aligned front-to-rear, on most the engine is mounted transversely—across the engine compartment. The transmission is attached to the

rear of the engine, but is shaped so that part of it tucks under or to one side of the engine to permit it to fit. The transmission transfers the power off to one side into the differential, and from there the power goes through individual shafts to each wheel (see fig. 12-12).

Unlike the axle shafts from the rear axle to the rear wheels, the shafts on a FWD are equipped with universal joints and a telescoping arrangement. These are required for two reasons:

1. The front wheels are an independent suspension, and if the wheel hits a road irregularly and rises, the shaft must be able to flex—and it does so at the universal joints. The telescoping joint allows changes in the operating length of the shaft—necessary when it rises and falls because of changes in road surfaces. The axle shafts in these respects are similar to the propeller shaft in a conventional front-engine, rear-drive car.

2. The front wheels receive power and turn to steer the car. The axle shafts, to which the wheels are attached, must permit them to pivot left or right, and a universal joint on the outboard end of the shaft serves that purpose.

Although many FWD cars have no-service wheel bearing at front and rear, some have conventional wheel bearings. Like the conventional front-engine, rear-drive car, they're on the wheels that are along for the ride. In the conventional setup, they're the front wheel bearings, but in FWD, they're the rears.

Most routine service on a FWD car is similar to that of a front-engine, rear-drive arrangement. The access to parts may be slightly different, however. For example, the ignition timing marks will still be on the front or rear of the

Figure 12-11. Layout of a typical rear-drive car. Engine is in front, followed by transmission. At the back of the transmission is a propeller shaft that carries the power to the rear axle-differential. There it is transferred to the rear wheels that drive the car. The front wheels are just along for the ride.

ENGINE

TRANSMISSION

PROPELLER SHAFT

REAR AXLE—DIFFERENTIAL

Figure 12-12. Here is a typical front-wheel-drive car with a transversely mounted engine, followed by the transmission-differential combination, commonly called a trans-axle. Power is transferred from the transmission out the rear side into the differential, and then across (by drive axle shafts) to each front wheel.

engine, but when the engine is mounted sideways (called a transverse engine), the physical location in the engine compartment is different. The transverse mounting also makes it difficult to use a mechanical fan because the radiator still is usually at the front of the compartment, whereas the belt-driven pulleys are at the side. Therefore, an electric fan is commonly installed. Some FWD engine compartments are laid out so that the radiator and AC condenser must be side-by-side across the front. This mandates a separate electric fan for each.

Suspension Service—Rear Wheel and Front Wheel Drive

The suspension and steering systems do not require a lot of routine service but they do need some, namely replace-

ment of shock absorbers, lubrication and adjustment of wheel bearings (on most cars), and grease application to the steering (and perhaps suspension ball joints) of most cars. Tires also need regular care. The rest of this chapter is devoted to the performance of these services.

CHASSIS LUBRICATION

All cars have some chassis and/or steering joints that should be lubricated with grease. The joint will typically have a nipple (also called a grease fitting) for a grease gun or a plug that can be removed to allow a nipple to be threaded in (see figs. 12-13 and 12-14).

Many cars today have just a few, in some cases only two, whereas others have perhaps a dozen or more. The

Figure 12-13. Unless a steering or suspension joint is prepacked for life with grease, it has a nipple-type fitting. Shown are the fittings on the upper and lower ball joints. Notice the flexible seals that hold in the grease.

Figure 12-14. This ball joint has a plug instead of a fitting. A box wrench is shown ready to fit on the hex-head of the plug, to remove it for replacement with a grease fitting.

typical lubrication points are each of the suspension ball joints and two to seven lubrication points on the steering linkage (see fig. 12-15). To lubricate them, you will need a grease gun, a tool that accepts a cartridge of grease and has a pump handle for dispensing it. The business end of the gun is a tube with a nozzle that fits onto the grease fitting nipple. The tube itself can be rigid or flexible, and each type has its advantages. Flexible permits you to twist the tubing to get to a less accessible fitting. Rigid means you can apply pressure with the gun to hold the nozzle in place on the fitting while you pump. You also can have the best of both worlds with a flexible tube with a rigid sleeve—just slide the sleeve forward when you want rigidity, backward if you want to be able to flex the tube. Another option is a lock-on adapter for a flexible tube— just thread it onto the nozzle end, push it onto the nipple, and turn a knurled lock to secure it (see fig. 12-16).

Finding the Fittings

Grease fittings are customarily covered by road film and mud and are hard to locate. Find them by feeling with your fingers, pulling off pieces of mud as you do. Look at the top end of an upper ball joint, the bottom end of a lower ball joint, and at each joint of the steering linkage (see fig. 12-15 for sample locations).

Original equipment universal joints on the propeller are packed with grease at the factory and require no regular lubrication, with the exception of some older full-size General Motors cars (and some Jeep four-wheel-drives) with a double-type rear universal joint. If a GM car has the double-joint, jack up the rear wheels, turn the propeller shaft, and look for a single grease fitting flush with the inside surface. This flush fitting must be lubed with a special pencil-point nozzle on the grease gun (see fig. 12-17). The nozzle is available at most well-equipped auto supply stores.

The typical replacement universal joint is equipped with a conventional grease fitting (see chapter 13, fig. 13-24).

Grease

Always choose a brand of chassis grease with a name you know. Grease is so inexpensive that it doesn't pay to take chances. Most of the leading refiners of engine oil also

Figure 12-15. Here's the typical front underbody with the location of grease fittings indicated. Notice that there are four fittings on the steering linkage, one on the pitman arm joint with the steering linkage, two on the idler arm and brack arm for the steering linkage. There is one on each of the four spherical (ball) joints.

Figure 12-16. Lock-on adapter on end of grease fun flexible hose is pushed onto grease fitting nipple, then knurled knob is turned as shown to lock the hose nozzle to grease fitting.

Figure 12-17. The double-cardan universal joint on older General Motors cars has one fitting. You must obtain a needlenose grease nozzle for your gun, as the fitting is flush with the surface into which it's threaded and won't accept a conventional grease gun nozzle.

PUMP GREASE INTO BALL FITTING UNTIL IT SHOWS AT CIRCLE

market chassis grease, so you should have no trouble finding a good brand. After finding a name, make sure the type of grease you select is a "multimileage lubricant No. 2," a premium chassis grease. You should grease the fittings every 6,000 miles or every 6 months, but never exceed a year, even if the manufacturer permits longer intervals.

Doing the Job

Wipe each fitting with a clean cloth. If you don't, you may force dirt into the joint. Inspect the rubber seal at the joint. If it is cut through, it must be replaced. You may be able to get a seal kit and install it yourself (instructions included with the kit). In some cases, the seal is not available as a replacement part and you must have the joint changed, a job for a professional.

If the joint has a grease plug in an inaccessible location, remove it and install a right-angle fitting (see fig. 12-18), available in most auto parts stores. Aim the right-angle fitting down or to the side so you can get the grease gun nozzle on it.

Before you pump, you must know what you are looking for. In some cases the grease will extrude from bleed holes at the base of the joint. In others, the seal will balloon. With this second case, the visual indication will be slight, so squeeze the seal before you start and in between pumping of the gun handle.

Figure 12-18. If you can't reach a conventional grease fitting with your gun because of clearance problems, you can remove it and install a right-angle grease fitting as shown. Aim the right-angle fitting down or to an open side, so the grease gun nozzle will go on easily.

HINGE PIVOTS

PP146

Figure 12-19. The indicated hood hinge pivots should be lubricated.

Stop pumping as soon as you see any grease extruding from the base of the joint, or if you can see or feel the seal ballooning or feel that the seal has filled with grease.

Note: If grease extrudes from between the nozzle and the nipple, the fitting is not taking grease. Stop immediately or you'll have a big mess. Remove the old grease fitting and install a new one.

Universal Joints

Although the original equipment universal joints of cars are packed and sealed for life, don't forget the fittings on replacement joints, and the double-type rear universal joint of some General Motors full-size cars. Just a couple of pumps on the handle should take care of the universal joint.

Dab It On

In addition to the grease fittings, chassis lubricant should be applied to joints of door and hood hinge, transmission and clutch underbody linkage, and parking brake levers. Just dab it on with your fingers and try to work it into the joints (see figs. 12-19 and 12-20). If there is dirt or mud on the joint, wipe it off first or spray it clean with solvent.

Figure 12-20. Transmission shift linkage joints, indicated by "G," should be lubricated.

TIRE BUYING AND TIRE CARE

The subject of tires could be an encyclopedia in itself. This section, therefore, is intended only as a primer on the important considerations in buying a tire and maintenance tips you should know.

Types of Tires

Tires are made in three basic types of construction: bias-ply, belted bias-ply, and radial. The construction refers to what's under the tread: layers of synthetic fiber cord or steel wire in various forms (see fig. 12-21).

The bias-ply is the smoothest riding tire, but the simple crossing of the cords results in squirming of the thread and short life because the tread gets hot and literally rubs out against the road. Longer tread life, cooler operation, and less rolling resistance is provided by the belted bias-ply, in which support belts are inserted between the tread and the layers of cord.

The radial is the kingpin. It runs the coolest and has the lowest rolling resistance, and because of the angles of the layers of cord and the belts the sidewalls flex to provide good tread contact with the road at all times. Radials have a tendency to provide a harsh ride, but suspension modifications by the car makers have reduced that. Steel-belted radials—belts with steel wire running through them—have a reputation for the greatest durability and resistance to road hazards but there also are synthetic fibers that perform well too. The low rolling resistance of the radial reduces fuel consumption, and in some cases radials provide 5 percent better gas mileage than the simple bias-ply. Most tires sold today are radials, although if you have an older car (1960s and early 1970s), its suspension may not be designed for radials. In that case, you can continue to use bias-ply or belted bias-ply. However, you also can switch to radials if you wish, but may experience some extra medium-speed harshness.

Tire Width

The wider the tire the more tread there is on the road and so the better the traction. Tires have gotten wider over the years, a fact reflected by a decrease in what is called the aspect ratio (relationship of width to height of the tire

Figure 12-21. Shown are the three types of tire construction. *At left* is the bias-ply, in which the tire cords cross each other at an angle. *In the center* is the radial, in which the tire cords run 90 degrees to the tread and are covered by cord belts that run at very slight angles to the tread. *At the right* is the belted bias-ply, in which the cords run at angles similar to the plain bias-ply and are covered by belts that run at slight angles.

section). A 60 tire has a section that is equal to 60 percent of the width. A 70 tire (narrower) has a section that is 70 percent of the width. Both tires may have the same section height, but the greater width of the 60 reduces the ratio.

There is a limit to how wide a tire you can install, compared with original equipment. The limits are imposed by the clearances in the fender well and the size of the wheel. You can install a different wheel, but you can't change the clearances. In any case, tread design and construction are equally important factors in traction.

Today's tire sizes are in metric dimensions. The letter "P" (for passenger car) precedes the number, which is in millimeters (such as 195). The next number is the aspect ratio.

Tread Designs

Many people, particularly owners of recreational vehicles, pick tires with very agressive-looking treads, even if the vehicles are always driven on relatively good roads. The aggressive tread—big, deep lugs in the design—looks good but doesn't provide good highway ride or gas mileage, so unless you really need something special, stick with a conventional ribbed tire (see fig. 12-22) or year-round type (see fig. 12-23). The year- round tire has become very popular for the straightforward family car and dominates the market. However, if you are driving a sporty car, you may want something closer to what was supplied as original equipment. A few sporty cars have had original equipment tires specifically tailored for each wheel.

Figure 12-22. This is a basic ribbed tire. The ribs are the grooves running around the circumference of the tread.

Load Range

Overloading is the most common cause of tire failure. You can overload either of two ways: by underinflating the tires, or by asking them to carry more weight than they are able.

All tires for passenger car use are in Load Range B, which means the tire can carry its maximum load (including the weight of the car) at 32 to 36 p.s.i. The information is on the tire sidewall and easy to read. If the total load-carrying capability of the four tires or either front or rear

Figure 12-23 This is a typical all-year-round tire. The dog-biscuit-shaped lugs help traction in mud and snow.

tires exceeds the rating of the tires, you must get either larger tires or ones in a higher load range (C,D,E, etc.). The higher load range means that the tire can be inflated to higher pressure to increase its load-carrying capability.

With a passenger car, ride considerations generally limit you to the largest possible tire in load range B. On a recreational vehicle, you can go to truck-type tires, which are in the higher load ranges.

As a practical matter, look at the load rating in pounds (or kilograms) for your present tires: A number (for each tire) appearing in raised letters on the tire sidewall (at a maximum specified pressure, also listed). If you need more load-carrying capacity, ask to consult an "upsize" booklet at a tire store. This will tell you what larger size tires your car can accept, and the load they will carry.

Tire Quality Markings

Since early 1979, sidewalls of some new tires have had important information on them: Ratings of treadwear, traction, and temperature resistance.

Traction. The letter *A* means maximum traction, *B* intermediate, and *C* means that the tire did not pass either the *A* or *B* tests.

High Performance. This is a temperature resistance grade that involves overloading, underinflation, and high speeds. A tire that passes the stiffest test gets an *A*, the next stiffest a *B*, and the easiest test a *C*.

Treadwear. A *100* means the tire passed a 30,000-mile test, *120* a 36,000-mile test (20 percent longer), an *80* a 24,000-mile test (20 percent shorter). The tests are standard ones, but do not constitute a guarantee of these tread mileages to the motorist.

Speed Rating

Some tires are rated by the industry for high-speed use, a practice adapted from Europe. An *H* means the tire is suitable for use up to 130 mph, a *V* up to 149 mph, and a *Z* for 149-plus mph (or the top speed of the car, if that is greater). Do not assume that a high-speed tire is your safest choice, as the speed rating is achieved at a compromise with other factors, such as tread life.

Tire Care

The best things you can do for your tires are to check the pressures regularly, using a gauge, and never overload them. Visual appearances are deceiving, particularly with radial tires, and the gauge on service station air meters is notoriously inaccurate.

Pressures should always be checked when the tire is cold (not driven more than a couple of miles at low speed in six hours). Never bleed air from a warmed-up tire.

Note: The typical tire provides the best ride at lower pressures, but you should realize that at those lower pressures the load-carrying capability is reduced. Periodically check the tires for stones in the tread and remove them.

If you have separate snow tires, buy a spare pair of wheels for them. The spare wheels, available from a wrecking yard, eliminate the twice-a-year service on both the snows and the regular tires they temporarily replace. This reduces the possibility of damage to the tire bead (the section that bears against the rim of the wheel and seals in the air) during service. Spare wheels also mean you can change the tires yourself.

When storing tires during the off season, reduce pressure to 15 p.s.i. and keep in a cool, dry place.

Tire Rotation

Tire rotation evens out the wear on tires and this can slighty extend their useful life and improve the car's ride. However, rotation does not make economic sense unless you do it yourself. Follow the rotation diagram in your owner's manual. Do not use any other.

Wear Patterns

When your tire treads wear down to $^1/_{16}$ inch, bars will appear across the width of the tread. These are wear indicators, designed to tell you to replace the tires immediately. With just $^1/_{16}$ inch of tread, the tire is effectively running bald.

Other wear patterns may indicate a suspension problem. If there is uneven wear on the outside or inside treads only, or scuff marks across the treads, that's wheel misalignment. Wear in the center is usually caused by overinflation; wear on both sides is usually caused by underinflation. Irregular spot wear around the tread circumference may be caused by wobbly wheels (the wheel could be bent or its bearings could be loose), worn shocks, or defective brakes. An across-the-tread wear pattern is typical of the rear tires of many front-drive cars.

FRONT WHEEL BEARINGS

The front wheels, or the rear wheels in a front-wheel-drive car, do not receive power from the engine. They simply support one end of the car and roll as the car is propelled by power transmitted to the other wheels. It might seem that aside from tire wear they should be of little concern. However, the bearings on which they roll (see fig. 12-24) are extremely important. If they aren't doing their job, the car will handle very poorly, wander, and even waste gasoline. If the bearings fail completely, the car is stuck.

Figure 12-24. This exploded view of a front wheel assembly shows how the hub and brake disc assembly fit on the spindle section of the front knuckle. Inside the hub and disc are two bearings, one on the inboard side of the disc and the other on the outboard side. The bearings are held to the spindle by the nut and lock. Because the bearings are tapered, retaining them also holds the disc-hub in place, although it can spin freely on the bearings.

These wheel bearings, therefore, should be periodically inspected, lubricated, and adjusted on most cars. Surprisingly, it is only the driven wheel bearings you may have to maintain. Those on the drive wheels are lubricated by axle grease (in most rear-drive cars), or are packed for life, as in all front-wheel-drive and some rear-drive cars.

Serviceable vs. Nonserviceable

On all American cars prior to 1979, the driven wheel bearings are serviceable. In 1979, nonserviceable (sealed for life) bearings made their debut on Buick Riviera, Cadillac Eldorado, and Oldsmobile Toronado (see fig. 12-25). The trend toward nonserviceable wheel bearings continues on GM "X" (Chevy Citation, etc.) and "J" (Chevy Cavalier, etc.) cars, and some imports.

If, however, you have one of the overwhelming majority of cars on which service is required, you should do the job every 20,000 miles or 2 years.

To determine if your wheel bearings are the serviceable type, just remove the hub cap or wheel cover on a driven wheel (rear on a FWD car, front on a conventional rear-drive car). If you see the bearing hub assembly in the center of the wheel, the bearings are nonserviceable.

Types of Serviceable Bearings

Although some cars have ball-type bearings, most driven-wheel bearings are made with tapered rollers assembled on a circular holder called a cage. The rollers bear against smoothly finished sleeves called races.

The wheel bearings actually don't support the wheel but a part of the braking system to which the wheel is bolted. If the car has front drum brakes, the drum is supported by the bearings and the wheel is bolted to the drum; if it has disc brakes, the wheel is bolted to the disc.

Each drum or disc has a cylindrical cavity in the center into which the bearings are installed. There is one bearing assembly on the inside half of the cavity, one on the outside half. The drum or disc, with its bearings, fits on a tapered shaft—called a spindle—which is part of the car's front suspension. The outer end of the spindle is threaded to accept a nut that holds the drum or disc in position on the spindle. When you adjust the wheel bearings you actually are setting the position of the nut on the threaded spindle. If the nut is too tight, the bearings are forced tightly against the spindle, and even with adequate lubrication, the friction of the tight fit will cause them to heat up and fail. If the nut is too loose, the vibration of the

Figure 12-25. The rear bearing assemblies typically are held by bolts accessible through holes in the rear axle flange, after the brake drum is removed. On GM cars the bolts are Torx-head, so have a suitable Torx wrench before you start.

wheels as they travel over road irregularities will shock the bearings, almost as if you were hitting them with hammers, and again they will fail.

Therefore, not only must you set the position of the nut properly, you must make sure the nut doesn't move. The manufacturer provides one of the following four means to hold the nut in place:

1. The top of the nut has cross slots and the spindle has one or two holes. A cotter pin, shaped somewhat like a lady's bobby pin, is inserted so it rests in the cross slots of the nut and goes through a hole in the spindle.

2. A hexagonal sleeve, called a nut lock, fits onto the nut. Like the nut in the previous example, it has cross slots and can be locked with a cotter pin through a hole in the spindle (see fig. 12-24).

3. A circular sleeve—another type of nut lock—fits onto the spindle and bears against the nut. The sleeve has slots for a cotter pin, which is installed in the same basic way as the first example.

4. Adjusting nut has a slit-through section, through which an Allen-head screw goes. To lock the nut, tighten the screw. To permit adjustment, first slacken the screw.

5. Nut has a flange that is bent up to "stake" the nut in place. The flange is moved up or down by hitting it with a hammer and chisel.

Wheel Bearings Service

Testing. Although some professional mechanics check wheel bearings only with a dial indicator, most still test the adjustment by feel, as follows: Hold the tire at the top and bottom and try to rock the wheel in and out. If you feel any more than just the slightest hint of movement, have a helper do the rocking as you look at the wheel's suspension. If the free play is in the suspension, reduce the rocking effort so the suspension joints do not show movement. If there still is more than barely perceptible free play when the wheel is rocked, an adjustment is apparently required.

Even if you believe free play is barely perceptible, the bearings should be removed for inspection and relubrication as a routine maintenance procedure at least every 2 years or 20,000 miles. Or if you are doing a brake job on the car, you should service the wheel bearings at that time.

Disassembly. To gain access to the wheel bearings for inspection and lubrication, you must jack up the car and support it on safety stands (see chapter 5).

Drum Brakes. Notice that most of the illustrations are of a disc brake car, as this job on a disc system starts with the removal of the wheel, which makes some of the steps photographically clearer, therefore easier to understand.

Begin the job on a drum brake car by removing the hub cap, then pry off the dust cap in the center. If you do not wish to obtain a special tool, you also can pry it off with two thin screwdrivers (inserted 180 degrees apart) or with large "water pump" pliers around the cap (see fig. 12-26). If you use pliers, be careful not to crush the cap.

With the dust cap off you'll see the nut lock or the wheel bearing nut. Remove the cotter pin (see fig. 12-27) or the locking screw, the nut lock if used (see fig. 12-28), and then the wheel bearing nut itself, using a socket wrench and ratchet.

With the nut off, grasp the tire at each side and jostle it toward you. As you jostle, a washer and the outer wheel bearing will pop outward. Remove them (see fig. 12-29). Continue jostling and the wheel and drum assembly will come off (see fig. 12-30).

If it sticks, turn the wheel slowly and listen for a scraping sound. If you hear a scraping noise, it indicates that the brake shoes are dragging against the brake drum, preventing the drum from coming off. You will have to turn an adjuster to back the brake shoes out of contact with the drum. See chapter 11 for details.

With the drum off you have complete access. Turn over the drum to inspect the inside, and you'll see a seal on the rim of the cylindrical cavity. Pry out the seal with a screwdriver (see fig. 12-31), then reach into the cavity and remove the inner wheel bearing.

Disc Brakes. Disc brakes pose a special problem, in that the disc must be removed. The caliper, a hydraulic clamp that squeezes the brake shoes against the sides of the disc, is mounted over it, so you must remove the caliper in order to take off the disc.

Begin by removing the wheel-tire assembly. Next, inspect the mounting of the caliper. In most cases, the caliper is held by two rods or by two guide brackets bolted to a mounting cage. If the method of unbolting the caliper is not obvious to you, refer to chapter 11, which covers the braking system.

Once you have unbolted the caliper, lift it away, and using coat hanger wire, tie it to the front suspension so there is no strain on the brake hose (see fig. 12-32). Do not let the caliper dangle by the hose, or the hose will be damaged (even if the damage is not something you can see).

Remove the dust cap, then the nut lock, cotter pin, wheel bearing nut, etc. Jostle the disc toward you, as you did with the wheel-drum assembly, and the washer and outer wheel bearing will pop out. Remove them. Continue jostling until the disc is off. Turn the disc over and you will see the same type of seal in the center as with the drum brake. Pry it out and lift out the inner wheel bearing.

Cleaning and Inspection. Clean out the bearing cavity in the drum or disc with automotive solvent and wipe clean. Reach into each end of the cavity and feel the cylindrical bearing race. If the surfaces against which the bearing roller rides are mirror smooth, the races are okay.

Figure 12-26. Removing the dust cap with "water pump" pliers. Although this job is illustrated on a disc brake car with the wheel already removed, on a drum brake car all you would have to do is remove the hub cap or wheel cover for access to the dust cap.

Figure 12-27. To remove the cotter pin, straighten the double end as shown, then pull it out from the opposite (eye) end.

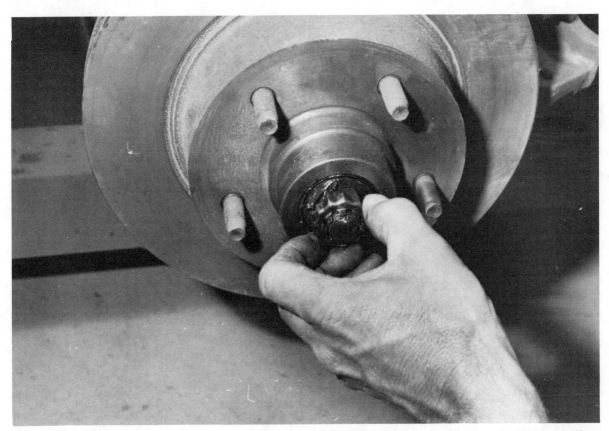

Figure 12-28. With the cotter pin out, the nut lock can be removed as shown.

Figure 12-29. Washer and outer wheel bearing come off next.

389

Figure 12-30. Whether it's a wheel and tire assembly, or just a disc, it can now be removed from the spindle. With a disc assembly, however, the caliper must be removed and hung out of the way first, as shown in figure 12-32.

Figure 12-31. Prying out a grease seal with a screwdriver. This job is illustrated with a disc, but it's the same on a drum.

Figure 12-32. Disc caliper has been unbolted from suspension, or from frame on some cars, then hung out of the way with wire, as shown. Disc can now be pulled off the spindle.

If they are rough or scratched, they must be replaced. Take a long, flat-end brass punch, insert it from the opposite end, and tapping on the inner edge of the race, tap it out. You must tap gently and move the punch around the edge circumference of the race so you don't cock the race in the cavity.

If the race does not budge, take the disc or drum to the machine shop of an auto parts store. The shop can remove a stuck race in seconds by using a press.

Caution: On a very few cars the race is held in place by a C-shaped spring clip. You should inspect the cavity adjacent to the race to determine if such a clip is used. If you find one, carefully pry it out with a thin screwdriver.

Inspection. Clean the roller or ball bearings in automotive solvent, then allow them to air dry. Turn the bearing cage as you hold the inner bearing race (it comes out with the roller or ball bearing cage and normally holds to it). If you feel any roughness, replace the bearing. Also inspect for the following:

Cracks in the cage or inner race.

Any wear pattern on the race or rollers that is not completely smooth.

Metal smear marks on the edges of the rollers. This indicates overheating, possibly from worn-out or inadequate lubricant.

Little steps worn into the edges of the rollers. This can be caused by dirt.

Wear on the outside diameter of the cage or in the pockets between the rollers or balls. This is caused by dirt or lubricant failure.

Indentations on the rollers or balls, or flaking of surface metal from the balls or rollers. This is caused by loose bearings, rough roads, and heavy loads.

Pockmarks on the bearing surfaces of the races. Often this is caused by poor lubrication.

Heat discoloration. A faint yellow or dark blue tint on the race and/or balls or rollers is a heat failure caused by heavy loads or poor lubrication.

Note: If the color is light brown to black, the problem is not severe, just some staining from moisture and the lubricant. Polish with a clean cloth, and if the bearings are otherwise in good condition they can be re-used. A simple test for heat failure is to draw a file over the roller or ball (while you restrain the ball or roller with your fingers). If the file glides over, the bearing is okay; if it grabs on the roller or ball, the bearing assembly should be replaced.

Reassembly. If any of the bearings have failed, obtain replacements. The inner and outer bearings are not of the same size, so watch when you install. Also obtain a new grease seal and a tube of wheel bearing grease (not chassis grease).

391

Clean out the bearing cavity in the disc or drum. If you had to remove the old bearing races, tap the new ones into place with a brass drift and hammer, working carefully all around to insure you don't cock them. If you had to take them to a machine shop for removal with a press, have the shop install the new ones.

With the races in place, smear a thin coat of grease over the inside wall of the drum or disc cavity and the races. Apply a generous coat of grease to the cage and rollers, carefully working it onto each roller (see fig. 12-33).

Install the inner wheel bearing, then tap the new grease seal into place. You can obtain a seal driver (see fig. 12-34) or use a socket wrench of the same size as the seal, or exhaust pipe connector of a suitable diameter (sold in auto parts stores). Place the seal driver, socket, or exhaust pipe connector onto the seal and tap it with a hammer.

Reinstall the drum or disc, install the outer bearing, the washer, and the adjusting nut. On a disc system, refit the caliper.

Adjustment. Begin the adjustment by tightening the nut to the specified torque (or 7 lbs.-ft. if you don't have the specifications), using a torque wrench while spinning the wheel or disc by hand. This will seat the bearings in place on the spindle.

Caution: Excessive torque could damage the bearings, so don't overdo it.

Loosen the nut until it is just free, then install the nut lock and cotter pin, or the screw. If the cross slot in the nut or nut lock does not align with a hole in the spindle, you may loosen the nut up to an additional one-half of one flat on the hexagonal nut (that's one-twelfth of a turn, very little).

Note: Ford products' wheel bearings are adjusted somewhat differently (see fig 12-35).

If you have a cotter pin arrangement, spread the stems of the pin, trim them if necessary with cutting pliers, and bend them back against the nut or lock so they don't touch the wheel cavity.

Check the bearings for free play by rocking the wheel in and out as you did for the predisassembly test. If they are too loose, readjust the nut. Smear a coating of grease over the inside surface of the dust cap, then tap the cap into place with a rubber mallet.

SHOCK ABSORBERS

The shock absorber, actually a spring damper as explained earlier in this chapter, stops the movement of the spring by dissipating it in the form of heat.

As the spring tries to oscillate, so must the shock absorber, for both are operating in the same location. The shock absorber, however, is a cylinder filled with oil and contains a piston. The piston has to force its way through a cylinder of oil (see fig. 12-36). This brings it to a quick stop as the energy is converted to heat, and the hot oil quickly dissipates the heat into the atmosphere.

Figure 12-33. Applying wheel-bearing grease to rollers. Use a generous amount. *Caution:* Do not use chassis grease.

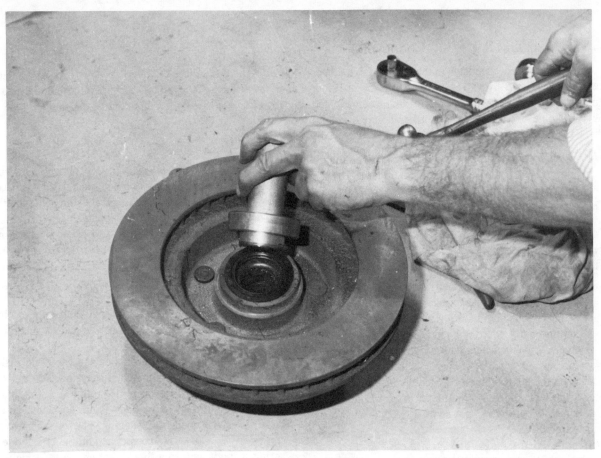

Figure 12-34. Using a seal driver. Grease seal is in position. Place driver shown squarely on top of it and hammer on driver top to seat the seal. Inner wheel bearing must be in place first, of course.

Figure 12-35. Illustration shows adjustment procedure for Ford wheel bearings.

WITH WHEEL ROTATING, TORQUE ADJUSTING NUT TO 17–25 FT.-LBS.

BACK ADJUSTING NUT OFF ½ TURN

TIGHTEN ADJUSTING NUT TO 10–15 IN.-LBS.

INSTALL THE LOCK AND A NEW COTTER PIN

ROD

PISTON

VALVE

A
C
B

A
C
B

COMPRESSION STROKE

REBOUND STROKE

Figure 12-36. How a shock absorber works. "A" is an oil-filled chamber above the piston, "B" is an oil-filled chamber below the piston, and "C" is an outer oil-filled chamber. When an end of the car goes down, the shock compresses. The piston must force its way through the resistant oil. Some oil passes through calibrated holes and valves in the piston to rise into the upper chamber. Other oil is pushed through the valve at the base of the shock into chamber "C." When the shock extends, as when a wheel bounces up, oil is drawn through the valve from the outer chamber into "B," and some oil passes through the piston holes from "A" to "B." In all cases, the piston movement is slowed by the oil-absorbing energy from the piston and rod. In so doing, the piston becomes hot. It dissipates this heat into the atmosphere. The damping action of the shock absorber stops the spring from oscillating.

The movement of the piston in the oil-filled cylinder is carefully regulated by valves and holes in the chamber and the piston, making the shock a pretty complicated device. Some shocks are even further complicated by these special features:

They are gas-charged. The gas exerts pressure on the oil to prevent it from aerating. This improves shock absorber performance.

They are adjustable. Some shock absorbers have an arrangement in which one of the valves can be preset for a normal, firm, or soft ride (see fig. 12-37).

They have air chambers. Some rear shocks have, in addition to the oil chamber, an air chamber built into the upper half. When air is added, as on a tire, the load-carrying capacity of the spring is increased. On some cars this is done automatically by means of an electric air compressor under the hood and a height sensor in the rear. When the height sensor determines that the car is too low in the rear (because of a heavy load), it triggers the air compressor. When the load is removed and the rear end rises, the height sensor triggers an electric valve in the compressor to deflate the air shocks (see fig. 12-38).

They have assist springs. The springs on a car may sag after a few years, particularly when heavy loads are carried. Some replacement shocks have a coil spring around them, much like a strut, to help the car's regular spring, whether coil, torsion bar, or leaf type (see fig. 12-39).

Even the conventional shock absorber is available in several types: standard, heavy-duty, and extra-heavy-duty. The differences are internal, chiefly in the diameter of the piston and the rod to which it is attached, the size of the oil chambers and the quantity of oil, and the type of valves.

Selecting a Shock

For most conditions, a conventional shock is all you need. The standard type duplicates original equipment, and the heavier-duty designs are the most popular for replacement use. The average driver with a suspension in otherwise good condition should find the heavy-duty design provides a good compromise for ride, extra handling control, and extra life over the original equipment type. The extra-heavy-duty, unless it is adjustable, may be too firm a ride, although some of this type are heavy-duty only in construction, not in the ride they provide. Check manufacturer's literature.

If the springs are sagging when the car is normally loaded, install a shock with an assist spring. You can see sag if you look at the car from the profile, and straight on at the front and rear. If the body is not horizontal in all these views, the springs are sagging. The torsion bar-type spring can be adjusted to correct height, but coil and leaf springs cannot, and so a shock with an assist spring will be helpful.

If you carry heavy loads in the rear, install shocks with air chambers. They come with extension tubes so you can install the inflation valves in a convenient place, such as the trunk compartment. Or you can install a compressor kit with dashboard controls, to inflate or deflate the shocks' air chambers from the driver's seat.

Figure 12-37. How an adjustable shock absorber works. The adjustable valve in the base of a shock engages specially shaped base of piston when the shock is completely collapsed. *At right,* note that when piston rod is turned, the adjustment on the valve is altered.

HEIGHT SENSOR

ELECTRIC AIR COMPRESSOR

AIR HOSE

AIR SHOCKS

Figure 12-38. This is an automatic rear-leveling system that uses shocks with built-in air bags, a height sensor, and an automatic compressor. When sensor, bolted to car body, senses that car rear is hanging low, it triggers the compressor, which pumps up the shocks to raise the car. When the ride height sensor determines that car rear is too high, it opens a valve in the compressor assembly and shocks automatically deflate.

Figure 12-39. This shock absorber has a coil spring included, making it suitable for cars with slight spring sag.

Testing the Shocks

The best way to check is with a road test. If the car has poor control on hard cornering and shakes badly on washboard roads, the shocks probably are bad. Check on smooth pavement at 10 to 15 mph by tapping the brakes repeatedly. If this sets up a rocking motion, in which the front dips while the rear rises, the shocks are defective.

Also, visually inspect the shocks (see fig. 12-40). Replace them if you see deep dents in the shell, oil leakage (more than minor seepage), or a pitted piston rod (visible when wheels hang down, so when you jack up the car, do it by the chassis).

Most original equipment shocks have had it at 20,000 miles, and the heavier-duty replacements will last up to 30,000. Shock life is not really predictable, however, because of the great variation in the condition of roads on which people drive.

Replacing a Shock

Shocks should be replaced in pairs—both fronts or both rears—for balanced results. Most shocks are outboard of the coil springs. To get the old ones off, begin by looking

Figure 12-40. Visually inspect your shocks for oil seepage, dents, and a pitted piston rod.

at the shock's upper and lower mountings to determine if there is enough clearance to work with the wheel in place. If not, loosen the wheel lug nuts.

Next, jack up the car (see chapter 5) and support it on safety stands. Remove the wheels if necessary and unbolt the shock at the top and bottom (see fig. 12-41 and 12-43). Some shock studs are specially shaped at the top, so they can be held with a wrench or pair of locking pliers while you loosen the retaining nut with a wrench (see fig. 12-42). If not, you can buy an inexpensive special tool to hold a stud. If the upper mounting is recessed, and the retaining nut is rust-frozen in place, first try spraying with penetrating solvent.

If that doesn't work, put a deep socket on the stud and with the ratchet wrench try rocking side to side to snap the stud (you're replacing the shock, so breaking the stud doesn't matter). If the stud won't snap, the best remaining choice is a nut cutter designed for shock work. It fits into the recess around the stud, and when turned with a wrench from the top will neatly cut the nut, permitting you to lower the upper portion of the shock and remove it. If that doesn't work, see what special tools are available from an auto parts store. One type (see fig. 12-44) has a long, hollow hex that fits onto the nut (and you can turn the hex with a wrench while holding the stud with a tool inserted into the hollow hex). Or you can break off the stud with another special tool (see figs. 12-45, 12-46 and 12-47). The tool, made by Lisle Corp., Clarinda, IA, and sold in auto parts stores, threads onto the stud up against the nut. Then a handle is attached to the tool and the handle is rocked up and down until the stud snaps below the nut, so removal is easy.

If a shock is inside the coil spring, it is lowered out. Look at the lower mounting and you will find some form of plate that can be unbolted to provide clearance for shock removal.

As you remove a shock absorber, notice the use of rubber bushings at the top and bottom. When you install the new shock, you must install the new bushings and any washers in exactly the same manner unless (as is common) the replacement shock comes with its own set of bushings (see fig. 12-48). In this case, the bushings can be different but still will do the job. Just follow the bushing instructions that come with the replacement shock. When you tighten the shock nuts, you want the shock to be secure, but you also don't want to overtighten. If the bushing under a washer is squeezed so that it protrudes from the exterior circumference of the washer, you've probably overtightened (see fig. 12-49). Normally the bushing should be flush with the edge of the washer.

Figure 12-41. Loosening an upper shock mounting bolt in the engine compartment. On other cars the shock mount may be a stud-and-nut type and may only be accessible from under the car.

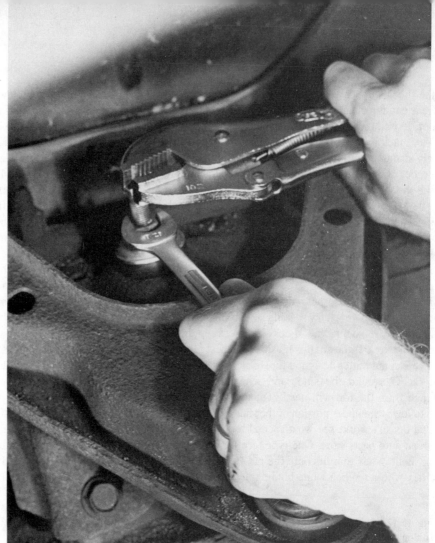

Figure 12-42. Hold rectangular tip of shock stud with locking pliers as shown while you loosen nut with a wrench.

Figure 12-43. Loosening a shock's lower mount.

Figure 12-44. Hollow hex fits over stud onto the nut. Additional special wrench goes into hollow hex onto top of stud, so stud can be held while open-end wrench turns hollow hex to loosen nut.

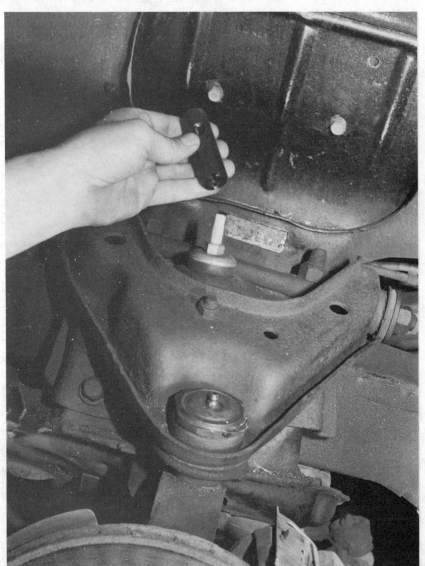

Figure 12-45. Special tool threads onto stud, up to and against nut.

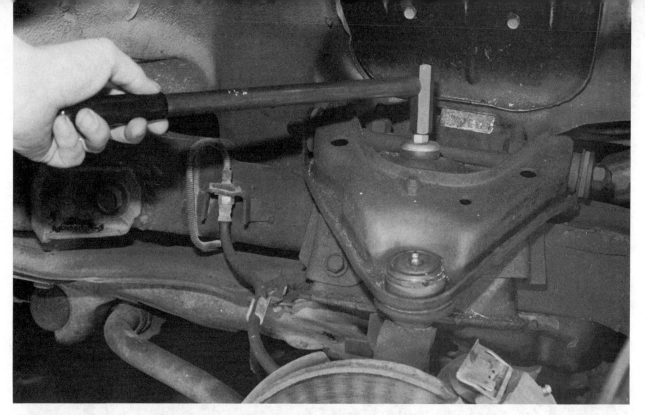

Figure 12-46. Handle is threaded into side of special tool, and handle is rocked up and down.

Figure 12-47. Stud breaks below the nut as shown, and old shock can be lowered out.

Figure 12-48. Replacement shock comes with its own bushings, a pair for top and a pair for bottom. This arrangement eliminates differently shaped bushings, washers, and other hardware used as original equipment.

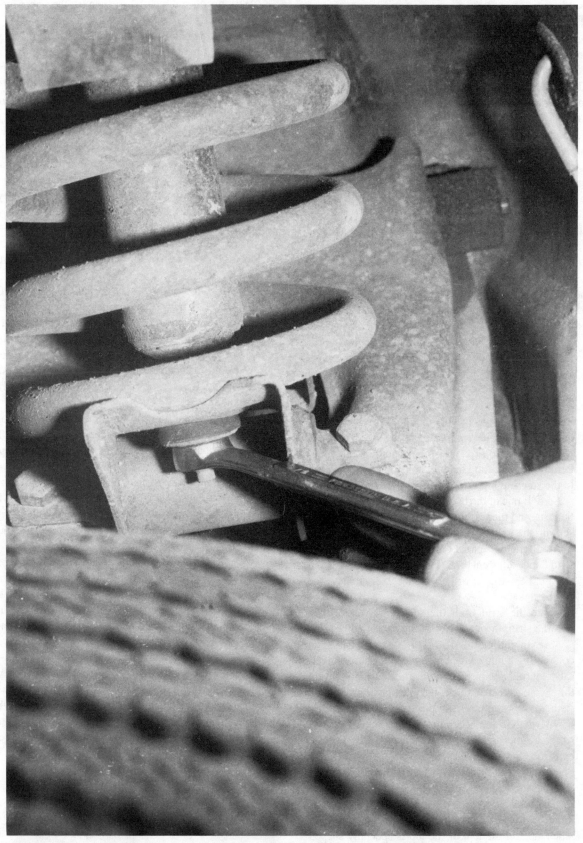

Figure 12-49. Tightening a shock's lower mount. Rubber bushing under the nut washer should not protrude measurably from the outer circumference of washer, or nut is too tight.

Strut Replacement

The front strut used on so many cars, particularly with front-wheel drive, is serviced somewhat differently than the conventional shock absorber.

There are many possible replacement procedures, depending on how the strut is attached to the steering knuckle. On the typical American-built, transverse-engine, front-wheel-drive car and VW Super Beetles, the strut is attached to the knuckle by two bolts. If there is a provision to set camber, you must take the car to a wheel alignment shop for immediate readjustment. If you don't, tire wear and handling will be affected (and in severe cases, you'll hear the tires squeal).

To replace this type of strut, you must have a suitable spring compressor. Although inexpensive ones can be purchased, you will do better and enjoy greater safety if you rent a high-quality spring compressor from a rental center. The basic procedure is as follows: Refer to figures 12-50 to 12-59 for replacement of a typical (General Motors car) strut.

1. Loosen the front wheel lugnuts, then jack up the car and place safty stands under chassis jacking points (see your owner's manual if their location is not obvious).
2. Remove the wheel.
3. Remove the screws or nuts that hold the strut upper mount in the engine compartment. Loosen but do not remove the piston-rod nut (the nut in the center).
4. Remove the nuts and the two bolts that hold the strut to the steering knuckle.

    Note: If one of the two bolts has an eccentric (cam) built in, and there is the possibility you will be reinstalling the strut (as explained later, in Step No. 10), make alignment marks on the cam surface and the strut flange adjacent to it. If you reinstall the strut and realign the marks, it will not be necessary to have the camber reset.

5. Separate the strut from the steering knuckle, then pull the strut down and out of the car.

    Note: In pulling the strut down on some cars, you could bring it into contact with the axle-shaft, universal-joint rubber cover damaging the cover. To prevent this, wrap a piece of thick, flexible plastic around the rubber cover and tape it in place. In some cases you may have to disconnect a brake line for clearance. If so, bleed the brakes after reconnecting the line, as explained in chapter 11.

6. Place the strut in a large vise, and with a spring compressor, compress the spring until the spring tension is released.
7. Remove the piston-rod nut. Most piston rods have Allen slots in the top, or the top is specially shaped for a wrench, so you can hold them while you remove the nut with a box wrench.

8. With piston-rod nut off, you can lift the upper mount up and off, then take off the coil spring.
9. Turn the upper mount bearing by hand, and if you feel roughness, replace the bearing assembly.

    Note: Some cars do not have a bearing in the upper mount. Rather, they use a rubber bushing and washer(s). If this is what you have, the wheels must face straight ahead when you reassemble and you must tighten the piston-rod nut to specifications with torque wrench.

10. Some struts have replaceable shock inserts, others do not. However, you may be able to get a replacement strut with an insert that can be changed, and if you do, the next time you have to service the strut you won't need the complete part. And because you will be refitting the strut, you can make alignment marks as explained in Step No. 4 and not have to get camber reset.

    Note: On some cars, such as many Hondas and GM "J" cars (Chevy Cavalier, etc.), the strut cap is welded in position and the welds must be ground off before the cap can be removed for replacement of the shock insert. This is not a practical matter for a weekend mechanic. Just install a complete strut assembly. If you shop carefully, the extra cost will be minimal.

11. When reassembling, be sure the coil spring fits into its mounting pads at top and bottom. Complete installation basically as reversal of the removal procedure.

    Ford cars with struts and rear drive (Fairmont—Zephyr—Mustang—Capri) are the easiest to service. The strut spring is separate and the strut unbolts from the steering knuckle. Camber is fixed, so no readjustment is needed.

    Note: This does not mean it is difficult to reset camber if necessary. Typically, these cars have the top strut mounted with a rivet through a slot that provides a range of camber adjustment, so the rivet can be drilled out and a bolt and nut installed in its place.

    After the lower mounting is free, disconnect the upper, noticing how the parts are assembled so you can install the new ones correctly. Most struts have a bearing assembly in the upper mounting, so when you take out the strut, spin the bearing by hand, feeling for any roughness and listening for any bearing noise. If there is either, replace the bearing.

Easy-change Strut Inserts

MacPherson strut inserts that can be easily changed from the top of the engine compartment appeared for the first time on three 1988 General Motors front-drive cars: Oldsmobile Cutlass Supreme, Buick Regal, and Pontiac Grand

Figure 12-50. Begin strut replacement by wrapping sheet of hard plastic (such as cut from bleach or milk container) around the universal joint boot as shown. Secure with household duct tape. This will protect boot from possible damage during the job.

Figure 12-51. Remove two bolts holding strut to steering knuckle. On some cars, particularly Japanese makes, the ball joint may have to be taken apart or a steering knuckle clamp opened.

Figure 12-52. After removing the bolts from the strut and knuckle, wire the knuckle flange to the steering linkage to hold it nearly vertical.

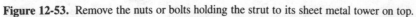

Figure 12-53. Remove the nuts or bolts holding the strut to its sheet metal tower on top.

Figure 12-54. Lower strut out of car.

Figure 12-55. Attach spring compressor recommended for particular car and connect safety catches if provided. If not, wrap and tie heavy braided wire around top coil and top of compressor, and bottom coil and bottom of compressor. Apply anti-seize compound to compressor screw threads. Then operate compressor with wrench. Strut is shown in inexpensive special holder, but job also can be done on floor.

Figure 12-56. Using two wrenches, one to hold piston rod at top, loosen the piston rod nut with open-end (or box) wrench as shown.

Figure 12-57. Remove piston rod nut after loosening.

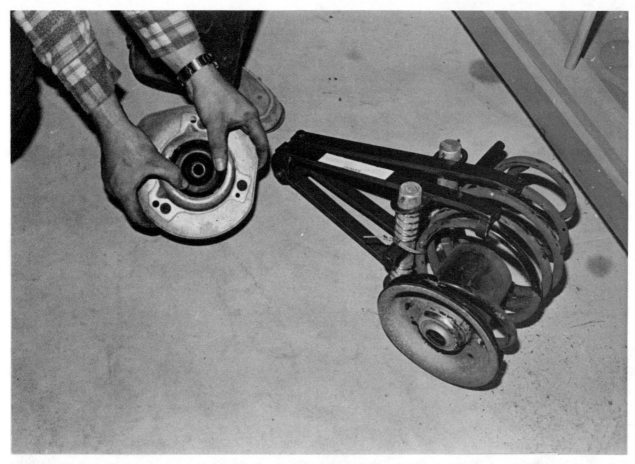

Figure 12-58. Lift off upper mount, and hold one end and turn the other to feel bearing for roughness or free play. If bearing is rough or has free play, replace upper mount. With upper mount off, coil spring (still compressed) can be lifted off old strut and installed on new one. Install upper mount and piston rod nut. Tighten nut securely, using a torque wrench with a crowfoot wrench bit. Remove spring compressor.

Figure 12-59. Install new strut assembly. Tighten flange bolts to specifications with torque wrench.

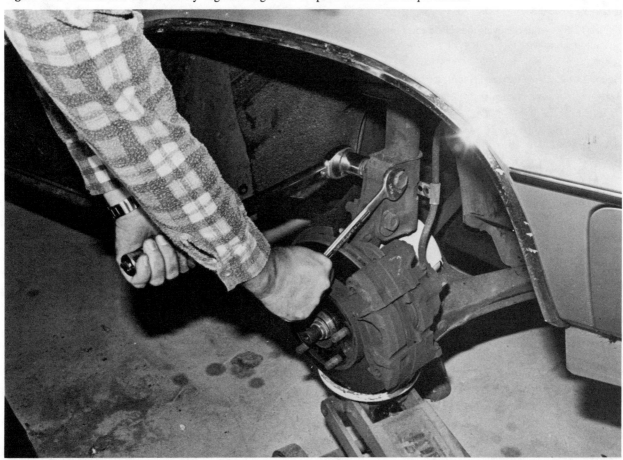

Prix. The procedure requires special tools that can be obtained from Kent-Moore tools (1-800-345-2233) and possibly at auto parts stores. One tool permits you to remove a flange at the top of the strut tower in the engine compartment; the other is a deep, hollow spanner wrench that, when used with a ratchet, permits you to reach and loosen the cap nut on the strut, so the insert can be lifted up and out through the top of the engine compartment. Installation of a new insert is the reverse of removal. See figures 12-60, 12-61, 12-62, and 12-63.

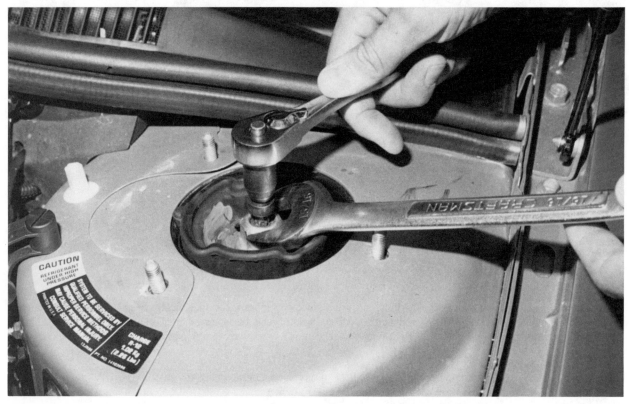

Figure 12-60. After removing the plastic cover on top of the spring tower and the three nuts that hold the strut, loosen and remove the piston rod nut as shown.

Figure 12-61. Using one special tool, remove the bracket as shown to provide clearance for strut to come up.

Figure 12-62. This is the deep, hollow spanner wrench. Insert it into the opening until you can feel the pins engage the slots in the cap of the strut. Then loosen the cap with a ratchet wrench in the spanner.

Figure 12-63. When the cap is loose, remove the spanner, then reach down and pull out the strut as shown (a plastic dust cover has already been lifted out).

13 Drive Train Fundamentals

Manual Clutch

The manual clutch is a mechanical device that can disconnect the engine from the transmission to permit stopping the car without turning off the engine and to allow gear changes. Here's how the typical clutch works (see fig. 13-1):

The key part of the clutch is the friction disc, a disc with friction material (like brake lining) on both sides. It has a splined center hub that fits onto the front of the transmission shaft, which is splined to mesh with those on the hub. The splined arrangement means that the disc will always turn with the transmission shaft but can move fore or aft on the transmission shaft.

A large plate called the pressure plate, with spring fingers, fits over the friction disc and is bolted to the engine flywheel. When the clutch is engaged, the fingers press down on the friction disc and hold it firmly to the flywheel. This provides a friction contact between the engine (the flywheel is bolted to the rear of the engine crankshaft) and the transmission shaft. Thus power from the engine can flow to the transmission.

When you want to separate the engine from transmission, to stop the car or change gears, you press down on the pedal, which operates linkage (or a cable and linkage) that pushes a throwout bearing assembly against the pressure-plate fingers, disengaging them from contact with the friction disc. The spinning flywheel then pushes the friction disc rearward (the disc slides along the splines) and the connection between the engine and the transmission is broken.

If the pressure plate spring fingers lose a bit of their grip, or if the friction disc wears down (or becomes contaminated with grease), the friction connection between engine and transmission deteriorates. You step on the gas and the engine speeds up, but the car seems to lag behind. This is called "clutch slippage," and the only cure is to replace the clutch, a job for professional mechanic.

Figure 13-1. A typical clutch. When you step on the clutch pedal, linkage pivots the fork-pivot, pushing on the sleeve and bearing that, in turn, depresses spring-loaded fingers on the clutch plate. This releases pressure on the disc, a plate coated with friction material on both sides. When the pressure on the friction disc is released, the transmission can be shifted into neutral, separating engine from the transmission and the remainder of the car's drive train.

There is another common cause of a slipping clutch, however, and this one you can do something about if you catch the problem in time.

As the friction disc wears, the spring fingers pivot and come in contact with the throwout bearing assembly that is pressed to disengage them. It is important to maintain some clearance between the throwout bearing assembly and the fingers, in order to allow the other ends of the fingers to keep full spring pressure on the friction disc as the disc wears. This clearance is translated into free play at the clutch pedal. If you slowly depress the normal clutch pedal, you'll feel a point at which you're really pushing down on something. Up to that point is the free play, and it should be $3/4$ to $1^3/8$ inches on most cars. If there is no free play, the clutch may not fully engage. If, however, there is too much free play, another problem can occur:

With too much play, the full travel of the linkage and the bearing assembly may not be sufficient to fully depress the spring fingers. Only a partial disconnection between engine and transmission results, and this causes three problems:

1. Because the friction disc is never really disengaged from the flywheel when the pedal is depressed, the flywheel spins against it and causes excessive wear of the friction disc.

2. When you try to shift gears, the transmission shaft will not be stopped, as it is when the clutch is fully disengaged. Parts in the transmission clash and wear out prematurely.

3. The throwout bearing is in constant contact with the fingers and wears out prematurely.

On many new transverse-engine, front-drive cars, the clutch free play is self-adjusting to prevent these possible problems. Or the clutch may require a minor adjustment you can make (check your owner's manual). The typical adjustment of this type should be done this way every 5,000 miles: Just slip your foot under the pedal, lift it up to a stop, then depress the clutch to complete the adjust-

ment. On other models, there also is a clutch play adjustment you can make to correct or prevent these problems.

You can correct any of these problems with a clutch linkage adjustment. The exact procedure varies from car to car, but the following are typical (although not exhaustive for the makes mentioned). Jack up the front of the car (see chapter 5) and support it on safety stands. If you have trouble finding the clutch linkage, have a helper operate the clutch pedal so you can trace it.

American Motors Rear-drive Cars (see fig. 13-2). Loosen the lockscrew on the outer end of the bellcrank to the throwout lever rod, then turn the adjusting nut (in the inner side) to change the operating length of the rod.

Chrysler Rear-drive Cars (see fig. 13-3). Turn the self-locking adjusting nut on the fork rod. On front-wheel-drive Omni and Horizon, see figure 13-4 for the proper adjustment.

Most General Motors Rear-drive Cars (see fig. 13-5). Disconnect the return spring at the clutch fork, then rotate the clutch lever and shaft assembly until the clutch pedal is firmly against the rubber stop on the dashboard brace. Push the outer end of the clutch fork to the rear until you can feel the throwout bearing just touching the pressure plate fingers. Loosen the locknut on the rod and shift the

Figure 13-2. Clutch adjustment for American Motor's cars: Loosen lockscrew on outer end of rod that goes from bellcrank to throwout lever, then turn adjusting nut.

Figure 13-3. This is a typical Chrysler Corp. rear-drive car clutch linkage. Turn adjusting nut on fork rod to change free play.

Figure 13-4. On Chrysler's front-wheel-drive Omni and Horizon, lift up on threaded bracket as shown to unseat the bracket, then turn it on the threaded cable end to change pedal free play. Newer designs have self-adjusting clutches.

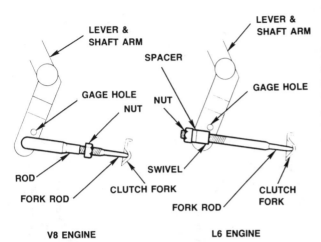

LEVER &
SHAFT ARM

LEVER &
SHAFT ARM

SPACER

GAGE HOLE

GAGE HOLE
NUT
NUT

NUT

ROD

SWIVEL

CLUTCH FORK

FORK ROD

CLUTCH
FORK

FORK ROD

CLUTCH
FORK

V8 ENGINE

L6 ENGINE

Figure 13-5. This is typical General Motors clutch free play arrangement. To adjust play, disconnect the return spring (not shown) at the clutch fork. Rotate the clutch lever and shaft assembly until the clutch pedal is firmly against the rubber bumper on the dashboard brace. Push the outer end of the clutch fork rearward until the throwout bearing just touches the pressure plate—something you can feel, not see. Install the pushrod or swivel in the gage hole and adjust the pushrod length until there is no free play in the system. Remove the rod or swivel from the gage hole and refit to the lower (operating hole). Install the washer and tighten the locknut, being careful not to change the length of the rod. Refit spring.

rod up to the gage hole. Turn the forward end of the rod until there is no free play in the system. Move the rod back to its original hole, then tighten the locknut, being careful not to change the length of the rod. Install the rod retainer and the clutch fork return spring. Pedal play should be within specifications.

Note: Chevy Citation and other GM front-drive compacts have a self-adjusting clutch setup.

Many GM front-wheel-drive cars have a self-adjusting

clutch or a lift-the-pedal-with-your-foot arrangement, as explained earlier in this chapter.

Ford Motor Rear-drive Cars Refer to figure 13-6 to 13-8. As with other types of linkage adjustments, such as parking brakes, you may not make the adjustment the correct way on the first shot. Be prepared for a second or even third try. Once you become familiar with it, however, it will be a quick job.

Figure 13-6. This is a common type of Ford rear-drive car free play adjuster on the linkage. With this type, begin adjustment by disconnecting clutch release lever spring, then move release fork rearward by hand until you feel the throwout bearing just touching the pressure plate. Loosen and back off both nuts at the swivel and place the specified feeler gauge (0.136-inch) between inner nut and swivel. Turn inner nut until feeler gauge is just touching nut, then run outer nut up to inner nut and lock them together. Reconnect the spring.

FREE PLAY ADJUSTER

.136 ± .035

CLUTCH CABLE

RELEASE LEVER

BRAKE SUPPORT

BRAKE BOOSTER

CLUTCH CABLE

BOOT

CABLE LOCK UNIT

FACE OF TAB

NYLON ADJUSTER NUT

NYLON ADJUSTING NUT

NOTE: CABLE ROUTING SHOULD FOLLOW A SMOOTH ARC AND MAINTAIN ADEQUATE
CLEARANCE OF ALL OTHER COMPONENTS

Figure 13-7. This is another type of Ford clutch linkage arrangement. To adjust free play, loosen locknut for cable and pull cable toward front of car until tabs on nylon adjuster nut are clear of the flywheel housing boss. Then turn adjusting nut about a quarter inch. Release the cable, then pull it forward again, until there is no free play at the clutch release lever. Turn the adjusting nut until it touches the face of the index tabs and the flywheel housing, then index tabs so they drop into the nearest housing groove. Finally, tighten locknut.

414

Figure 13-8. Third type of Ford free play adjuster. To set free play, remove cable retaining clip at dash panel. Remove screw holding cable bracket to fender apron, then pull cable toward front of car until it is possible to turn adjusting nut. Turn nut away from adjustment sleeve about a quarter inch. Release cable, then pull again until free movement of the clutch release lever is eliminated. Turn adjusting nut toward the adjustment sleeve until it just touches, then index into the next notch. Refit cable clip and attaching bracket.

ADJUSTMENT SLEEVE

SURFACE A

RETENTION SPRING

ADJUSTMENT NUT

CLUTCH CABLE

FREE PLAY ADJUSTER

415

AUTOMATIC TRANSMISSION MAINTENANCE

When an automatic transmission fails, it's an expensive proposition to repair. Although that work is not for weekend mechanics, you can give your automatic routine maintenance and other care to extend its life.

Most important, check the fluid level regularly. After the car has been driven a few miles, apply the brakes and move the shift lever from "Park" to "Low," then back again, stopping in "Neutral" on Chrysler and American Motors cars, and "Park" on General Motors and Ford automobiles. Let the engine idle and pull the automatic transmission dipstick. Wipe dry, reinstall (be sure to get it down all the way), then remove and read the dipstick level. Even if the dipstick shows only a half pint low, add that half pint, using a long hose and funnel. Cap the oil can and save for future needs.

Use "Dexron II" fluid on all cars except some Ford products, for which Type F fluid is specified. Check your owner's manual to be sure. If the Ford owner's manual lists a Type "CJ" fluid, you can use Dexron II in that transmission too. These names appear on the appropriate cans. Some Fords call for Type H fluid. Use a high-quality Dexron II fluid, preferably one approved by the oil refiner as a substitute, or listed as meeting the "Mercon" specifications.

Save your transmission from a fast burnout—don't try to rock yourself loose if you're stuck in snow or mud. You may eventually get out, but the transmission oil will often have overheated so badly and adversely affected transmission parts that the victory will be short-lived. The cost of a tow truck will be far less than the loss of useful transmission life.

Changing Oil and Filter

Most transmissions have a replaceable filter or cleanable screen in the oil pan. It's good maintenance practice to remove the oil pan, change the filter or clean the screen in solvent, and discard the oil that drains out with pan removal. Only a fraction of the total oil content of the automatic transmission comes out (perhaps $2\frac{1}{2}$ to $3\frac{1}{2}$ quarts) when you drop the pan, but this amount of fresh oil is enough to revitalize the remainder.

Jack up the car (see chapter 5) and support it on safety stands, preferably at all four wheels, but if you only have two stands, jack as high as possible at the front.

Place a large drain pan just under the transmission oil pan (support it on a box if necessary to bring it as close as possible to the oil pan).

Remove all the screws holding the transmission pan (see fig. 13-9) and carefully lower it so that any spillage goes into the drain pan. Empty the remainder into the drain pan.

Service the oil pan and its mating surface as with any gasketed engine joint (see chapter 5).

Remove the screen or filter, which is held by screws or

Figure 13-9. Removing transmission oil pan screws.

Figure 13-10. After removing the retaining screws, lower the oil filter. When installing the new one, be sure O-ring on filter seats against neck on pipe. Or if O-ring is furnished separately, install it against neck on pipe.

bolts. If the old filter has a neck with a rubber O-ring, the replacement will have the O-ring too.

Install the cleaned screen or new filter (see fig. 13-10), refit the pan (see fig. 13-11), then top off the transmission with fresh oil approximately equal to what was drained. As with other gasketed joints, you should tighten the oil pan screws in a crisscross fashion or in a spiral manner, starting in the center and working alternately toward the ends.

Note: Before pan installation inspect bolt holes, and if they appear to aim up, place the pan on a steel surface and whack them flat with a ball-peen hammer (fig. 13-12). High-quality, rubber-cork or rubber-fiber gaskets are generally supplied with the better brands of automatic transmission filters, so there is rarely a problem of gasket shrinkage or danger of tearing during installation.

Run the engine with the brakes firmly applied and move the shift lever through all positions while a helper looks underneath to see if there are any leaks. If there are, stop the engine and recheck the tightness of the oil pan screws.

Make a precise fluid level check as soon as possible and add oil if necessary.

Vacuum Modulator

Some transmissions use a vacuum diaphragm device threaded into the transmission case to help regulate shifting. Called a vacuum modulator, it is connected by a hose to the carburetor base or intake manifold, and because it's the only part threaded into the transmission with a vacuum hose (or two, on some cars), it's easy to spot. If the car suffers from rough or erratic shifting, disconnect the vacuum hose(s) and probe the neck(s) with a pipe cleaner. If the pipe cleaner comes out oily, replace the modulator. It's an inexpensive part that in most cases can be changed with a simple wrench or large pliers. On some Ford products, a special wrench (see fig. 13-13) is helpful. On GM cars, the modulator typically is held by a bracket and bolt. Just remove the bolt and bracket and pull out the modulator.

Figure 13-11. Refitting transmission oil pan with new gasket can be a problem because gasket may slip. The type shown has undersize bolt at the corners, so you can thread the bolts as shown and they'll hold the gasket in place.

Figure 13-12. If bolt holes aim up, flatten them to improve oil pan gasket sealing by leaning the pan against a hard surface and whacking on the holes with a ball-peen hammer as shown.

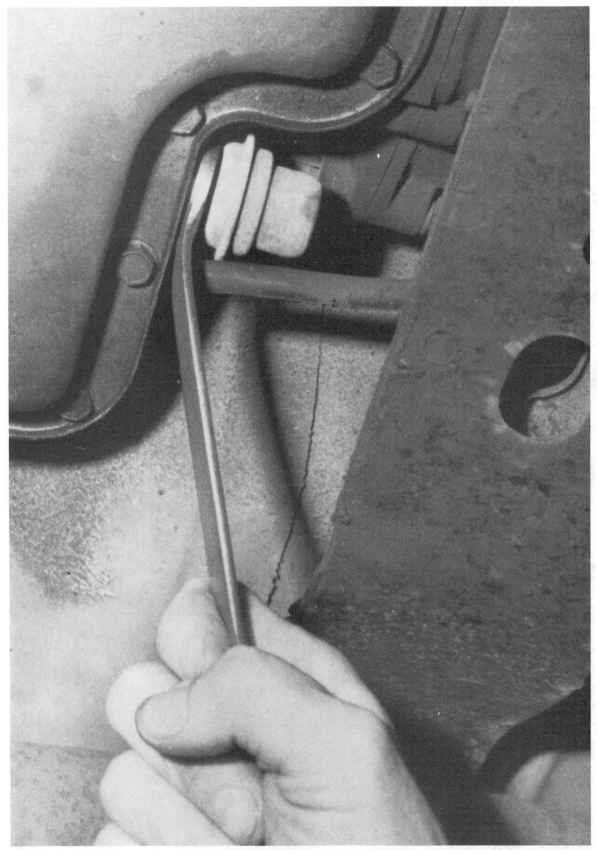

Figure 13-13. Removing a Ford modulator with a special wrench. This wrench also is useful for tightening the new modulator in place.

UNIVERSAL JOINTS

If you hear a clunk in the drive train when you take off or come to a stop, loose universal joints in the propeller shaft may be the problem, if you have a conventional front-engine, rear-drive car. Check by jacking up the car (see chapter 5), at all four wheels if possible, support on safety stands, and check the universal joints.

Hold the propeller shaft on each side of a universal joint and try to turn one part of the shaft clockwise, the other counterclockwise; then reverse the procedure (see fig. 13-14). If you feel any free play at all, the universal joint is defective and should be replaced. Rebuilding kits are inexpensive and readily available.

Most front-engine, rear-drive cars have simple cross-and-roller universal joints (see figs. 13-15 and 13-16) that you can replace yourself. If a car has what appears to be a double universal joint at the rear (see fig. 13-17), even a professional may not be able to service it. Only a few shops are equipped to repair that type of joint, and even they may not be able to guarantee the results. The normal cure is to change the entire propeller shaft.

Removing the Propeller Shaft

To replace the universal joint, you must remove the propeller shaft and service it on a workbench with a vise.

To remove the propeller shaft, you disconnect it at the rear axle. It is commonly held in one of three ways:
1. By U-bolts and nuts that also secure the rear universal joint (see fig. 13-18).
2. By straps and screws that also hold the rear universal joint (see fig. 13-16).
3. By a flange on the rear of the propeller shaft (just to the rear of the universal joint) that mates with a similar flange on the rear axle. The two flanges are held together by nuts and bolts (see fig. 13-19).

Begin by making alignment marks (with dabs of paint, nail polish, etc.) at the rear axle connection, either on the propeller shaft and rear axle flange, or on both mating flanges. These alignment marks will permit you to reattach the propeller shaft to the rear axle in exactly the same position as it was, maintaining the balance. Failure to take this step could result in vibration afterward.

Next, detach the propeller shaft from the rear axle by removing the bolts and/or nuts. Have a helper hold the

Figure 13-14. Checking a universal joint. If you feel any free play while attempting to turn one section clockwise and the other counterclockwise, the universal joint is defective and should be replaced.

Figure 13-15. This is a simple front cross-and-roller universal joint. Bushings are bearing cups that contain the rollers—also called needles—that support the cross. Sliding yoke—also called slip yoke—fits on transmission shaft.

Figure 13-16. This is a rear universal joint. The hub actually is bolted to the rear axle, and when you remove the propeller shaft, you *do not* remove the nut and washer, but do remove the two clamps (also called straps) and screws. The parts supplied in the repair kit are identified and serviced as an assembly, and the number refers to the quantity supplied.

Figure 13-17. If you see this type of universal joint at the rear, it is not one you can service. If defective, replace the entire propeller shaft.

shaft at the front, so it doesn't drop to the ground and suffer damage that also could throw it out of balance.

If the rear universal is to be reused, be careful when you remove U-bolts or straps to make sure the two bearing cups they held do not fall off.

Lower the propeller shaft so it is clear of the rear axle, then pull it rearward, out of its slip joint in the transmission at the front. Place a catch pan under the back of the transmission and stuff a clean rag into the back of the

transmission, around the transmission shaft, to minimize oil spillage.

Place the shaft on the bench. In most cases you will notice that the bearing cups in the propeller shaft ears are held by snap rings, but in a few cases you may see nothing. Those on which there is no retainer readily visible actually have injected, formed-in-place plastic retainers, and the replacement universal joint has the snap rings.

If you're working on the front universal, make align-

Figure 13-18. This type of rear universal joint is held together by U-bolts and nuts.

Figure 13-19. This rear universal joint has a flange that mates with a flange from the rear axle. Just remove the nuts and bolts holding the flanges together.

ment marks on front and rear sections here too, so they can be reassembled for original balance.

Remove the snap rings with a small screwdriver and needle nose pliers (see fig. 13-20). If you have the design with the plastic retainers, they will break apart later in the disassembly, so no special action is required.

Support the universal joint in a vise and then whack down on the cross with a hammer and chisel (see fig. 13-21). The bearing cup on one side will be partly pushed out. Next, lock the bearing cup in the vise and tap away

the propeller shaft (see fig. 13-22). Repeat this procedure to remove the other three bearing cups if you are working on a front universal or a rear of the mating flanges type.

If you're replacing a rear universal of one of the other types, just pull off two bearing cups. Only two must be forced out.

Discard the old bearing cups and cross.

Now inspect the sliding (slip) yoke, the part that splines onto the transmission shaft (see fig. 13-23). If the exterior has any burrs, remove them with fine crocus cloth. Burrs

Figure 13-20. Using screwdriver and needlenose pliers to remove snap ring from propeller shaft ear. On some cars, the snap rings are on the inboard side of the propeller shaft, and fit in a groove in the cup. Pry out this type with a screwdriver.

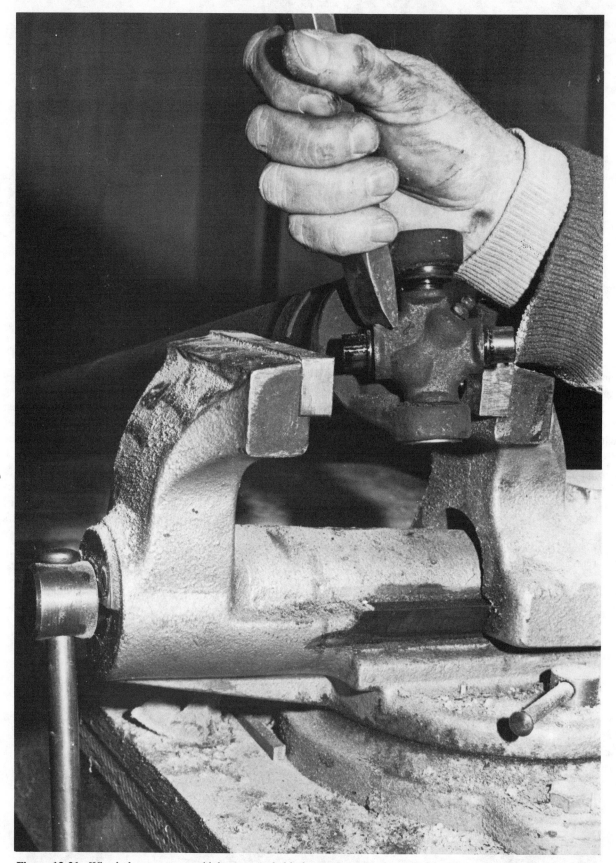

Figure 13-21. Whack down on cross with hammer and chisel to push out bearing cup at bottom.

Figure 13-22. If a bearing cup doesn't come all the way out, just lock it in a vise as shown and tap propeller shaft away with hammer.

Figure 13-23. The slip yoke end of the propeller shaft. If outer surface is badly scored, or splines inside are damaged, replace it.

won't come off? Replace the sliding yoke or you may damage a transmission seal when you attempt to reinstall the yoke.

Look at the universal joint side of the sliding yoke, and if it has a vent hole the yoke splines must be lubricated with universal joint grease. Also, check the vent hole to make sure it is open. If necessary, run a pipe cleaner through it. If there is no vent hole, the splines are lubricated by transmission fluid.

Assembly

Inspect the cross of the new universal joint to see if there is a grease fitting (see fig. 13-24) and if the grease seals are fitted onto the cross stems (called the journals). If they are not, push them on. Do they fit too tight? Position the seals on the outer edges of the cross journals, put sockets of the same diameter against them, and place the cross inside the jaws of the vise. Close the vise jaws against the sockets, and they will push the seals into place.

Next, inspect the bearing cups, which should be well greased inside. If not, apply a thick coat over the needle bearings (see fig. 13-25) and make sure all are up against the inner wall of the cup.

Position the propeller shaft in the vise with a pair of ears parallel to the jaws, one ear against a jaw and the other a couple of inches away. Place a bearing cup between the second ear and the other vise jaw and close the vise jaw and shift the bearing cup so it is aligned with the bearing cup hole in the ear. Continue to close the vise and the jaw will push the bearing cup into the ear. Stop when the cup is about halfway into the ear.

Next, put the cross into place, making sure the grease fitting faces the propeller shaft (so that it can be greased properly when the propeller shaft is installed). Be sure that the cross journal slips smoothly into the bearing cup (see fig. 13-26).

Now place the opposite side bearing cup up against the propeller shaft ear hole. Close the vise very slowly while you handle the cross, to make sure its journal slips smoothly into the second bearing cup. Continue to close the vise until the cups are flush with the outer ends of the propeller shaft ears.

The bearing cups will not be fully seated, so you can't install the snap rings just yet. Take a socket smaller in diameter than the bearing cup and place it against a cup (or if the vise opens wide enough, place a socket against each cup). Close the jaws and the smaller socket will push the cup in a bit further (see fig. 13-27). Check repeatedly, so you push the cup in only far enough to expose the groove in the ear for the snap ring. Install the snap ring. On front universal joints, or rears of the mating flange

type, repeat the procedure to install the other two bearing cups. Be careful to maintain the alignment.

Installation

When you are ready to install the propeller shaft, put on the two rear bearing cups that are held by the U-bolts or straps and screws and then tape them lightly into place.

Remove the cloth in the transmission end and have your helper start the sliding yoke onto the transmission shaft (see fig. 13-28). Raise the rear end of the propeller shaft and push the sliding yoke in as far as it will go. If you've aligned the marks on the rear axle and propeller shaft, then install the straps and screws or U-bolts loosely. Remove the tape and tighten down the rear connections. On a mating flanges type, just align the marks and bolt the flanges together. If the marks do not align, remove the shaft, turn as necessary, and reinstall.

Front Wheel Drive

If you hear a click as you make a turn on a car with front wheel drive, the likelihood is that the universal joint in a front-wheel axle shaft is nearing the end. Servicing it requires special tools and is a job for a professional. However, much of the time a failure is caused by the grease leaking out of the joint, past a damaged boot (rubber cover over the joint). If you inspect the boots as a routine matter whenever you do an oil change, you may find a nicked boot before a problem has developed. In that case, you have two alternatives:

Clean the nicked area of the boot with detergent and water, wipe dry, and seal with silicone paste.

Remove the boot and install a replacement. Although boot replacement would appear to require removal of the axle shaft, a significant job, there are kits with factory-split boots. Cut the old clamps and the boot and remove, then fit the factory-split boot in place. There are two designs, one which requires application of a glue to the joint, another which has screws and bolts to hold the boot. Although the glued type is more durable, it is often difficult to apply the glue and join the boot sections in the tight quarters inboard of the wheel. The service kits often come with special clamps that require no special tools to install (compared with most original equipment–type clamps, which often require special tools). In any case, you should check the replacement boots for looseness or damage even more frequently than the originals. See figures 13-29 and 13-30. The typical useful life of split boots is 1 to 2 years in areas with good roads.

Figure 13-24. This replacement cross has grease fitting. Install cross so you can reach fitting with grease fun when propeller shaft is installed in car.

Figure 13-25. A look inside a bearing cup. If the needle bearings inside are not properly lubricated, apply a thick coat of universal joint grease. Do not pack the cup with grease.

Figure 13-26. Pressing bearing cup into propeller shaft ear with vise.

Figure 13-27. Using socket between bearing cup and vise jaw to seat cup fully, so snap ring can be refitted. If the snap ring goes on the inboard side, into a groove in the bearing cup, you may not have to perform this step. Merely seating the bearing cup flush with the exterior of the propeller shaft ear may expose the snap ring groove in the cup.

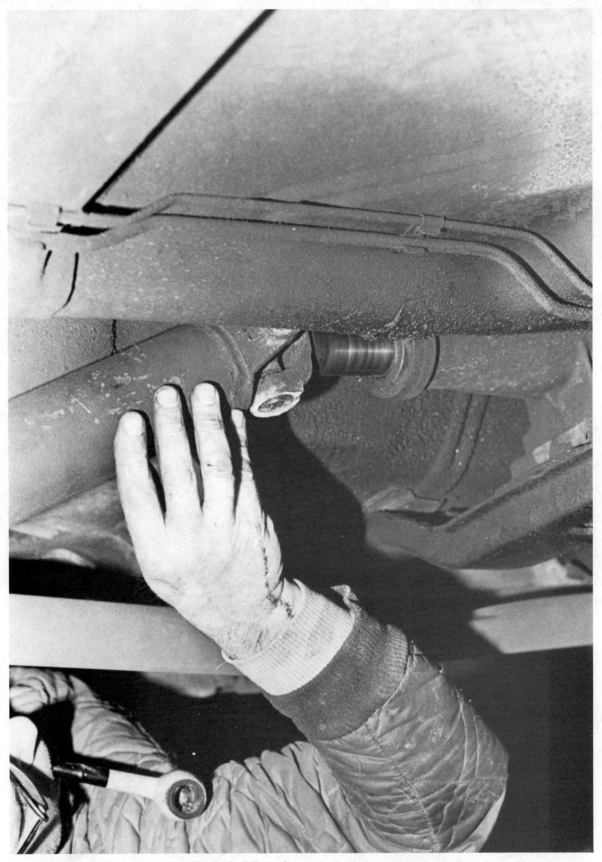

Figure 13-28. Have helper start propeller shaft sliding yoke onto transmission shaft as shown.

Figure 13-29. This is a typical split boot for a constant velocity outer joint. It is fitted in place and its seam is glued.

Figure 13-30. This is another type of split boot. The seam is secured with small nuts and bolts through the holes in the projecting tabs.

14 BODY REPAIRS

Minor dents, scratches to bare metal, and rustouts are three of the most common body repair jobs you can do with simple tools and easy-to-use patching products available in discount stores and auto supply shops.

Note: If your car has a "clear-coat" finish, it takes special equipment to refinish it. Minor scratches can be removed from the clear-coat with extremely fine sandpaper made for this work. If your car has larger damage, restrict your work to restoring the surface (the most expensive part of most body repair jobs) and let a professional shop apply the color and clear coats.

Very minor damage to clear-coat finishes can be repaired using aerosol cans of clear-coat or touch-up paint and clear-coat formulated for use with the Pre-Val sprayer (an aerosol-type power unit atop a glass bottle of liquid paint). The Pre-Val is available in many auto parts stores.

SCRATCHES

Surface preparation, as in any body work, is very important. Clean the area around the scratched (or chipped) area with a soap-and-water solution, then wipe dry and apply a wax and grease remover. Unless these steps are taken, the paint you apply later will not adhere properly.

Using wet-or-dry, very fine sandpaper, wet-sand the area (see fig. 14-1). Sand until you have a featheredge, that is, until there is a continuous smooth surface from bare metal to the paint on adjacent undamaged areas.

Mask off the area to be painted, including a small area beyond the featheredge (see fig. 14-2). If you are working near chrome, glass parts, wheels, and tires, be sure to mask them off too, using newspaper or wrapping paper and masking tape to protect them from overspray (see figs. 14-3 and 14-4).

Wipe the area to be painted with a tack cloth to remove any dust, then apply a coat of automotive primer from a spray can (see fig. 14-5). Do not move the can toward and away from the metal, but hold it the same distance (generally eight inches) and move it from side to side or up and down. After the primer has dried thoroughly, wet-sand with wet-or-dry very fine paper, dipping the paper in water repeatedly. Be careful not to sand through the primer coat, but if you do, wipe the area dry and reapply primer.

After sanding, wipe the area with a tack cloth and use a spot putty (sold in squeeze tubes) to fill pinholes and minor scratches (see fig. 14-6). Wet-sand as before, wipe dry, then apply two additional coats of primer. Permit them to dry, then wet-sand with wet-or-dry, super-fine paper. Use rubbing compound to remove overspray. Dry and clean with a tack cloth, then spray on the color coats (see fig. 14-7).

Note: If the paint is available only in liquid form, and you do not have a paint sprayer, obtain a Pre-Val sprayer.

Note: With acrylic lacquers only, you can improve the finish by lightly wet-sanding the color with wet-or-dry, ultrafine paper to remove any overspray and surface irregularities from dust. Finish up by carefully rubbing the repaired area with rubbing compound and a damp cheesecloth (see fig. 14-8). This procedure should be done only after allowing the color coat to dry overnight.

MINOR DENTS

Begin by cleaning the surface as for deep scratches (see fig. 14-9). If the dent is more than $1/4$ inch deep, it should be knocked out (as best you can) to the normal surface. If you have access from behind, use a hammer. If you can't get behind the dent (such as in a door), drill a $1/16$-inch hole in the center of the dent, or if it's a crease, drill holes along the crease about 2 or 3 inches apart (see fig. 14-10). Thread an oversize sheet metal screw into the hole

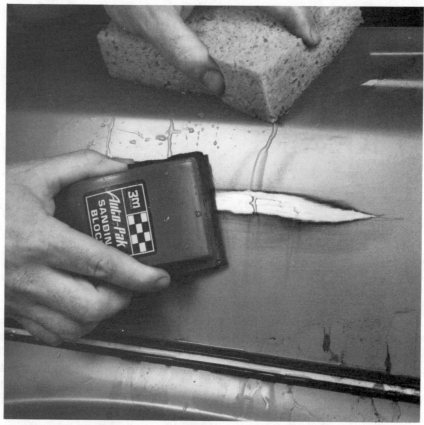

Figure 14-1. Flood area with wet sponge, and using wet-or-dry sandpaper, sand scratched area down to featheredge.

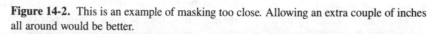

Figure 14-2. This is an example of masking too close. Allowing an extra couple of inches all around would be better.

Figure 14-3. Masking an emblem with tape.

Figure 14-4. Using wrapping paper to mask a wheel to protect from overspray.

433

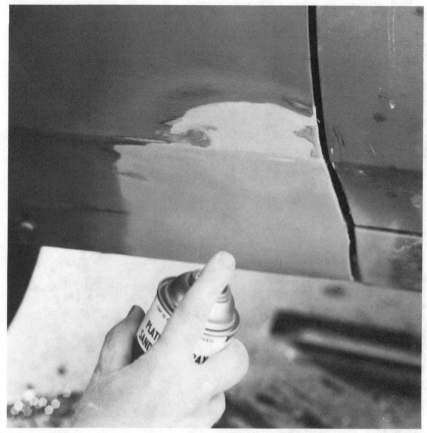

Figure 14-5. Spraying on primer coat. Be sure to hold can the same distance from the metal as you move it up or down and side to side.

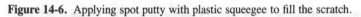

Figure 14-6. Applying spot putty with plastic squeegee to fill the scratch.

Figure 14-7. Applying color coat from an aerosol can. Only a spray will give you a professional look. Brushes leave stroke marks.

Figure 14-8. After the color coats are dry, finish the job by rubbing the repair gently with rubbing compound and damp cheesecloth.

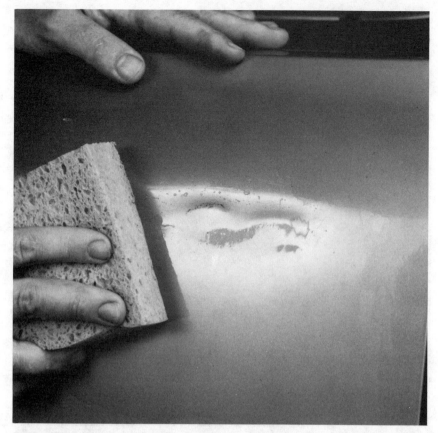

Figure 14-9. Clean dented surface with sponge and soap-water solution, then apply a wax and grease remover.

Figure 14-10. If you don't have access to knock out dent from rear, drill small holes as shown about two to three inches apart along the crease. Thread in oversize sheet metal screws and pull out on them with vise-type locking pliers.

Figure 14-11. Grind away all paint in and just around the dent with a coarse sanding disc on an electric drill. Hold disc at a slight angle to the sheet metal as shown.

(because it is oversize it will protrude) and lock vise-type pliers onto the head. Pull on the pliers to draw the sheet metal out as close as possible to the normal surface. Follow this procedure along the dent until you have done the best you can.

Next, grind away all the paint in and just around the dent with a coarse sanding disc on a ¼-inch electric drill (see fig. 14-11), holding the disc at a slight angle to the sheet metal. Wear safety glasses when performing this operation.

Mix a suitable amount of plastic filler, following the manufacturer's instructions for proportions of base material and the hardener (see fig. 14-12). Mix very thoroughly and apply immediately, for it will start to harden in minutes. Use a plastic squeegee to apply the filler and put pressure on it to force out any air bubbles (see fig. 14-13). Make the coat as smooth as possible, but don't skimp. After it dries, sand it down to shape, and if there are any low spots mix some more filler and apply. Finally, paint the repaired surface as described for deep scratches.

RUSTOUTS

A small rustout (under 36 square inches) can be repaired in much the same manner as a small dent, using any one of the various types of patches to bridge the opening.

Prepare the surface as for deep scratches (see fig. 14-14). Sand away rust and the paint immediately surrounding the rustout with a coarse sanding disc on a ¼-inch drill. You should have about two inches of good metal showing around the rustout, and as you sand you may find that more metal weakness from rust has occurred than was obvious before you started. As with any power-sanding operation, wear safety glasses.

Bend in the edges of solid metal to outline the opening, using a small hammer (see fig. 14-15). This will recess the patch slightly to allow an application of plastic filler.

There are several good choices for bridging the opening:

1. A fiberglass patch.

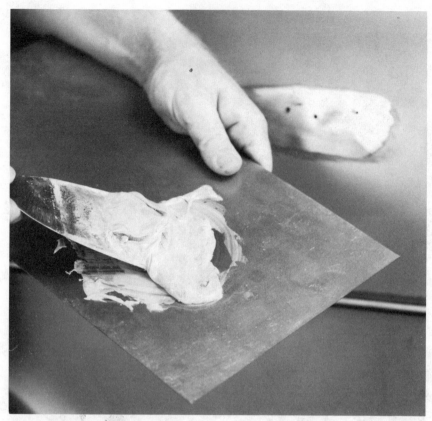

Figure 14-12. Mix base material and hardener very carefully, following manufacturer's instructions for proportions.

Figure 14-13. Apply putty mixture immediately as shown, for it will start to harden very quickly. Apply pressure with plastic squeegee to force out any air bubbles.

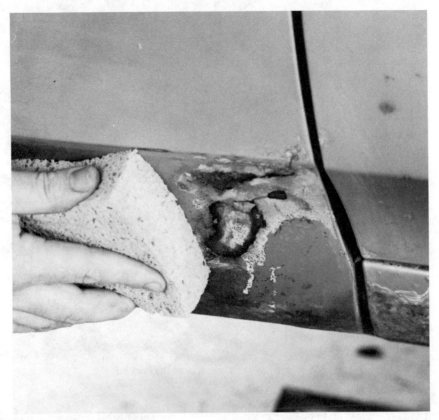

Figure 14-14. Cleaning rustout area.

Figure 14-15. Bending in edges of solid metal to outline the opening. This will recess the patch (to allow application of filler).

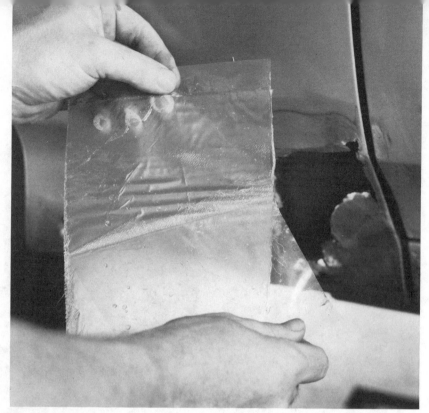

Figure 14-16. Peeling a Lay-It-On patch from the backing.

2. A "Lay-It-On" fiberglass and polyester patch.
3. Metallic auto body repair tape or patch. Instructions for application are furnished with each type, but there are special cautions to observe with each.

With the Lay-It-On patch, you cut the patch with scissors to size it to cover the entire sanded area, then moisten your fingers (so the patch won't stick to them), peel the patch from the backing (see fig. 14-16), and apply (see fig. 14-17). Cure the patch in direct sunlight (up to 2 hours at 80° F in bright sun, as long as 8 hours if it's partly sunny). At lower ambient temperatures it takes much longer (up to 24 hours in partial sun at 50° F), often an impractical length of time. A better choice is an ultraviolet sunlamp, 6 inches from the patch, for 12 to 20 minutes (see fig. 14-18). Heat alone will not work. Be careful not to allow overcuring, or the patch could become brittle.

Once the patch is hard, scuff-sand it with 80-grit paper, from the edges toward the middle until you have close to a featheredge from the bare metal to the patch (see fig. 14-19).

With the metallic tape there is no need for curing. However, the tape is only two inches wide, so to bridge most rustouts you must apply slightly overlapped strips (see fig. 14-20). Cut excess tape (past the bared sheet metal) with a razor blade and use a screwdriver handle to press the tape into good contact with the bared sheet metal. If you can use the metallic patch, you eliminate the need to apply and overlap the strips, and the need to get good adhesion at the overlap points. The single patch should bridge the small rustout completely.

The fiberglass patch is similar to the other types in method of application, and it is heat-cured. After applying a metallic or fiberglass patch, scuff-sand as with the Lay-It-On type to help the plastic filler adhere. Complete the job by applying plastic filler as for minor dents and paint as for scratches.

WAXING AND POLISHING

To get the best results from a wax job, you should start with a clean body. Remove tar with a mild solvent. Touch up any nicks and allow paint to dry for a couple of days.

Note: If you have repaired and repainted a panel, or part of it, wait 30 days before waxing the car.

If the body finish is severely weathered (chalky-looking), clean it first with a mild abrasive polish. Do not use rubbing compound, which is very abrasive and will thin out the color coat. If the finish shows only mild weathering, use a combination polish and wax. With a new car, use only a wax, which is commonly advertised for new car use only.

Never use a buffing wheel driven by an electric drill. It is next to useless at sharply bent edges (of which there are many on the car) and, unless handled with great care and skill, could result in color coat removal at sharp bends. Your hand still is the best polishing and waxing cloth holder available.

Polishes, waxes, and polish-wax combinations are available in paste, softened paste, and liquid forms. You probably will find the liquid the easiest to use, with the softened paste a close second choice.

440

Figure 14-17. When applying the Lay-It-On patch, smooth it down with fingers and make sure it adheres all around.

Figure 14-18. If curing in sunlight is impractical, you may use an ultraviolet sunlamp as shown. The lamp, set 6 inches from the patch, will cure it in 12 to 20 minutes.

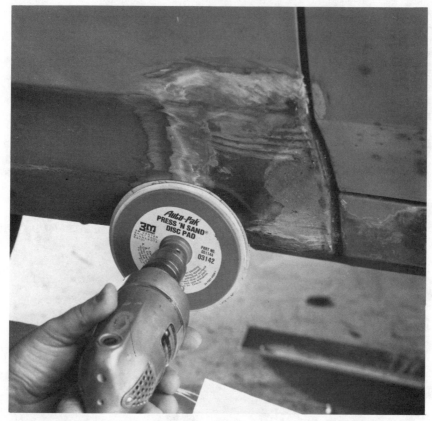

Figure 14-19. After patch cures (becomes hard), scuff-sand with 80-grit disc as shown until you have close to a featheredge to the bare metal.

Figure 14-20. If you are using auto body tape, slightly overlap the layers as shown, then use a screwdriver handle to press tape into good contact with the sheet metal, also as shown.

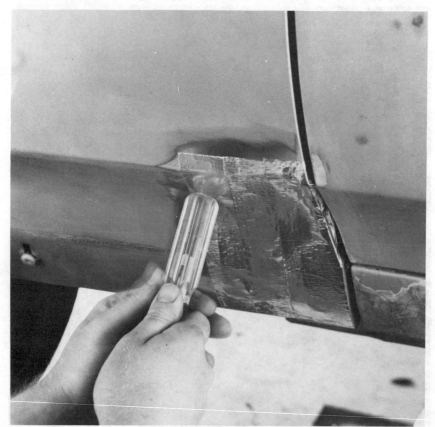

15 PARTS BUYING GUIDE

The kind of part you buy—new, rebuilt or used—is an important factor in the cost of auto repairs. The best choice is not a single one, but depends on the part itself.

A new part is exactly what the adjective says—brand-spanking new. A rebuilt part is one in which all defective contents have either been repaired or replaced by new items. A used part is one that has been salvaged from a car that was wrecked or removed from service by an insurance company for some reason, whether the result of an accident, flooding, fire, or other minor disaster.

It might seem that you could buy almost anything new, but you really can't in many cases without a struggle. The reason: The new part is so expensive that practically no one buys it, so the manufacturers turn out very few in addition to what is needed for the automobile production lines. Rebuilts save you 40 to 60 percent off the price of new parts—if you could get new. Some examples: starters, alternators, ignition distributors, and water pumps.

Other parts more commonly sold in rebuilt form than new include: carburetors, brake shoes, clutches, power steering gear, manual steering gear (particularly rack-and-pinion-type), engines, transmissions, windshield wiper motors, power steering pumps, and air conditioning compressors. Rebuilts also are coming on strong for power brake boosters, disc brake calipers, and brake master cylinders. In addition, radiators are commonly rebuilt (a process called recoring) by specialty shops. The saving over a new radiator is small (perhaps less than 15 percent), but recoring reduces the shop's stocking requirements, and the result is about as good as new.

A high-quality rebuilt part can provide very satisfactory service. Only two rebuilders have national distribution—Arrow and Champion; the remainder are regional operations so numerous it would be impossible to list them here. Therefore, when it comes to a rebuilt, you probably will not be able to find a national name. If you buy at a parts store that serves the professional, however, you should get a quality rebuilt, for professional mechanics will not long patronize a parts store that sells unreliable rebuilts.

You should be wary of some rebuilts that you might be tempted to buy. Rebuilt spark plugs and voltage regulators are the two prime examples that just can't compare with a new part. Rebuilt fuel pumps are also available and, although usually reliable, they cost so little less than a new part that their sales are low and, therefore, so is stock in the typical parts store.

Rebuilt batteries are available in some parts of the country, but the workmanship varies so greatly that it represents a risk which is not recommended.

You should be aware that replacement versions of some components do not come complete. You may have to take a pulley off an old water or power steering pump; brackets, solenoid, and vacuum diaphragm unit off the old carburetor. This not only is true with new or rebuilt parts but with a part from a wrecking yard. (Because the same part goes on different cars, the brackets, pulleys, etc. on the part may not match the one on your car, even though the basic part is the same. However, always inspect carefully to be sure the part really is the same.) With a pulley, make sure you can remove it. Some pulleys can only be removed safely with a special tool.

USED PARTS

The used part is often a best buy. When it comes to body parts, you can't beat the wrecking yard. You can buy a fully assembled door, often in the right color, for much less than the individual parts would cost new—and you save the time of assembly and painting. Interestingly, availability of used body parts is usually much better than for new parts, particularly if the car is a few years old.

Note: Aftermarket (rather than from the car maker)

443

body panels are also available for many cars. Once of poor quality, these panels are getting better, and are worth consideration if the price is right.

After body parts, the wrecking yard is an excellent source for the following:

Batteries. A good used battery from a late-model wreck is a reasonably good risk, at perhaps one-fourth the price of a new one. If you're not planning to keep the car very long, you could save big money.

Tires and spare wheels. These also cost just a fraction of the price for new ones, even less than retreaded tires. Spare wheels for snow tires save the cost of seasonal mounting and demounting, and if you're planning to sell the car soon the much lower cost of used tires makes them a best buy.

Electrical parts. A used electrical part is much cheaper than even a rebuilt, and in some cases the rebuilt may not be available, such as for some imports. Starters, alternators, ignition distributors, wiper motors, horns, power window and seat motors, and some multipurpose stalk switches (the ones on the steering column) are low-risk items. The wrecker can test the part with jumper wires and a battery, so you know if it works before you buy it.

Carburetors and power steering pumps. These parts cannot be tested before you buy, but they normally are not time-consuming items to install, so if the part doesn't work you haven't invested a lot and can return it for a quick exchange or refund. The prices will be much lower than rebuilts. The power steering pumps on many transverse-engine, front-drive cars are an exception, often very difficult to remove. In this case, where you are investing a lot of labor, you may want the extra security of a quality rebuilt.

Brake discs and drums. You can't get a rebuilt drum or disc, so the choice is either new or used. The used part can be inspected for cracks and other defects, so the risk is really very low. The savings, however, can be 70 percent.

Although major components—engines, transmissions, and differentials—are sold by wrecking yards, there is greater risk involved. You can see if an engine starts and runs and if a manual transmission shifts into all gears, but that's about it. If you ever attempt a major component replacement, you should, of course, consider the wrecking yard as a source. The wrecker will exchange or refund, as with smaller components, but the labor investment you have is very substantial, so don't go by component price alone.

Wrecking Yard Prices

Most small wrecking yards don't post a price list. The wrecker just quotes what he thinks he can get, based to some vague degree on the price of rebuilts and new parts, whichever is the competition. You can, therefore, do some bargaining and often save some money. If a part is in great demand, however, the price may be very close to a rebuilt, so always know the cost of the alternatives.

However, there are many "super wreckers" who not only calatog their prices by computer, but have computerized prices lists too.

COPING WITH CATALOGS

Most of the parts you will buy—plugs, filters, drive belts, lubricants, etc.— will be new. You want to get the best price possible, so you'll check with auto parts stores, discount houses, and mail order firms. Generally, the discount house and mail order firm will be cheaper than the auto parts store but, in may cases, you must read the catalogs and application charts to find the part number, then pick the part off the shelf. Parts manufacturers selling to discount houses try to offer easy-to-read catalogs and charts but, in many cases, the listings must be condensed to keep them from being thicker than a phone book. The first thing you can see that you may have to know is what the numbers mean. A 235 6-cylinder is a 6-cylinder with a cubic-inch displacement of 235. Or the listing may be given in metric terms, such as 3.8L (for liter). Displacement is the volume of all cylinders added together.

The term 4B carb means 4-barrel carburetor. 2B is 2-barrel. In some cases 2V or 4V are used, with the V referring to venturi, a section of the carburetor barrel.

The abbreviation FI means fuel injection, and EFI means electronic fuel injection (which could be TBI or MPFI)—TBI means throttle body fuel injection (a single injector assembly with one or two injectors in place of the carburetor), MPFI means multipoint fuel injection (a separate injector for each cylinder).

In some cases, the displacement number will be on the air cleaner or engine top cover, or on an exterior body emblem. To tell which carburetor you have, remove the air cleaner cover and count the number of holes (one, two, or four). An in-line engine with four or six cylinders will have a one- or two-barrel carburetor; a V-6 or V-8 will have two or four barrels (see fig. 15-1).

Let's assume you have a 1973 model with the 325 V-8. In that case, you don't care what carburetor it has, for all take Part No. 1472-D. If you have a 1974 with air conditioning, but only a two-barrel carburetor, the part number also is 1472-D, because No. 1503-R is only for cars with the four-barrel *and* air conditioning.

If you have a 1979 Hummer with the 385 V-8 and power steering, the part number is 1704-M, not 1828-Z, which is only for those with *both* air conditioning and power steering.

Figure 15-1. Top view of a four-barrel carburetor. You will notice that it has four distinct circular sections, or barrels. Some carburetors have only one, others two.

Some catalogs give interchange listings between the manufacturer's make and competitors. If you have a competitive part, you may be tempted to take the number off the part and look at the interchange listing. With many parts, however, particularly spark plugs, this information is often inapplicable. Always use the make-of-car listings only, or you could end up with the wrong part.

Don't be surprised (even with the same brand) if you find that the catalog lists a different part from the one in your engine. Either the old part may have been superseded by the new number, or the last installation could have been in error. It happens all the time.

You should, therefore, know how to read a catalog listing. Below is a sample and what it means.

		Part No.
1971–80	All Models with 235 6-cylinder	1471-D
1971–76	All 325 V-8 except below	1472-D
1974–75	325 V-8 with air conditioning, 4B carburetor	1503-R
1971–77	385 V-8 except below	1468-N
1973–76	Charger, Rammer 325 V-8	1525-L
1977–82	All 325 V-8 except below	1516-A
	385 V-8 except below	1704-M
	Charger, Rammer 325 V-8, 385 V-8 except below	1851-C
	All 385 V-8 with air conditioning and	
	power steering	1828-Z
1983–85	2.4-liter 4-cylinder 1B	1831-X
	2.4-liter 4-cylinder TBI	1833-Z
	3.0-liter V-6 2B	1902-R
	3.0-liter V-6 MPFI	1904-R
	All 325 V-8	1516-A
1986–88	All 2.4-liter 4-cylinder	1833-X
	All 3.0-liter V-6	1904-R

Metric Conversions

As the conversion to the metric system continues, you may find that you must convert American/English dimensions to metric. It's particularly easy with a pocket calculator, and here are the formulas you will need.

INCHES TO MILLIMETERS: Multiply by 25.4. — Ex.: .001-inch equals .0254-mm.

MILLIMETERS TO INCHES: Multiply by .04. — Ex.: .05-mm equals .002-inch.

INCHES TO CENTIMETERS: Multiply by 2.54. — Ex.: 3.41 inches equals 8.66 cm.

CENTIMETERS TO INCHES: Multiply by .4. — Ex.: 8.4 cm equals 3.36 inches.

CUBIC INCHES TO LITERS: Divide by 61. — Ex.: 122 cubic inches equals 2 liters.

LITERS TO CUBIC INCHES: Multiply by 61. — Ex.: 3 liters equals 183 cubic inches.

LITERS TO CUBIC CENTIMETERS: Multiply by 1000. — Ex.: 1.4 liters equals 1400cc

PRESSURE—POUNDS PER SQUARE INCH (PSI) TO KILOPASCALS (kPa): Multiply by 6.9. — Ex.: 10 p.s.i. equals 69 kPa.

PRESSURE—KILOPASCALS TO POUNDS PER SQUARE INCH: Divide by 6.9 — Ex.: 138 kPa equals 20 p.s.i.

TORQUE—POUNDS-FEET (LBS.-FT.) TO NEWTON-METERS: Multiply by 1.356. — Ex.: 100 lbs.-ft. equals 136n-m.

TORQUE—NEWTON-METERS TO POUNDS-FEET: Divide by 1.356. — Ex.: 225 lbs.-ft. equals 166 n-m.

QUARTS TO LITERS: Multiply by .946. — Ex.: 16 quarts equals 15.1 liters.

LITERS TO QUARTS: Divide by .946. — Ex.: 10 liters equals 10.6 quarts.

DEGREES FAHRENHEIT TO DEGREES CELSIUS: Subtract 32, then multiply by .5555. — Ex.: 212 degrees F. equals 100 degrees C.

DEGREES CELSIUS TO DEGREES FAHRENHEIT: Multiply by 1.8, then add 32. — Ex.: 80 degrees C. equals 176 degrees F.

OUNCES TO MILLILITERS: Multiply by 30. — Ex.: 2 oz. equals 60 ml.

MILLILITERS TO OUNCES: Divide by 30. — Ex.: 45 ml equals 1.5 oz.

The conversions are based on the use of new metric standards. If you have an old imported-car shop manual, it may refer to pressure in terms of atmosphere (atm). One atmosphere equals 15 p.s.i. Or it may refer to torque in kilograms-meter (kgm). One kilogram-meter equals 7.2 pounds-feet.

Index

A

Accelerator pump, 101, 102
Air cleaner, 4, 5, 7, 116, 167, 172
  basic description of, 175–76
  filter, 115, 139, 167, 174, 210
  gasket, 203
  troubleshooting, 176–77, 188
Air conditioning, 262
  AMC, 308–9, 311
  basic description of, 307–9
  Chrysler, 310, 311
  Ford, 307, 308, 311, 314
  GM, 307, 308, 309, 310–11, 312, 313
  Renault, 311
  servicing, 315–17
  troubleshooting, 309–14
Air pollution controls
  air cleaner, 4, 5, 7, 115, 116, 139, 167, 172, 174, 175–77,
      188, 203, 210
  air pump, 172, 183–86
  basic description of, 3
  catalytic converter, 172, 183, 264, 266
  EGR system, 172, 177–81, 266
  Ford, 176, 177
  fuel vapor control, 172, 181–82
  GM, 176, 183
  oil burning and, 210
  PCV valve, 4, 5, 28, 172–74, 210, 236
  Pulsair, 183, 186, 187
  tuneup checklist and, 186, 188
  vacuum hoses, 66, 186, 187
Air pump, 172
  basic description of, 183, 184
  computer and, 183
  troubleshooting, 183, 185–86
  V-8 engine, 185
Alignment, 373
Allen wrench, 10, 17, 33, 132, 327, 328
Alternator, 4, 5
  Chrysler, 254
  no charge, 284, 285
  output test, 285, 287
  overcharge, 284, 285
  replacing, 288–90
  troubleshooting, 284–87

  undercharge, 284, 285
American Motors Corporation (AMC)
  air conditioning, 308–9, 311
  automatic transmission, 416
  brake system, 357, 359
  electrical system, 292–94, 295–96, 297
  four-cylinder engines, 62
  four-wheel drives, 357, 359
  fuel system, 128, 138, 223
  ignition system, 58, 62, 79
  six-cylinder engines, 62, 128
Antifreeze, 237, 247, 248

B

Battery, 23, 275, 284, 285, 291, 292, 294, 296–97, 298, 304
  amp-hour capacity, 277
  basic description of, 21–22, 276–77
  diesel engines and, 225, 228, 294
  engine size and, 277
  maintenance, 278
  reserve capacity, 278
  servicing, 279–83
  side-terminal versus top post, 278–79
  warranties, 279
  zero cold rating, 277
Belts, drive, 252, 285, 288, 290
  installing, 257–61
  removing, 253–57
Body repairs
  dents, 431–37
  rustouts, 437–42
  scratches, 431
  waxing and polishing, 440
Brake system
  AMC 357, 359
  antilock brakes, 361
  basic description of, 318–20
  Chrysler, 333–34, 360, 361
  disc type
    basic description of, 318–20
    servicing, 320–22, 324–41
    wheel bearings and, 387–92, 393
  drum-type
    basic description of, 318–20, 323

Brake system (*continued*)
    servicing, 341–56
      wheel bearings and, 387–92, 393
  fluid, 318, 357
  Ford, 354, 356
  four-wheel-drive, 357, 359
  friction operation, 318, 320
  front-wheel-drive, 322, 333, 337, 346, 354–56, 357, 359
  GM, 320, 333–34, 335, 337, 338, 346, 350, 357, 359
  Honda, 357, 359
  hydraulic system
    operation, 318, 319
    servicing, 357–62
  master cylinder, 318, 319, 322, 326, 357, 360, 361–62
  parking brake, 320, 354, 355, 363–65
  power brakes, 361, 365–67
  rear-wheel-drive, 327, 333, 334, 349–53
  Toyota, 359
  VW, 354, 356, 357, 359
  wheel cylinders, 347, 348, 357, 358
Breaker points, 13, 17, 28, 58
  basic description of, 22–26
  Datsun, 32
  Ford, 35
  gaps for, 30–31
  GM, 30, 35, 188
  replacing, 34–38, 47
  servicing, 28–34, 66
  troubleshooting, 44, 45, 46

C
Carburetor, 4, 7, 208, 219
  accelerator pump, 101, 102
  air cleaner, 4, 5, 7, 26, 115, 116, 139, 167, 172, 174, 175–77, 188, 203, 210
  basic description of, 100
  choke, 102–5, 115–27
  Chrysler, 138
  cleaning, 186
  computer-controlled, 108–9, 128, 134–39
  fuel bowl, 101, 105, 107
  gasket, 203–4, 223
  GM, 75, 123, 125, 127–28, 176, 223
  idle circuit, 100, 101
  idle speed adjustments, 127–34
  replacing, 140–47
  servicing, 109–34
  throttle, 69, 70, 78, 100, 101, 203
  troubleshooting, 134–39
  venturi, 100, 106, 107
Catalytic converter, 172, 183, 264, 266
Chassis lubrication, 376–81
Choke
  basic description of, 102–5
  Chrysler, 126–27
  GM, 123, 125
  heaters, 126–27
  servicing, 115–26
Chrysler Corporation, 11, 12
  air conditioning, 310, 311
  alternator, 254
  automatic transmission, 416
  brake system, 333–34, 360, 361
  clutch, 412
  cooling system, 243, 244, 254, 256, 263

  drive belts, 254, 256
  electrical system, 254, 293–94, 295–96, 297
  VW, 79, 128
Condenser, 28
  basic description of, 25
  Ford, 35
  GM, 35
  replacing, 34–38, 46, 47
  troubleshooting, 46
Cooling system
  antifreeze, 237, 238, 242–44, 246, 247, 248
  Audi, 249
  basic description of, 234–36
  Chrysler, 243, 244, 254, 256, 263
  drive belts, 252–61, 285, 288, 290
  fan, 4, 5, 234–36, 262–63
  flushing, 238–41
  Ford, 203, 243, 244, 249, 254, 257, 263
  four-cylinder engines, 243, 244, 251, 256, 263
  GM, 202, 203, 243, 244, 251, 257, 263
  heater, 236, 261–62
  heater hoses, 240, 241, 246
  overflow reservoir, 237–38, 244
  overheating, 246–52
  pressure cap, 237, 238, 239, 246, 247, 251–52
  radiator, 202, 234–44, 246–48
  radiator hoses, 234, 241, 244–46, 247
  thermostat, 7, 202, 234, 236–37, 243, 248–51
  V-6 engines, 243, 244, 254, 263
  VW, 243, 244, 249, 254–55, 260, 261
  water pump, 7, 202–3, 234
  four-cylinder engines, 62, 243, 244, 256
  front-wheel drives, 50, 78, 93, 254, 375, 412
  fuel system, 50, 53, 55, 78, 79, 126–27, 138, 164, 167
  ignition system, 21, 47, 50, 53, 54, 55, 56, 57, 61, 62, 63, 68, 69, 72, 93, 98, 99
  rear-wheel drives, 47, 56, 61, 63, 126–27, 212, 334, 412
  six-cylinder engines, 62, 208
  valve lifters, 208
  valve stem guides and seals, 212
  V-8 engines, 62
Clamps, exhaust, 266, 268, 270, 274
Clutch, manual transmission, 410–15
Coil, ignition, 4
  basic description of, 23
  Chrysler, 50, 53, 54, 55
  Ford, 47, 48
  GM, 47, 48, 50, 87
  troubleshooting, 44, 47, 50
Coil springs, 368, 369, 370, 373, 374
Compression gauge, 14, 15
Compression test, 85, 87, 186, 231
Computer, 5
  air pump and, 183
  AMC, 128, 138
  carburetors and, 108–9, 128, 134–39
  Chrysler, 50, 53, 55, 72, 78, 98, 99, 138
  EGR system and, 178
  electronic fuel injection and, 162
  Ford, 55, 71, 75, 99, 137–38, 162
  GM, 73, 75, 98, 99, 128, 138–39
  Renault, 138
  self-diagnosis, 98–99, 137–38
  spark advance and, 68–80
  timing and, 58, 68–80, 138, 169
  turbocharging and, 169

D

Datsun
  four-cylinder engines, 62
  ignition system, 32, 62
Diesel engines, 224–33, 257, 294
Distributor, 4, 5, 7, 17, 27, 205
  basic description of, 23–26, 41–43
  Chrysler, 11, 47, 53, 54
  Ford, 35, 38, 43, 53, 55–56, 69, 76
  GM, 11, 28, 29, 32–33, 35, 39, 42–43, 47, 48, 50, 51,
    58, 73, 75, 87, 93, 188, 210
  servicing, 27–58
  timing and, 68
  troubleshooting, 50
Drive train
  automatic transmission, 4, 5, 198, 382, 416–19
  manual transmission clutch, 410–15
  universal joints, 378, 381, 420–30
  See also Front-wheel-drive vehicles;
    Rear-wheel-drive vehicles
Dwell, 19, 32, 47, 136–37
Dwellmeter, 32, 136

E

EGR system, 172, 266
  basic description of, 177–78
  computer-controlled, 178
  intake manifold and, 178, 179
  troubleshooting, 177–81
Electrical system
  alternator, 4, 5, 254, 284–90
  AMC, 292–94, 295–96, 297
  basic description of, 21–22, 275–76
  battery, 21–22, 23, 275, 276–83, 284, 285, 291, 292, 294,
    296–97, 298, 304
  Chrysler, 254, 293–94, 295–96, 297
  diesel engines and, 225, 228
  drive belts, 252–61, 285, 288, 290
  exterior bulbs, 302–5
  Ford, 292–94, 295–96, 297
  generator, 254–55
  GM, 287, 297
  headlights, 299–302, 304
  horn, 297–99
  ignition switch, 23, 42, 46, 291–92, 293, 295, 296
  interior bulbs, 305–6
  starter, 4, 5, 291–97
  voltage regulator, 284, 285, 286, 287, 291
  VW, 254–55
Exhaust manifold, 5, 102, 104, 125–26, 175, 183
  basic description of, 102
Exhaust system
  catalytic converter, 172, 183, 264, 266
  clamps, 266, 268, 270, 274
  exhaust manifold, 5, 102, 104, 125–26, 175, 183
  hangers, 266, 272–73, 274
  inspecting, 264–66
  muffler, 264–70, 272, 274
  pipes, 264–74
  replacing, 272–74
  servicing, 266–72

F

Fan, 4, 5
  basic description of, 234–36
  troubleshooting, 262–63

Feeler gauge
  for breaker points, 13, 30–31
  for spark plugs, 12–13, 87–88
Firing order chart, 62
Ford Motor Company, 11
  air conditioning, 307, 308, 311, 314
  air pollution controls, 176, 177
  automatic transmission, 416, 417, 419
  brake system, 354, 356
  clutch, 413–15
  cooling system, 203, 243, 244, 249, 254, 257, 263
  drive belts, 254, 257
  electrical system, 292–94, 295–96, 297
  four-cylinder engines, 62, 243, 244
  front-wheel drives, 375
  fuel system, 115, 137–38, 158, 162, 164, 167
  ignition system, 35, 38, 39, 43, 47, 48, 53, 55–56, 57, 58,
    62, 68, 69, 70, 71, 75, 76, 99, 137, 188
  in-line six-cylinder engines, 62
  power steering pump, 254
  rear-wheel drives, 212, 370, 413
  suspension system, 370, 392, 402
  valve lifters, 206
  valve stem guides and seals, 212, 219
  V-8 engines, 62, 206
  V-6 engines, 62, 243, 244, 254
Four-cylinder engine(s)
  AMC, 62
  battery and, 277
  Chrysler, 62, 243, 244, 256
  cooling systems, 243, 244, 251, 256, 263
  cylinder numbering for, 62
  Datsun, 62
  firing order for, 62
  Ford, 62, 243, 244
  fuel system, 147
  GM, 62, 95–96, 197, 208, 243, 251
  self-diagnosis, 137–38
  side view of a, 7
  spark plug removal, 95–96
  Toyota, 62
  valve lifters, 198
  VW, 226
Four-wheel-drive vehicles
  AMC, 357, 359
  brake system, 357, 359
  Jeep, 378
  suspension system, 378
Front-wheel-drive vehicles
  brake system, 322, 333, 337, 346, 354–56, 357, 359
  Chrysler, 50, 78, 93, 254, 375, 412
  clutch, 410–13
  Ford, 375
  GM, 97, 346, 357, 359, 375, 413
  illustrations of, 6, 376
  rear-wheel-drive compared to, 375–76
  suspension system, 370, 373–76, 385, 386, 402, 408,
    426, 430
  universal joints, 426, 430
  VW, 59, 354
  water pump, 202–3, 236
Fuel bowl, 101, 105, 107
Fuel filter, 5, 107–8, 113, 160
  diesel engines and, 228
  replacing, 108, 111–15, 167, 228
  troubleshooting, 147, 150, 160, 167

Fuel injection, electronic
  basic description of, 155, 156–58
  Chrysler, 50, 53, 55, 164, 167
  computer and, 162
  diesel engines and, 228–30
  Ford, 158, 162, 164, 167
  GM, 159–60, 164, 167, 229, 230, 231, 232
 - servicing, 155, 159–67
  VW, 226, 228, 229, 230, 231, 232
Fuel pump, 4, 5, 7, 160
  basic description of, 147
  gasket, 198
  replacing, 150–54
  troubleshooting, 147–50, 167
Fuel system
  accelerator pump, 101, 102
  air cleaner, 4, 5, 7, 26, 115, 116, 139, 167, 172, 174,
      175–77, 188, 203, 210
  AMC, 128, 138, 223
  basic description of, 3
  carburetor, 4, 7, 26, 69, 70, 75, 78, 79, 100–138, 140–47,
      167, 172, 203–4, 208, 219, 223
  choke, 102–5
  Chrysler, 50, 53, 55, 78, 79, 126–27, 138, 164, 167
  Ford, 115, 137–38, 158, 162, 164, 167
  fuel bowl, 101, 105, 107
  fuel filter, 5, 107–8, 111–15, 147, 150, 160, 167, 228
  fuel pump, 4, 5, 7, 147–54, 160, 167, 198
  GM, 75, 123, 125, 127–28, 138–39, 152, 158, 159–60,
      164, 167, 168, 169, 176, 223, 229, 230, 231, 232
  idle circuit, 100, 101
  idle speed adjustments, 127–34, 228–30
  intake manifold, 4, 26, 100, 102, 104, 162, 167–71, 178,
      179, 203–4, 210, 212, 219–23
  Renault, 138
  throttle, 69, 70, 78, 100, 101, 203, 208
  turbochargers, 167–71
  venturi, 100, 106, 107
  VW, 114, 128, 166, 171, 226, 228, 229, 230, 231, 232
  See also Fuel injection, electronic
Fuel vapor control, 172, 181–82

G
Gaps, 19
  for breaker points, 30–31
  for spark plugs, 87–88, 188
Gaskets, 210, 223, 247
  air cleaner, 203
  air-holding, 203–5
  basic description of, 196
  carburetor, 203–4, 223
  cooling system pressure cap, 247, 251
  engine oil pan, 197
  formed-in-place, 201
  fuel pump, 198
  intake manifold, 203–4, 210, 212
  oil sealing, 196
  replacing, 196–205
  thermostat, 202, 251
  throttle, 203
  timing belt cover, 197–98
  transmission oil pan, 198, 418
  valve cover, 196–97, 198, 205
  water pump, 202–3
  water-sealing, 202–3

General Motors (GM), 11, 12, 17
  air conditioning, 307, 308, 309, 310–11, 312, 313
  air pollution controls, 176, 183
  automatic transmission, 416, 417
  brake system, 320, 333–34, 335, 337, 338, 346, 350, 357,
      359
  clutch, 413
  cooling system, 202, 203, 243, 244, 251, 257, 263
  dicsels, 225, 228, 229, 230, 231, 232, 233, 257
  drive belts, 257
  electrical system, 287, 297
  four-cylinder engines, 62, 95–96, 197, 208, 243, 251
  front-wheel drives, 97, 346, 357, 359, 375, 413
  fuel system, 75, 123, 125, 127–28, 138–39, 152, 158,
      159–60, 164, 167, 168, 169, 176, 223, 229, 230,
      231, 232
  ignition system, 11, 28, 29, 30, 32–33, 35, 39, 40–41, 42,
      43, 44, 45, 47, 48, 50–53, 54, 58, 61, 62, 68, 69,
      73–74, 75, 77, 87, 93, 95–97, 98, 99, 188, 210
  in-line six-cylinder engines, 62
  oil changes, 190
  suspension system, 378, 379, 381, 386, 402–8
  valve lifters, 206, 208, 210
  valve stem guides and seals, 219
  V-8 engines, 17, 28, 29, 32–33, 39, 40–41, 62, 202, 206,
      225, 228
  V-6 engines, 62, 96–97, 244
Generator, VW, 254–55
Glow plugs, 225, 227, 228, 233

H
Hall Effect switch, 41–42, 55
Hangers, exhaust, 266, 272–73, 274
Headlights, 299–302, 304
Heater
  basic description of, 236, 261–62
  hoses, 240, 241, 246
  troubleshooting, 262
Honda
  brake system, 357, 359
  suspension system, 402
Horn, 297–99

I
Idle circuit, 100, 101
Idle speed adjustments, 127–34, 228–30
Ignition electronic
  basic description of, 41–43
  computer spark advance, 68–80

  Hall Effect switch, 41–42, 55
  pickup coil, 41–42, 44, 47, 50, 51, 53, 55, 56, 58
  reluctor, 43, 44
  servicing, 47–58, 188
  timing and, 66
  troubleshooting, 43–58
Ignition system
  AMC, 58, 62, 79
  basic description of, 3, 21–26
  breaker points, 13, 17, 22–26, 28–38, 44, 45, 46, 47, 58,
      66, 188
  Chrysler, 21, 47, 50, 53, 54, 55, 56, 57, 61, 62, 63, 68,
      69, 72, 78, 79, 93, 98, 99
  coil, 4, 23, 44, 47, 48, 50, 53, 54, 55, 87
  computer, 5, 50, 53, 55, 58, 68–80, 98, 99
  condenser, 25, 28, 34–38, 46, 47

distributor, 4, 5, 7, 11, 17, 23–58, 68, 69, 73, 75, 76, 77, 87, 93, 188, 205, 210
    Ford, 35, 38, 39, 43, 47, 48, 53, 55–56, 57, 58, 62, 68, 69, 70, 71, 75, 99, 137, 188
    GM, 11, 28, 29, 30, 32–33, 35, 39, 40–41, 42, 43, 44, 45, 47, 48, 50–53, 54, 58, 61, 62, 68, 69, 73–74, 75, 77, 87, 93, 95–97, 98, 99, 188, 210
    Peugeot, 62, 83
    Renault, 58, 79, 80
    resistor, 23, 42, 47, 56, 57
    rotor, 23–25, 28, 29, 33, 38–39, 44, 56, 57, 58, 93, 205
    starter, 4, 5, 291–97
    switch, 23, 42, 46, 291–92, 293, 295, 296
    timing, 19, 58–80, 138, 169
    Toyota, 62
    troubleshooting, 43–47
    vacuum advance unit, 4, 26, 39–41, 51
    VW, 59, 61, 62, 79, 80
In-line six-cylinder engines, 4, 62
Intake manifold, 4, 26, 162
    basic description of, 100, 102
    EGR system and, 178, 179
    gasket, 203–4, 210, 212
    heat riser, 219–23
    oil burning and, 210, 212
    turbocharging and, 167–71
    V-8, 104, 198, 222
    V-6, 220, 222

J

Jeep four-wheel-drive suspension, 378

L

Lights
    exterior bulbs, 302–5
    headlights, 299–302
    interior bulbs, 305–6

M

Manual clutch, 410–15
    AMC, 411
    Chrysler, 411
    GM, 411–12
    Ford Motor, 412
Master cylinder, 326, 357, 360
    basic description of, 318, 319, 322
    servicing, 361–62
Mercedes-Benz diesels, 230
Metric conversion, 446
Muffler, 264–70, 272, 274
Multi-meter, 16

O

Ohmmeter
    basic description of, 14, 16
    using an, 49, 50–52, 90–92, 127
Oil burning, curing, 210–19
Oil changes
    diesel engines and, 228
    GM, 190
    how to perform, 189–96
    interval for, 171, 189, 195, 228
    selection of oil, 195, 294
    turbocharging and, 171
    valve lifters and, 205, 208
    V-8 engines, 195

    VW, 195
Oil filter, 4, 5, 7
    replacing, 171, 189–96, 228
    selection of, 195
    turbocharging and, 171
    wrench for, 190, 193, 194
Oil pan, engine, 4, 5
    gasket, 197
Oil pan, transmission, 416–17
    gasket, 198, 418
Overflow reservoir, 237–38, 244
Overheating, cooling system, 246–52

P

Parts buying guide, 443–45
PCV valve, 4, 5, 236
    basic description of, 172–73
    clogged, 28, 173, 174
    oil burning and, 210
Peugeot ignition system, 62, 83
Phillips screwdriver, 10, 89
Pickup coil, 44, 47, 50, 51, 53, 55
    basic description of, 41–42
    replacing, 56, 58
Pipes, exhaust system, 264–74
Piston engine, basic description of, 14
Piston rings, oil burning and, 210
Pliers, 10
Posi-driv screwdriver, 10
Power steering pump, 5, 259
    Ford, 254
    oil reservoir for, 4
Pressure cap, 237, 238, 239, 246
    gasket, 247, 251
    replacing, 251–52
Pulsair, 183, 186, 187

R

Radiator, 202, 234–44
    hoses, 234, 241, 244–46, 247
    plugged, 246–48
Ratchet, spark plug, 17, 18, 83–85
Rear-wheel-drive vehicles
    AMC, 411
    brake system, 327, 333, 334, 349–53
    Chrysler, 47, 56, 61, 63, 126–27, 212, 411
    clutch, 410–13
    Ford, 212, 370, 413
    front-wheel-drive compared to, 375–76
    GM, 411
    illustration of, 375
    rear wheel cover plate, 198
    suspension system, 370, 373, 375–76, 386, 402, 420
    universal joints, 420
    valve stem guides and seals, 212
    water pump, 202, 236
Reluctor, 43, 44
Renault
    air conditioning, 311
    fuel system, 138
    ignition system, 58, 79, 80
Resistor, ballast, 23, 42, 47
    dual, 56, 57
Rotor, 28, 29, 33, 205
    basic description of, 23–25
    Chrysler, 93

Rotor (*continued*)
 Ford, 38, 39, 56, 57
 GM, 39
 replacing, 38–39, 58
 servicing, 38–39, 56, 57, 58
 troubleshooting, 44

S
Screwdrivers, 10, 89
Self-diagnosis, computer, 98–99, 137–38
Shock absorbers, 370, 373, 374, 376, 395
 basic description of, 368, 392–94
 buying, 394
 replacing, 396–401
 testing, 396
Six-cylinder engines
 AMC, 62, 128
 battery and, 277
 Chrysler, 62, 208
 cylinder numbering for, 62
 firing order for, 62
 fuel system, 147
 slant, 208
 See also In-line six-cylinder engines;
  V-6 engines
Spark advance, computer-controlled
 AMC, 79
 basic description of, 68–69
 checking timing, 75–80
 Chrysler, 68, 69, 72, 78, 79
 failure of, 75
 Ford, 68, 69, 70, 71, 75
 GM, 68, 69, 73–74, 75
 Renault, 79, 80
 retarding, 58, 169
 VW, 79, 80
Spark plugs, 4, 5, 7, 23–25, 44
 basic description of, 3, 81
 checklist for, 188
 feeler gauge for, 12–13, 87–88
 gaps for, 87–88, 188
 ratchet for, 17, 18, 83–85
 replacing, 39, 81–90, 95–97, 188
 socket wrench for, 8, 9, 83–85
Spark plug wires, 5, 23–25, 42, 43
 disconnecting, 27, 44, 49, 81–83, 160
 inspecting and testing, 90–92
 replacing, 92–95
 routing of, 188
Starter, 4, 5
 AMC, 292–94, 295–96
 basic description of, 291–94
 Chrysler, 293–94, 295–96
 Ford, 292–94, 295–96
 relay, 292–94, 295–96
 replacing, 296–97
 troubleshooting, 294–96
Steering
 basic description of, 368, 370, 371
 rack-and-pinion, 372
Stethoscope, 17, 162, 163
Struts
 basic description of, 370
 MacPherson strut inserts, 402–8
 replacing, 402–9
Suspension system

 alignment, 373
 basic description of, 368–74
 chassis lubrication, 376–81
 coil springs, 368, 369, 370, 373, 374
 Ford, 370, 392, 402
 front-wheel-drive, 370, 373–76, 385, 386, 402, 408, 426,
  430
 GM, 378, 379, 381, 386, 402–8
 Honda, 402
 Jeep, 378
 leaf springs, 373
 GM, 378
 rear-wheel-drive, 370, 373, 375–76, 386, 402, 420
 shock absorbers, 368, 370, 373, 374, 376, 392–401
 steering, 368, 370, 371, 372
 struts, 370, 402–9
 tie-rod ends, 371
 tires, 382–85
 universal joints, 378, 381, 420–30
 VW, 402
 wheel bearings, 376, 385–92, 393
Switch, ignition, 42
 basic description of, 23, 291–92, 293
 troubleshooting, 46, 295, 296

T
Tachometer
 basic description of, 11
 for Chrysler, 11
 connections for, 47–49
 for Ford, 11
 for GM, 11, 47
 using a, 47–49, 56, 68, 169, 170, 228, 230
Test light
 basic description of, 16–17
 using a, 44, 46, 47, 50, 127, 153, 160, 233
Thermostat, 7, 234, 243
 basic description of, 236–37
 gasket, 202, 251
 replacing, 249–51
Throttle, 101, 208
 basic description of, 100
 gasket, 203
 timing and, 69, 70, 78
Tie-rod ends, 371
Timing, ignition, 19
 basic description of, 58
 checking and adjusting, 58–68
 computer and, 58, 68–80, 138, 169
 distributor and, 68
 electronic ignition and, 66
 retarding, 58, 169
 throttle and, 69, 70, 78
Timing belt cover, 7
 gasket, 197–98
Timing light
 basic description of, 11–12
 for Chrysler, 12
 for GM, 12
 using a, 61, 66–68, 169, 170
Timing marks, 60, 68
 basic description of, 58, 61
 Chrysler, 61, 63
 finding, 61
 GM, 61
 making new, 61, 64, 65

V-8, 63

V-6, 63
VW, 59, 61
Tires
  buying, 382–84
  care of, 384–85
Torque, 19
Torque wrench, 18, 19, 259, 337
Torx wrench, 10, 327, 328
Toyota
  brake system, 359
  four-cylinder engines, 62
  ignition system, 62
Transmission, automatic
  AMC, 416
  Chrysler, 416
  fluid, 416
  Ford, 416, 417, 419
  GM, 416, 417
  lubrication of, 382
  oil pan, 198, 416–17, 418
  oil pan gasket, 198, 418
  servicing, 198, 416–19
Transmission, clutch for manual, 412–15
Tuneups, basic
  basic hand tools, 8–10
  buying tuneup parts, 20
  checklist for, 186, 188
  engine systems, 3–7
  how to get started, 20
  specifications, 19
  specific tuneup tools, 11–19
Turbochargers, 167–71

U
Universal joints, 378, 381
  basic description of, 420, 421
  front-wheel-drive, 426, 430
  rear-wheel-drive, 420
  servicing, 420, 422–30

V
Vacuum advance unit, 4
  basic description of, 26
  GM, 39, 40–41, 51
  servicing, 39–41
Vacuum gauge test, 266
Vacuum hoses, 66, 186, 187
Valve cover gasket, 196–97, 198, 205
Valve lifters
  basic description of, 205–6
  Chrysler, 208
  cover gasket, 196–97, 198, 205
  Ford, 206
  four-cylinder, 198, 208
  GM, 206, 208, 210
  oil changes and, 205, 208
  replacing, 208–10
  slant six-cylinder, 208
  troubleshooting, 205–9
  V-8, 205, 206, 208
  V-6, 206, 208
Valve stem guides and seals, 210–19
V-8 engines
  air pump, 185

battery and, 277
Chrysler, 62
cylinder numbering for, 62
firing order for, 62
Ford, 62, 206
fuel system, 147
GM, 17, 28, 29, 32–33, 39, 40–41, 62, 202, 206, 225, 228
intake manifold, 104, 198, 222
oil changes, 195
self-diagnosis, 137–38
side views of, 5
timing marks, 63
valve lifters, 205, 206, 208
Venturi, 100, 106, 107
Voltage regulator, 286, 287
  basic description of, 284
  replacing, 285, 291
V-6 engines
  cooling systems, 243, 244, 254, 263
  firing order for, 62
  Ford, 62, 243, 244, 254
  GM, 62, 96–97, 244
  intake manifold, 220, 222
  spark plug removal, 96–97
  timing marks, 63
  valve lifters, 206, 208
Volkswagen (VW)
  brake system, 354, 356, 357, 359
  cooling system, 243, 244, 249, 254–55, 260, 261
  diesels, 226, 227, 228, 229, 230, 231
  drive belts, 254–55, 260, 261
  electrical system, 254–55
  four-cylinder engines, 226
  front-wheel-drives, 59, 354
  fuel system, 114, 128, 166, 171, 226, 228, 229, 230, 231, 232
  generator, 254–55
  ignition system, 59, 61, 62, 79, 80
  oil changes, 195
  suspension system 402
Voltmeter, 56, 92, 99, 284–85

W
Water Pump, 7
  basic description of, 234
  front-wheel-drive, 202–3, 236
  gasket, 202–3
  rear-wheel-drive, 202, 236
Wheel bearings, 376
  basic description of, 385–87
  servicing, 387–92, 393
Wheel cylinders, 347, 348, 357, 358
Wrenches
  Allen, 10, 17, 33, 132, 327, 328
  box, 8
  C-shaped distributor, 17
  for GM V-8s, 17
  for oil filters, 190, 193, 194
  open-end, 8
  socket, 8–9, 83–85
  for spark plugs, 8, 9, 83–85
  torque, 18, 19, 259, 337
  Torx, 10, 327, 328